Cornell Studies In Security Affairs

edited by Robert J. Art *and* Robert Jervis

Liddell Hart and the Weight of History, by John J. Mearsheimer

Inadvertent Escalation: Conventional War and Nuclear Risks, by Barry R. Posen

The Sources of Military Doctrine: France, Britain, and Germany between the World Wars, by Barry R. Posen

Dilemmas of Appeasement: British Deterrence and Defense, 1934–1937, by Gaines Post, Jr.

Winning the Next War: Innovation and the Modern Military, by Stephen Peter Rosen

Israel and Conventional Deterrence: Border Warfare from 1953 to 1970, by Jonathan Shimshoni

Fighting to a Finish: The Politics of War Termination in the United States and Japan, 1945, by Leon V. Sigal

The Ideology of the Offensive: Military Decision Making and the Disasters of 1914, by Jack Snyder

Myths of Empire: Domestic Politics and International Ambition, by Jack Snyder

The Militarization of Space: U.S. Policy, 1945–1984, by Paul B. Stares

Making the Alliance Work: The United States and Western Europe, by Gregory F. Treverton

The Origins of Alliances, by Stephen M. Walt

The Ultimate Enemy: British Intelligence and Nazi Germany, 1933–1939, by Wesley K. Wark

The Tet Offensive: Intelligence Failure in War, by James J. Wirtz

Deterrence and Strategic Culture: Chinese-American Confrontations, 1949–1958, by Shu Guang Zhang

Myths of Empire

DOMESTIC POLITICS AND INTERNATIONAL AMBITION

JACK SNYDER

Cornell University Press

ITHACA AND LONDON

First published 1991 by Cornell University Press.
First printing, Cornell Paperbacks, 1992.

International Standard Book Number 0-8014-2532-8 (cloth)
International Standard Book Number 0-8014-9764-7 (paper)
Library of Congress Catalog Card Number 91-55052
Printed in the United States of America

Librarians: Library of Congress cataloging information appears on the last page of the book.

⊗ The paper in this book meets the minimum requirements of the American National Standard for Information Sciences— Permanence of Paper for Printed Library Materials, ANSI Z39.48-1984.

Contents

Acknowledgments

At times while working on this book, I felt as overextended as the empires I was studying. Fortunately I had many friends and allies who tried their best to pull me out of the quagmires I blundered into. Stephen Van Evera unquestionably heads the list. Many of the basic concepts I used to organize my research are based on his work. It will come as no surprise to those who know him that he was extremely generous in offering creative, lucid comments throughout the project.

Michael Brown, John Gaddis, Joseph Grieco, Robert Jervis, David Lake, Marc Trachtenberg, and Stephen Walt read the whole manuscript and left a significant imprint on some of its main arguments. Michael Desch, Michael Doyle, Jeff Frieden, Robert Gilpin, Ted Hopf, Chaim Kaufmann, Paul Kennedy, Charles Kupchan, Robert Legvold, Helen Milner, and John Mearsheimer read large parts and provided helpful suggestions on both theory and substance. Jeff Frieden also tutored me on the political economy of interest groups.

Michael Barnhart, Miles Kahler, James Morley, and Scott Sagan provided expert criticism of the Japan chapter. Lynn Eden's knowledgeable, thorough, and theoretically astute critique of the America chapter was a model of how to provide constructive comments on other people's work. Kenneth Bourne and the late Roger Bullen, the leading experts on Palmerston, were patient and incisive in their attempts to curb the excesses of a political scientist who knew just enough to be dangerous. Among the many students and colleagues who commented on the argument of the Soviet chapter, I must especially mention James Richter, on whose interpretations and advice I relied heavily. Other helpful contributions on specific points are acknowledged in the notes.

Teresa Pelton Johnson provided extremely useful advice on the organization and presentation of the argument. She also did a miraculous job of editing the *International Security* article that formed the basis of the Soviet chapter, as those who saw the "before and after" can readily attest. Alice Bennett copyedited the manuscript, making many improvements throughout. Holly Bailey made several key suggestions during the initial stages of the editorial process at Cornell University Press. Kathleen McNamara prepared the index.

The National Council for Soviet and East European Research provided financial support. I am grateful to *International Securty* and the MIT Press for permission to reprint parts of "The Gorbachev Revolution: A Waning of Soviet Expansionism?" vol. 12 (Winter 1987–88), and to *World Politics* and the Johns Hopkins University Press to quote from George Breslauer, "Ideology and Learning in Soviet Third World Policy," vol. 39 (April 1987).

The book is dedicated to my parents, Robert E. and Irene E. Snyder.

J. S.

New York, New York

Myths of Empire

[1]

The Myth of Security
through Expansion

Great powers in the industrial age have shown a striking proclivity for self-inflicted wounds. Highly advanced societies with a great deal to lose have sacrificed their blood and treasure, sometimes risking the survival of their states, as a consequence of their overly aggressive foreign policies. Germany and Japan proved so self-destructive in the first half of this century that they ended up in receivership. Most other great powers, including the United States and the Soviet Union, have exhibited similar tendencies from time to time, but they were better able to learn from the adverse reactions their aggressive behavior provoked.[1]

In this book I try to explain why overexpansion has been so common among the great powers, and also why some states have been particularly inclined toward extreme overexpansion. I offer a two-step explanation, stressing the role of strategic concepts and their function as ideologies in domestic politics.

Counterproductive aggressive policies are caused most directly by the idea that the state's security can be safeguarded only through expansion. This idea, the central myth of empire, was the major force propelling every case of overexpansion by the industrialized great powers. In the more egregious cases, the belief in security through expansion persisted tenaciously despite overwhelming evidence that aggressive policies were actually undermining the state's security.

The myth of security through expansion originated in each case as a justification for the policies of domestic political coalitions formed among groups having parochial interests in imperial expansion, mili-

---

1. This history of overextension is recorded in Paul Kennedy, *The Rise and Fall of the Great Powers* (New York, 1987); Robert Gilpin, *War and Change in World Politics* (Cambridge, 1981); and Michael Doyle, *Empires* (Ithaca, N.Y., 1986).

tary preparations, or economic autarky. These groups, including economic sectors and state bureaucracies, logrolled their various imperialist or military interests, using arguments about security through expansion to justify their self-serving policies in terms of a broader public interest in national survival.

These opportunistic strategic justifications were propounded not only by the narrow interest groups themselves but also by the statesmen who tried to reconcile the groups' competing programs within the ruling coalition. Often the proponents of these strategic rationalizations, as well as the wider population, came to believe them. The political and intellectual entrenchment of these myths hindered strategic learning and reinforced the impetus toward overexpansion. Even the pro-imperial elites became entrapped in this political and ideological dynamic, which in several cases hastened their departure from positions of power and privilege.

Understanding the myth of security through expansion and its origins is the first step toward solving the recurrent problem of self-defeating aggression among the great powers. This introductory chapter identifies the recurrent myths of empire, describes the varieties of overexpansion those myths have led to, and sets my arguments in the context of traditional explanations for overexpansion offered by historians and political scientists. The next chapter lays out competing theories of overexpansion in more detail. Subsequent chapters test those theories in the light of case studies of Germany, Japan, Britain, the Soviet Union, and the United States at the height of their expansionist impulses.

HYDRA-HEADED RATIONALES FOR EXPANSION

Statesmen and strategists have typically envisioned a world in which security is scarce and expansion is the best route to it. Like Catherine the Great, they have commonly contended that empires must either expand or die: "That which ceases to grow begins to rot." They have often argued that costly wars must be fought in the hinterlands to prevent the empire from collapsing like a row of dominoes. Encircling alliances can best be broken up, they have claimed, by threats and preventive aggression rather than by appeasement. Reasoning this way, statesmen and strategists have recurrently created situations in which expansion and war have seemed unavoidable, even for states motivated primarily by the desire for security.[2]

2. On insecurity as a cause of international conflict, see Robert Jervis, "Cooperation under the Security Dilemma," *World Politics* 30 (January 1978): 167–214; Kenneth Waltz, *Theory of International Politics* (Reading, Mass., 1979); and Stephen Van Evera, "Causes of War" (Ph.D., diss., University of California at Berkeley, 1984).

In making these arguments, statesmen have exaggerated the benefits of expansion for both themselves and their opponents while underrating its costs. Likewise, they have exaggerated the probable success of offensive or expansionist strategies while underrating the prospects of defensive measures and retrenchment.[3] Such views, though present to some degree in all the great powers, have been most extreme in Germany and Japan.

Underpinning the central idea that security requires expansion are a variety of more specific strategic conceptions that in varying mixtures have provided hydra-headed justifications for aggressive policies. These concepts can be grouped under three general premises: gains and losses are cumulative; the offense has the advantage; and offensive threats make others more cooperative. Together, these assumptions portray the international system as a place where the balance of power does not operate and where opponents are made more tractable by having their vital interests threatened.

The Domino Theory: Cumulative Gains and Losses

The first category of myths of empire, cumulative gains, purports to explain why expansion will add to the state's strength and, consequently, to its ability to defend itself.[4] Conquest increases power, in this view, because it adds resources, both human and material, that can be used in further competition against other great powers. Vulnerable areas at the periphery are depicted as El Dorados, cheap to conquer yet harboring vast resources that must be acquired lest they fall into the hands of opponents. The lure of conquest is especially strong for states that are just short of self-sufficiency in the resources needed for war, since it can be argued that a grab for autarky can fundamentally improve their security. Imperial Japanese expansionists in particular stressed this rationale, though they found that with each outward push autarkic security was still out of reach.

Just as proponents of expansion have promised that cumulative gains will lead to imperial security, so too they have warned that losses in the empire's periphery can easily bring a collapse of power at the imperial core, through any of several mechanisms: a cumulative erosion of economic and military resources; the increasing difficulty of imperial defense owing to the loss of strategic forward positions; or the progressive abandonment of the state by its allies, who might infer that it would not live up to its commitments.

3. Van Evera, "Causes of War."
4. In addition to Van Evera, see Robert Jervis and Jack Snyder, eds., *Dominoes and Bandwagons: Strategic Beliefs and Great Power Competition in the Eurasian Rimland* (New York, 1991).

[3]

Relatively satisfied powers like Britain and the United States have been especially prone to this domino theory. In a particularly inventive instance, accepted even by the skeptical and astute prime minister Lord Salisbury, Britain anticipated that a handful of French explorers might claim the outpost of Fashoda in the trackless hinterlands of the Upper Nile and somehow dam the river, destroying Egypt's economy and provoking an anti-British revolt that would lead to the loss of the Suez Canal, thus cutting the royal navy off from India, which would lead in turn to an Indian mutiny and ultimately to the collapse of the entire British economy. Though none of the steps in this chain of reasoning stands up to scrutiny, it seemed plausible enough to both the French and the British to bring them to the brink of war in 1898.[5]

Offensive Advantage

A second category of imperial myths holds that the best defense is a good offense.[6] This view asserts that cumulative gains in the imperial periphery can be reaped through aggressive action, whereas passivity will bring cumulative defeats. For example, the solution to security problems at the "turbulent frontier" of the empire is to conquer still more territory in order to punish or prevent harassment by contiguous barbarians.[7] Likewise, it is held that the cheapest way to forestall cascading dominoes is to prevent the fall of the first one by a forward defense. Like the deployment of a few good Greeks in the pass at Thermopylae, active measures at the periphery allegedly allow a cheap defense of empire, whereas defending farther back, after the dominoes gather momentum, might be impossible at any price. Over the past two centuries, great powers have repeatedly fought costly, unsuccessful wars in Afghanistan, all justified by the alleged cost-effectiveness of forward defense of vulnerable imperial holdings.[8]

Likewise in direct military showdowns between great powers, attack is often held to be advantageous. States must always be prepared, in this view, for preventive aggression against competitors whose rising power might someday outstrip them. Moreover, the benefits of sur-

5. Ronald E. Robinson and John A. Gallagher, *Africa and the Victorians* (London, 1961), 285–86. The French focused only on the initial part of the causal chain.

6. Stephen Van Evera, "The Cult of the Offensive and the Origins of the First World War," *International Security* 9 (Summer 1984): 58–107; Van Evera, "Causes of War," 250–54, 280–324; and Barry Posen, *The Sources of Military Doctrine: Britain, France, and Germany between the World Wars* (Ithaca, N.Y., 1984).

7. John S. Galbraith, "The 'Turbulent Frontier' as a Factor in British Expansion," *Comparative Studies in Society and History* 2 (January 1960): 150–68.

8. Malcolm Yapp, *Strategies of British India, 1798–1850* (Oxford, 1980).

prise and of forcing the opponent to fight at times and places of the attacker's choosing create major first-strike advantages.

Paper Tigers and Bandwagons: Faith in Threats

A third contribution to the belief in security through expansion is the idea that threats make other states compliant. This belief leads to the paper tiger image of the adversary: the main opponent is seen as an implacable foe posing an immense security threat, yet at the same time as too weak, inert, or irresolute to combat aggressive countermeasures. Applied to allies and neutrals, this idea leads to "bandwagon" predictions. That is, third parties, instead of forming alliances to balance the power of the most threatening state, are expected to jump on the bandwagon and support its emerging hegemony.[9] Threatening behavior is expected to attract allies and to intimidate opponents. In other words, the basic principles of the balance of power are held to operate in reverse.

Though moderate forms of such paper tiger and bandwagon beliefs have been common among most great power statesmen and strategists, they have been most extreme in Germany and Japan. Wilhelmine naval strategists argued, for example, that Britain would use its naval superiority to strangle Germany's world trade, yet would not seriously contest a German attempt to close the gap.[10] Likewise, the Germans saw the encircling Entente as unalterably bent on Germany's destruction, yet so irresolute that a showdown would lead to the Entente's humiliation and disintegration.[11] The Japanese concocted similarly paradoxical views of their opponents. Colonel Ishiwara Kanji, a staff officer who played a key role both in instigating the occupation of Manchuria and in devising a strategy for an autarkic empire, decided in the early 1920s that all-out war between Japan and the United States was inevitable, given America's inherently rapacious nature. At the same time, Ishiwara counted on the United States and Japan's other foes to be so somnolent that they would allow Japan to conquer, piecemeal, the resource base that would let it successfully prosecute this war.[12]

---

9. On bandwagoning, see Stephen Walt, *The Origins of Alliances* (Ithaca, N.Y., 1987), 19–33. Stephen Van Evera coined the term.

10. Paul Kennedy, *Strategy and Diplomacy, 1870–1945* (London, 1983), chaps. 4 and 5.

11. Glenn Snyder and Paul Diesing, *Conflict among Nations* (Princeton, N.J., 1977), esp. 248–49 and 262–76 on the Moroccan crises of 1905 and 1911.

12. Michael Barnhart, *Japan Prepares for Total War: The Search for Economic Security, 1919–1941* (Ithaca, N.Y., 1987), 49, 86, describes these contradictions; Van Evera, "Causes of War," 394, explains them theoretically.

Soviet theories of détente under Khrushchev and Brezhnev had a similar ring: the United States was so aggressive that it would accept détente only if handcuffed by a shift in the military and political "correlation of forces" in socialism's favor; yet it was so passive that it would allow the handcuffs to be slipped on.[13] The main difference is that the Soviets retreated when this image of the United States was disconfirmed, whereas the Germans and Japanese pushed the theory to its ultimate test, hoping that a preventive war would decisively weaken their paper tiger opponents.

Together these strategic concepts create a powerful justification for a policy of security through expansion. If the world really were as these ideas portray it even status quo states would have to embark on endless war and expansion to maintain their security. This book will show that imperial overexpansion correlates closely with the prevalence of these concepts in a state's discourse on national security. The states in which these ideas were most prevalent adopted the most self-defeating aggressive policies and were the least able to correct their overexpansion."

OVEREXPANSION: THE CONSEQUENCE OF IMPERIAL MYTHS

The strategy of gaining security through expansion is rarely effective because the ideas underlying it contradict two of the most powerful regularities in international politics: the balance of power and the rising costs of expansion. Statesmen who base their strategy on the myths of empire are likely to undermine their power and security by provoking an overwhelming coalition of opposing states, which I call "self-encirclement," and by persistent expansion into the hinterland beyond the point where costs begin to outstrip benefits—or "imperial overextension."

Scholars have typically treated these two problems separately; some studies address the great powers' wars in Europe, for example, while others study "imperial overstretch" at the periphery. But since I argue that the two have common roots in strategic myths and domestic politics, I refer to them jointly as overexpansion. Some states, because of their strategic situation and domestic political alignments, have suffered primarily from self-encirclement; others, primarily from imperial overextension; some have experienced both.

Self-encirclement results from a basic principle of the balance of

13. See the discussion of the "second image" in Franklyn Griffiths, "The Sources of American Conduct: Soviet Perspectives and Their Policy Implications," *International Security* 9 (Fall 1984): 3–50.

power: that the most aggressive states make the most enemies.[14] When a state indiscriminately threatens many of its neighbors, they normally coalesce against it. In response, if it is incapable of evaluating its own role in causing the encirclement, it may embark on "preventive" war to break the ring. But if the balance of power works as it normally does, this attempted breakout will entail high risk and a low probability of success, and the aggressor will normally find overwhelming power ranged against it. For example, at the onset of war in 1914, Britain, France, and Russia enjoyed a three-to-two advantage over Germany and Austria in most indicators of industrial capacity. Even after Germany knocked Russia out of the war, the ratio climbed to five to two once the United States joined in.[15] Similarly, in the Second World War, Germany, Japan, and Italy provoked an opposing coalition that by 1943 was outstripping them three to one in armaments production, despite the conquests by the Axis powers.[16]

States that are better learners may provoke an encirclement but then shy away from war or even begin to appease some of their enemies. Britain, for the most part, has been a good learner and an astute appeaser, which explains, as Paul Kennedy put it, "why the British Empire lasted so long."[17] When Lord Palmerston flirted with the idea of expanding the Crimean War into a world war to extinguish Russian power permanently, neutral powers and Palmerston's own allies objected and the British cabinet convinced him to sign a compromise treaty.[18] Likewise, Britain's aggressive colonial expansion in the scramble for Africa left it at odds with every major European power by the turn of the century. Calculating the disastrous erosion of the naval balance this could cause, Britain quickly ended its "splendid isolation," settling disputes with Japan, France, and Russia and thereby strengthening its hand in the competition with Germany.[19]

Some argue that Britain learned the lessons of appeasement and retrenchment too well between the world wars, jeopardizing its security through strategic passivity. In this view a preventive war against

14. Realist theory has been ambiguous about whether states balance against the most powerful state or the most threatening state, taking into account both power and intentions. Walt, *Origins of Alliances*, 21–26, 263–66, argues unambiguously and persuasively for the latter view.

15. Paul Kennedy, "The First World War and the International Power System," *International Security* 9 (Summer 1984), reprinted in Steven Miller, ed., *Military Strategy and the Origins of the First World War* (Princeton, N.J., 1985), 21, 25.

16. Kennedy, *Rise and Fall*, chap. 7.

17. Kennedy, *Strategy and Diplomacy*, chap. 8.

18. This is argued most vigorously by Winfried Baumgart, *The Peace of Paris, 1856* (Santa Barbara, Calif., 1981), though note the qualifications that I add in chapter 5.

19. On the British tradition of appeasement, see Kennedy, *Strategy and Diplomacy*, chap. 1.

Germany in 1936 or 1938 would have forestalled the conquest of France and enhanced Britain's security.[20] Indeed, if there was any instance of "underexpansion" by the great powers in the industrial era, this was it. But even this case is doubtful. Britain and France may have been too weak to launch a preventive attack, which would have been divisive domestically and onerous diplomatically. Moreover, one of the reasons Neville Chamberlain had to appease Hitler at Munich was that so much of Britain's strength was diffused throughout a far-flung empire. France had similar problems.[21] So pervasive is overextension that even the archappeasers and archretrenchers suffer from it.

Another state that combined overassertiveness with quick learning is the Soviet Union. Belligerent behavior in the Berlin crises, the Korean War, and the Sino-Soviet rift provoked an array of potential enemies that outnumbered the Warsaw Pact nations by more than three to one in national income.[22] But, the Soviets have been good learners in the short run and have followed each of their counterproductive militant phases with attempts to defuse opposition through self-restraint and overtures toward détente.[23]

There is also imperial overextension. Aggressors get into trouble not only because they provoke balancing coalitions by other great powers, but also because they get stuck in quagmires in the hinterland. Up to a point, imperial expansion may be a paying proposition for a strong power. Sometimes resources and markets can be gained more cheaply and reliably by military than by economic means.[24] The historical experience of all empires shows, however, that at some point the costs of additional expansion begin to outstrip its benefits.[25] Easy, nearby targets that yield a high return are exhausted. The logistic burdens of further expansion make it easier for an opposing coalition to impose heavy costs by resisting.

All the industrial great powers have at times expanded past the point

20. Williamson Murray, *The Change in the European Balance of Power, 1938–1939* (Princeton, N.J., 1984).

21. Brian Bond, *British Military Policy between the Two World Wars* (Oxford, 1980); Stephen Schuker, "France and the Remilitarization of the Rhineland, 1936," *French Historical Studies* 14 (Spring 1986): 299–338; Miles Kahler, *Decolonization in Britain and France* (Princeton, N.J., 1984); Charles Kupchan, *The Vulnerability of Empire* (forthcoming).

22. Stephen Walt, "Alliance Formation and the Balance of World Power," *International Security* 9 (Spring 1985): 42–43.

23. Marshall Shulman, *Stalin's Foreign Policy Reappraised* (New York, 1969); Deborah Welch Larson, "Crisis Prevention and the Austrian State Treaty," *International Organization* 41 (Winter 1987): 27–60.

24. David Lake, *The State and Grand Strategy* (forthcoming), argues that this is especially true for certain types of "rent-seeking" states.

25. Gilpin, *War and Change*, chap. 4. When I use the term "empire" or "imperial," I refer to any expansionist great power.

where marginal costs equal marginal benefits, in terms of both economic and security interests.[26] Even Britain had its Boer War and its recurrent forays into Afghanistan in the face of repeated lessons that this remote land was beyond the perimeter of Britain's sustainable power. Britain, however, was relatively successful at calculating the marginal costs and revenues of expansion; it almost always learned to retrench in the face of negative feedback.[27] Similarly, the Vietnam War caused most of the outcomes it was designed to forestall: it touched off more than a decade of inflation, starved America's regular military forces of funds, demobilized domestic support for America's global role, sowed dissension in NATO, and encouraged Soviet geopolitical assertiveness in the 1970s. As a consequence, Americans learned fairly quickly that Vietnam, and many other places in the Third World, were beyond America's sustainable perimeter of empire.[28]

Britain and America were good learners, but Japan drew exactly the wrong conclusions about overextension. Japan strove to conquer China so as to have an autarkic military-industrial base. By 1937 the China campaign was in fact eating up Japan's industrial base, diverting expenditures from industrial investment into current military consumption.[29] But unlike Britain, Japan did not appease and retrench. Instead it gambled on still more expansion to cut off supplies to China and conquer resources even farther afield, in Southeast Asia. As a consequence, Japan wound up both mired in China and with an overwhelming great power, the United States, against it.

THE ORIGINS OF OVEREXPANSION AND IMPERIAL MYTHS

Why has self-punishing overexpansion been so prevalent among the industrialized great powers? And why has the myth of security through expansion been so widespread? Existing explanations are inadequate for several reasons. Many writers fail to distinguish between the

26. Gilpin, *War and Change*, chaps. 3 and 4, argues that states expand to the cost-benefit equilibrium, but then the equilibrium line recedes as a result, inter alia, of the diffusion of the expansionist's technological and organizational innovation to its competitors and subjects. In this interpretation, disequilibrium comes not from expanding past the equilibrium line, but from the failure to retrench when the equilibrium line recedes. Though the process Gilpin describes undoubtedly occurs, in the cases I examine states also overexpand in the direct sense of pushing beyond the cost-benefit equilibrium in the first place.

27. For examples, see Yapp, *Strategies of British India*, 335, 341–43.

28. This is apparent in Defense Secretary Caspar Weinberger's exclusionary criteria for the use of American military forces abroad; see *Department of Defense Annual Report, Fiscal Year 1987* (Washington, D.C., 1986), 78–79.

29. Barnhart, *Japan Prepares*, 95–96, 103.

specific problem of overexpansion and the more general "imperialism" or "expansionism." Much imperial expansion is unproblematic: the strong conquer the weak because it pays. And many explanations are flawed because they take the justifications of statesmen and strategists at face value—they accept the myths of empire advanced by imperialists as plausible depictions of the realities of international politics and hence as adequate reasons for overexpansion. For example, Ronald Robinson and John Gallagher, extremely influential historians of Victorian overseas expansion, argued that "if the papers left behind by the policy-makers are to be believed, they moved into Africa, not to build a new African empire, but to protect the old empire in India."[30] But newer research suggests that those papers are *not* to be believed: the oblique strategic justifications found in them were largely debating points masking a variety of economic, bureaucratic, and political interests.[31] Finally, some theories do treat strategic ideas as myths, but they omit key aspects of the origins and workings of those myths.[32] Though on the right track, these accounts are not fully satisfying, theoretically or empirically.

Interpretations of overexpansion offered by historians and political scientists can be grouped into three general types: "Realist" explanations, stressing the exigencies of the state's position in the international system; cognitive explanations, stressing purely intellectual errors in strategic assessment; and domestic political explanations, stressing interest groups, ruling classes, and the strategic ideologies they propound.

Realist Explanations

Realism contends that the costs and risks of aggression may be unavoidable in an anarchic international environment that forces states to use warlike means to guarantee their own security. Realists argue, in

---

30. Robinson and Gallagher, *Africa and the Victorians*, 464.

31. A. G. Hopkins, "The Victorians and Africa: A Reconsideration of the Occupation of Egypt, 1882," *Journal of African History* 27 (1986): 363–91. For discussions of works by historians who accept that imperial expansion was a reasonable strategic reaction to international circumstances, including crises in the periphery, see Tony Smith, *The Pattern of Imperialism* (Cambridge, 1981), chaps. 1 and 2; and Doyle, *Empires*, 146–48 and chaps. 8 and 9.

32. Van Evera, "Causes of War," is the most important work in this category. I borrow heavily from Van Evera's arguments in developing my own. The main difference between us is that he stresses the crucial role of the state as the main source of strategic myth, whereas I stress the process of forming coalitions among a variety of state and nonstate actors. Several historians, especially of imperial Germany, implicitly use a concept of strategic mythmaking that is close to mine. See especially Eckart Kehr, *Battleship Building and Party Politics in Germany, 1894–1901* (German ed., 1930; Chicago, 1973).

essence, that the "myths of empire" are not always myths. Sometimes offense really does have an advantage, and dominoes do fall. Sometimes it does make sense, they claim, to seek a more self-sufficient empire with a more geographically defensible frontier. In general, they argue, the more vulnerable states are to the depredations of others, the more aggressive they must become, if only in self-defense.[33]

On its face it sounds paradoxical to explain counterproductive overexpansion as a rational expedient, but it is not. Political scientists, drawing an analogy between international politics and the mathematical game "Prisoners' Dilemma," have shown how states' rational, defensive choices can draw them into competitive interactions that leave everyone less secure. If a nonexpansionist policy would have left the state even more vulnerable to its competitors, a grab for security through expansion would then be rational despite its predictably high costs and low chance of success.[34]

Historians have sometimes explained instances of overexpansion in much this way. Germany and Japan, for example, are sometimes portrayed as driven to expand by the logic of their disadvantaged, vulnerable position in the international system.[35] Surrounded by potential enemies on whom they were economically dependent, these latecomers to imperial competition had little choice but to use force to break out of the hostile encirclement. Though their bids for security through expansion may have had relatively little chance of success, less aggressive strategies might have been even riskier.

There are two general problems with Realist explanations for overexpansion, one logical and one empirical. The logical difficulty is that Realists themselves claim that states typically form balancing alliances to resist aggressors. Therefore, at least in the long run, the balance of power that arises out of international anarchy punishes aggression; it does not reward it. Consequently, strategies of security through expansion violate the basic principles of international politics that the Realists themselves have articulated.

To resolve this contradiction, it may be helpful to distinguish between two variants of the Realist argument. Both accept that security is normally the strongest motivation of states in international anarchy, but they have opposite views about the most effective way to achieve

33. In addition to Waltz, see Jervis, "Cooperation," and John Mearsheimer, "Back to the Future: Instability in Europe after the Cold War," *International Security* 15 (Summer 1990): 5–56.

34. Both Jervis and Van Evera develop these arguments.

35. David Calleo, *The German Problem Reconsidered* (Cambridge, 1978), argues this explicitly; James Crowley, *Japan's Quest for Autonomy* (Princeton, N.J., 1966), includes Japan's international position as well as domestic factors. See also Mearsheimer, "Back to the Future," 25.

it. One variant, which might be called "aggressive Realism," asserts that offensive action often contributes to security; another, "defensive Realism," contends that it does not.[36] My arguments, though stressing the domestic determinants of grand strategy, are fully consistent with the defensive version of Realism. States with myth-resistant domestic political orders behave in accord with the tenets of defensive Realism. They form defensive alliances to contain the expansion of aggressive states. In contrast, states with myth-producing domestic political orders engage in preventive aggression to forestall hypothetical future threats from states that have not yet taken significant menacing actions.

The empirical problem with Realist explanations for overexpansion is that they accept decision makers' own estimates of their incentives for making their strategic choices. They accept, for example, that Japan's aggressive bid for autarky was a plausible response to the situation it faced. They accept, moreover, that the European powers' scramble for formal colonial control was an almost unavoidable reaction to rising nationalist turmoil at the periphery. They accept, likewise, that American decision makers' concern over the reputational consequences of defeats in Korea and Vietnam adequately explains why those wars were fought.[37] In general, such Realist accounts accept superficially plausible reasons given by imperial policymakers for strategies of security through expansion but fail to evaluate these strategies in light of their predictable costs and the availability of more effective alternatives.

Two additional rationalist accounts of overexpansion merit discussion. One is that under uncertainty statesmen are bound to make errors, including overexpansion. But this fails to tell why the error of overexpansion is so much more common than the error of under-expansion. Nor does it explain why some states fail to retrench even after clear evidence of overexpansion emerges.

The second account relies not on uncertainty but on perverse preferences. In this view, self-destructive expansionists have been rational in the sense that they were willing to jeopardize the state's security in a self-consciously risky attempt to achieve other aims. The chance to achieve glory, plunder, *la mission civilisatrice*, the worldwide victory of socialism, "a place in the sun," or the domination of the master race simply outweighed the risk to national security in the calculations of

---

36. Walt, *Origins of Alliances*, is the quintessential example of what I call the defensive Realist position. Mearsheimer, "Back to the Future," 12, comes close to the aggressive Realist position, especially in his statement that "the international system creates powerful incentives for aggression." Waltz, *Theory of International Politics*, has a foot in both camps. For elaboration, see chapter 2, below.

37. On Korea, see William Stueck, *The Road to Confrontation: American Policy toward China and Korea, 1947–1950* (Chapel Hill, N.C., 1981).

overexpansionist empire builders.[38] Open-eyed, they gambled for great stakes but lost. The problem with this view is that such statesmen and strategists rarely were open-eyed or candid about the security risks of their aggressive policies. On the contrary, they always argued that expansion was the best way to solve the state's security problems. Retrenchment and stand-pat passive defense were always portrayed as riskier than aggression.

Judging from the experience of the industrialized great powers, rational reaction to compelling international circumstances never suffices to explain overexpansion. Yet international conditions, including the behavior of other great powers, did increase the plausibility of myths of empire. The more closely the real international system approximated the Hobbesian caricature of it, the easier it was to sell imperial myths in domestic political debates.[39] In this sense, I do not deny that international conditions affect grand strategy. I simply argue that they are not by themselves an adequate reason for overexpansion or for the conflictual character of great-power relations.

Two additional theories, rooted in cognitive psychology and in domestic politics, agree that the belief in security through expansion is erroneous. They disagree, however, about the source of the error.

Cognitive Explanations

It is sometimes claimed that the ideas I call the myths of empire have their origins in purely intellectual biases—that strategic ideas, like other beliefs, are learned from formative experiences. For simplicity, people reduce these lessons to schematic, ossified axioms that persist in the face of disconfirming evidence.[40]

Consequently statesmen and strategists—indeed, whole generations—might come to believe in falling dominoes, bandwagons, and paper tigers if they faced such conditions during their intellectual development. The Munich analogy, for example, is often blamed for the United States' exaggerated concern over the disgrace of backing down in peripheral disputes. Historians of other empires as well often identify some purportedly formative lesson that predisposed imperial statesmen toward costly, self-defeating strategies.

Yet though such lessons should be rare, the myths of empire are common. Formative experiences might occasionally lead to a belief in

38. For example, see the characterization of Adolf Hitler by Robert Jervis, *Perception and Misperception in International Politics* (Princeton, N.J., 1976), 51.

39. See Jack Snyder, "International Leverage on Soviet Domestic Change," *World Politics* 42 (October 1989): 1–30.

40. Jervis, *Perception and Misperception*, esp. chap. 6.

security through expansion, but overall the available stock of lessons points in the other direction. Any straightforward reading of history should produce many more statesmen predisposed against such strategies than in favor of them.

In fact, statesmen pick and choose among the available lessons of history until they find one that fits the strategy that they want, for other reasons, to adopt. For the same reason, moreover, the lessons they draw from events are often perverse. Observing the fate of Germany in World War I, for example, the Japanese military concluded not that aggression leads to diplomatic isolation and defeat, but that Japan needed to conquer an autarkic economic base in order to fight a long war successfully.[41]

Purely intellectual errors may sometimes contribute to imperial myths, through the influence of formative lessons as well as other kinds of cognitive biases.[42] But the beliefs of imperial policymakers—the "official mind" of the Victorian empire builders, the "operational code of the Politburo," the Japanese Bushido warrior code, and the American Cold War consensus—must be understood primarily as social, political, and ideological, not cognitive.

Domestic Political Explanations

Existing domestic political explanations for overexpansion contend that self-serving imperialist groups "hijack the state" and pervert national policy in the pursuit of private interest.[43] Two of the most famous theories of imperialism are of this type: the Hobson-Lenin thesis blames the drive of monopoly capitalists to export surplus capital so as to forestall declining returns to investment, and the Schumpeter thesis blames atavistic military-feudal elites whose social predominance depends on maintaining a rationale for their obsolete warrior function.[44]

Though they point to different culprits, the logic of these two

41. Some historians, insufficiently critical of documents written by the officials they study, accept these "lessons" at face value. Even a tough critic of Japanese militarism like Michael Barnhart slips into this error. See, for example, Barnhart, *Japan Prepares*, 9, 18, 270, on Japanese learning from World War I.

42. The historiographical literature stays mainly on the plane of beliefs and historical lessons. Therefore, in the case studies, this is the only cognitive explanation I try to test. In chapter 2, however, I pull together a somewhat broader cognitive explanation for strategic misperceptions based on hypotheses in Richard Nisbett and Lee Ross, *Human Inference* (Englewood Cliffs, N.J., 1980); Jervis, *Perception*; and Deborah Welch Larson, *The Origins of Containment* (Princeton, N.J., 1985).

43. This is the characterization of interest group theories offered by P. J. Cain, "J. A. Hobson, Financial Capitalism and Imperialism in Late Victorian and Edwardian England," *Journal of Imperial and Commonwealth History* 13 (May 1985): 1–27, esp. 2.

44. J. A. Hobson, *Imperialism* (1902); V. I. Lenin, *Imperialism: The Highest Stage of Capitalism* (1916); Joseph Schumpeter, *Imperialism and Social Classes* (1919).

theories runs parallel and can be expressed as a more general explanation: though overexpansion hurts the society as a whole, it is attractive to some groups within society. The benefits of expansion are disproportionately concentrated in their hands, while the costs of expansion are largely borne by the state and thus diffused throughout the society in the form of taxes, conscription, or (for imperial tariff protection) higher prices for consumer goods. By justifying their parochial interests in terms of national security, imperialist and military interest groups seek to pass the costs of aggressive policies on to society as a whole. The more powerful and persuasive such groups are, the more the state will be inclined toward self-defeating aggression.[45]

The problem for this kind of theory is to explain how narrow interests can succeed in hijacking state policy. Groups with very narrow interests normally lack the power or authority to harness the state for their own ends. Other interests that are harmed by costly, counterproductive imperialist policies—not least the interests of the state itself—should stand in their way. Effective propaganda might sometimes persuade the people and their leaders of the benefits of expansion, but studies have shown that interest groups' direct appeals are viewed skeptically. The credibility of narrow interest groups normally is far outstripped by that of national leaders, if they are popular, and disinterested experts.[46] For these reasons, interest group theories bear a heavy burden of proof in showing how narrow groups can dominate state policy and national perceptions.

Another kind of domestic explanation faces the opposite problem. These theories blame not a particular narrow class or sectoral interest, but the state apparatus or the ruling class as a whole. They argue that the governing elite may exaggerate foreign threats and glorify imperial projects to justify extracting resources from society, to cloak its rule in the legitimacy of nationalism, and to defuse domestic challenges to its domination. The ruling elite, in this view, does not necessarily benefit from war and expansion per se, but it profits from the nationalism, social solidarity, and social mobilization that go along with it. War and overexpansion are merely the unintended by-product, produced when the governing elite or the society comes to believe the mobilizing propaganda, or when other states react aggressively to the social-imperialist fanfare.[47]

45. The progenitor of this line of argument is Hobson, *Imperialism*. Closer to my own formulation of it is Van Evera, "Causes of War." My use of the terminology of rent-seeking cartels to describe imperialist interest groups derives from Mancur Olson, *The Rise and Decline of Nations* (New Haven, Conn., 1982).

46. Benjamin Page and Robert Shapiro, *The Rational Public* (Chicago, 1991), chap. 8.

47. See Van Evera, "Causes of War"; Hans-Ulrich Wehler, *The German Empire, 1871–1918* (Leamington Spa, N.H., 1985); Jack Levy, "The Causes of War: A Review of Theories and

These theories have no trouble explaining how the governing elite harnesses state power or exploits the inherent credibility and vast propaganda resources of the state. Their problem is not with power, but with motivation. Powerful interests such as "the ruling class" have a major stake in the long-run health of the society as a whole. They suffer directly from the costs of overexpansion. Up to a point, these costs can be passed on to the society at large, but this risks alienating the population and undercutting its productivity.[48] Unless quickly corrected, this is a self-defeating strategy for the ruling elite. Theories of this type, therefore, must demonstrate how a unified elite that is rational enough to devise a strategy of social imperialism nevertheless loses the ability to pull back when the costs of the strategy outweigh its benefits.

There is thus a paradox in existing domestic theories of overexpansion. The power to implement a strategy leading to overexpansion is inversely related to the motive for doing so. Theories that focus on narrow imperialist interest groups can easily explain the motive, but they must strain to explain how the groups gain power over policy. Conversely, theories that focus on the social imperialism of the state have no trouble explaining the power to implement the policy, but they find it hard to explain why the state fails to pull back when costs mount.

This paradox is not necessarily crippling; various supplementary hypotheses can be invoked to explain it away. This can be done by showing, for example, that parochial groups enjoy huge propaganda advantages owing to monopolies of information; that state mythmakers somehow come to believe their own propaganda;[49] that the domestic legitimacy crisis is so grave that long-run foreign policy consequences must be disregarded; or that precipitous reactions of other states cut short the opportunity to pull back. The case studies in this book suggest there is some truth in all these arguments. Indeed, some of them play major roles in explaining one or another of the cases. Nevertheless, this ad hoc mixture of auxiliary hypotheses lacks a unifying logic.

Domestic theories of overexpansion would be more satisfying, consequently, if the paradox of power and motivation could be solved in a way that is more integral to the domestic political process. Thus my

Evidence," in Philip Tetlock et al., eds., *Behavior, Society, and Nuclear War* (New York, 1989), 209–334, esp. 271–74; Arno J. Mayer, *The Persistence of the Old Regime: Europe to the Great War* (New York, 1981), chap. 5.

48. On limits to the ability of the "predatory state" to pass costs along to its society, see Douglass North, *Structure and Change in Economic History* (New York, 1981), 23, 27, and Margaret Levi, *Of Rule and Revenue* (Berkeley, Calif., 1988), 13, 33–38.

49. Van Evera, "Causes of War."

theory of coalition logrolling and coalition ideology draws on and subsumes earlier domestic theories, strengthening their explanatory power by rooting them more securely in a rational-choice foundation.

Coalition Logrolling and Coalition Ideology

Overexpansion is indeed a product of the political and propagandistic activities of imperialist groups. The crucial element in the explanation, however, lies not with the power and persuasiveness of these groups taken separately, but with the process by which they form coalitions of several such groups and with how these coalitions justify their policies.

Narrow imperialist interests overcome their weakness and hijack national policy in two ways. First, they gain control over national policy by joining in logrolled coalitions, trading favors so that each group gets what it wants most and costs are diffused to society through taxes imposed by the state.[50] In all the cases examined here, the state's overexpansion was more extreme than any individual group would have preferred, owing to the compounding of separate imperial programs through the logrolling process. Thus, logrolling was crucial to empowering interests favoring expansion and to exacerbating the overexpansion.

Second, by capturing the state, groups in the imperial coalition can harness its propaganda resources. Selling myths is easier for coalition leaders than for individual interest groups, because the instruments and credibility of the state can be exploited for the task and because self-serving strategic arguments become less traceable to the parochial interests that benefit from them. Moreover, coalition leaders have their own need for mythmaking, since they must justify the overcommitment that is endemic to logrolling.

This perspective explains several of the puzzles presented by other domestic explanations. It explains how narrow interests can hijack state policy: they do it by pooling their power in a coalition. It also explains why the state may be unable to pull back when the costs of imperialism rise: the state's leadership is not a unitary rational actor, but rather is the manager of a heterogeneous coalition that constrains the leadership's ability to adjust policy. This perspective explains, moreover, how strategic myths come to capture even those who invent them: because the myths are necessary to justify the power and policies of the ruling coalition, the leaders must maintain the myths or else jeopardize their rule. Overexpansion and imperial myths are so

50. On logrolling, see Dennis Mueller, *Public Choice* (Cambridge, 1979), 49–58. See also the discussion of "distributive issue areas" in Theodore Lowi, "American Business, Public Policy, Case Studies, and Political Theory," *World Politics* 16 (July 1964): 677–715.

widespread because logrolling is a feature of most political systems, to one degree or another. By its nature logrolling pays off concentrated group interests and ignores diffuse interests, like taxpayers, which are hard to organize. Since interests in expansion and militarism are typically more concentrated than the interests opposed to them, logrolling is inherently more apt to produce overexpansion than underexpansion.

Coalition theory also explains variations in the intensity of overexpansion and imperial mythmaking. When logrolling is the dominant feature of a political system, self-defeating overexpansion and the myths justifying it are more extreme. The degree of logrolling in a political system depends, in turn, on the distribution of power and interests in the society and on the character of its political institutions. In Wilhelmine Germany and imperial Japan, the social consequences of late industrialization gave rise to logrolling among narrow interest groups, producing overcommitted expansionist policies and extreme imperialist ideologies.[51] In contrast, the democratic systems of Britain and the United States, which are especially characteristic of early industrializing societies, strengthened diffuse interests opposed to overexpansion.[52]

My theory yields weaker, mixed predictions about unitary political systems like that of the Soviet Union or Hitler's Germany. On the one hand, the comparatively unitary Soviet system, whose origins lay in the dynamics of "late, late" industrialization, strengthened the hand of the Politburo oligarchy vis-à-vis parochial imperialist and military interests. As a result, the central leadership was able to keep imperialist logrolling in check. On the other hand, in unitary systems dominated by a single individual, like Hitler and Stalin, there is no countervailing political force to keep the dictator in check. If the dictator believes in the myths of empire, overexpansion is quite possible. When everything hinges on a single, unpredictable personality, there is no political counterweight to correct whatever strategic myths the leader may happen to believe in. Mythmaking begun for purposes of social mobilization, as in Stalin's case, or left as a holdover from an earlier period of imperial logrolling, as in Hitler's case, can spin out of control. For these reasons, democratic systems and systems dominated by a unitary oligarchy have been less prone to overexpansion and strategic mythmaking

51. On the differences between early, late, and "late, late" industrializers, see Alexander Gerschenkron, *Economic Backwardness in Historical Perspective* (Cambridge, Mass., 1962). On logrolling among expansionist interest groups in Wilhelmine Germany, see Eckart Kehr, *Economic Interest, Militarism, and Foreign Policy* (Berkeley, Calif., 1977).

52. This argument is derived from Anthony Downs, *An Economic Theory of Democracy* (New York, 1957), which is summarized, qualified, and contrasted with logrolling by Norman Frohlich and Joe Oppenheimer, *Modern Political Economy* (Englewood Cliffs, N.J., 1978), 127–30.

than have systems dominated by logrolling among cartels or by individual dictators.[53]

WHY IT MATTERS

These findings have both theoretical and practical significance. Theoretically, Realism must be recaptured from those who look only at politics between societies, ignoring what goes on within societies. Realists are right in stressing power, interests, and coalition making as the central elements in a theory of politics, but recent exponents of Realism in international relations have been wrong in looking exclusively to states as the irreducible atoms whose power and interests are to be assessed.[54] These truncated Realists have also been wrong in ignoring the role ideology plays in enhancing the power and shaping the perceived interests of political groups, especially when information is monopolized and interests are uncertain.

Machiavelli, Thucydides, and even Hans Morgenthau understood political realism in this broader way, but for the most part more recent Realists have not.[55] Morgenthau believed that "domestic and international politics are but two different manifestations of the same phenomenon: the struggle for power."[56] Contemporary political scientists are beginning to conceive of the state not as a unitary billiard ball in a system of other billiard balls, but as a pivot adjudicating between international *and* domestic pressures.[57] But even if this view is accepted, Kenneth Waltz argues that the international game board is decisive. "In self-help systems," he says, "the pressures of competition weigh more heavily than ideological preferences or internal political pressures."[58]

53. Margaret Hermann and Charles Hermann, in "Who Makes Foreign Policy Decisions and How?" *International Studies Quarterly* 33 (December 1989): 361–88, distinguish among systems ruled by a "predominant leader," by a "single group," and by "multiple autonomous actors."

54. Waltz, *Theory of International Politics*, has presented the most sophisticated justification of this narrow view of Realism, though he did not invent it. The "primacy of foreign policy" over domestic politics has a long history in German Realist thought.

55. For some recent debates on Realism, see Robert Keohane, ed., *Neorealism and Its Critics* (New York, 1986). For examples of analyses rooted in power, interest, and coalition politics but operating across the international-domestic boundary, see Ronald Rogowski, "Structure, Growth, and Power: Three Rationalist Accounts," *International Organization* 37 (Autumn 1983): 713–38, and Rogowski, *Coalitions and Commerce* (Princeton, N.J., 1989).

56. Hans Morgenthau, *Politics among Nations*, 5th ed. (New York, 1973), the first sentence in chap. 4.

57. Robert Putnam, "Diplomacy and Domestic Politics: The Logic of Two-Level Games," *International Organization* 42 (Summer 1988): 427–60.

58. Kenneth Waltz, "Reflections on *Theory of International Politics*: A Response to My Critics," in Keohane, *Neorealism*, 329.

The classics of realist political philosophy and contemporary research findings both cast doubt on this view. Hobbes himself argued that individuals formed a state precisely in order to mitigate the pressures of anarchy. And Adam Smith, in noting that "there is a great deal of ruin in a nation," understood that the survival of great states does not normally hang by a mere thread.[59] More recently, Peter Katzenstein has found that the domestic political arrangements of small states are determined by their vulnerable position in international markets; conversely, the domestic structure of large states determines their strategy in world markets.[60] My own work finds that, among the great powers, domestic pressures often outweigh international ones in the calculations of national leaders.

This book's findings also have practical significance. A new understanding of the domestic political origins of strategic myths should affect how people assess strategic debates in their own states, and how policies affect strategic mythmaking in opposing states. A theory of the link between domestic politics and foreign policy is indispensable for thinking through the international consequences of Mikhail Gorbachev's domestic innovations and the appropriate American response to them.[61] More broadly, such a theory can help in assessing claims that the end of the Cold War division of Europe reflects the growing obsolescence of great-power war, as well as counterclaims that it may mean the end of the long post-1945 peace. The practical and theoretical implications of my findings will be taken up in the concluding chapter.

59. As quoted by Bernard Brodie, *Strategy in the Missile Age* (Princeton, N.J., 1965), 6.

60. Peter Katzenstein, *Small States in World Markets* (Ithaca, N.Y., 1985); Katzenstein, *Corporatism and Change: Austria, Switzerland, and the Politics of Industry* (Ithaca, N.Y., 1984); Katzenstein, ed., *Between Power and Plenty: Foreign Economic Policies of Advanced Industrial States* (Madison, Wis., 1978).

61. For attempts to do this, see Jack Snyder, "The Gorbachev Revolution: A Waning of Soviet Expansionism?" *International Security* 12 (Winter 1987–88): 93–131; Snyder, "International Leverage," 1–31; and the Soviet chapter and concluding chapter of this volume.

[2]

Three Theories of
Overexpansion

The idea that security can be achieved through expansion is a pervasive theme in the grand strategy of the great powers in the industrial era. What explains the prevalence of this idea and variations in its intensity?

THE REALIST EXPLANATION: RATIONAL RESPONSE TO ANARCHY

Realists argue that statesmen who believe expansion is the best means of achieving security are often making reasonable judgments. In their view states are doomed to unending competition in an anarchic setting, like Hobbes's state of nature. In the absence of a supranational sovereign to enforce rules, states must constantly be wary of depredations by others, looking to themselves for security and material strength. Even status quo powers may resort to aggression to gain control over scarce resources that might otherwise be turned against them. Thus, though aggressive behavior may make life "nasty, brutish, and short," the scarcity of security in an anarchic environment often makes preventive aggression necessary.[1]

Even when hindsight shows that a bid for security through expansion turned out to be a costly failure, Realists could—and do—argue

1. Robert Jervis, "Cooperation under the Security Dilemma," *World Politics* 30 (January 1978): 167–214, argues that the requirements of self-help under anarchy may force even status quo states to become aggressors. Likewise, Kenneth Waltz says that "states facing global problems are like individual consumers trapped by the 'tyranny of small decisions.'" He also remarks that "early in this century Winston Churchill observed that the British-German naval race promised disaster *and* that Britain had no realistic choice other than to run it." See his *Theory of International Politics* (Reading, Mass., 1979), 110–11.

that the attempt was a rational response to international circumstances. Given the information available, they argue, it may have been reasonable to take a risk on achieving security through expansion, if statesmen had good reason to believe retrenchment would have been even riskier. For vulnerable states in a highly competitive anarchic environment, all strategies for achieving security are likely to have low success rates. In this sense it may not be contradictory to argue that a case of overexpansion was a rational response to the objective constraints and incentives of the state's international position.

But anarchy is not in itself sufficient to predict an expansionist security strategy. Realist scholars argue that the normal response to threat is to form a balancing alliance.[2] Therefore states should expect that expansion will reduce their security insofar as it threatens other states and provokes an opposing coalition. In light of that, the simple facts of anarchy and insecurity should not be enough for a Realist to expect states to adopt strategies of expansion. Other conditions, which would outweigh or nullify the fear of a balancing response to aggression, must be added to explain this strategic choice. Some might be conditions that prevail throughout the international system at a particular time, encouraging aggressive solutions to security problems for many states. For example, when the prevailing military technology available to all the great powers makes offense easier than defense, strategies of security through expansion should be widespread. Some of the conditions promoting expansion might be peculiar to the position of the individual state, giving it special incentives to solve its security problems through aggression.

The following Realist hypotheses about conditions that should give rise to expansionism are derived from the theories of political scientists and from historians' interpretations of individual cases. When these conditions are present, Realists would expect the state to adopt a strategy of security through expansion; when they are absent, Realists would expect the state to adopt a nonaggressive strategy.

Offensive Advantage

Whenever prevailing military technology favors the attacker, expansionist security strategies should be attractive.[3] An aggressive strategy

2. Waltz, *Theory of International Politics*, and Stephen Walt, *The Origins of Alliances* (Ithaca, N.Y., 1987).

3. Jervis, "Cooperation"; Stephen Van Evera, "Causes of War" (Ph.D. diss., University of California at Berkeley, 1984); Stephen Van Evera, "Why Cooperation Failed in 1914," in Kenneth Oye, ed., *Cooperation under Anarchy* (Princeton, N.J., 1985), 80–117, a special issue of *World Politics* 38 (October 1985).

would allow states to capitalize on surprise and exploit the advantages of the attacker to compensate for weakness. They would have strong first-strike incentives to destroy opponents' military forces and seize their war-making capacity before others did the same to them.

Such situations of global offensive advantage are rare, however. Authorities on ground warfare usually claim that the defender almost always enjoys a net advantage, which may be smaller or larger depending on various technological and geographical conditions. Air power theorists predicted that the rise of long-range bombers and later of intercontinental missiles would create first-strike incentives if the forces of one side were vulnerable to a preemptive attack by the other. In fact, first-strike knockout blows have been rare. Though surprise attacks often succeed tactically at the outset of a war, the attacker normally finds that the diplomatic onus of aggression outweighs its fleeting operational benefits.[4] Most theorists argue, moreover, that the nuclear stalemate aids the side that is defending the status quo, since the threat to use nuclear force in defense of vital interests is more credible than its use in conquest.[5] In short, technological conditions aiding the attacker may exist in isolated instances and therefore may help explain some cases of expansionist strategies. Overall, however, they have not been common enough to account for the more general inclination toward such strategies.

Geography may place greater or lesser obstacles in the path of the attacker.[6] In land warfare, rough terrain and narrow frontages aid the defender, whereas flat terrain and wide frontages aid the attacker. In all forms of warfare, the logistical burden of projecting power over a distance tends to reduce the relative fighting power of the attacker. But if the attacker is invading weakly defended territories near its own home base and the defender must transport forces to support a distant client, distance will aid the attacker.[7]

---

4. On the reasons for the defender's advantage, see John Mearsheimer, "Why the Soviets Can't Win Quickly in Central Europe," *International Security* 7 (Summer 1982): 15–20. Richard Betts, "Conventional Deterrence: Predictive Uncertainty and Policy Confidence," *World Politics* 37 (January 1985): 153–79, has shown persuasively that surprise gives the attacker significant advantages at the outset of a military campaign. In all of his cases in which numerically inferior attackers won opening engagements, however, surprise proved to be a wasting asset—that is, the attacker ultimately lost the war, especially as a result of balancing behavior that the aggressor's victories provoked.

5. Robert Jervis, *The Meaning of the Nuclear Revolution* (Ithaca, N.Y., 1989), 30–31, 35, 41, 227.

6. Jervis, "Cooperation," 195; Mearsheimer, "Why the Soviets Can't Win Quickly."

7. For a complete listing of the conditions in which offensive strategies are necessary or enjoy an advantage, see Stephen Van Evera, "Offense, Defense, and Deterrence: When Is Offense Best?" paper delivered at the annual meeting of the American Political Science Association, Chicago, September 1987.

Geography and technology may interact in shaping the incentives for expansionist strategies. For example, innovations in transportation technology, such as the building of railroads in the colonial periphery in the 1890s, may reduce the difficulty of projecting power into the hinterlands[8] and thus bring new territories and new strategic resources inside the cost-benefit frontier of the empire. Nonetheless, security problems on the turbulent frontier opened up by the new technology may still lure the empire beyond the cost-benefit equilibrium.[9]

Political conditions may also affect a Realist's calculations about offensive security strategies. Even if the defender enjoys military advantages, the instability of the political status quo may make a positional defense impossible. After the Second World War, for example, the political status quo in Europe was fluid. Each side had potential fifth columns in the other's camp, and the dividing line between the blocs ran down the middle of formerly united countries. Moreover, many of the European states were weak internally and militarily and consequently would have reason to join the bandwagon with the rising power rather than balance against it. Given this fluid situation, there were plausible reasons to believe that a political offensive was the best defense.[10]

Cumulative Resources

Whenever states can make significant net additions to their power resources through conquest, Realists would expect them to adopt strategies of security through expansion.[11] But open-ended strategies of cumulative gains, counting on a never-ending cycle in which new conquests provide the resources for still further conquests, are highly dubious.[12] At some point, according to Robert Gilpin's historical review of the experience of empires, costs always outstrip revenues from additional conquest.[13] Yet under some conditions more limited attempts to strengthen the state's position through conquest might in principle be worthwhile.

8. Daniel Headrick, *Tools of Empire* (New York, 1981).

9. Robert Gilpin, *War and Change in International Politics* (New York, 1981).

10. Scott Parrish, "Soviet Reactions to the Security Dilemma: The Sources of Soviet Self-Encirclement, 1945–1950" (Harriman Institute certificate essay, Columbia University, April 1990), and his forthcoming dissertation.

11. Van Evera, "Causes of War," has the best discussion.

12. Robert Jervis, "Domino Beliefs and Strategic Behavior," in Robert Jervis and Jack Snyder, eds., *Dominoes and Bandwagons: Strategic Beliefs and Great Power Competition in the Eurasian Rimland* (New York, 1991), 20–50, and other essays in the volume; Van Evera, "Causes of War."

13. Gilpin, *War and Change*, chap. 4.

The clearest case is a situation of near autarky. If a state could achieve direct physical control over the resources it needs to fight a long war against its strongest opponents, its security would be greatly enhanced. Blockades would not deprive it of crucial war matériel or food for its population. Moreover, once autarky was achieved, the state could take advantage of all the tactical and operational benefits of standing on the defense. Consequently a strategy of limited expansion might make sense for a security-conscious, nearly autarkic power. Still, this incentive would have to be weighed against the risk of provoking an overwhelming balancing alliance.[14]

Similarly, expanding to achieve a natural defensive frontier or to seize a strategically crucial defensive bottleneck might make sense for a security-conscious state. The problem is, however, that other states are likely to want to hold the strategic point, such as the Turkish Straits, for their own defensive reasons. Holding the position might make defense easier, but fighting to seize it may undermine security. In the extreme case, such a position could be so crucial that whoever holds it can render the other insecure, so that the opponents must fight over it, even if the fighting itself endangers their security. But in many cases the strategic value of the bottleneck may be exaggerated, and the struggle for it counterproductive.

Shifts in Relative Power

A state has an incentive for preventive aggression whenever its relative power is expected to decline.[15] By attacking immediately and conquering its rising opponent, the state can enhance its chances for long-run security. This should be true even if the chances of success in the preventive attack are low, as long as the chances of success in a defensive war later would be lower still. But this incentive must be weighed against the diplomatic and operational disadvantages of being the attacker. It must be compared, moreover, with the alternative strategy of appeasing the rising power.

14. The two cases of this type are Germany and Japan. David Calleo, *The German Problem Reconsidered* (Cambridge, 1978); James Crowley, *Japan's Quest for Autonomy, 1930–1938* (Princeton, N.J., 1968). Michael Barnhart, *Japan Prepares for Total War: The Search for Economic Security, 1919–1941* (Ithaca, N.Y., 1987), 104, summarizes a December 1937 Japanese Planning Board meeting as acknowledging that "even if Japan occupied all of China and Southeast Asia, it would still find itself unable to wage a long war without relying on Anglo-American resources." Arguing for the rationality of a nonimperialistic, cooperative strategy for powers in this kind of situation are Davis Bobrow and Robert Kudrle, "How Middle Powers Can Manage Resource Weakness: Japan and Energy," *World Politics* 39 (July 1987): 536–65.

15. Jack Levy, "Declining Power and the Preventive Motive for War," *World Politics* 40 (October 1987): 82–107.

In calculating their incentives for preventive aggression, states assess not only long-run shifts in underlying power resources, but also short-run shifts in the degree to which those resources are mobilized for war. The paper tiger image of the opponent rests in part on the argument that the opponent, though hostile, is not yet fully mobilized for war, materially or politically. Therefore there is an incentive to conquer the resources needed for self-defense, or to defeat potential enemies piecemeal before they are ready to move. The problem is that these conquests are likely to provoke the feared mobilization. Even so, if the mobilization is really inevitable in the long run, and if sufficient resources can be conquered in the short run, the strategy can in principle be a rational response to the state's international situation.

Multipolarity

Strategies of security through expansion make more sense in multipolar situations than in bipolar ones.[16] In multipolarity, an expansionist power may be able to defeat its opponents piecemeal if they fail to unite because they cannot agree on who should bear the costs of resistance. At the same time, great powers in multipolarity may have strong incentives to expand to achieve autarky, since they are less likely to be self-sufficient in the resources needed for national security than are bipolar powers. The most dangerous situation would be one in which some great powers were autarkic in security resources but others were not. To avoid one-way dependency, the latter would have a strong incentive to expand. Arguably, this aptly describes the situation of Germany and Japan vis-à-vis the United States and the Soviet Union before the Second World War. Yet the failure of their bids for autarky, snuffed out by the balancing reaction of the other powers, shows that this incentive must be weighed against other factors that affect its probability of success.

THE COGNITIVE EXPLANATION: MISLEADING MENTAL SHORTCUTS

Some common strategic myths may be artifacts of the shortcuts the human brain takes when processing information under uncertainty. To

16. Waltz, *Theory of International Politics*; John Mearsheimer, "Back to the Future: Instability in Europe after the Cold War," *International Security* 15 (Summer 1990): 5–56; Thomas Christensen and Jack Snyder, "Chain Gangs and Passed Bucks: Predicting Alliance Patterns in Multipolarity," *International Organization* 44 (Spring 1990): 137–68. Waltz, *Theory of International Politics*, 169, 178, 199, 207–8, stresses that bipolarity mitigates the effects of anarchy; one reason is that the certainty of each pole's internal strength makes it less tied to the fate of smaller powers.

simplify decision making, people focus inordinately on the most available data, use ready-made theories to impose order on the data, and employ rules of thumb to draw inferences.[17] Some of these shortcuts may introduce biases that predispose decision makers toward overexpansion.

Cognitive theory, unlike the Realist theory discussed above, is not organized in a tightly deductive form. Nor has anyone attempted to show systematically how hypotheses deduced from cognitive theory can explain patterns of great-power overexpansion.[18] Implicitly, however, many of the explanations offered for individual instances of overexpansion—those stressing beliefs and lessons of the past, for example—are cognitive in nature. Consequently it should be worthwhile to try to establish a coherent theoretical basis for those interpretations and to derive testable hypotheses from it.

Most cognitive hypotheses can be at least loosely derived from what is called the "cognitive miser" model.[19] Its central principle is economy of cognitive operations. Under complexity and uncertainty, people use several devices to simplify assessment and choice. The ones most pertinent to the study of strategic myths are, first, belief systems, and second, cognitive heuristics and biases.

People store what they have learned in simplified, structured form in belief systems. Incoming information is categorized in accordance with the preestablished categories of these beliefs. Consequences of alternative courses of action are assessed with the aid of causal beliefs. Belief systems serve the need for cognitive economy in several ways. They reduce the need for information, since expectations embedded in the belief system can be used to fill in gaps in information. They promote efficient theoretical thinking by organizing beliefs into hierarchies, subordinating a plethora of details under more general concepts. Moreover, stable belief systems protect against the mental burden of constant fundamental reassessments by resisting change in the face of disconfirming information. When disconfirming evidence is so overwhelming that it cannot be ignored, its disruptive impact on the economy of cognitive operations is managed by first adjusting only the beliefs lower down in the hierarchy of generalization, revising more central concepts only when absolutely necessary, and perhaps not even then. In this way the decision maker, though partially responsive to

17. Robert Jervis, *Perception and Misperception in International Politics* (Princeton, N.J., 1976); Deborah Welch Larson, *Origins of Containment* (Princeton, N.J., 1985); Daniel Kahneman, Paul Slovic, and Amos Tversky, *Judgment under Uncertainty: Heuristics and Biases* (Cambridge, 1982); Harold Kelley and John Michela, "Attribution Theory and Research," *Annual Review of Psychology* 31 (1980): 457–501.

18. Ralph White, *Fearful Warriors* (New York, 1984), is a quasi-popular book that uses several cognitive hypotheses to explain great-power conflict and enemy images.

19. Susan Fiske and Shelley Taylor, *Social Cognition* (New York, 1984), 15.

information from the environment, is buffered from the intellectual burden of dealing with its full complexity, uncertainty, and variety.

This system has tremendous advantages for cognitive economy, though its benefits are purchased at the price of being heavily dependent on the initial structuring of the beliefs. Future events will be seen as reruns of formative experiences or as the playing out of patterns instilled in early training. Consequently, for explaining strategic ideas and behavior, formative lessons drawn from early, vivid, or firsthand experiences take on special importance. When a whole generation undergoes the same formative experiences, such as the lessons of Munich, the strategic policy of the whole state is likely to be affected for many years.[20]

Such a process could explain variations in beliefs about the wisdom of strategies of security through expansion. When formative experiences of pertinent decision makers have taught them that dominoes fall, that states join bandwagons, that attackers win quickly through surprise, or that passivity jeopardizes security, then the belief in expansionism should be prevalent and difficult to reverse. A generation steeped in the lessons of appeasement at Munich would be quick to imagine dominoes falling and would feel a need to nip an opponent's growing assertiveness in the bud. Conversely, the opposite formative experiences should lead to the opposite strategic beliefs. A generation raised on the lessons of Vietnam would be quick to foresee quagmires resulting from an overextended containment policy.

At least some historians and area specialists have tried to explain the American Cold War belief system, the Bolshevik operational code, and German and Japanese imperialism in terms of such formative lessons. To test these explanations, I examine whether people learned the same lessons from the same experiences, whether they drew conclusions in a logically plausible way, and whether their conclusions preceded or followed the adoption of policies implied by the lessons.

Formative experiences could in principle explain why imperial myths have occasionally appeared, but it is puzzling that such beliefs should be fairly common among all the great powers. If lessons were being absorbed in an unbiased way, then paper tiger and domino beliefs should be widespread only if they were generally true. Since these beliefs contradict fairly well-established scholarly knowledge about the balance of power, it is necessary to explain why conclusions might be drawn in such a skewed way. Some additional features of information

20. Jervis, *Perception*, chap. 6; also Larson, *Origins of Containment*, 50–57, on processing information according to preestablished templates, called "schemas." For some qualifications, see Shelley Taylor and Suzanne Thompson, "Stalking the Elusive 'Vividness' Effect," *Psychological Review* 89 (March 1982): 155–81.

processing by the "cognitive miser," called "heuristics and biases" in the psychological literature, might in principle explain this.

For example, the common tendency to adopt a paper tiger image of the adversary might be explained by typical biases in the way we attribute causes to behavior. People tend to explain their own actions in terms of environmental constraints (a "situational attribution"), whereas they explain others' actions in terms of innate disposition (a "dispositional attribution"). A purely cognitive explanation is that environmental pressures stand out in our minds when we reconstruct our own actions, whereas the actor is the most salient object in the field of vision when we reconstruct the actions of another.[21] Situational attributions consequently require less mental work in explaining our own actions, but more work in explaining others'. In conflict relationships, this leads to attributions like "he acted aggressively because that's his nature, but I stood firm because circumstances forced me to."[22] Raymond Garthoff has extensively documented this kind of mutual double standard in how states cast blame in his study of the decline of Soviet-American détente in the 1970s.[23]

Some psychological studies suggest that people make dispositional attributions when adversaries behave aggressively but situational ones when they behave cooperatively. A purely cognitive explanation is that we expect our own actions to elicit the desired results, so that when they do we say, "My strategy worked." But if our actions are counterproductive, we blame the other person for being incorrigible rather than our own actions for being ineffective.[24] Over time, this bias in historical bookkeeping could foster an image of the enemy as an innate aggressor who will bow to forceful resistance—a paper tiger. For example, this fits perfectly Brezhnev's "correlation of forces" theory of détente: when America behaved as Brezhnev desired, he said it was because the power of the socialist camp gave America no alternative; but when America misbehaved, it was a reflection of the innate aggressiveness of capitalism.

Satisfying cognitive explanations for the domino theory are harder to think up. Laboratory findings suggest that people overrate the cumulative probability of a series of events. Thus, if three events must occur to produce an outcome and the independent probability of each is 0.8,

---

21. The relevant research is cited by Kelley and Michela, "Attribution Theory and Research," 477–78.

22. Jervis, *Perception*, chap. 3, traces these consequences in terms of a spiral theory of international conflict.

23. Raymond Garthoff, *Detente and Confrontation* (Washington, D.C., 1985).

24. Robert Jervis, "Deterrence and Perception," *International Security* 7 (Winter 1982–83): 20–22. Kelley and Michela, "Attribution Theory and Research," 478–79, note that experimental evidence is somewhat contradictory on this point.

people tend to estimate the probability of the outcome as 0.8, when it is in fact only 0.5.[25] This might help explain the ready acceptance of the domino theory.

One test for this argument is whether statesmen who exaggerate cumulative probabilities in the domino theory also exaggerate it in other circumstances. For example, the same bias should lead them to fear that firm deterrence strategies might set off a conflict spiral with the adversary. For example, a statesman who estimated that the chance of provoking a military mobilization was 0.8, that the chance that a mobilization would inadvertently trigger a war was 0.8, and that the chance that the war would become nuclear was 0.8, would erroneously calculate the cumulative probability of the whole chain as 0.8. In fact, people who worry the most about connections between falling dominoes probably worry the least about connections between rungs on the ladder of escalating hostility, and vice versa.[26] If so, this suggests that some different, probably noncognitive dynamic drives the domino theory.

More generally, the case studies in this book will cast doubt on cognitive explanations for strategic concepts by showing that beliefs and "lessons" correlate more strongly with personal and institutional interests than with formative experiences. It is more accurate to say that statesmen and societies actively shape the lessons of the past in ways they find convenient than it is to say they are shaped by them. Both Germany and Japan had numerous opportunities to learn from their own experiences that big stick diplomacy provokes opposition and that defenders attract allies while aggressors lose them. Bismarck was misremembered by subsequent German militarists as the man of "blood and iron, who used his sword to cut the tangles of politics on the battlefield,"[27] whereas in fact he had been careful to isolate his opponents by making them appear to be the aggressors.[28] Similarly, Japanese militarists might have learned a lesson when their assassina-

---

25. Amos Tversky and Daniel Kahneman, "Judgments of and by Representativeness," in Kahneman, Slovic, and Tversky, *Judgment*, 90–98; Nancy Kanwisher, "Cognitive Heuristics and American Security Policy," *Journal of Conflict Resolution* 33 (December 1989): 652–75, esp. 663–65.

26. Tversky and Kahneman attribute bias in assessing cumulative probability to the "representativeness heuristic," which suggests that people classify events and their causes in terms of superficial resemblance rather than a deep analysis of underlying processes. For example, the fall of Vietnam "resembles" the fall of Western Europe and thus seems like a plausible cause of it. But the war in Vietnam also "resembles" a Soviet-American war over Europe, and so by this same psycho-logic should be seen as a cause of it—and a deterrent to intervention.

27. Quoted in Jack Snyder, *The Ideology of the Offensive* (Ithaca, N.Y., 1984), 133.

28. Stephen Walt, "The Search for a Science of Strategy," *International Security* 12 (Summer 1987): 163–64.

tion of the queen of Korea in 1884 drove the king to collaborate with the Russians. But in 1928 their murder of the relatively pliable warlord of Manchuria drove his son into an alliance with the Chinese nationalists.[29] In both Germany and Japan some important figures, like Bernard von Bulow and Kijuro Shidehara, came close to learning the right lessons, but they were ejected by a political system that could not tolerate accurate self-evaluation.[30]

Mental scripts and operational codes used by statesmen are not, at bottom, strictly cognitive. Rather, they are bound up with the social order, the political balance of power within it, its legitimation, and the justification of policies favored by particular social groups. Strategic beliefs exist more in the realm of ideology than in that of pure cognition. The next section presents my own explanation of the ideological origins of strategic ideas.

THE DOMESTIC EXPLANATION: COALITION POLITICS AND IDEOLOGY

The myths of empire arise as rationalizations for the interests of groups that derive parochial benefits from expansion, from military preparations associated with expansion, or from the domestic political climate brought about by intense international competition. Individually and in coalitions, such groups propagate the myth of security through expansion in order to advance their parochial interests in the guise of the general interests of the whole society.

Overexpansion and the myths of empire have been widespread among the great powers because imperialist groups enjoy at least some political advantages in most political systems, owing to their ability to organize for collective action, their monopolies on information, and their ties to the state. The extent of these political advantages is determined in large part by the type of political system in which these imperialist groups must operate. Their success is easiest in what I call "cartelized" political systems. In cartelized systems power assets— including material resources, organizational strength, and information— are concentrated in the hands of parochial groups, each with very narrow interests focused in a particular economic sector or bureaucratic sphere. In such systems, ruling coalitions are formed by logrolling among these concentrated interests, and their policies are justified by

29. John G. Roberts, *Mitsui* (New York, 1973), 155, 266.

30. Van Evera, "Causes of War," devotes a chapter to the subject of strategic nonevaluation. On Bulow's learning and political problems, see Gerhard Ritter, *The Sword and the Scepter*, vol. 2 (Coral Gables, Fla., 1969), 161; Geoff Eley, *Reshaping the German Right* (New Haven, Conn., 1980), chap. 9.

[31]

mythmaking. Since interests favoring expansion tend to be disproportionately represented in such systems, overexpansion is more likely. In
democratic systems, by contrast, power is diffused widely by the ballot
and by norms of free debate. Diffuse interests opposed to expansion
are more strongly represented and are more able to check the logrolling
and mythmaking of concentrated imperial interests. In unitary systems, power is concentrated in the hands of a single dictator or a
unitary oligarchy, which has diverse interests in a variety of economic
and bureaucratic sectors. This concentration gives the unitary elite a
relatively encompassing view of the state's interests and an incentive to
keep overexpansion, imperialist mythmaking, and imperialist logrolling in check. In the case of the single dictator, however, incentives
rooted in distributions of power and interest yield weak predictions,
since there are no political checks on whatever strategic notions the
dictator may happen to hold. Though overexpansion is not structurally
required in this case, there is no political counterweight to prevent it.

The experience of the industrialized great powers suggests that
coalition politics and ideology offer the single best explanation for the
strategic ideas that contribute to overexpansion. Though the international factors stressed by Realism also play an important role, their
effects are skewed by domestic coalition making and ideological
mythmaking.

Political Advantages of Imperialist Groups

Overexpansion and imperial myths are common among the great
powers because groups benefiting disproportionately from expansion
or from the ideas that promote it often enjoy advantages in organization and persuasiveness. These advantages help such groups to sell
imperial myths to state leaders and the public and thus to "hijack"
state policy. Though the extent of these advantages varies greatly over
time and across political systems, imperialist groups normally enjoy at
least some net political advantage over anti-imperialist interests. In
particular, pro-expansionist groups typically enjoy (1) organizational
and motivational advantages owing to the comparative compactness
and concentration of interests of those who benefit from imperialism;
(2) a partial monopoly of information bearing on the costs and benefits
of imperialism; and (3) close ties to the state.

Compact groups with concentrated interests. The benefits of empire are
normally more concentrated than its costs, which are in most cases
diffused through taxes. Private investors in imperial enterprises pay
their own operating costs, but it is the state—the taxpayers—that pays

[32]

for infrastructure and military protection. This diffusion of anti-imperial interests among all taxpayers is in itself a major reason for their chronic political weakness. The theory of collective goods explains that it will be easy to organize a compact group, in which each member derives a large benefit from the successful promotion of the shared interest. But when benefits are diffused throughout a much larger group, each member will have a weaker incentive to work for the common goal, and coordinating common action will be more cumbersome.[31] An exhaustive study of the costs and benefits of the British Empire in the late nineteenth century has borne out these predictions of the theory of collective action. During this period the empire served to transfer income from a large number of middle-class taxpayers and regional economic elites to a more compact London commercial elite who had invested heavily abroad.[32] Military expenditure in defense of foreign economic interests was the most costly item in what the authors call the "imperial subsidy."[33]

Both economic sectors and bureaucratic organizations may have concentrated interests in expansion. Militaries and colonial bureaucrats are especially prominent throughout the case studies as compact groups having concentrated interests in expansion, big stick diplomacy, and arms races. Though militaries may not want war per se, their interest in organizational growth, wealth, prestige, and autonomy is usually served by ideas and policies that tend to create war as their "waste by-product."[34] Thus Admiral Alfred von Tirpitz, the chief of Wilhelmine Germany's naval staff, sought a fleet that inadvertently made war more likely because it provoked Germany's encirclement, then found himself unable to head off the war that he knew the fleet was unprepared for.[35] Likewise, the Kwantung army sought Manchuria as its own quasi-autarkic industrial empire to enhance its autonomy from the vagaries of politics in Tokyo, but in doing so it led Japan down the path to an open-ended war on the Asian mainland.[36] The relative compactness of

---

31. Mancur Olson, *The Rise and Decline of Nations* (New Haven, Conn., 1982); Olson, *The Logic of Collective Action* (Cambridge, Mass., 1965); Russell Hardin, *Collective Action* (Baltimore, 1982).

32. Lance Davis and Robert Huttenback, *Mammon and the Pursuit of Empire: The Political Economy of British Imperialism, 1860–1912* (Cambridge, 1986), esp. 212, 221, 250, 252. For qualifications stemming from their focus on foreign investment rather than trade, see Michael Edelstein, "Discussion," *Journal of Economic History* 42 (March 1982): 131–32.

33. Davis and Huttenback, *Mammon*, 304.

34. Van Evera's phrase and analysis, from "Causes of War." See also Barry Posen, *Sources of Military Doctrine* (Ithaca, N.Y., 1984).

35. Fritz Fischer, *War of Illusions* (New York, 1975), 162–63.

36. On this point, in addition to Barnhart, see Sadako Ogata, *Defiance in Manchuria* (Berkeley, Calif., 1964).

the professional military—its hierarchical nature, its habituation to discipline, the lack of an alternative employer for its specialized skills— has enhanced its dedication to and effectiveness in pursuit of its concentrated interests in imperial projects.[37]

Economic groups also figure from time to time as compact interests receiving concentrated benefits from expansionism. The motives and characteristics of these groups have been quite varied: in 1882 holders of Egyptian bonds wanted military intervention to secure their invest- ment; in the 1890s noncompetitive Birmingham industrialists and workers sought protected markets in an expanded empire; highly competitive Manchester textile merchants half a century earlier had demanded that force be used to open up closed markets abroad; Ruhr steel makers cared about the German empire only because it justified the steel- hulled fleet.[38]

Not all compact economic groups have had a clear-cut interest in expansionism, however. Actively anti-imperialist economic groups ap- pear in some of the case studies, but their motivations regarding imperial overexpansion were typically ambivalent and changeable. For example, Manchester industrialists mobilized by Richard Cobden funded the popular anti-interventionist propaganda of the Anti–Corn Law League, but once mass pressure was successfully exploited to push through free trade in grain, the industrial magnates dumped Cobden's peace program and instead backed Palmerston's trade-promoting gun- boat diplomacy.[39] Likewise, Junkers and some Tory landlords disliked paying taxes for fleets and foreign interventions, but this interest was not their highest priority. The *zaibatsu*, large trading and manufacturing conglomerates that dominated the Japanese economy of the 1920s, depended on access to American raw materials and markets, and so they favored Shidehara's policy of cooperating with the democracies. But they also counted on expanded access to Chinese markets and resources, so they simultaneously helped fuel the expansionist side of Japanese diplomacy.[40]

Because the costs of empire are diffused through the state, few compact groups have strong interests opposed to empire. In light of collective goods theory's conclusions about the difficulty of effectively

37. Van Evera, "Causes of War"; Francis Rourke, *Bureaucracy and Foreign Policy* (Bos- ton, 1969), chaps. 2–4.

38. All of these are discussed in the case-study chapters below.

39. William Grampp, *The Manchester School of Economics* (Stanford, Calif., 1960), esp. 117; Asa Briggs, *Victorian People*, rev. ed. (Chicago, 1970), 17, 23.

40. For example, Mitsui was one of two *zaibatsu* that controlled three-fourths of Japanese colonial investment, but it also had a diversified portfolio of banking, trading, mining, and some manufacturing concerns, making it "a splendidly balanced money machine that functioned well in war or peace, in boom or depression." Roberts, *Mitsui*, 5, 135.

organizing diffuse interests, this helps explain the endemic bias toward overexpansion.

As collective goods theory would predict, imperial interests were especially concentrated in the two most extreme cases of overexpansion, Germany and Japan. German state-financed colonialism, for example, benefited the navy, Krupp steel, and other contractors while providing essentially zero return on the public's investment.[41] In Japan, very narrow army and navy concerns, speciously rationalized in terms of the national interest, dominated strategic calculations.[42]

British and American internationalist business enterprises fall at the other extreme. As a rule, they made economically productive investments abroad at low military overhead while using cheap food prices or social welfare programs at home to win mass allies away from competing protectionist interests.[43] Thus economic calculations by German and Japanese imperialists and protectionists, who extracted rents from other sectors of society, had no relation to marginal costs and benefits to society as a whole. Calculations by American and British internationalists, who earned profits from productive ventures, came closer to mirroring the costs and benefits to society as a whole.

Information monopolies and other propaganda advantages. Another cause of endemic overexpansion is that self-interested groups favoring militarism and imperial expansion often enjoy an information monopoly. Those who engage in imperial activities and preparation for war automatically gain special knowledge about key elements in strategic cost-benefit calculations, such as local conditions in the hinterland, the strength of the opponent, and the effectiveness of various techniques of fighting.

Such groups exploit their reputation for expert knowledge to justify their self-serving policies in terms of diffuse national interests. Rationales that explain the need for expansion in terms of national security are especially convenient for this purpose. Thus the German navy under Tirpitz invented the theory of the "risk fleet" to explain why naval expansion was needed to forestall imminent strangulation of the German economy. By using the German navy's own internal studies, Paul Kennedy can today destroy the logic of the Tirpitz risk fleet theory in thirty pages. But at the time, those studies were tightly held,

41. Woodruff Smith, *The German Colonial Empire* (Chapel Hill, N.C., 1978).

42. Barnhart, *Japan Prepares*, 268–69.

43. Thomas Ferguson, "From Normalcy to New Deal," *International Organization* 38 (Winter 1984): 41–94; Peter Gourevitch, "International Trade, Domestic Coalitions and Liberty: Comparative Responses to the Crisis of 1873–96," *Journal of Interdisciplinary History* 8 (Autumn 1977): 281–313.

unavailable to those who might have used them to counter the potent propaganda of the Navy League.[44]

Likewise, the "man on the spot" at the edge of everyone's empire was always inventing domino theories to explain why a small investment in pacifying that part of the "turbulent frontier" would forestall the loss of more lucrative adjacent dominions.[45] For example, a major role in promoting Russophobia in Great Britain in the years before the Crimean War was played by a cabal of Near Eastern experts who literally conspired to oversell the Russian threat to India and the Turkish Straits, thus propelling themselves into high parliamentary, military, and diplomatic positions.[46] Similarly, those with a stake in British economic penetration of Egypt in 1882 exaggerated the threat to Suez, a "domino" linked to India, in order to sell a policy of military intervention.[47] In all the cases I examine, overexpansion was to some degree promoted by exploiting information monopolies and reputed expertise.

Success in propaganda battles hinges not only on information monopolies, but also on having the organizational and material resources to support favorable politicians, buy journalists, and fund mass organizations and think tanks. Hobson's argument focused on the ability of capital exporters to buy off or co-opt the press and the intelligentsia to help sell expansionism.[48] Industrialists' money and Tirpitz's organizational resources were important factors in Wilhelmine imperialist mass movements.[49] In the British case, Palmerston gained a favorable hearing in the press for his assertive policies by giving exclusive information to journalists who toed the line and diplomatic posts to their sons.[50]

The effectiveness of propaganda depends on the vulnerability of the target as well as the propagandist's advantages. This factor also favors elite groups with concentrated interests in empire over mass groups

44. Paul Kennedy, *Strategy and Diplomacy, 1870–1945* (London, 1983), chap. 5.
45. Malcom Yapp, *Strategies of British India, 1798–1850* (Oxford, 1980), 127 and passim.
46. Florence Macalister, *Memoir of Rt. Hon. Sir John McNeill* (London, 1910), 132–33, 175.
47. A. G. Hopkins, "The Victorians and Africa: A Reconsideration of the Occupation of Egypt," *Journal of African History* 27 (1986): 363–91, at 384, says: "It remained only to make the occupation palatable to parliament and the public. This was achieved by emphasizing the national interest rather than by referring to specific business and financial concerns, and by stressing the spurious danger to the Canal and to the freedom of the seas."
48. J. A. Hobson, *Imperialism* (Ann Arbor, Mich., 1965), 56–61.
49. Eley, *Reshaping*, 140–47 and passim, documents and qualifies this.
50. Kenneth Bourne, *Palmerston: The Early Years, 1784–1841* (New York, 1982), 474–91, 614–17.

with more diffuse interests. Imperial ideologies have sold best among people whose minds can be swayed by new, persuasive "information," such as groups with uncertain or cross-pressured interests, or those newly mobilized into the political process.

The mass constituencies for the Wilhelmine Navy League and Agrarian League, Palmerston's "liberal" imperialism, Stalinism, and McCarthyism all fit that profile; the case of Japanese militarist populism is especially instructive. Objectively, Japanese farmers suffering from the depression of the early 1930s had little interest in empire as a solution to their problems. Indeed, rice from the colonies of Korea and Taiwan depressed the price of domestically grown rice by about a fifth during the 1920s.[51] For this reason, as late as 1930 the platform of the major peasant league featured Marxist-style denunciations of imperial expansion. Nonetheless, farmers were ambivalent on the issue, since wars and the army had traditionally provided one of the few paths of upward mobility for rural youth. Moreover, the wealthier farmers, who played a key organizing role in agrarian organizations, had no sympathy for anything that smacked of Marxist appeals to the rural proletariat. In these circumstances the army's populist imperial propaganda, reinforced by well-established reservist organizations in the villages and the arrest of anti-imperialist agrarian organizers, succeeded in creating an enthusiastic mass base for expansionism.[52] In such ways, imperialist elite groups have often been able to use their inherent advantages in organization and information to mobilize groups with uncertain or contradictory interests.

Yet groups with concentrated interests in expansion suffer one disadvantage in the propaganda battle: the transparency of their self-interest. At least in America, some studies have shown that obviously self-interested propaganda hurts the case of its proponents, whether business or labor.[53] Consequently, unless more credible sources like the press or the state can be bought or co-opted, the group's propaganda may be discounted as coming from an obviously biased source.

The propaganda advantages typically enjoyed by imperialist interests help explain the endemic bias toward overexpansion in all great powers. Extreme advantages help explain the extreme overexpansion in the

51. Hugh Patrick, "The Economic Muddle of the 1920s," in James Morley, ed., *Dilemmas of Growth in Prewar Japan* (Princeton, N.J., 1971), 218.

52. Ronald P. Dore, *Land Reform in Japan* (London, 1959), 89–91, 97, 116–20; Richard Smethurst, *A Social Basis for Prewar Japanese Militarism: The Army and the Rural Community* (Berkeley, Calif., 1974).

53. E. E. Schattschneider, *The Semisovereign People* (New York, 1960), 53; Benjamin Page and Robert Shapiro, *The Rational Public* (Chicago, 1991), chap. 8.

worst cases. In Germany and Japan, militarists and navalists enjoyed greater monopolies on strategic information and analysis than did their counterparts in societies with a free press and systematic oversight by the cabinet and Parliament. In the Soviet Union, tighter control from the top counteracted the unavailability of competing analysis from below. In each case, however, the extent of the propaganda advantage seems to hinge more on the social environment in which the interest groups operated than on the characteristics of the groups themselves.

Ties to the state. Another explanation for endemic overexpansion is that representatives of parochial imperialist groups are often over-represented in the highest organs holding legitimate state power. In Britain, financial circles geared toward foreign investment were so socially intertwined with the political elite that most of them saw little distinction between national interests and those of the City of London.[54] In the early Cold War years in America, the upper echelons of the State Department were disproportionately staffed by Wall Street internationalists, including both Republicans like John Foster Dulles and Democrats like Robert Lovett and Averell Harriman, who had spent the interwar years investing abroad, representing European clients, and setting up global market-sharing cartels.[55] Germany and Japan were much more extreme cases of interest group penetration of the state. Meiji Japan was founded by a military coup, and a military clique oversaw the selection of government leaders, often choosing military men for key positions.[56] In Germany, Junker landowners, statesmen, and soldiers likewise formed an elite that mingled parochial interests and legitimate public authority. Its direct interests, however, were more noticeably protectionist and militarist than expansionist per se. Much of the imperialist impetus in Wilhelmine Germany came from bourgeois groups that were more peripheral to the Junker "power elite."

Arguably, the state itself has an interest in war and empire. As Charles Tilly has put it, "war made the state and the state made war."[57] War provides a justification for strengthening the state against other

54. This is argued by P. J. Cain and A. G. Hopkins, "Gentlemanly Capitalism and British Expansion Overseas, II: New Imperialism, 1850–1945," *Economic History Review* 40 (February 1987): 1–26; and Hopkins, "Victorians and Africa," overturning the very narrowly argued view of D. C. M. Platt, *Finance, Trade, and Politics in British Foreign Policy, 1815–1914* (Oxford, 1968).

55. Ronald Pruessen, *John Foster Dulles: The Road to Power* (New York, 1982); Walter Isaacson and Evan Thomas, *The Wise Men* (New York, 1986).

56. Peter Duus, *Party Rivalry and Political Change in Taisho Japan* (Cambridge, Mass., 1968).

57. Charles Tilly, "Reflections on the History of European State-Making," in Charles Tilly, ed., *The Formation of National States in Western Europe* (Princeton, N.J., 1975), 42.

domestic groups so it can compete with other states. In war, the state commands more resources and gains more extensive legal preroga- tives. This parochial interest is mitigated, however, by the state's encompassing interest in the long-run health of the society it governs.[58] Sovereigns who squander their nations' resources in unproductive wars will be impoverished, defeated by other states, and deposed by their subjects, whom they exploit and fail to protect. On balance, the interests of the state and of parochial groups tied to the state provide an endemic, though limited, bias in favor of overexpansion.

Domestic Political Context: Empowering Parochial Interests

The characteristic advantages of imperial groups—compactness, in- formation monopolies, and ties to the state—are more valuable or easier to achieve in some political contexts than in others. Without specifying the broader political context, these characteristics are insuffi- cient to explain how parochial groups influence state policy for their own benefit. Compactness and concentration of interests, for example, can be a disadvantage in some political contexts. A compact group by definition encompasses fewer individuals than the diffuse groups to which it hopes to pass the costs of its preferred policies. In a democrat- ic system, where political power hinges in part on getting a large number of votes, compactness is at best a two-edged sword. It may help in organizing lobbying, but it must overcome the inherent lack of numerical strength. Similarly, concentration of interests by definition implies that the parochial group's policies are at odds with the interests of the general mass of voters, most of whom do not share this concentrated interest. Consequently, persuading the majority of voters to approve a parochial agenda is inherently difficult. In such a political system, the power of parochial imperial groups depends greatly on their information monopolies or on their direct penetration of the state. But these too depend in part on the broader character of the political system.

Fully developed democracies normally have institutions that break down or limit information monopolies. For example, a pluralistic press guarantees access to a broad range of viewpoints. Universities provide independent experts to analyze public questions. Representative branches of government have the right to extract information from state bureau- cracies. Though these institutions can sometimes be captured by lobby- ists or defeated in argument by parochial propagandists, the political

---

58. On encompassing interests, as the opposite of parochial interests, see Olson, *Rise and Decline,* 47–53, 90–93.

context makes the parochial group's task more difficult and limits its success.

The feasibility of penetrating the state also depends on the broader political context. In a democracy, the state must consider the cost in votes of pursuing policies desired by compact groups with parochial interests. If the state is strong vis-à-vis its society, it might be able to ignore such constraints. But at the same time, such a strong state could also ignore the pleas and inducements of parochial groups lobbying for empire. In that case, overexpansion and imperial mythmaking could occur only if the state itself—or "the ruling class"—had a parochial interest in such policies.

A strong state or an encompassing ruling class, with diverse interests spread across various economic and bureaucratic sectors, might have some parochial interests in overexpansion and mythmaking, but they should be limited. The strongest and most persuasive groups, those at the core of the ruling class and those staffing legitimate state institutions, may have an incentive to rake off modest excess profits from imperial activities while passing costs on to taxpayers, conscripts, and consumers. Such groups may also have an incentive to engage in modest inflation of foreign threats to get the population to perceive national conflicts of interests as more salient than class conflicts. They may likewise have an incentive to portray international conflicts and foreign policy fiascoes as the fault of another state.[59]

Such groups should have a healthy sense of when to stop, however, lest this behavior kill the goose that lays the golden egg.[60] Unified ruling groups that are firmly in the saddle have almost no incentive to pocket "superprofits" or to propagate nationalistic myths at the cost of ruining their societies in costly wars. "Structural Marxists," for example, argue that there is no reason to expect Wall Street monopoly capitalists to be so foolish as to run their system into the ground through mindless overexpansion.[61] Instead, it is more plausible to expect them to cede power to the bourgeois state to act in the enlightened, long-term interest of the imperialist system as a whole and the capitalists that derive such disproportionate benefits from it. Indeed, all the unified oligarchies surveyed in this book—the American East Coast foreign policy Establishment, the Soviet Politburo, the

59. Van Evera, "Causes of War," stresses this motive for mythmaking and the falsification of history.
60. Ronald Rogowski, "Structure, Growth, and Power: Three Rationalist Accounts," *International Organization* 37 (Autumn 1983): 722; Douglass North, *Structure and Change in Economic History* (New York, 1981).
61. Stephen Krasner, *Defending the National Interest* (Princeton, N.J., 1978), 21–26; Franklyn Griffiths, "The Sources of American Conduct: Soviet Perspectives and Their Policy Implications," *International Security* 9 (Fall 1984): 3–50.

British Whig oligarchy, and the founding fathers of the reformed Meiji state (the *genro*)—demonstrated some ability to limit overexpansion for this reason.[62]

In short, there is a paradox in simple interest group theories of overexpansion: narrow, peripheral interest groups have the strongest motives for reckless overexpansion, but their ability to "hijack the state" to that end remains insufficiently explained; conversely, core interest groups have the power but lack a strong motive. Groups with a small stake in the fate of the society as a whole should be the ones most strongly swayed by a parochial interest in passing along the costs of ruinous imperial enterprises. But these groups should be the weakest politically. Almost by definition, their ties to the ruling class and power within the state must be weak if they take such a parochial view of their interests. Thus the power to force through self-interested policies of overexpansion should in most cases vary inversely with the motive for doing so.

This paradox might be resolved in several ways. For example, members of the ruling group might come to believe their own propaganda, or their short political time horizons might leave them insensitive to the long-run costs of overexpansion. A more satisfactory resolution of the paradox stresses the logrolling of individually weak parochial groups into a single, powerful coalition. The following sections examine these various approaches.

Self-delusion, or "blowback" from propaganda. The paradox would disappear if the state and ruling class came to believe the imperialist propaganda they used to mobilize nationalistic support and justify extracting resources from society. Thus a politically strong group could become the agent of extreme overexpansion if cynical, mobilizing elites inadvertently socialized successor elite generations to believe the imperial myths, failing to explain their instrumental origins. It could also happen as a result of subconscious psychological processes, which convince people that what is good for them is good for their country. In either case, the line between fact and fiction could become blurred in the elite's own mind, an outcome that Stephen Van Evera calls "blowback."[63]

Indeed, the blurring of sincere belief and tactical argument has been common, and it would not be surprising if the elites purveying such

---

62. On the *genro*, see Richard Ned Lebow, *Between Peace and War* (Baltimore, 1981), 303–5.

63. On motivated bias in perception and belief, see Irving Janis and Leon Mann, *Decision Making* (New York, 1977); and Lebow, *Between Peace and War*, chap. 5. "Blowback" originally referred to the recoil of anti-tank weapons.

arguments were unable to maintain the distinction between valid strategic concepts and opportunistic strategic rhetoric. "If we made our points clearer than the truth," said Dean Acheson of Cold War containment rhetoric, "we did not differ from most other educators and could hardly do otherwise.... The purpose of NSC 68 was to so bludgeon the mass mind of 'top government' that not only could the President make a decision but that the decision could be carried out."[64] Likewise, John Foster Dulles wrote in a 1942 pamphlet that all empires had been "imbued with and radiated great faiths" like "Manifest Destiny" and the "White Man's Burden," adding that we too "need a faith . . . that will make us strong, a faith so profound that we, too, will feel that we have a mission to spread it through the world." Two years before, Dulles had remarked that all states "attempt to cloak self-interest in ways which will appeal to those of its members who have moral standards."[65]

Even if the elite avoids internalizing its own myths, it may nonetheless become politically entrapped in its own rhetoric. Insofar as the elite's power and policies are based on society's acceptance of imperial myths, its rule would be jeopardized by renouncing the myths when their side-effects become costly. To stay in power and to keep central policy objectives intact, elites may have to accept some unintended consequences of their imperial sales pitch. For example, Harry Truman and Dean Acheson used the universalist rhetoric of global confrontation with communism to sell their containment policy for Europe, but then were constrained to accept the logic of critics who turned their arguments against them, demanding a similar anticommunist crusade in East Asia and in domestic politics. In this way, the blowback of imperial myths may depend not only on the elite's intellectual confusion, but on the political context that forces elites to live up to their own rhetoric.

Elite time horizons. The paradox between the parochial motive for overexpansion and the power to authorize it would also disappear if the ruling interest group had a short time horizon. For example, a declining core interest group that still controlled some of the levers of military power might use them recklessly to try to retain its slipping position. A long-shot gamble on a successful war might make sense as a last-ditch attempt to shore up the declining elite's prestige and social role. In Germany and Japan, the impending eclipse of traditional

64. Dean Acheson, *Present at the Creation* (New York, 1969), 374–75. NSC 68 was a 1950 strategic planning document advocating a policy of global containment, discussed in John Lewis Gaddis, *Strategies of Containment* (New York, 1982), chap. 4.
65. Pruessen, *John Foster Dulles*, 200, 258.

oligarchies—the *genro*, the Junkers, and their military offshoots—might be seen as providing just such an incentive for increasing recklessness.

In both these cases, however, the problem was not just that declining oligarchs became reckless, but that their decline left the polity without responsible centralized leadership. The *genro* and old-style Prussians like Bismarck and the elder Moltke were gone, and with them went their encompassing, long-run social vantage point. In their place were a plethora of contending bureaucracies, military factions, or interest groups, logrolling their concentrated interests in ways that produced expansionist ideas and policies much more overcommitted than any of the interest groups sought individually.

Indeed, at some point in each of the cases, the expansionism that resulted from the process of domestic coalition making was more extreme than that advocated by any single group. Tirpitz wanted a fleet but opposed a preventive war. Colonel Ishiwara, who had planned the 1931 fait accompli in Manchuria, recoiled when Prince Konoye's cabinet insisted in 1937 on a quick, victorious campaign to finish the war in China.[66] The Soviet military-industrial complex wanted an arms race with the West, but not the Berlin crisis that Khrushchev cooked up in a misguided effort to head off an arms race.[67] Neither the East Coast internationalists nor the Republican neoisolationists wanted land wars in Asia, but the Cold War consensus forged from the programs and rhetoric of each made such wars hard to avoid.[68] Victorian Toryism and radicalism both had strong anti-interventionist components, but Palmerston's governing formula of "liberal" imperialism abroad and social stasis at home realigned politics in such a way that reformists and anti-imperialist elements were isolated and checkmated.[69]

Thus a simple interest group explanation for overexpansion faces a double paradox: First, how do weak parochial interests hijack the state? Second, how do they produce a degree of expansion that none of the interests individually desires? To explain this fully, it is necessary to look beyond individual groups to the underlying political structures that shape how those groups interact in the domestic political process.

The Cartelized System

Parochial interests in imperial overexpansion have the greatest opportunity to control state policy in a cartelized political system. A

---

66. Barnhart, *Japan Prepares*, 99–101.

67. Jack Snyder, "The Gorbachev Revolution: A Waning of Soviet Expansionism?" *International Security* 12 (Winter 1987–88): 93–131.

68. I argue this in the American case, below.

69. This is argued briefly in Richard Shannon, *The Crisis of Imperialism, 1865–1915* (London, 1974), 20, and more extensively in the British case, chapter 5 below.

cartelized system is dominated by a number of interest groups or "cartels," each with concentrated interests different from those of other such groups. Because imperial and military interests are commonly more concentrated than anti-imperial and antimilitarist interests, a cartelized political system will give a chair at the bargaining table to imperial interests whereas diffuse groups with diffuse interests, like taxpayers and consumers, are excluded.[70] Although not everyone around the table will be actively imperialist, some are enough, because of the way a group of cartels will integrate their diverse interests.

Bargaining among compact groups with different, highly concentrated interests proceeds by logrolling. In this arrangement each group gets what it wants most in return for tolerating the adverse effects of the policies its coalition partners desire. Short-run costs are passed to groups outside the coalition. Long-run social costs remain uncalculated because of the highly parochial perspectives of the groups participating in the logrolled coalition.

Cartelized politics can produce somewhat different forms and degrees of overexpansion, depending on precisely which groups are represented and on the strength of the coalition leaders who act as brokers. Two principal forms of logrolled overexpansion are multiple expansion and offensive détente.

Multiple expansion. Multiple expansion means pursuing several distinct imperial projects; each may individually involve some small risk of overexpansion, but when combined they produce an overwhelming strategic overcommitment and self-encirclement. This occurs when several competing imperial or militarist interests sit at the table with neither anti-imperial interests nor strong brokers. Each interest group insists on its own program of expansion, so the result is far more overcommitted and provokes far more enemies than any of the individual interests thinks is wise. Yet none is strong enough to bar the others' programs, and none is willing to sacrifice its own highly concentrated interests to make the national policy solvent as a whole.

A fairly simple example is the case of the Japanese military in the late 1930s. The army insisted on a mainland empire, which created a resource-eating quagmire in China and led to armed clashes with the Soviet Union. This in itself was overextension, which naval policy compounded. The navy did not want to fight a war with America, but they wanted to prepare for one on a massive scale. Given the drain on

70. On logrolling (or "vote trading"), see Dennis Mueller, *Public Choice* (Cambridge, 1979), 49–58; William Riker and Steven Brams, "The Paradox of Vote Trading," *American Political Science Review* 67 (December 1973): 1235–47.

imperial resources from the China War, the navy could hardly justify maintaining—let alone expanding—its own share of the budgetary pie unless war with America was imminent or the naval operations could somehow extricate Japan from this geopolitical impasse. In this atmosphere, the navy accepted the strategy of a southern advance toward the Indonesian oil fields. Though fearing this would get Japan into a hopeless war with America, the navy leaders recognized that their budgetary and political position would evaporate the instant they admitted that war with America would be unthinkable no matter what resources the navy was given. Separately, the army and the navy would have undertaken moderate overexpansion and a counterproductive arms race, but each might have avoided a fight to the finish with America. But in logrolling and interacting together, they produced a more extreme strategic insolvency.[71]

An overcommitted coalition policy can cause a variety of second-order complications that mire the cartels still further. As the consequences of overexpansion become apparent, groups within the coalition jockey to shift the burdens of adjusting to overexpansion onto others. They may use imperialist appeals to mobilize mass allies in support of their own particular program, becoming captives of the success of this rhetoric. At the same time, coalition leaders must invent further strategic myths to explain why the state has become encircled. With multiple groups strongly committed to their own programs and no strong broker to enforce priorities, these secondary effects of the logrolling process deepen the overexpansion.

In the case of Wilhelmine Germany,[72] the interests of the navy and heavy industry in building a fleet made an enemy of Britain, while the army's rigid war plan ensured that France would be an enemy. Russia was an enemy in part because of her rivalry with Germany's ally Austria, but also because Germany kept trying to coerce Russia to accept a one-sided tariff arrangement, excluding Russian grain from Germany to please the Junkers while demanding low Russian tariffs for German manufactures to please the Ruhr. Complicating matters further, neither the Junkers nor the industrialists were willing to bear the tax burden to pay for the land and naval arms races these policies provoked.

---

71. On army-navy logrolling, see Barnhart, *Japan Prepares*, 36–38, 211, 266, 268–69; placing this in a broader political context, Gordon Berger, *Parties out of Power in Japan, 1931–1941* (Princeton, N.J., 1977), 79, 81, 114–15.

72. The following account draws on Kehr and his modern follower, Hans-Ulrich Wehler, *The German Empire, 1871–1918* (Leamington Spa, N.H., 1985), who stress elite interests and social imperialist manipulation, and on Eley, *Reshaping*, who stresses the autonomous impetus for imperialism from the middle class.

Recognizing that the general insolvency of the "marriage of iron and rye" was jeopardizing their individual programs, each cartel used strategic ideologies to mobilize mass support to pass the costs of overcommitment to its coalition partners. In turn, mass groups exploited the elites' imperialist ideologies to argue that if the world was really as the cartels portrayed it, then the old elite groups were not acting aggressively enough to parry its dangers. Coalition makers caught in this maelstrom had to develop their own strategic ideologies to explain how their program would succeed—or later, why it was running into so much trouble abroad. The more overcommitted Germany's foreign policy became, the more the individual cartels needed to mobilize support to protect their programs, and the more the coalition leaders had to invent myths to justify German overexpansion. The whole process was like riding a tiger: the impetus for overexpansion and its ideological justification fed on itself to the point that the only safe option for the players and the coalition makers was to stay on the tiger, making a desperate gamble that would result in either world power or collapse.

Offensive détente. A more moderate outcome of logrolling is offensive détente. In these cases both imperial and anti-imperial interests were represented among the ruling cartels. In Taisho Japan in the 1920s, for example, military and naval imperialists had seats at the table, but so did light industrial trading cartels (*zaibatsu*), which needed good relations with America and China. The logrolling problem was to devise a formula that would give each of several key players what they wanted most: an autarkic mainland empire for the army, a capital ship building program for the navy, and détente and free trade for the *zaibatsu*. Shidehara diplomacy, which envisioned America's acquiescence to Japan's gradual "Finlandization" of China, was the strategy for meeting most of these irreconcilable interests simultaneously.[73] Like most strategies of offensive détente, it was too clever by half and broke down by provoking Chinese and ultimately American resistance.

Soviet General Secretary Leonid Brezhnev also pursued a strategy of offensive détente. He offered an arms buildup to the military, Third World expansion to the orthodox ideologues, and détente and technology transfer to the cultural and technical intelligentsia.[74] His rationale was the "correlation of forces" theory, which held that unilateral Soviet gains and détente were not only compatible, but mutually reinforcing.

73. Akira Iriye, *After Imperialism* (New York, 1978), 301–2.

74. Apart from Snyder, "Gorbachev Revolution," the work that comes closest to making this argument is Harry Gelman, *The Brezhnev Politburo and the Decline of Detente* (Ithaca, N.Y., 1983).

In both of these cases, pro-expansionist and pro-détente cartels failed to cancel each other out and reach a compromise at some midpoint. Rather, each insisted on getting what it wanted most. Incompatibilities were ignored, deferred, or rationalized away. Cartel deals and their legitimating ideologies blocked criticism of dubious imperialist policies by anti-imperialist elites. Thus incompatible or unreachable goals were not evaluated, scaled down, and reconciled, as a unitary rational actor would have handled them, through a value-integrating compromise at some optimum point.

Despite these similarities, the Brezhnev and the Shidehara cases differed radically in their ultimate outcome. The Soviets ultimately learned that the "correlation of forces" theory was, as Gorbachev has implied, a "world of illusions."[75] The Japanese pushed on further, still clinging to the paper tiger theory that the rapacious United States would somehow not resist Japanese hegemony until it was too late. The main difference was that in the Soviet case relatively strong central authorities controlled the logrolling, as in the late Brezhnev era, or moved to end the pernicious game entirely, as in the Gorbachev years. With the passing of the *genro*, Japan had no similar body to impose a more encompassing perspective on the parochial contending factions.[76]

In most of these examples of cartelized politics, the logrolled policy created an outcome that was disastrous even for the logrollers themselves. In such cases, why don't at least some of the logrollers defect from a coalition agreement that is turning out to have negative payoffs? Several answers are possible, and one or more may apply in any given case of overexpansion. In some, coalition dynamics are central to the failure to retrench; in others, the coalition setting is an exacerbating factor.

Collective action problems within the coalition. Self-restraint among the participants in a logroll contributes to the collective good. But each logroller has a stronger incentive to pursue its parochial interest in expansion than to promote the collective interest in restraint. This problem of collective action is complicated by uncertainty about the long-run costs of expansion. Theorists of logrolling (or "vote trading") note that the negative consequences of a particular deal may be difficult to foresee.[77] Logrollers can easily calculate the direct concentrated

75. *Izvestiia*, 19 August 1986. Thanks to Robert Legvold for this citation.

76. Duus, *Party Rivalry*, 249, notes that "by dividing the powers of decision making among so many competing elements, the [*genro*] oligarchs had forced anyone who assumed power to adopt the tactics of compromise." After the passing of the Meiji *genro* by the late 1920s, this led to a system of logrolling among cartels.

77. Steven Brams, *Paradoxes in Politics* (New York, 1976), 102–4, notes the negative consequences of vote trading may be difficult to foresee.

benefits to themselves from the deal, whereas their costs accrue only through the indirect, long-run effects of overcommitment. Once these costs become apparent, the logrollers have three basic choices.

The first is to dissolve the coalition and agree to sacrifice their concentrated benefits in the overall interest of a solvent policy. Any group that follows this course risks discrediting itself by admitting that its former arguments were based on self-seeking myths. It also risks the danger that other groups will continue logrolling even if it defects. In that case it would lose the benefits of logrolling but still bear its costs.[78]

The second option is to jockey for advantage within the coalition, making other groups bear the rising costs of the logroll. This requires intensified mythmaking and mobilizing mass allies, both of which exacerbate the problem of overexpansion.

The third option, which can be combined with the second, is to keep the coalition intact, hoping that some risky gambit will succeed in making the logroll solvent. With luck this might be achieved, for example, by a successful preventive war, by the achievement of cumulative gains through empire, or by successful coercive diplomacy to break the encircling alliance. Justifying this route within the coalition and to the mass public requires still further salesmanship on behalf of the myths of empire.

Pressure from above and below. In some political systems, the destructive dynamic of cartel logrolling may be prevented by pressure for imperial retrenchment from above (from central state authorities) and from below (from the mass population). But in cartelized systems, such pressure is likely to be part of the problem rather than part of the solution. State leaders are not autonomous, farsighted authorities, focused on long-run state interests. Instead, they are coalition managers whose position depends on keeping the logroll going. Of course, where the broker has significant independent authority, this problem is mitigated. The stronger the coalition broker vis-à-vis the separate groups participating (that is, the more the cartelized system resembles a unitary system), the more likely it is that the state will retrench from overexpansion.

Similarly, mass pressures in a cartelized system are more likely to be a source of trouble than a salutary constraint. Under such conditions, the interests of the general public are not articulated through well-institutionalized, competitive elections. Rather, mass groups are mobi-

78. Brams, *Paradoxes*, 102–4, argues that even when externalities from other vote trades outweigh the benefits from one's own trade, continued trading may remain rational for the individual, out of fear of exploitation (that others will continue to trade votes anyway).

lized through ideological appeals by elite cartels in ways that simply contribute to the cartelized nature of politics. In the absence of developed democratic institutions, mass mobilization is a spur to reckless political behavior by elites rather than a check on it.[79]

Blowback. Mythmakers can become trapped by their own myths in any kind of political system. This is especially likely in cartelized systems, for two reasons. First, through logrolling, parochial interests capture the state's propaganda apparatus and don its mantle of disinterested authority. Thus the state obscures the parochial origins of the myths of empire, which are therefore more likely to be mistaken for truth, even by a large part of the elite. Second, cartels' competitive mobilization of mass groups is especially likely to cause severe blowback. The political position of the cartels may become heavily dependent on their mass backers, who in a cartelized system are unlikely to have access to the information and analysis needed to distinguish myth from reality.

Immobile interests and short time horizons. One reason groups in cartelized systems have such concentrated interests is that their assets are not very mobile. Such cartels frequently find themselves wedded to a narrow economic sector or bureaucratic skill that is becoming obsolete. As a result, they have an incentive to adopt reckless strategies, which sometimes include war and expansion, to recoup waning advantages and forestall social change. Their declining prospects lead them to discount the long-term costs and risks of such policies.

The Democratic System

When political power is highly dispersed throughout society, as in an electoral system with universal suffrage and administrative institutions beholden to elected officials, diffuse interests will have a stronger voice.[80] Thus democracy creates checks on concentrated interests that would promote overexpansion.

79. Samuel Huntington, *Political Order in Changing Societies* (New Haven, Conn., 1968); Jack Snyder, "Averting Anarchy in the New Europe," *International Security* 14 (Spring 1990): 5–41.

80. Anthony Downs, *An Economic Theory of Democracy* (New York, 1957); Mueller, *Public Choice*, 98–106; and especially Norman Frohlich and Joe Oppenheimer, *Modern Political Economy* (Englewood Cliffs, N.J., 1978), 127–29, who directly contrast logrolled "coalitions of minorities" with two-party competition for the middle of the spectrum. George Rabinowitz and Stuart Macdonald, "A Directional Theory of Voting," *American Political Science Review* 83 (March 1989): 93–122, at 93, claim of Downs's theory that "no other formal paradigm has had such wide use or such great impact on how people think about politics."

In the simplest case, there is a spectrum of voters with interests ranging from strongly pro-imperial to strongly anti-imperial. In a democratic system, parties must present platforms to try to capture the voters in the middle of this spectrum if they are to have a chance to win.[81] Median voters are likely to have a variety of diffuse interests for and against empire and military programs. They object to taxes and to the conscription of their sons to conquer and administer the empire. Their other interests affected by empire tend to be mixed. Some may have jobs that depend on military programs or imperial trade, and they may have investments in imperial enterprises, but for some their wages may be lower because capital has been exported abroad. They may purchase products that cost less because they come from an exploited colonial economy—or that cost more because they come from a subsidized, protected, autarkic empire. Their physical security may be greater because of astute imperial expansion or military expenditure— or less because of foolish expansion or an arms race. Thus, subject to a plethora of diffuse, cross-cutting interests, median voters face net incentives that reflect those of the society as a whole. On average, they will tend to support only imperial enterprises that are profitable for the society and reject those that are not.

In this they roughly mirror the incentive structure of the unitary rational actor or the ruling oligarchy with encompassing, long-run interests.[82] The structural incentive to compete for the middle of the spectrum in competitive democratic politics forces politicians to reject the appeals of concentrated interests if they would alienate median voters. Strongly pro-imperial interests therefore have the choice of voting for slightly pro-imperial candidates or not voting at all.[83]

The classic example is Gladstone's Midlothian campaign of 1880, the first attempt at modern mass politics after the Second Reform Bill of 1867 vastly widened the franchise. By appealing to the widespread sense that Disraeli's interventionist policies and costly brushfire wars represented a perversion of the national interest, Gladstone co-opted

---

81. Though the classic statement of this view restricts this hypothesis to the case of two-party, winner-take-all competitions, Ronald Rogowski, "Trade and the Variety of Democratic Institutions," *International Organization* 41 (Spring 1987): 209, argues that proportional representation systems have similar effects.

82. Peter Aronson and Peter Ordeshook, "Public Interest, Private Interest, and the Democratic Polity," in Roger Benjamin and Stephen Elkin, *The Democratic State* (Lawrence, Kans., 1985), 87–178, esp. 110–11, argue on similar grounds that a Downs type of two-party democracy should produce an optimal level of a public good.

83. Likewise, under these political conditions, governments that want to pursue imperial activities must chose low-cost, low-publicity strategies, like the Reagan doctrine. Thanks to Stephen Walt for discussion on this point.

median voters and won a striking victory.[84] Although this electoral strategy does not always prevail in mass democracies, that democracy empowers people with diffuse anti-imperial interests is a major factor explaining why the overexpansion of the American and British empires has been moderate.

The "intelligence of democracy" does not always work so perfectly, however. Several impediments may prevent outcomes from matching the predictions of the median voter model. One reason is that cross-pressured median voters, sometimes lacking good information or analysis regarding their own interests, are good targets for demagogic propaganda. Nixon can oversell détente to them, or Truman can oversell the Cold War.[85] If elite groups collude to withhold information and rig public debates on behalf of a logrolled coalition, formal democratic voting may make little difference.

Another reason is that representative institutions may work imperfectly and create cartelized blocs within different segments of the elected government. In the United States, for example, power over foreign affairs is shared between the presidency and various congressional bodies. Though these institutions are all made up of politicians subject to the preferences of voters, they are elected at different times by different constituencies, some of them parochial or manipulatable. When this is the case, policy-making necessarily involves bargaining among various party and regional factions and specialized legislative committees, as well as unelected bureaucratic professionals. Even in a democracy this bargaining process, which provides opportunities for logrolling, may resemble a limited form of cartelized politics.

A further problem is that some blocs of voters may have concentrated interests in predatory behavior. In Britain in the 1890s, for example, voters in Birmingham's declining industries were a significant constituency behind Joseph Chamberlain's bid for a protected, autarkic empire. Junker and Nazi promises of Ukrainian *Lebensraum* for German farmers had similar effects. If these interests vote as blocs, then democratic politics may resemble cartel politics.[86]

Finally, as some rational-choice theorists argue, the striving of politi-

---

84. John Vincent, *The Formation of the Liberal Party* (New York, 1966), 124, 162, 247. Once in office, Gladstone approved the occupation of Egypt, but this was not in itself costly overexpansion.

85. John Lewis Gaddis, *The United States and the Origins of the Cold War, 1941–1947* (New York, 1972), chap. 10.

86. Frohlich and Oppenheimer, *Modern Political Economy*, 130, suggest that the cutoff line between the two kinds of politics is the point at which "50 per cent of the voters are in a minority position on some issue and feel more strongly about that issue than they do about all others combined."

cal parties to co-opt the middle of the political spectrum may operate inefficiently when opinion is ranged along more than one dimension.[87] There may be no unique, stable strategy when views on empire vary independently from views on, say, tariffs or the welfare state. During partisan realignments in American politics, the existence of competing lines of cleavage has tended to turn voters into cartelized blocs, available for recruitment to a logrolled coalition. This gives concentrated elite interests, including imperial interests, a chance to lead coalitions in directions they favor. For example, disagreements about European and Asian commitments during the early Cold War period were not settled in a presidential electoral showdown, in part because partisan divisions did not coincide with foreign policy cleavages. Rather, foreign policy disputes were settled through congressional logrolling, in which support for Asian commitments was traded for support for European commitments in a global Cold War consensus.[88] Especially when cartelized blocs are recruited into political coalitions by elite interest groups, outcomes in democratic political systems may resemble a less extreme version of the outcomes found in cartelized systems.[89]

The Unitary Political System

A unitary system is dominated by a single ruler or by a ruling group sharing common interests, which I will call a unitary oligarchy. As an ideal type, the unitary oligarchy has group interests that are diffuse and encompassing, not parochial. The unitary oligarchy's interests are

87. A formal proof, related to the Arrow Paradox, is offered by Richard McKelvey, "Intransitivities in Multidimensional Voting Models and Some Implications for Agenda Control," *Journal of Economic Theory* 12 (June 1976): 472–82. For a formal argument that convergence toward median preferences will occur even in multidimensional policy spaces, see Gary Cox, "The Uncovered Set and the Core," *American Journal of Political Science* 31 (May 1987): 408–22. Also generally supporting Downs is Gary Cox, "Electoral Equilibrium under Alternative Voting Institutions," *American Journal of Political Science* 31 (February 1987): 82–108.

88. James Sundquist, *Dynamics of the Party System* (Washington, D.C., 1973), on realignment; on the Cold War logroll, H. Bradford Westerfield, *Foreign Policy and Party Politics: Pearl Harbor to Korea* (New Haven, Conn., 1955); for the American case, see chapter 7 below.

89. Democracies have been about as likely to become involved in wars as nondemocratic states, but virtually all great power wars have been provoked primarily by nondemocratic states. Also, democracies have never fought each other. Michael Doyle, "Liberalism and World Politics," *American Political Science Review* 80 (December 1986): 1151–69; Jack S. Levy, "Domestic Politics and War," *Journal of Interdisciplinary History* 18 (Spring 1988): 653–73, esp. 658–62; Zeev Maoz and Nasrin Abdolali, "Regime Types and International Conflict," *Journal of Conflict Resolution* 33 (March 1989): 3–36; Steve Chan, "Mirror, Mirror on the Wall . . . : Are the Freer Countries More Pacific?" *Journal of Conflict Resolution* 28 (December 1984), 617–48.

diffuse insofar as its assets and skills are mobile across economic and bureaucratic sectors. In managing the flow of resources to and from varied sectors of society, the unitary oligarchy has no parochial reason to back the success of some sectors over others. Similarly, the unitary oligarchy's interests are encompassing insofar as it is the steward of the whole national economy and has the biggest stake in the long-run survival of the state. Moreover, by definition, the interests of the unitary oligarchy are relatively homogeneous within the oligarchical group, so it has no parochial factions to engage in logrolling.

In this ideal case, the unitary oligarchy has little incentive for imperial overexpansion. Perhaps such a ruling group might have an incentive to use threat inflation and symbolic victories to enhance its power at home when the legitimacy of its rule is in doubt,[90] but this incentive should normally be held in check by its encompassing concerns. As the proprietor of the national economy, the unitary ruler has a powerful incentive not to provoke a self-encirclement or to drain resources in counterproductive overexpansion.[91] Thus the unitary ruling group should tend to weigh both the costs and the benefits of empire from a broadly national point of view. Trade-offs should be resolved not by ignoring diffuse interests, as logrolling cartels would do, but by seeking the optimal point where the sacrifice of some interests in the pursuit of others is minimized.[92] Calculating in this way might occasionally result in some overexpansion, but it should usually be limited, and corrective learning should be prompt.

This reasoning fits fairly well with the policies adopted by the unitary oligarchies studied in this book—the Meiji founding fathers, the Whig aristocracy, the Soviet Politburo, and to some extent, the U.S. East Coast foreign policy Establishment. In these cases, when interest groups or individual leaders were about to embark on programs of excessive expansion, the oligarchy as a whole tended to check their excesses.

Some qualifications must be added in moving from the ideal type to the real cases of unitary oligarchy, however. In some cases the real

90. Jack Levy, "The Diversionary Theory of War: A Critique," in Manus Midlarsky, ed., *Handbook of War Studies* (Boston, 1989), 258–86.

91. As Rogowski, "Structure, Growth, Power," 722, puts it in his useful review of North, *Structure and Change*, "Rulers are motivated to maximize profits, that is, the surplus of their revenues over the costs to them of providing protection and justice. Yet rulers are constrained against simple depredation by the requirements of social efficiency and the availability of substitutes." This constraint should operate with some stringency in the case of imperial expansionists, since they are competing with other imperial powers.

92. On value trade-offs by rational actors, see John Steinbruner, *The Cybernetic Theory of Decision* (Princeton, N.J., 1974), or the discussion on indifference curves in any economics textbook.

unitary oligarchy had a mixture of parochial and encompassing interests, which affected its choices about imperial expansion. These partly parochial interests typically stemmed from the organizational or economic origins of the ruling group. For example, in two cases the unitary ruling group had especially strong connections to a narrow interest: the ties of the Meiji *genro* to the Japanese military, and the ties of the Soviet Politburo to the Communist party apparatus. The stronger the ties of the unitary oligarchy to a narrow imperial interest, the greater the likelihood that it would tolerate some overexpansion. Still, such ties to narrow interests had to be weighed against the oligarchy's encompassing interests as the proprietor of the national polity and economy.

An even more fundamental qualification is necessary when all power lies in the hands of one person. As with a unitary oligarchy, the diffuse and encompassing interests of a single dictator should in principle check any inclinations toward overexpansion. But the validity of this hypothesis depends greatly on the dictator's continuing ability to calculate long-run costs and benefits rationally. Though the dictator may face no social incentive for overexpansion, there may be no immediate social sanction either. Thus there is no direct check on the leader's personal quirks or strategic mythology. Blowback is a particular risk when the dictator's political ideas were formed in an environment dominated by mythmaking cartels (as in Hitler's case) or the use of foreign threats for national mobilization (as in Stalin's). The logic of unitary rule does not impel a Hitler toward overexpansion, but likewise it does nothing to check him.[93]

Conclusions and Caveats on Coalition Politics

The domestic structure explanation can account both for the endemic bias toward overexpansion and for variations in its intensity. All three types of domestic structure—unitary, cartelized, and democratic—offer some opportunities for concentrated interests in empire, militarism, and threat inflation to push to the fore. Yet concentrated interests in empire have a much greater chance to dominate political decision making in the cartelized system than in the others. It is easier for their programs to get adopted and harder for them to be reversed.

Some qualifications, which may already be obvious from the examples above, should be made more explicit. The three systems are ideal types. Real systems are likely to be hybrids that entail some unique consequences of their own. Thus, Wilhelmine Germany combined

93. Olson, *Rise and Decline*, 52, argues that this is a problem not only for single dictators but for all encompassing groups.

dominant cartels with nascent democracy in a way that made the outcome worse than if the cartels had simply logrolled among themselves. In another hybrid pattern, Brezhnev's Russia combined some of the stabilizing features of a unitary oligarchy with some of the expansionist characteristics of interest group logrolling. Gorbachev's Russia has been attempting a different combination, aligning the strong center with democratizing forces against the orthodox ideological, old industrial, and military cartels. If this works, it could produce a favorable alignment for empowering diffuse anti-imperial and antimilitarist interests. The ideal types may yield some gross predictions that help explain very general variations across the cases, but more precise analysis depends on complex variations on the main patterns that are peculiar to the individual case.

FACTORS SHAPING DOMESTIC STRUCTURE

Given the different consequences that flow from unitary, cartelized, and democratic political structures, it will be useful to determine the origins of those structures. For example, understanding and evaluating Gorbachev's attempt to break the Soviet Union's imperialist cartels requires a theory of the origins of domestic structures and the conditions that promote changes in them.[94]

Building on the work of Alexander Gerschenkron, I hypothesize that the timing of a state's industrialization correlates closely with the concentration of power in its society and with the concentration of its elites' interests.[95] Early industrialization, as in Britain and the United States, is associated with diffuse elite interests and the development of mass democracy. Late industrialization, as in Germany and Japan, is associated with immobile, concentrated elite interests and cartelized politics. "Late, late industrialization," as in the Soviet Union, is associated with a hypercentralized political and economic system, producing a relatively unified elite with relatively encompassing interests.[96] This is

94. Snyder, "Gorbachev Revolution."

95. In addition to Alexander Gerschenkron, *Economic Backwardness in Historical Perspective* (Cambridge, Mass., 1962), this argument also rests on Barrington Moore, *The Social Origins of Dictatorship and Democracy* (Boston, 1966), and in part on arguments about the mobility of capital by Jeff Frieden, *Debt, Development, and Democracy: Modern Political Economy and Latin America, 1965–1985* (Princeton, N.J., 1991), chap. 1. I do not claim that the timing of industrialization *causes* a particular distribution of power and interests in society. The reverse seems just as likely. That is, the preexisting distribution of power and elite interests affects the timing and nature of the state's industrialization. For my present purpose, it is sufficient to hypothesize that they correlate.

96. In addition to Gerschenkron, *Economic Backwardness*, see James Kurth, "The Political Consequences of the Product Cycle: Industrial History and Political Outcomes," *International Organization* 33 (Winter 1979): 1–34; Peter Katzenstein, "Conclusion," in

borne out by my cases, in which the type of political system generally correlates with the timing of industrialization. Moreover, for all types of system, the distribution of power and interests in the political system fluctuates during the period of most rapid industrialization. At this juncture, the large number and heterogeneity of distinct social groups causes some cartelization of politics even in early industrializers, though this effect is temporary.

Though domestic structure correlates most strongly with the character of the industrialization process, other factors may also affect the domestic distribution of power and interests. The international environment, for example, may affect the cartelization of the political system. The cases discussed here offer several examples in which cartelization was increased by international economic depression, protectionism in other states, or the rise of other kinds of external threats. Such international challenges strengthened the domestic political hand of military and autarkic cartels by demonstrating the need for expansion to achieve a self-sufficient empire and by undercutting the resources of liberal, free-trading interests. External threats were insufficient to cartelize early industrializing states, but they exacerbated the cartelization of late industrializers.

The Timing of Industrialization

Early industrialization is associated with diffuse elite interests, mobile capital, and the diffusion of power in a democratic political system. In Britain, capital accumulation for the small-scale, decentralized textile industry was achieved gradually and early through the commercialization of the landed upper class. As early as the eighteenth century, landed aristocrats were receiving much of their income from their commercial ventures, not just from agricultural rents. Their capital was mobile, and their interests were diffuse. They shared many economic interests with the bourgeoisie, so they were not sharply threatened by a controlled devolution of power. When it became clear that agricultural protection was becoming a drag on economic development, many of them were willing to give it up rather gracefully, because of the cushion provided by their commercial interests.[97]

Peter Katzenstein, ed., *Between Power and Plenty* (Madison, Wis., 1978), esp. 323–32; and Moore, *Social Origins*. Ronald Rogowski, *Commerce and Coalitions: How Trade Affects Political Alignments* (Princeton, N.J., 1989), 163–65, points out that Gerschenkron's arguments do not hold in Latin America because labor scarcity there created different coalition incentives than in late nineteenth-century Germany. For a general critique of Gerschenkron's work, see Charles Maier, "Foreword to the Cornell University Press Edition," in Alexander Gerschenkron, *Bread and Democracy in Germany* (Ithaca, N.Y., 1989), vii–xxx.

97. In addition to Barrington Moore, see David Spring, ed., *European Landed Elites in the Nineteenth Century* (Baltimore, 1977).

In Germany, by contrast, late industrialization correlated with a pattern of concentrated, immobile elite interests and a cartelized political system. Junker economic assets were not diversified into mobile, commercial investments, either before or after Germany's industrialization. Rather, they were tied to the exploitation of immobile factors of production. The "expansion of grain-growing" in East Elbia rested on "a repressive labor system using labor dues and serfdom" and depended on the "Junkers' personal economic control." This contrasted sharply with the British pattern of enclosures for sheep raising, the "gradual release of labor power" that became available for manufacturing, and the natural diversification of capital from sheep raising into the financing of textile production and other commercial ventures.[98]

When Germany finally did industrialize, it exploited what Alexander Gerschenkron has called the "advantages of backwardness," adopting off-the-shelf technology and knowing in advance what industrialization should look like. Germany's industrialization was centrally financed by bank capital; it truncated the textile stage to focus on large-scale iron and steel production and proceeded rapidly. This produced centralized industrial structures with concentrated interests and left the preexisting military-feudal elite unintegrated into the nation's economic transformation.[99] Rapid industrialization also caused rapidly increasing demands for expanded political participation, which could be accommodated to prevailing elite interests only by the selective recruiting of mass groups as fractious junior partners in elite cartels.[100]

Japan's variant of late development was different in many respects from Germany's but similar in the essentials. Unlike Germany's rapid industrialization, Japan's proceeded from a textile base and at the outset broke the power of the top level of the landed elite. Nonetheless, it manifested many of the key characteristics of late, "top down" industrialization.[101] It was to a significant degree centrally financed, and it worked through the medium of highly concentrated commercial and industrial cartels, which counted on coercive state power to keep wages down at home and to conquer exclusive markets abroad. The ruling oligarchy provided pork-barrel subsidies for rural landlords in exchange for limited mass support in an electoral system skewed

98. Hanna Schissler, "The Junkers," in Robert G. Moeller, *Peasants and Lords in Modern Germany* (Boston, 1986), 24–51, esp. 40.

99. Gerschenkron, *Economic Backwardness*, 25–26; Ralf Dahrendorf, *Society and Democracy in Germany* (London, 1968), 37–40, 48.

100. Eley, *Reshaping*; Hans Jurgen Puhle, "Lords and Peasants in the Kaiserreich," in Moeller, *Peasants and Lords*, 81–109.

101. Kazushi Ohkawa and Henry Rosovsky, "A Century of Japanese Economic Growth," in William W. Lockwood, *The State and Economic Enterprise in Japan* (Princeton, N.J., 1965), 47–92, esp. 51–52; G. C. Allen, *A Short Economic History of Japan* (New York, 1981).

against the working class.[102] And most important, the transformation was carried out by a modernizing military elite that retained many of its parochial corporate interests along with its more encompassing national concerns. Thus politics was cartelized among a number of elite sectors with distinct, concentrated interests—especially the army and the navy, but also the local landlords and the *zaibatsu*.

Russia's variant of the pattern of late development was so extreme that it created a new pattern, different in kind from Germany's. Extreme backwardness led to the destruction of the old elite and urban classes, largely through international competition, allowing a modernizing Bolshevik elite to create and dominate an extremely centralized political and economic structure. But the partial devolution of totalitarian institutions into concentrated military-industrial and party interest groups produced a comparatively mild form of cartelization, mitigated by the relatively encompassing interests of the Politburo elite.[103]

In short, variation in the type and timing of industrialization explains most of the variation on three other dimensions in the causal chain leading to overexpansion. Late industrialization produces a cartelized political structure, which magnifies the effectiveness of concentrated interests in expansion, favors the development of expansionist strategic myths, and promotes self-encirclement and imperial overextension. In contrast, early industrialization produces a democratic political structure, which empowers diffuse interests opposing overexpansion, promotes learning when strategic myths are proved false, and keeps expansion relatively close to the point where its marginal benefits make up for its marginal costs. Late, late industrialization produces roughly similar results by vesting power in a unified elite with relatively encompassing interests.

Table 1. Timing of industrialization and overexpansion

	Early	Late	Late, Late
Cases[a]	U.S., G.B.	Germany, Japan	USSR
Elite interests	Diffuse	Concentrated	Encompassing
Type of politics	Democratic	Cartelized	Unitary
Strategic mythmaking	Moderate	Extreme	Moderate
Strategic learning	Prompt	Backward[b]	Prompt
Overexpansion	Moderate	Extreme	Moderate

[a]The real cases do not conform precisely to the ideal types and often reveal combinations of two patterns.

[b]By this I mean that failure leads to ever more reckless attempts at expansion.

102. Duus, *Party Rivalry*.

103. Gerschenkron, *Economic Backwardness*, chap. 6; Snyder, "Gorbachev Revolution."

The Process of Industrialization

The very process of industrialization, regardless of its type and timing, tends to produce some cartelization of political interests. Rapid economic change crowds the social spectrum with groups and classes from seemingly disparate epochs: the atavistic, the currently dominant, and the newly emerging. In extreme cases, atavists such as hereditary monarchs, traditional military castes, and landed aristocrats share the historical stage with the bourgeoisie and an organized working class. Even if no single group has extremely concentrated interests, it will be hard to reconcile all their interests through an integrative compromise. Under such conditions, older social groups need, to a greater or lesser degree, to defend entrenched interests that emerging groups fundamentally challenge.[104]

As a result, industrialization tends to produce a sociopolitical stalemate at the point when new groups have grown in strength but old ones have not yet been eliminated or sufficiently adapted to the new order. In the British case, historians call this the "mid-Victorian equipoise."[105] In these circumstances, ruling majorities can be formed only by logrolling deeply opposed interests. Moreover, the sudden social mobilization caused by rapid industrialization creates mass targets vulnerable to imperial ideologists. The German "marriage of iron and rye" and the Palmerstonian formula of liberal imperialism abroad and social stasis at home both reflect this dynamic.

Though the pileup of classes caused cartelization and logrolling in both the early and the late industrializers, in Britain cartelization was a passing phase. The relatively diffuse interests of the old elite made it possible to adjust gradually to the diffusion of power to new social groups, resulting by the 1880s in two-party mass politics. In Germany cartelization was more permanent. Even after the First World War curtailed the power of the Junkers, the relative immobility of many groups' economic assets, whether in agriculture or heavy industry, helped recreate the Wilhelmine social stalemate in a new Weimar form.[106] Finally, the Soviet case was different from either of these. Since the breaking of the old classes largely preceded the rapid industrializa-

---

104. Though Peelite Tories took the long view and accepted the repeal of agricultural protection in 1846, for example, most Tories remained unreconciled to this and other reforms for decades. J. B. Conacher, *The Peelites and the Party System* (Hamden, Conn., 1972).

105. W. L. Burn, *The Age of Equipoise* (London, 1964).

106. David Abraham, *The Collapse of the Weimar Republic*, 2d ed. (New York, 1986); Thomas Childers, *The Nazi Voter* (Chapel Hill, N.C., 1983); Robert G. Moeller, "The Kaiserreich Recast? Continuity and Change in Modern German Historiography," *Journal of Social History* 17 (Summer 1984): 655–83.

tion of the 1930s, there was no pileup of diverse social groups at that point.[107]

TESTING THE COMPETING EXPLANATIONS

Three competing explanations for self-encirclement and overexpansion have been proposed: Realist, cognitive, and coalition politics and ideology. Five case studies are used in constructing a variety of tests of covariation, many pitting two or more theories head to head in conditions where they should make opposite predictions. The purpose is to eliminate theories that fail many tests and to show in what ways the surviving theories contribute to explaining the outcomes of the cases.

What Is to Be Explained?

All three theories seek to explain counterproductive aggressive behavior—specifically the presence, absence, and extent of "overexpansion." Overexpansion comes in two general forms, "self-encirclement" and "imperial overextension." The degree of self-encirclement is measured primarily by the ratio of the war-waging resources of one's enemies to those of one's allies: where a country manages to get its side outnumbered, it is said to be self-encircled. Defeat in a major war, persistence in a losing arms race, and counterproductive attempts to break the opposing alliance with threats are corroborating evidence of self-encirclement. "Imperial overextension" means expansion beyond the point where material costs equal material benefits, measured where possible in quantifiable economic and security terms.[108] Where hard measures are elusive, judgments by the protagonists' successors, by contemporary observers, and by historians serve as surrogates.

All three theories also claim to explain, as intervening variables, decision makers' advocacy of strategic concepts. These concepts are treated as simple dichotomies: advocacy of security through expansion or through retrenchment; expectation of dominoes or quagmires as the general rule; anticipation of balancing or bandwagoning in response to threats; images of the opponent as threatening but irresolute or defensive but provokable. Public statements and private beliefs are both important sources of evidence in measuring these intervening variables. Since the coalition politics theory argues that politicians may be constrained to act in accordance with their rhetoric, public statements

---

107. Sheila Fitzpatrick, "The Russian Revolution and Social Mobility," *Politics and Society* 13 (1984): 124–26.

108. Here I follow Gilpin's criteria.

are no less important than private ones in assessing the prevalence of particular strategic concepts.

Measuring the Causal Variables

I use two strategies, one direct and one indirect, for measuring the "independent" or causal variables of the three competing theories in the case studies. First, I measure the causal variable directly. For example, to measure the cartelization of group interests, I report the findings of economic historians regarding the concentration of groups' assets in particular sectors and their mobility between different uses. Second, I measure the causal variable indirectly, by a process tracing method.[109] Thus, to determine whether the political system is cartelized, I observe the political process to see if groups behave as they would in a cartelized system—that is, whether they logroll.

Case Selection

The five countries chosen have been the main contenders for power in the international system in the industrial era. The imperial behavior of each country is traced over two to four periods, including times of greater or lesser overexpansion. Periods in which the expansionism and the relative power of the country were at a peak are covered in extra detail. I do not cover the problems of decolonization faced by declining powers, though the coalition politics theory might be relevant to this.[110]

France and Italy, powers of a somewhat lesser rank, were excluded to make the research more manageable. They might well fit the coalition politics theory. Italy, a late industrializer with a ruling coalition mirroring the German marriage of iron and rye, was a chronic overexpander, spending twice the government's annual revenue to conquer useless Ethiopia.[111] Likewise, Napoleon III of France is often portrayed as the prototype social imperialist coalition manager, using a flamboyant foreign policy to help manage a heterogeneous society poised between tradition and modernity. In all likelihood his case would have many parallels with that of Palmerston.[112]

109. On process tracing, Alexander George and Timothy McKeown, "Case Studies and Theories of Organizational Decision Making," in *Advances in Information Processing in Organizations*, vol. 2 (Greenwich, Conn., 1985), 21–58.
110. Miles Kahler, *Decolonization in Britain and France* (Princeton, N.J., 1984).
111. Dennis Mack Smith, *Mussolini's Roman Empire* (New York, 1976), 67, 99.
112. Charles Maier, "'Fictitious Bonds...of Wealth and Law': On the Theory and Practice of Interest Representation," in Suzanne Berger, ed., *Organizing Interests in Western Europe: Pluralism, Corporatism, and the Transformation of Politics* (Cambridge, 1981), 40.

Tsarist Russia was also omitted, though it too might fit the coalition theory. Russia's rapid industrialization at the end of the nineteenth century corresponded with a period of imperial expansion, though Russia was expansionist in earlier periods as well. One study of Russian foreign policy-making between 1905 and 1914 shows that Russia was least expansionist in the period of strong unitary government under Stolypin and most expansionist when various bureaucratic cartels advanced their own imperial schemes under weak premiers.[113]

Preindustrial states, including the prominent case of Napoleonic France, were excluded for two reasons. First, many of them had absolute rulers, and the predictions of the coalition theory are weakest and least interesting in such cases. These cases would not test the main claims of the coalition politics theory. Second, preindustrial societies, lacking modern class, sectoral, and bureaucratic structures, would be more difficult to compare with the contemporary cases that are of greatest interest. Qualitatively different categories would be required for identifying groups, interests, institutions, and cleavages.[114]

Also absent are cases of overextension or self-encirclement by small powers. I would not expect the coalition politics theory to fit small powers. The literature on political economy suggests that domestic structure is a good predictor of foreign economic strategy for big powers, but for small powers foreign economic circumstances shape domestic political institutions. Cartelization has opposite effects in big and small powers. In big countries, cartels try to use state power to conquer or to "beggar their neighbors." In small countries, cartels work out arrangements for sharing the unavoidable burdens imposed by international pressures.[115]

113. David M. McDonald, "Autocracy, Bureaucracy, and Changes in the Formation of Russian Foreign Policy (1895–1914)" (Ph.D. diss., Columbia University, 1988). I make a similar argument about tsarist military policy in Snyder, *Ideology of the Offensive*, 163, 196.

114. A ready-made scheme for identifying preindustrial social cleavages may be found in S. M. Lipset and Stein Rokkan, "Cleavage Structures, Party Systems, and Voter Alignments," in *Party Systems and Voter Alignments* (New York, 1967). In the case of preindustrial France, the Wars of the Revolution were touched off by the Brissotin faction's calculated use of social-imperialist bombast to forge a ruling majority in the stalemated assembly. T. C. W. Blanning, *The Origins of the French Revolutionary Wars* (London, 1986), chap. 3.

115. Peter Katzenstein, in *Small States in World Markets* (Ithaca, N.Y., 1985) and *Corporatism and Change: Austria, Switzerland, and the Politics of Industry* (Ithaca, N.Y., 1984) argues that small states' domestic structure is shaped by the need to adjust to the international environment; conversely, Katzenstein, in *Between Power and Plenty*, shows that large states' foreign economic strategies are shaped by their domestic structures, as shaped in turn by the timing of their industrialization. Also, a Gerschenkron-based coalition theory may not apply to "late, late" developing countries in the Third World, because their resource endowments differ from those of the European states that Gerschenkron studied. Rogowski, *Commerce and Coalitions*, 163–65.

The cases permit three kinds of tests of the rival explanations for variations in overexpansion and strategic beliefs. Tests of covariation across countries—extremely overexpansionist powers like Germany and Japan versus moderately overexpansionist powers like the United States, Britain, and the Soviet Union—assess whether these variations in outcome match variations in strategic circumstances (the Realist explanation), intellectually formative experiences (the cognitive explanation), or type of political system (the coalition politics explanation).

Second are tests of covariation over time within a country. Do periods of isolation and expansion follow from changes in political structure—for example, Shidehara diplomacy during "Taisho democracy" and the southern advance under militarist logrolling (the coalition theory)? Or do they follow from an intensification of the security dilemma (the Realist theory) or from salient new lessons (the cognitive theory)? Or does a combination of two theories explain the outcome? For example, does a moderate intensification of the security dilemma trigger big domestic changes, which lead to overexpansionism?

Third are tests of covariation across individuals and groups within cases. Do variations in beliefs line up with variations in interests or in information or formative experiences? This test is an important hurdle for the interest group and cognitive theories. It cannot be used to eliminate the rational actor theory, however, because even though the views of many statesmen and strategists may coincide with their parochial interests, the political system may nonetheless have selected the winner of the strategic debate on the merits of the arguments.

Finally, tests can discriminate between the different kinds of domestic politics explanations. Can the outcome of the cases be explained by the process of logrolling alone, without invoking the role of strategic ideology? Conversely, can interest group ideology in itself explain the outcome without reference to logrolling? Or are both logrolling and strategic ideology necessary to explain the outcome?

In principle, these tests might have concluded that only one of the theories had any explanatory power. In fact my findings are more complicated. The single most successful explanation was the theory of coalition politics and ideology. Cognitive explanations were the least successful. By itself, the international system explanation was insufficient to explain the cases of overexpansion. In conjunction with preexisting domestic conditions, however, international circumstances occasionally played a key role in strengthening the hand of imperialist cartels. Realistic adaptation to international conditions explained the behavior of democratic states quite well. For these cases, domestic structure explained why the state was able to adapt well to the incentives of its position in the international system.

Thus the two explanations that achieved some success, the domestic and Realist theories, were both rooted in the concepts of power, interests, and coalitions among conflict groups. Using the broadest sense of the term, these are both realist theories. This pattern of findings suggests a need to develop hypotheses about power, interests, coalitions, and ideology that can operate simultaneously at the domestic and international levels. It is useful to know that the domestic aspects of coalition making strongly influence a state's conflict behavior, but it would also be useful to have a theory that would explain parsimoniously how domestic and international coalition politics interact. I make no attempt to do this here, but my results suggest that it is a necessary next step.

Criteria for Historical Judgments

Primary research covering the domestic and international politics of five great powers over a span of 150 years is not feasible for one author. Therefore I have had to rely on the work of historians. When historians addressed a question I was investigating, and when a consensus existed among them, I have followed that consensus. Often, however, I have asked questions that cut across the categories historians have worked within. In many cases there existed a fairly well developed historical literature on separate aspects of the larger question I was asking. Thus there was typically a literature on strategic ideas, another on domestic sources of foreign policy, another on economic change and political development, and so forth, but there was little available on the connections among them. In most instances I have assembled an overall interpretation of the case that combines existing interpretations of its separate aspects. Thus I have relied on historians and area studies specialists to provide the building blocks for my arguments, but I have combined them in ways that historians, for the most part, have not used.

The most innovative historical interpretation is of the Palmerston case study. Because as a whole it is significantly different from any existing interpretation, I develop the argument in extra detail to demonstrate my case. The other cases offer arguments that are more closely drawn from existing literature, so I often cite sources rather than recite details. In part of one case, Soviet foreign policy in the late 1940s, there is insufficient evidence to choose among competing explanations.

Overall, I make no claim that the case studies in this volume offer a conclusive test of the theories. Because many of the issues I confront are subject to continuing historical debate, and because many others involve questions that historians have not directly addressed, my interpretations are far from definitive. Nonetheless, I do claim that these cases go beyond mere illustrations of theoretical points. They rely on the best, most recent, and—when possible—most widely shared judgments of historians. They are set up as systematic tests, using methods of controlled comparison. In this sense the cases constitute a preliminary test, subject to further historical and theoretical scrutiny.

[3]

Germany and the Pattern of Late Development

In the first half of the twentieth century the word Germany became a synonym for self-destructive aggression. German belligerence in crisis and war twice provoked overwhelmingly powerful coalitions that fought at great cost to impose a decisive defeat on the German nation. Any theory that attempts to explain self-defeating expansionism must begin with this quintessential case.

The Germans who embarked on this course of expansion did not, of course, see themselves as engaged in quixotic folly. They contended, and for the most part believed, that the dangers and opportunities inherent in Germany's position in the international system required an expansionist course. Both Wilhelmine and Nazi expansionists believed that Germany's hemmed-in territorial base was insufficient to support its economic prosperity or its military security in the face of aggressive competition from states enjoying large colonial or continental-scale resource bases. Moreover, they depicted a world in which conquest was relatively easy, because of the alleged advantages of offensive military operations, because allies would jump on the bandwagon of a rising power, because conquered resources could be plowed back into increased military strength, and because opponents were paper tigers who exploited the circumspect but collapsed under pressure from the fierce.

The German experience offers four main lessons about the sources of overexpansion and imperial myths. First, it shows the connection between cartelized politics and imperial overexpansion. The pattern of late development left German politics dominated by several elite groups, many having highly concentrated interests in various projects of imperial expansion, economic protectionism, or military preparations. These groups logrolled their interests, producing a policy outcome that was

[66]

more expansionist and overcommitted than any group desired individually.

Second, within that broad pattern of late development and cartelized politics, variations in the character of the German political system between 1870 and 1945 correlated with variations in German over-expansion. German overexpansion was most extreme when political cartelization and logrolling were extreme, during the rule of Kaiser Wilhelm between 1890 and 1918, and when power was in the hands of a single dictator, under Hitler from 1933 to 1945. Conversely, German foreign policy was most moderate when the political system was most democratic, during the Weimar Republic of the 1920s, and when it was dominated by the unitary oligarchy of the Second Reich's founding fathers, especially Chancellor Otto von Bismarck and Field Marshal Helmuth von Moltke, between 1870 and 1890. This pattern conforms to the predictions of the coalition politics theory outlined in chapter 2.

Third, the German case shows the independent role of strategic ideology. Interest groups and coalition leaders exploited information monopolies and propaganda resources to justify their imperial pro-grams, especially among the broad middle classes being mobilized into politics for the first time. These ideas became deeply engrained in the thinking of German middle-class nationalists and thus took on a life of their own even apart from the political circumstances that gave rise to them. Hitler's strategic thinking, for example, was largely shaped by pre-1914 myths of empire, which for this reason continued to exert a determining influence in the radically changed political conditions under the Third Reich.

Finally, the German case undermines Realist and cognitive explanations for overexpansion. German expansionists themselves offered such explanations for their counterproductive strategies, but these accounts were opportunistic justifications that do not stand up to scrutiny. International circumstances did affect German expansionist policy, but only by influencing the domestic political strength of imperialist groups and the persuasiveness of their strategic myths. They hardly constitute a sufficient explanation for German overexpansion.

TRENDS IN OVEREXPANSION: PROVOKING SELF-ENCIRCLEMENT

For the Second and Third Reichs, overexpansion was not a matter of blundering into colonial quagmires. Although this happened, notably in the war against the Herero of South-West Africa, it was on a small scale. Rather, overexpansion occurred when German pretensions to continental or overseas expansion provoked opposition from other great powers whose prior claims or security were threatened by German assertiveness. In this context the simple way to measure overexpansion is by the strength of the opposing coalition provoked by German belligerence.

In two periods, roughly 1898–1918 and 1933–45, threatening German behavior provoked increasingly overwhelming balancing responses from other powers, leading to German military defeat. In both periods Germany took the initiative in the arms race, attempting to achieve one-sided improvements in the military and naval balances. This includes the naval race against Britain between 1898 and 1914 and Hitler's rapid rearmament in the 1930s. Germany's blame for the land arms race after 1910 is more ambiguous, since in part that spiral was triggered by Germany's legitimate need for security in the face of the Russian military's recovery from its nadir after the Russo-Japanese War. But even here the underlying engine of the arms spiral was Germany's unnecessarily offensive strategy for a decisive invasion of France, which virtually required the defensive-minded Russians to switch to a robust, offensive force capable of invading Germany's exposed rear. Also, by posing an almost impossible task, German military strategy required military superiority in order to have any hope of success.[1] Thus, in all these instances, German ambitions or strategies triggered arms races against opposing alliances. In these arms competitions, which continued into the two world wars, Germany lacked the economic capacity to win.[2]

Likewise, in both the Wilhelmine and Nazi periods, Germany manufactured a series of international crises, aimed at extracting concessions on imperial or territorial issues, splitting the opposing alliance, or justifying a limited war of expansion. Admittedly, in the crises of the Wilhelmine era over Morocco and the Balkans, Germany was in part responding to bids by France and Russia for unilateral gains. But Germany's penchant for displaying military force, issuing ultimatums, and refusing to accept reasonable compensation quickly unified France, Russia, and Britain against it.[3] Eventually, in both periods, Germany felt compelled toward preventive military action to defeat piecemeal the members of the opposing encirclement.[4]

Two periods, the Bismarckian and the Weimar, stand in partial contrast to this more general penchant for provoking overwhelming opposition. Until his fall in 1890, Chancellor Otto von Bismarck studiously

1. Jack Snyder, *The Ideology of the Offensive* (Ithaca, N.Y., 1984), chaps. 4 and 5.
2. See Paul Kennedy, *The Rise and Fall of the Great Powers* (New York, 1987), chaps. 5 and 6.
3. Eugene N. Anderson, *The First Moroccan Crisis, 1904–1906* (Hamden, Conn., 1966).
4. Fritz Fischer, *War of Illusions* (New York, 1975), chaps. 18–22; Norman Rich, *Hitler's War Aims* (New York, 1973), 81–82, 204–11, 245–46.

avoided any adventurous policy that would drive France, Britain, and Russia together in a "nightmare of coalitions." Though occasionally exploiting the electoral value of overseas imperial expansion and European war scares, Bismarck assiduously sought to remain in the good graces of at least two others within the balancing system of five great powers.[5] In particular, he tried to ensure that the alliance with Austria remained defensive only, so that the onus for aggression would always lie with other parties. In this way aggressive Russian behavior would stimulate British resistance, and aggressive French behavior would not be assisted by Russia, while Germany would make sure that Austria would not engage in the reckless activities that might unify Russia, France, and Britain against the Germanic powers. Even before 1870, when Bismarck's strategy was not the maintenance of the status quo, he always tried to place the onus of aggression on his opponents, while reassuring third parties that his limited aims did not extend to overturning the European balance of power. Moreover, he rejected the schemes for decisive, preventive wars that the German General Staff tried to force on him. Consequently, the "natural" balancing alliance between Russia and France failed to form until after Bismarck's fall from power.[6]

On the other hand, Bismarck's assertive diplomacy often skated close to the line that would trigger an encircling alliance. Manipulated war scares, gratuitous colonial demands, and the retention of Alsace-Lorraine after the Franco-Prussian War, set in the context of the General Staff's offensive military strategies that inherently threatened France and Russia, sustained a widely shared assumption that security in Europe depended on a finely tuned balance. Bismarck's diplomacy, though defensive, nonetheless fostered the belief that security was precarious, that predation was normal and possibly lucrative, and that only an assertive defense of one's prestige and interests could maintain the precarious balance. In particular, Bismarck's commercial war against Russia, in which Germany tried to use financial and tariff pressure to force the tsar to accept a one-sided combination of high agricultural and low industrial tariffs, set the stage for the breakdown of defensive diplomacy under Bismarck's successors.[7]

The diplomacy of the Weimar Republic was even more successful in

---

5. Bruce Waller, *Bismarck* (London, 1985), 44.

6. The most recent biography of Bismarck is Lothar Gall, *Bismarck*, 2 vols. (London, 1986). On the lack of balancing behavior in the 1880s, see Brian Healy and Arthur Stein, "The Balance of Power in International History: Theory and Reality," *Journal of Conflict Resolution* 17 (March 1973): 33–62.

7. Hans-Ulrich Wehler, *The German Empire, 1871–1918* (Leamington Spa, N.H., 1985), 190–92; Dietrich Geyer, *Russian Imperialism: The Interaction of Domestic and Foreign Policy, 1860–1914* (Leamington Spa, N.H., 1987), 150–68.

avoiding an encirclement by hostile powers. Weimar first emerged from its diplomatic isolation after its defeat in World War I through the Rapallo Treaty for limited political, economic, and military cooperation with the other pariah power, Soviet Russia. Then the Locarno Agreement guaranteed Germany's boundaries to the west, dovetailing with economic arrangements that ensured the flow of American capital to finance industrial recovery and social programs while largely deferring reparations payments. The "success" of this policy was of course limited, in that it did nothing to recapture lost territories apart from the French-occupied Rhineland or to renounce restrictions on the German military, while making Germany highly vulnerable to the vagaries of world markets for goods and capital.[8]

In short, the German case shows considerable variation in the "dependent variable": two periods, from 1898 to 1918 and 1933 to 1945, of aggressive foreign policy and overextension, defined in terms of the provocation of an overwhelming opposing coalition; and two periods, from 1870 to 1890 and 1924 to 1930, of largely defensive or cooperative foreign policy, defusing potential opposing coalitions.

THE INTERNATIONAL SYSTEM: COMPELLED TO EXPAND?

Those who contend that Germany's expansionism was compelled by its position in the international system stress Germany's vulnerable position as a late developer hemmed in by powerful competitors. As a latecomer to national unification and industrialization, Germany became a military power only after other imperial powers had appropriated the world's spoils. Consequently, its bid for its fair share necessarily embroiled it in European wars and colonial disputes against status quo powers who resisted a redivision of the spoils. In this view a greater share was not just fair, but indispensable. Germany, limited to its pre-1914 dimensions, would always be intolerably vulnerable in both economic and military terms. Militarily, it was vulnerable to continental-sized competitors who commanded superior resources for a long war and enjoyed control of the sea, so as to bar Germany from importing resources during a war. Moreover, its central location in Europe made it fear all its neighbors and made them in turn fear Germany. Economically, the lack of political control over necessary markets and resources left Germany vulnerable to the vagaries of the world political economy. It simply was not a large enough political or economic entity to be

8. On economic issues, see William C. McNeil, *American Money and the Weimar Republic* (New York, 1986).

secure against sharp competition and unpredictable onslaughts in the anarchic international system and world market. Consequently Germany was forced by circumstances to expand in order to be secure.[9]

This argument was put forth by German expansionists themselves and has been accepted by some subsequent historians and political scientists. The logic behind it gains support from Realist theories of international politics. Nonetheless, the argument is fundamentally unconvincing. Even a cursory look at Germany's international position will show that the nation's vulnerability and insecurity were caused by its own aggressive policies.

Nothing could be further from the truth than the assertion that Wilhelmine Germany needed imperial expansion to secure its economic prosperity. The two decades before 1914 were a time of worldwide economic growth, in which Germany secured more than its share. Far from Germany's being stifled by the allegedly jealous British hegemon, Britain was the country's largest trading partner. Even though Germany pursued protectionist policies, Britain largely maintained its policy of unconditional free trade, giving Germany the opportunity to compete effectively against Britain's goods in Britain's home market and colonial empire. Germany, the only major industrial state to increase its share of world trade during the pre-1914 years, ran a growing trade surplus with Britain in this period.[10]

In no way was Britain using its naval or economic position to stifle German trade. Though it did occasionally use its fleet to stop contraband or unilaterally impose solutions to minor colonial disputes, Britain's overall role was undoubtedly positive, providing liquidity, insurance, secure sea lanes, and generally free markets from which Germany could profit.[11]

Moreover, colonial trade was peripheral to the health of the German economy. Three-quarters of German trade was with Europe, over 60 percent with the Entente countries. German colonies absorbed less than 1 percent of Germany's foreign trade and 2 percent of its foreign investment. More important, absolute levels of colonial investment were low, because German banks had little capital left over after

9. David Calleo, *The German Problem Reconsidered* (Cambridge, 1978), 3–5 and passim; Ludwig Dehio, *Germany and World Politics in the Twentieth Century* (New York, 1959).

10. Martin Kitchen, *The Political Economy of Germany* (London, 1978), 229–30; Daniel Garst, "Capitalism and Liberal Democracy: State Structures in Britain and Germany prior to World War I" (Ph.D. diss., University of Minnesota, 1988), chap. 4, p. 8, citing Paul Bairoch, "Geographical Structure and Trade Balance of European Foreign Trade from 1800 to 1970," *Journal of European Economic History* 3 (1974): 557–608.

11. Gerhard Ritter, *The Sword and the Scepter: The Problem of Militarism in Germany*, 4 vols. (Coral Gables, Fla., 1969–72), 2:144.

investing in domestic industry, which German investors, unlike the British, preferred to overseas projects. Nor is it true that Germany had to provide an outlet for its heavy industrial production by building a navy, which accounted for only 2 percent of total iron and steel output.[12]

In short, Germany had no fundamental foreign economic problem in 1914. David Calleo notes that one-sided trade treaties with Russia and Austria were due to expire shortly after 1914, but this could hardly outweigh Germany's generally positive foreign economic prospects.[13] Since Britain's economy was complementary to Germany's and British voters had soundly defeated Joseph Chamberlain's push for protectionism, Germany had no reason to suspect that this favorable situation would change fundamentally in the near future.[14] Ironically, Germany's own choice of a policy of aggression created the very conditions—war, encirclement, and blockade—that necessitated the conquest of a larger, autarkic economic base.

Arguments that stress the strictly military aspects of Wilhelmine Germany's insecurity are only slightly more convincing. Germany's encirclement was not a geographical given. Rather, it was a consequence of the country's belligerent diplomacy and the Schlieffen Plan, which made the Entente powers fearful and strategically united. Even given the Franco-Russian alliance, Germany could have achieved security by adopting a defensive military strategy, which would have used German military power more efficiently and kept Britain neutral. Finally, Germany's incentive for preventive war, stimulated by anticipation of Russia's impending military buildup, was largely an artifact of the Schlieffen Plan, which denuded the Russian frontier in order to pursue a chimerical knockout blow against France.[15] In short, Germany's military vulnerability in Central Europe was a consequence, not a cause, of its peculiarly offensive behavior.

In the Nazi period, the alleged need for autarky provides the most plausible explanation for German aggression at the level of the international system. In this account, the vulnerability of Weimar Germany to the cycles of the world economy demonstrated the necessity for Germany to gain political control over its own markets and sources of raw materials. Nazi Germany was able to pull out of the depression through rearmament, public works, and other largely internal efforts, but by the late 1930s this hothouse economy was at an impasse. By 1936 German gold reserves were exhausted. To balance its payments,

12. Kitchen, *Political Economy of Germany*, 198, 231.
13. Calleo, *German Problem*, 39.
14. Garst, "Capitalism," chap. 4.
15. Snyder, *Ideology*, chaps. 4 and 5.

Germany would have to reduce arms spending, which would risk turning off the "military Keynesian" engine of recovery, devalue the mark, which would reduce living standards and raise the specter of inflation; or become autarkic, which would require conquering the resources the economy needed.[16]

There are three problems with the argument that necessity dictated the choice of the third option, autarky and expansion. First, economic recovery preceded remilitarization, so we must assume that cutting military spending would not necessarily have ruined the German economy.[17] Second, there is evidence that Hitler sought autarky as a preparation for war, not war as the means to achieve autarky. The economic impasse of the late 1930s was almost entirely caused by the attempt to have guns and butter at the same time. The hard currency crisis, for example, was due to the attempt to maintain civilian imports at previous levels while vastly accelerating imports to fuel expanded military production. The downturn of American demand for German exports, associated with renewed depression in 1938, exacerbated this contradiction but was not its root cause.[18] Third, key economic interests and experts opposed the policy of excessive military production, autarky, and aggression. Hjalmar Schacht, overseer of the economy, wanted to pursue a strategy based on high levels of foreign trade. In Eastern Europe he thought his trade agreement had already acquired much of the hinterland that the German economy needed, without conquest and colonial settlement. Schacht, like the Ruhr coal and steel interests, expected to buffer Germany from fickle international market forces not by territorial conquest, but through international cartel agreements, which were proceeding successfully.[19] In sum, the economic crisis was not a cause of Hitler's aggression, but rather a consequence of his policy of "strip mining" the German economy to prepare for war.[20]

16. John Hiden and John Farquharson, *Explaining Hitler's Germany: Historians and the Third Reich* (Totowa, N.J., 1983), 143; William Carr, *Arms, Autarky and Aggression: A Study in German Foreign Policy, 1933–1939* (London, 1972), 51–58; Williamson Murray, *The Change in the European Balance of Power, 1938–1939* (Princeton, N.J., 1984), 14.

17. Harold James, *The German Slump: Politics and Economics, 1924–1936* (Oxford, 1986), 371–86.

18. Hiden and Farquharson, *Explaining Hitler's Germany*, 144–49; Murray, *Change in the European Balance*, 4–19.

19. Hiden and Farquharson, *Explaining Hitler's Germany*, 127, 142; R. J. Overy, "Heavy Industry and the State in Nazi Germany: The Reichswerke Crisis," *European History Quarterly* 15 (July 1985): 313–40, at 332; Woodruff Smith, *The Ideological Origins of Nazi Imperialism* (New York, 1986), 244; John Gillingham, *Industry and Politics in the Third Reich: Ruhr Coal, Hitler and Europe* (New York, 1985).

20. Peter Hayes, "Polycracy and Policy in the Third Reich: The Case of the Economy" (unpublished manuscript, Northwestern University, n.d.), 9.

Realists would argue in rebuttal that it is not necessary to show that some immediate economic or military threat compelled Germany to seek security through expansion. In international anarchy, they would remind us, the problem is not just that opponents are out for conquest now, but that they may turn predatory at some time in the future. Consequently, they argue, statesmen must aggressively seek secure markets and borders as a hedge against future developments.[21] Though statesmen surely must consider this danger, it does not in itself explain how anarchy compels unthreatened states toward aggression. Against the benefits of autarky and empire, statesmen must weigh the risk that efforts to achieve them will bring on precisely the consequences they seek to avoid: encirclement by an overwhelming coalition before a self-sufficient, defensible position has been achieved. Reflecting on the fates of both Napoleons, the German Reichs, Fascist Italy, and imperial Japan, it seems clear that behaving too aggressively is a very good way for the state as a ruling organization to go out of business. In anarchy, the risks associated with a low-profile foreign policy seem a better bet.

Proponents of rationalistic explanations for German behavior make one final argument: that German statesmen valued expansion more than security and thus were not irrational in running great risks to achieve it.[22] Indeed, the younger Moltke, irritated by German pusillanimity in the second Moroccan crisis, remarked that Germany might as well "abolish the Army and . . . place ourselves under Japanese protectorate; we shall then be in a position to make money without interference and develop into ninnies."[23] But for this line of argument to hold, it must be shown that the Germans understood that they were running great risks and that there were safer alternatives available. It is true, for example, that the German General Staff before 1914 had a fairly realistic view of the difficulties of implementing the Schlieffen Plan. It is not true, however, that they recognized that defensive alternatives, whether diplomatic or military, were feasible. On the contrary, the whole thrust of Wilhelmine strategic mythology was the assumption that offense and expansionism, no matter how risky, were less risky than defensive and cooperative approaches. In this sense it is incorrect to argue that German statesmen were adopting a rational but risk acceptant policy in view of Germany's position in the international system.

Though international circumstances are in no way a sufficient explanation for German aggressiveness, they did influence the tugging and hauling of domestic politics. World depressions twice undercut domes-

21. Robert Jervis, "Cooperation under the Security Dilemma," *World Politics* 30 (January 1978): 167–214.

22. Robert Jervis, *Perception and Misperception in International Politics* (Princeton, N.J., 1976), 51.

23. Snyder, *Ideology*, 148.

tic political constituencies for liberal, cooperative foreign policies. Strategic competitors inadvertently enhanced the plausibility of expansionists' arguments, either by creating the impression that they would not resist German expansion or by fostering the opposite idea that they were bent on Germany's encirclement and strangulation.

For example, the protectionist coalition of iron and rye, which strongly shaped Germany's whole foreign policy, was triggered by the so-called Great Depression of 1873–96. Likewise, the defeat of Caprivi's free-trading interlude was due not only to Junker political agitation but also to a drop in world grain prices.[24] Weimar's labor-export coalition unraveled as a result of the world economic downturn, the drying up of foreign credit, and the closing of foreign markets. At a deeper level, Otto Hintze argued that the military character of the Prussian state was due to Prussia's exposed position in Central Europe, which forced it to adapt its domestic institutions to the exigencies of constant military conflict.[25] The international setting, in both its immediate and its long-term effects, thus helped shape German foreign policy by influencing the nature of its domestic actors, their interests, and the plausibility of the arguments they put forward against each other. Germany's international circumstances ensured that there would be a constituency for autarky, militarism, and expansion and that arguments for such policies would seem plausible in some circles.

But saying that international events affected the plausibility of bad arguments in German domestic politics is not the same as saying that international circumstances made expansionism a rational gamble for the German state or nation. They did not. The competitive character of the international system cannot in itself explain German aggressiveness, because Germany was not sharply threatened by its powerful competitors, economically or militarily, until Germany itself forced the issue. It is therefore not surprising that the most recent exponent of the realpolitik account of German expansionism, David Calleo, often falls back on purely domestic factors at crucial parts of his story.[26]

STRATEGIC CONCEPTS: THE BANDWAGON AND THE BIG STICK

German militarists and imperialists articulated almost every argument in the panoply of rationales for security through expansion.[27] In

---

24. Hans Jürgen Puhle, "Lords and Peasants in the Kaiserreich," in Robert G. Moeller, ed., *Peasants and Lords in Modern Germany* (Boston, 1986), 82.

25. Otto Hintze, "Military Organization and the Organization of the State," in Felix Gilbert, ed., *The Historical Essays of Otto Hintze* (New York, 1975), 178–215.

26. Calleo, *German Problem*, 78–84, endorses the views of Eckart Kehr.

27. This section generally follows the theoretical and historical analysis of Stephen Van Evera, "Causes of War" (Ph.D. diss., University of California at Berkeley, 1984).

contrast, Bismarck and Gustav Stresemann, the architect of the Weimar policy of international cooperation, held an opposite view of how to create security for Germany. Though the imperialists' views were often, though not always, sincerely held, their worldview seems designed to employ every conceivable double standard and analytical sleight of hand in the service of rationalizing a policy of diplomatic bluster, military procurement, and imperial expansion.[28] Thus the very character of German strategic concepts suggests that they were myths rather than rational reactions to Germany's position in the international system.

German international social Darwinism portrayed a world in which security was scarce, competition was intense, and an aggressive policy was required by the situation in which Germany found itself. This view can be expressed in terms of a number of interrelated strategic concepts.

The Strategic Concepts

The paper tiger image of the adversary. Proponents of expansionist *Weltpolitik* held an oddly self-contradictory view of the competition with Great Britain. Britain was seen as an immensely powerful, aggressive foe yet as unlikely to resist German efforts to redress the imbalance of power. On the one hand, German strategists held that "two great trading nations could not coexist" without their economic competition turning into a military "struggle for survival." Britain, incensed with "trade envy," was trying to throttle Germany's worldwide economic development.[29] This was hardly an accurate perception, though Britain's seizure of German vessels suspected of carrying contraband during the Boer War did give a vivid example of how vulnerable Germany's worldwide economic interests might be to the British fleet. If Britain was indeed unappeasable, Germany would have to checkmate Britain by building a battle fleet of its own. The German navy argued that even a somewhat inferior German fleet would deter an attack by the superior British, who would fear that the loss of ships in fighting Germany would leave Britain vulnerable to the navies of France and Russia.

Proponents of this "risk fleet" concept held that the British would for some reason fail to compete intensely in the naval construction race, although the navy mattered more to Britain and the British did not have to support a large continental army. Moreover, they ignored the possibility that Britain would react to the rising German naval threat by

28. On the sincerity question, Smith, *Ideological Origins*, 237.
29. Jonathan Steinberg, *Yesterday's Deterrent* (London, 1965), 27, 42–43; Paul Kennedy, *Strategy and Diplomacy, 1870–1945* (London, 1984), 156.

aligning with France and Russia, who were also threatened by offensive German war plans and belligerent German diplomacy.

In short, German strategy rested on an inherently contradictory image of a key adversary: paper tiger Britain would voraciously snuff out German trade if unopposed on the high seas, yet would acquiesce to German *Weltpolitik* without a fight or a serious arms race if Germany built a token, numerically inferior fleet. Bolstered by this "logic," Chancellor Bernhard von Bülow could contend that "the purpose of the Navy Law is above all to secure peace for us against England."[30]

The paper tiger image of Britain served to reinforce aggressive policies, no matter which aspect of the tiger's character was stressed at the given moment. Thus, in the final years and even days before August 1914, Chancellor Theobald von Bethmann-Hollweg's strategy for backing Austria against Serbia and Russia was bolstered by the thought that Britain might stay out of a war fought over these issues. But at the same time, the German General Staff rejected the civilians' suggestion that the march across neutral Belgium might be given up in exchange for a pledge of British neutrality, on the grounds that no such pledge could be trusted.[31] In effect, Britain might fail to fight out of lack of resolve, but no concessions to the concerns of the devious, hostile British could possibly be considered to increase that likelihood. In short, the Germans' paper tiger image put Britain under a double whammy, whereby any British act of moderation might be taken as indicating lack of resolve, while any act of firmness might be taken as confirming the need for aggressive German counteraction to break the encirclement.[32] As Paul Kennedy has noted, German pessimists in 1914 argued for preventive war, while optimists argued that Germany was strong enough to brush aside any resistance to its expansion.[33]

Bandwagon and big stick assumptions. German imperialists and militarists assumed that the balance of power operated in reverse and that

30. To the Reichstag, 27 March 1900, in Paul Kennedy, "Tirpitz, England and the Second Navy Law of 1900: A Strategical Critique," *Militärgeschichtliche Mitteilungen* 2 (1970): 33–58, at 35. On the underestimation of Britain's ability to keep up in a naval race, see Weyer's 1902 memorandum, cited in Walther Hubatsch, *Die Ära Tirpitz* (Göttingen, 1955), 74n.69.

31. Snyder, *Ideology*, 149. Similarly, in 1905 Britain was taken to be so aggressive that it might preventively attack the German fleet, yet so passive that it would shy away from backing France in Morocco. The former was taken to be an argument for expanding the fleet more quickly to get through the danger period, while the latter was taken as an invitation to coerce France with impunity.

32. The recent debate between John Orme, "Deterrence Failures: A Second Look," *International Security* 11 (Spring 1987): 96–124, and Richard Ned Lebow, "Deterrence Failure Revisited," *International Security* 12 (Summer 1987): 197–213, needs to be reconsidered in this light. For further remarks, see the conclusion to this chapter.

33. Paul Kennedy, *The Rise of Anglo-German Antagonism, 1860–1914* (London, 1980), 454.

the best way to make friends was to wave a big stick. In the Moroccan crises of 1905 and 1911, German diplomats calculated that threats of war directed at France would tend to separate it from its allies, but in fact they had the opposite effect. Despite this, Chancellor Bethmann-Hollweg stuck to the same strategy in July 1914, telling his private secretary Kurt Riezler that a local war in the Balkans would crush Serbia, humiliate Russia, and disrupt the Entente.[34] German imperialists thought not only that threats would break apart the opposing alliance, but also that offensive military capabilities were a prerequisite for attracting allies. As early as 1883 Admiral Albrecht von Stosch, the predecessor and tutor of Alfred von Tirpitz, invented the concept of "alliance worthiness," which held that a navy capable only of coastal defense would make Germany a worthless ally.[35]

Dominoes and the interdependence of commitments. Proponents of big stick diplomacy justified their belligerent tactics with the argument that retreats on small issues would have a domino effect by tarnishing Germany's reputation for resolve. Since some authorities have contended that an obsession with "saving face for the sake of deterrence" is peculiar to the United States in the nuclear era, it is worth quoting some remarks of Friedrich von Holstein, the chief strategist in the German Foreign Office, that have a decidedly contemporary ring.[36] "If we let ourselves be trampled on in Morocco, we invite similar treatment elsewhere. Not for material reasons alone, but even more for the sake of prestige must Germany protest against the intended appropriation of Morocco by France," Holstein asserted.[37] "We stand here before a test of strength; a German retreat in the face of Anglo-French resistance would in no way be conducive to bringing about better German-English relations, but would on the contrary give the English, the French, and the rest of the world practical proof that one gets most from Germany by treating her badly. . . . In this way, instead of getting peace we should only be preparing the way for further conflicts."[38]

He drew the same inferences about the consequences of the retreats

34. Van Evera, "Causes of War," 489, citing Imanuel Geiss, *German Foreign Policy, 1871–1914* (London, 1976), 167; see also Wayne C. Thompson, *In the Eye of the Storm: Kurt Riezler and the Crises of Modern Germany* (Iowa City, 1980), 75. Van Evera, "Causes of War," 487–90, discusses German bandwagon thinking.

35. Steinberg, *Yesterday's Deterrent*, 66.

36. Patrick Morgan, "Saving Face for the Sake of Deterrence," in Robert Jervis, Richard Ned Lebow, and Janice Gross Stein, *Psychology and Deterrence* (Baltimore, 1985), 125–52, discusses the American analogue.

37. G. P. Gooch, *Before the War: Studies in Diplomacy*, 2 vols. (1938; New York, 1967), 1:247.

38. Norman Rich, *Friedrich von Holstein*, 2 vols. (Cambridge, 1965), 2:683, letter of 5 June 1904. For other examples, see Steinberg, *Yesterday's Deterrent*, 155; Anderson, *First Moroccan Crisis*, 150.

of other powers. He worried, for example, that a German retreat in Morocco would "stand on the same level with [Prussia's humiliation in 1850 at] Olmütz and cause the [French retreat in 1898 at] Fashoda to be forgotten." But he failed to consider that Fashoda had actually turned out to be a boon to French diplomacy, disabusing France of her self-defeating colonial aims and setting the stage for a highly advantageous alliance with Britain.[39]

Offensive advantage. German militarists and navalists argued that the necessity for offensive action was axiomatic, notwithstanding their keen appreciation of tactical and logistic considerations that played into the hands of the defender. Best documented among army circles, this held true for the German navy as well. Paralleling General Schlieffen's views on land warfare, Tirpitz contended that any successful naval strategy had to rest on decisive offensive action threatening to achieve total command of the sea.[40] Yet when Tirpitz's argument required it, he could also invoke the tactical advantages of the defensive. Explaining to the kaiser in 1912 how the inferior German fleet might inflict heavy losses on the British, Tirpitz insisted that the British offensive spirit and sense of prestige would lead them to fight in disadvantageous waters near the German coast.[41] But privately Tirpitz and his lieutenants had understood for years that Britain would be hard to lure into such an obvious trap. As it turned out, both Tirpitz and the British fought the surface naval war in a tactically defensive way, the British mounting a standoff blockade and the German surface fleet refraining from challenging it.[42]

Tirpitz's rhetoric insisted on the necessity of gaining sea control through a decisive offensive, explaining why Germany needed a battle fleet; the tactical advantages of the defense, explaining how an inferior German fleet could win; and the British appreciation for the necessity of the offensive, explaining why the British would not exploit the tactical advantages of the defensive. The welter of contradictions in these arguments and the discrepancies between Tirpitz's public and private pronouncements on strategy suggest that these were largely opportunistic arguments, not true beliefs. Though Tirpitz's strategy was criticized by a variety of German politicians, army men, and diplomats, he managed to maintain the technical credibility of the risk fleet concept by keeping secret the naval staff studies that irrefutably

39. Anderson, *First Moroccan Crisis,* 202.
40. Kennedy, "Tirpitz, England and the Second Navy Law," 45; Snyder, *Ideology,* chaps. 4 and 5.
41. Ritter, *Sword,* 2:150.
42. Ibid., 2:151; Paul Kennedy, "The Development of German Naval Operations Plans against England, 1896–1914," *English Historical Review* 89 (January 1974): 48–76, at 64.

pointed out its flaws and by deterring leaks through firing naval critics.[43]

The importance of windows of vulnerability. Seeing others as hostile, war as inevitable, and offense as easy, German imperialists and militarists repeatedly argued for preventive attacks to forestall an adverse shift in the balance of power. While well documented in the area of land warfare,[44] the use of the concept in naval strategy is especially revealing. Tirpitz argued that the initial burst of German naval building had to proceed very rapidly to reduce the duration of a dangerous window of vulnerability, when Britain might choose to attack the German fleet preventively just as it had preventively attacked—or "Copenhagened"— the Danish fleet in its own harbor during the Napoleonic War. Holstein believed Tirpitz had exaggerated this danger, "for this fear is the most effective argument in favor of either giving up our colonies [which was unthinkable] or increasing our fleet."[45]

The El Dorado myth. Proponents of German imperialism naturally exaggerated the expected benefits of colonies, calling the utterly undeveloped wastes of *Mittelafrika* "a second India," and understated their costs. Weighing costs and benefits was discouraged by the argument that costs were necessarily front loaded, whereas benefits would appear only in the long run.[46]

Evaluation of the Myths

These strategic arguments constitute, above all, a promiscuous, hydra-headed rationale for imperial expansion, military procurement, and big stick diplomacy. Surely many of them were sincerely believed by their proponents. Bethmann-Hollweg would have had little reason to dissemble in conversations with Kurt Riezler, his personal secretary. But some arguments, especially those Tirpitz put forward, were thought by skeptical contemporaries to be purely opportunistic concoctions. Yet sincere or not, they uniformly have the character of arguments skewed to a predetermined outcome. This bias is especially apparent in the

43. Kennedy, *Antagonism*, 417–19; Ritter, *Sword*, 2:152–53; Kennedy, "Tirpitz, England and the Second Navy Law."

44. Jack Levy, "Declining Power and the Preventive Motivation for War," *World Politics* 40 (October 1987): 82–107.

45. Jonathan Steinberg, "The Copenhagen Complex," in Walter Laqueur and George L. Mosse, *1914: The Coming of the First World War* (New York, 1966), 39–40, citing Norman Rich and M. H. Fisher, eds., *The Holstein Papers*, 4 vols. (Cambridge, 1955–63), 4:81–82.

46. For examples, see Woodruff Smith, *The German Colonial Empire* (Chapel Hill, N.C., 1978).

convenient use of logical double standards. Tirpitz, for example, reversed his views on the offense/defense question at different junctures of his argument so as to make a plausible case for the risk fleet. More fundamentally, the paper tiger image of Britain used social Darwinist assumptions to explain why Germany was in an "expand or die" situation but then used liberal arguments to explain how expansion could be achieved successfully, safely, and at low cost.

A particularly clear example is Riezler's 1913 textbook on international politics, which Bethmann apparently encouraged him to write as a rebuttal to Pan-German extremists.[47] Riezler argued that commercial and cultural rivalry inevitably made for a zero-sum competition between Germany and Britain, in which Germany must either expand its world political presence or fall by the wayside. He also argued, however, like the British liberal Norman Angell, that wars had become too costly for anyone to undertake rationally. But Riezler's conclusions were more like those of the American theorist of nuclear brinkmanship, Thomas Schelling, than like Angell's. Riezler deduced that Germany could—indeed, given social Darwinist imperatives, had to—exploit other powers' fear of war by extorting concessions from them in intense international crises. Only if public opinion got out of control and wrecked the delicate game of brinkmanship, Riezler contended, would such tactics backfire and lead to war.[48]

The logic of this argument manifests significant internal tensions. It depicts zero-sum struggle as both inevitable and impossible, Britain as both implacable and easy to face down in a crisis. As Riezler's biographer suspects, these contradictions may grow out of the political contradictions that Bethmann had to manage: on the one hand, the domestic political necessity of pursuing an imperialist course, but on the other hand, the domestic *and* international necessity of countering the dangerous excesses of the Pan-Germans.[49]

In short, the very structure of the arguments put forward in Riezler's "risk theory" smacks of a finely-balanced political program, manipulating contradictory strategic assumptions to mask its real costs and risks.[50] Similarly, the self-contradictory structure of Tirpitz's "risk fleet" idea and Holstein's concept of a "world-historical game of chance" suggests prima facie that these notions were myths and rationalizations.

47. Thompson, *Eye of the Storm*, chaps. 2 and 3, esp. p. 23.
48. J. J. Ruedorffer [pseud. for Kurt Riezler], *Grundzüge der Weltpolitik in der Gegenwart* (Berlin, 1914), esp. 214–32; Thompson, *Eye of the Storm*, chaps. 2 and 3; Andreas Hillgruber, *Germany and the Two World Wars* (Cambridge, Mass., 1981), 22–24; Norman Angell, *The Great Illusion* (London, 1910); Thomas Schelling, *Arms and Influence* (New Haven, Conn., 1966).
49. Thompson, *Eye of the Storm*, 43–44.
50. Kitchen, *Political Economy of Germany*, 235.

VARIATIONS IN GERMAN STRATEGIC CONCEPTS

So far I have used illustrations from the Wilhelmine period, which capture the most striking features of German imperialist ideology particularly well. But tracing variations over time in German strategic ideas is also revealing and will help to establish three points that are important to the overall argument of this chapter. First, prevailing strategic concepts changed a great deal as the domestic and international environment changed. Though there were great similarities between Wilhelmine and Nazi strategic ideas, Bismarckian and Weimar concepts were quite different. Thus there was no simple, straight-line intellectual continuity that can be traced back to the alleged lessons of the Franco-Prussian War of 1870.

Second, even at the height of Wilhelmine imperial ideology, German elites retained considerable understanding of the true character of the balance of power system, though they were often politically constrained from acting on that knowledge. Each elite group expected that the imperialist projects promoted by other groups would provoke a balancing response from Germany's foes abroad, yet they failed to anticipate such responses to their own pet projects.

Third, under Hitler, Germany was governed by an elite that had completely internalized the imperialist myths that had become the common currency of popular political discourse in the late Wilhelmine period. The Nazis, not party to the cynical manipulations of a Bernhard von Bulow, were victims of what Stephen Van Evera has called ideological "blowback," wherein a state's official policy comes to be caught up in the unanticipated consequences of its own mythmaking.[51]

Bismarck's Strategic Concepts

Though Wilhelmine expansionists often claimed Bismarck as their model and inspiration, Bismarck's brand of realpolitik was in many respects based on principles opposite to theirs. Bismarck's Realism conceived of politics as an exercise in building temporary coalitions, based on the power and interests of the participants, which included both states and social groups within states. Indeed, Bismarck viewed domestic political alliances as potential substitutes for foreign alliances, if they could provide the power necessary to carry out his purpose of the moment.[52] There was a social Darwinist core to Bismarck's Realism:

51. Van Evera, "Causes of War."
52. Otto Pflanze, *Bismarck and the Development of Germany: The Period of Unification, 1815–1871* (Princeton, N.J., 1971), 99, shows that Bismarck saw an alliance with German national liberalism as an alternative to an alliance with France or Russia for the purpose of gaining political parity with Austria in 1854.

"Without struggle there can be no life and, if we wish to continue living, we must also be reconciled to further struggles." Also present was the resignation to the necessity of risk taking that Wilhelmine Realists-in-caricature later glorified: "My entire life," said Bismarck, "was spent gambling for high stakes with other people's money."[53]

These elements were offset, however, by a keen appreciation of the workings of the balance of power and the Realist expectation that others would coalesce to resist encroachments on their interests. Thus, to further one's own purposes, it was crucial to show others that they would profit more from an alliance with oneself than from an alliance with one's enemies. Tactically, this expressed itself in Bismarck's principle of always trying to occupy the pivot in any international or domestic political constellation. Bismarck always sought to retain the option of allying with any of a number of actors while trying to restrict his opponents' alliance possibilities.[54] Inevitably this had a moderating effect on Bismarck's tactics, since the pivot could normally be occupied only by accommodating the interests of a majority of the players and refraining from threatening their security.

Before 1870 Bismarck was less constrained, because France was universally considered a greater threat to the European balance than was Prussia, regardless of Bismarck's revisionist policy. But even then Bismarck understood that he must always make the opponent seem the aggressor and above all reject his military's advice to launch a cold-blooded preventive war, which would range neutral opinion against him.[55] Thus patience in awaiting the accretion of a winning coalition and a propitious moment was a principle of his: "I have often had to stand for long periods of time in the hunting blind and let myself be covered and stung by insects before the moment came to shoot."[56] The "exercise of caution," moreover, is required by "the possiblity that the opponent will at the last moment make another move than that expected and act accordingly. In other words, one must always have two irons in the fire."[57] In diplomacy, this meant concluding a reinsurance treaty with Russia as the second iron to go along with the alliance with Austria. The potential contradiction in this arrangement could be reconciled only if both alliances were interpreted as strictly defensive.[58]

53. Pflanze, *Bismarck*, 87–88.
54. Otto Pflanze, "Bismarck's *Realpolitik*," in James Sheehan, *Imperial Germany* (New York, 1976), 164–65; Pflanze, *Bismarck*, 91–92.
55. Snyder, *Ideology*, 128.
56. Pflanze, *Bismarck*, 90.
57. Pflanze, "Bismarck's *Realpolitik*," 163.
58. On Bismarck's defensive alliances, Stephen Van Evera, "The Cult of the Offensive and the Origins of the First World War," in Steven E. Miller, ed., *Military Strategy and the Origins of the First World War* (Princeton, N.J., 1985), 96–98; reprinted from *International Security* 9 (Summer 1984).

Even Bismarck found it difficult to maintain this "equilibrium of mutual frustration," because his domestic political allies demanded a more offensive policy against Russia.[59] The agricultural pillar of Bismarck's alliance of iron and rye required prohibitive tariffs against imports of Russian grain, whereas the industrial pillar demanded a contradictory policy of low Russian tariffs for German manufactured goods. To coerce the Russians into a one-sided trading relationship, which they ultimately accepted only at the nadir of their power during the Russo-Japanese War in 1904, Bismarck in 1887 cut off Russia's access to German capital markets, thus driving it into the arms of French finance and a step closer to a French military alliance. At the same time, the German General Staff's preparations for preventive war also undermined normal political relations with Russia. Bismarck invoked the strategic justification that the financial restrictions were necessary to curtail Russia's potential for war in the Balkans, which threatened to break out as a result of the Bulgarian crisis. But in fact this counterproductive move violated his own strategic principles by making France the diplomatic pivot, handing Germany's "second iron in the fire" to its enemies. Even under the astute Bismarck, the logic of domestic coalition maintenance was beginning to skew foreign policy tactics and turn sound balance of power practices on their heads.

Wilhelmine Strategic Concepts

Throughout the Wilhelmine era, German chancellors and diplomats drifted further and further from Bismarckian defensive realpolitik, both because of domestic pressures that required reckless policies and because German leaders eventually came to believe in the imperialist myths that were the common currency of political debate in the Wilhelmine polity.

The Caprivi period. Bismarck's successor, General Leo von Caprivi, pursued a moderately liberal policy at home and abroad. He argued that protectionism had not solved the problem of industrial overproduction; on the contrary, by provoking other states to close their markets to German goods, protectionism had exacerbated it. Attacking the agricultural protectionism of the Junkers as naked self-seeking, Caprivi negotiated treaties with Austria, Romania, and eventually Russia providing for reductions in industrial and agricultural tariffs. Caprivi pursued a domestic policy of reform and appeasement of the working class to create a domestic base for this policy. He and Holstein expected that a

59. This phrase is Pflanze's, *Bismarck*, 92; the domestic political argument follows Wehler, *German Empire*, 190–92.

"natural alliance" with England—liberal, free trading, anti-French, anti-Russian—would provide its international complement. Caprivi's policy in essence was a liberal version of *Mitteleuropa* and *Weltpolitik*: without a fleet, without the marriage of iron and rye, but with Britain's cooperation against Germany's continental and colonial opponents.[60]

This strategy foundered because of the lukewarm reaction of Britain, which saw insufficient incentive to abandon the policy of the free hand, and the opposition of the Junkers and other German farmers, who united in a politically potent pro-tariff Agrarian League. Failing to attract the British tie, the strategy nonetheless scuttled the Reinsurance Treaty with Russia, which was consequently propelled into an alliance with France. Thus Caprivi and Holstein managed to achieve the worst of all possible worlds, alienating the Junkers over grain imports from Russia while not even gaining a Russian diplomatic alliance to offset this heavy domestic political price.

The Bülow period. By 1898 the German ruling elite had shifted back to the uneasy marriage of iron and rye, which invoked the vague doctrines of social Darwinism and *Weltpolitik* to justify a heterogeneous mix of assertive foreign policies: an enlarged fleet to protect German commerce, increased grain tariffs to make Germany self-sufficient in food and protect the rural wellspring of folkish German culture, and colonial and continental expansion for purposes of both economic exploitation and emigration from crowded German farmlands. This was all to be achieved without war, however, through the risk fleet and coercive diplomacy, and without taxing Junker estates or inheritances, since small military programs would suffice to produce big political effects.[61]

Strategic concepts in this period are oddly contradictory. Even within a particular individual, big stick theories exist side by side with a clear understanding of balancing dynamics and the danger that threatening actions will provoke opposition and increase the likelihood of an unwanted war. Thus, on the one hand, Bülow's remarks reflect the assumptions of social Darwinism, the bandwagon, the domino theory, and paper tiger images. He asserted, for example, that "the German

---

60. John A. Nichols, *Germany after Bismarck: The Caprivi Era* (Cambridge, Mass., 1958); Kitchen, *Political Economy of Germany*, 208–14; John C. G. Rohl, *Germany without Bismarck* (Berkeley, Calif., 1967), chaps. 2 and 3; Calleo, *German Problem Reconsidered*, 18–20; Smith, *Ideological Origins*, 79–80.

61. Wehler, *German Empire*, chaps. 5–8; Smith, *Ideological Origins*, chaps. 4 and 5; David Kaiser, "Germany and the Origins of the First World War," *Journal of Modern History* 55 (September 1983): 442–74. Peter Winzen, *Bülows Weltmachtkonzept* (Boppard am Rhein, 1977), 43, fixes Bulow's shift from a continental to a *Weltpolitik* orientation in August 1897, coinciding with the development of Tirpitz's fleet plan.

people will either be the hammer or the anvil,"[62] that English irritation at the kaiser's visit to Morocco would somehow undercut the Anglo-French entente,[63] that a fleet would win allies for Germany,[64] that an Anglo-Russian alliance was impossible no matter how aggressively Germany behaved,[65] and that a retreat from the quagmire in South-West Africa would reflect on all of Germany's colonial endeavors.[66]

On the other hand, there is also strong evidence that Bülow was in fact a cautious cynic, using the language of *Weltpolitik*, for example, to win the "Hottentot election" of 1907 but actually having rather limited foreign policy aims. In 1908 he explained that "no war in Europe can bring us much. There would be nothing for us to gain in the conquest of any fresh Slav or French territory. If we annex small countries to the Empire we shall only strengthen those centrifugal elements which, alas, are never wanting in Germany." Defeat would trigger the fall of the dynasty, whereas victory would require compensation for the sacrifices of the populace.[67] Indeed, Bülow's real strategy, as distinct from his public strategy of bluff and brinkmanship, was probably to wait for an Anglo-Russian war and then dominate the ensuing peace conference, as Bismarck had done at the Congress of Berlin.[68]

This patient, reactive Bismarckian strategy of limited aims fit with a balancing view of international politics that was the opposite of the big stick theory. Bülow recognized more quickly than Holstein that the Moroccan gambit was going sour, warning that "pushing or threatening at this moment on account of Morocco would only press France still closer to England and at the same time cause the Emperor Nicholas to suspect that directly after Björkö he is to be forced to choose between us and France."[69] A forced alliance with Russia, he realized, would be worthless.[70] Likewise, he learned rather quickly that the risk fleet plan was backfiring, that it was provoking a balancing arms buildup by

---

62. Kennedy, "Tirpitz, England and the Second Navy Law," 34, quoting an 1899 speech.

63. Anderson, *First Moroccan Crisis*, 186–87.

64. Kennedy, "Tirpitz, England and the Second Navy Law," 35, to the Reichstag, 27 March 1900.

65. Rich, *Holstein*, 2:674–75; Barbara Vogel, *Deutsche Russlandpolitik* (Düsseldorf, 1973), 118–23.

66. George Crothers, *The German Elections of 1907* (New York, 1941), 105.

67. Bülow to the Crown Prince, October 1908, as reproduced in *Memoirs of Prince von Bülow* (Boston, 1931), cited in Kaiser, "Germany," 455–56; more generally, Winzen, *Bülows Weltmachtkonzept*, 238.

68. Kennedy, *Antagonism*, 227.

69. Anderson, *First Moroccan Crisis*, 263–64. Chaim Kaufmann, "Deterrence and Rationality in International Crises" (Ph.D. diss., Columbia University, 1990), chap. 4, shows that Bülow learned more quickly in the Moroccan affair than did Holstein, but less quickly than other German diplomats for whom the personal political stakes were lower.

70. Rich, *Holstein*, 2:690.

Britain.[71] To minimize the risks of provoking a Copenhagening, as well as the diplomatic and economic costs of an arms spiral, he favored arms control on terms favorable to Britain and asked Tirpitz whether mines, U-boats, and coastal fortifications might not provide an effective defensive substitute for an offensive battle fleet.[72] Tirpitz, threatening to resign, replied that backing down would humiliate Germany, demonstrate its weakness, and thus increase the danger of war.[73] In fact, it was Bülow who was fired as a result of his differences with Kaiser Wilhelm and Tirpitz over the fleet, his plan to tax Junker estates, and in general the frictions with Wilhelm and various interest groups caused by Bülow's attempt to pursue a new policy line.[74]

Overall, the picture that emerges is of a politician who basically understood the balancing character of the system and the limits it placed on big stick diplomacy, yet who engaged in the pretense of a vague *Weltpolitik* for purposes of domestic political prestige and minimal payoffs to constituencies who sought a strong, "national" foreign policy. Naturally he hoped that big stick diplomacy would work well enough to keep up the pretense, but his public orations about *Weltpolitik* overstated the results he expected to achieve.[75]

Holstein's strategic arguments also show a certain duality, though they are slanted more toward genuine faith in waving the big stick. On the one hand, Holstein consciously aimed to use the Moroccan crisis to break the Entente, increasing his demands in response to French concessions and rejecting "the naive view... that the more we give in to the French, the more grateful they will be to us. No, it is not to us that they will be grateful, but to England. The greater the success of France in Morocco, the closer she will draw to England as a result of this proof of the value of the entente cordiale."[76] "The French will only consider approaching us when they see that English friendship is not enough to obtain Germany's consent to the French seizure of Morocco."[77] Whereas Bülow came to see Morocco as a bribe to get France to accept a Russo-German treaty, Holstein hoped the tsar would get France to concede over Morocco. Holstein thought in terms of the Fashoda

71. Gooch, *Before the War*, 1:270, 274.

72. Arthur Marder, *The Anatomy of British Seapower* (Hamden, Conn., 1964), 171–73; Ritter, *Sword*, 2:161; Gooch, *Before the War*, 1:270; see also Kennedy, *Antagonism*, 238–39.

73. Ritter, *Sword*, 2:161; Gooch, *Before the War*, 1:271.

74. V. R. Berghahn, *Germany and the Approach of War in 1914* (New York, 1973), chap. 4, esp. 83–84.

75. For more evidence, Kaiser, "Germany," 450–51; Kennedy, *Antagonism*, 236–39, 365; Rich and Fisher, *Holstein Papers*, 4:236.

76. Rich, *Holstein*, 2:730, Holstein to Arthur von Brauer, 27 December 1905.

77. Christopher Andrew, *Théophile Delcassé and the Making of the Entente Cordiale* (London, 1968), 269.

model: squeeze the French, then dictate from a position of strength.[78] Holstein explained France's increasing intransigence as a reaction to concessionary statements by the kaiser, whereas it was in fact due to firm British backing, which had been heightened by evidence that Germany was unwilling to reciprocate reasonable concessions.[79]

Though Holstein often counted on the big stick as a tool for making friends with France and Russia, he was able to understand balancing dynamics when they interfered with Anglo-German friendship, which was the elusive cornerstone of his whole policy. Tirpitz's "naval policy is of benefit to the naval trust (armour-plating, etc.) and the promotion of naval officers," Holstein wrote to Bulow in August 1907. "For the rest of Germany it is detrimental and an indubitable danger both in foreign and domestic affairs. The Kaiser's speeches about the fleet, the Navy League, and the convulsive naval armaments—these are the things that have consolidated an overwhelming naval superiority against us. . . . The three dreadnoughts that are now being built in England owe their existence indirectly to the iron will of His Majesty."[80] In short, even Holstein was capable of thinking in balancing terms, when big stick policies threatened his own hobbyhorse and when appeasement would only offend someone else's bureaucratic interest.

Other political groups and figures also understood balancing dynamics, or at least recognized them when they happened. Liberal businessmen often backed the fleet less for immediate financial gain than because it fit with a social imperialist class ideology of Anglo-German condominium of the modern, technocratic, global economy. Such figures as Albert Ballin abandoned Tirpitz when they saw that the fleet was having the opposite effect.[81] Business circles were also keen to appease France in Morocco in order to get a share of the economic action, regardless of French political primacy.[82]

Likewise, General Moltke, chief of the General Staff, easily recognized that naval and overseas adventures, in which his department had no interest, were needlessly provoking other powers and siphoning funds away from the army. He favored negotiation to forestall a naval arms race, and he scoffed at the idea that Morocco would be a source of military manpower for France; rather, it would take 100,000 troops to occupy it.[83] On someone else's turf, Moltke was ready to see balancing

78. Rich, *Holstein*, 2:717.

79. Ibid., 2:709–10.

80. Rich and Fisher, *Holstein Papers*, 4:488, 29 August 1907; on the need to appease Britain, 4:377, 23 December 1905.

81. Smith, *German Colonial Empire*, 170–71; Smith, *Ideological Origins*, 61.

82. E. W. Edwards, "The Franco-German Agreement on Morocco, 1909," *English Historical Review* 78 (July 1963): 483–513, at 492–94.

83. Ritter, *Sword*, 2:158; Edwards, "Franco-German Agreement," 510n.2, Moltke to Bülow, May 1908, on Morocco.

behavior and quagmires. On his own turf, however, he retained the main features of the Schlieffen Plan, which provoked Britain's entry into the war and stuck the German army in a four-year morass on the Western Front.

Even Tirpitz himself understood that the fleet was a provocation to England, not simply a lever to gain British friendship. It was for that reason he insisted that "all policy hostile to England must be left alone until we have a fleet which is as strong as the English."[84] Thus he rejected the idea proposed by the kaiser and the Foreign Office that an alliance with Russia would deter Britain from Copenhagening the nascent German fleet, even though this scheme had some of the flavor of his own risk theory. Rather, he argued that such an alliance would trigger a preventive attack.[85] Similarly his lieutenant, Admiral Eduard von Capelle, argued that a big push in naval building could not have been taken during the Moroccan crisis, when it would be provocative, but could be taken in 1907, to exploit what he expected would be the wimpish liberal government of Campbell-Bannerman.[86] Finally, Gerhard Ritter has noted that behind the whole risk theory was the balancing assumption that "all second-rate naval powers had a common interest in breaking Britain's seagoing monopoly."[87] Of course Tirpitz's policy long outlived the falsification of this assumption. The most likely guess is that Tirpitz did not believe his own bandwagon argument, which held that the fleet would force Britain to accept Germany as a partner in global condominium. Rather, he seems to have used this as an argument to attract support from liberal industrialists and to explain in the Reichstag how the costs and risks would be kept down.[88] He seems to have understood all along that the fleet would produce at best a tense standoff with Britain, and that Germany in the long run would have to aim for naval superiority, not a 70 percent risk deterrent.[89] "If one wishes to achieve a great aim," admitted Tirpitz, "one is not always in the position to reveal one's final thoughts."[90]

The Bethmann period. Theobald von Bethmann-Hollweg is a controversial historical figure, portrayed by some as a moderate struggling against the militarists and populists who cavalierly welcomed war, but characterized by others as a true believer who failed to understand that

---

84. Kennedy, "Tirpitz, England and the Second Navy Law," 54, Tirpitz to Hohenlohe, 1898.
85. Kennedy, *Antagonism*, 274.
86. Ibid., 443.
87. Ritter, *Sword*, 2:148.
88. Smith, *German Colonial Empire*, 171–72.
89. On the latter point, Kennedy, *Strategy and Diplomacy*, 156.
90. Kennedy, *Antagonism*, 422.

Bülow's *Weltpolitik* had been only a cynical game of social imperialism.[91] His most substantial biography places him somewhere in between, claiming that he used brinkmanship to pursue liberal imperialist goals: that is, limited domestic liberalization, an Anglo-German alliance, and an empire in Central Africa and Asia Minor as Germany's "place in the sun," which would be the "legitimate reward of a growing [national] organization."[92] Despite accepting a fair amount of social Darwinist claptrap and personally selecting the belligerent Alfred von Kiderlen-Wächter as his foreign secretary, Bethmann largely held to a balancing view of the world.[93] For example, while the kaiser and the military took Lord Haldane's unwillingness to pledge British neutrality on his 1912 visit as an indication that war was coming, Bethmann argued that Haldane had "only affirmed what we have long known: now as before England follows a policy of balance of power and therefore will stand up for France if the latter is in danger of being annihilated by us."[94]

Moreover, he felt that the best way to loosen the Entente and protect Austria was by appeasement, not threats. By improving relations with Russia, he argued, "we calm France, facilitate our rapprochement with England, and will be able to envisage a future resolution of the Balkan question more confidently than if we were enemies."[95] In the aftermath of the Agadir crisis, he prophetically argued that if he had allowed a slide toward war, Germany's army would be stuck in France, its fleet would be sunk, and the German people "would rightly string me up on the nearest tree." Yet he also insisted that "we were driven by the necessity of maintaining our economic interests and of showing the world that we were firmly resolved not to be pushed aside."[96]

Bethmann's cautious yet belligerent "risk diplomacy" might be attributed to the two-sided nature of his views: social Darwinist yet attuned to the basic balancing character of the system. Underlying this, however, was his recognition that no matter how realistic his own view might be, he could operate politically only at the margins. Bethmann, realizing that neither the kaiser nor the Reichstag would accept a complete abandonment of the naval program, was forced to admit in intragovernment meetings that he lacked the naval expertise of Tirpitz. Therefore he could offer only mitigating arguments from a financial or diplomatic standpoint, not a decisive refutation of the German navy's strategic myths.[97]

Backed further and further into a corner by international events and

91. Kaiser, "Germany," 458–74.
92. Konrad Jarausch, *The Enigmatic Chancellor* (New Haven, Conn., 1973), 144–45.
93. Ibid., 111, 123, 141.
94. Ibid., 134; also 94–96.
95. Ibid., 118.
96. Ibid., 126.
97. Ibid., 113.

the German nationalists, Bethmann clung to the slim hope that Britain would stay neutral, telling his ambassador in London that "you see things somewhat too pessimistically if you believe that in case of war England will *undoubtedly* be found on France's side against us."[98] "The British *parties* favor an understanding with us and I hope to be able to overcome the resistance of Sir Edward Grey and especially his aides in the Foreign Office *in time*—if here everything were not dictated by the mood of the moment and by the political sophistication of a kindergarten."[99]

In summary, Wilhelmine statesmen were no doubt partially sincere about the social Darwinist doctrines and strategic myths that led them down the path of *Weltpolitik*, and they were perhaps increasingly so as time passed. Nonetheless, there is strong evidence that these statesmen understood quite well the balancing character of the system and the provocative and self-defeating nature of many of Germany's foreign policies. Despite this, they were constrained by domestic political circumstances from acting effectively on this understanding, and indeed were reluctant to apply it when it foiled their own pet projects.

Weimar Strategic Concepts

Gustav Stresemann, a comparatively moderate proponent of *Weltpolitik* in the Wilhelmine period, crafted a cooperative foreign policy that fit the exigencies of the Weimar Republic's international position and a labor-export coalition that gave it life in domestic politics. The Locarno accommodation with the Western powers was necessary, he explained, because "economic power is the only respect in which we are still a Grossmacht [great power], and it is only through it that we can conduct foreign policy."[100] Moreover, "autarky is impossible. Our economic problems can only be solved by a reconquest of the German position in the world market. In this task the advanced and processing industries [as opposed to coal, steel, or agriculture] will take the lead."[101] In short, even moderate former proponents of *Weltpolitik* understood that a policy of free trade and appeasement was necessitated by Weimar Germany's lack of military power and limited geographic base, as well as aided by the availability of foreign capital and the voting power of labor. This liberal strategy was no longer viable when

98. Ibid., 143, to Count Lichnowsky, June 1914.
99. Ibid., 126.
100. To the DNVP Central Committee, November 1925, quoted in David Abraham, *The Collapse of the Weimar Republic*, 2d ed. (New York, 1986), 125n.54. On the general point, Marshall M. Lee and Wolfgang Michalka, *German Foreign Policy, 1917–1933* (Leamington Spa, N.H., 1987), chap. 3.
101. Speech of April 1927, quoted by Abraham, *Collapse of the Weimar Republic*, 61.

these facilitating international and domestic conditions collapsed in the early 1930s.[102]

Nazi Strategic Concepts

Whereas the true believer interpretation of Bethmann-Hollweg has not won universal acceptance, the true believer interpretation of Hitler's foreign policy is nowadays held almost unanimously.[103] In this view Hitler's racial ideas, his social Darwinism, and his nationalism were incubated in the supportive environment of Viennese coffeehouses before World War I.[104] Hitler himself cites in *Mein Kampf* the "lessons" he learned in Vienna.[105] In the early and mid-1920s Hitler worked out the details of his ideas of race and living space until they hung together to his satisfaction, then he looked to them throughout his career as a lodestar for aggression.[106] These ideas drew together two strands of Wilhelmine imperial ideology—the folkish ideology of emigration into East European agricultural living space and the bourgeois ideology of economic imperialism on a world scale—elements that Hitler combined sequentially in his *Stufenplan*, or plan of stages, for world conquest.[107]

Hitler's strategic ideology centered on self-sufficiency in the means for "the people's sustenance." A Germany lacking the territory for self-sufficiency in raw materials and especially in food would always find itself exploited in peacetime and at a mortal disadvantage in war. In this zero-sum struggle, said Hitler in a 1928 speech, "the path to this [autarkic] goal will, in the final analysis, always be war."[108] "If we had at our disposal the Urals, with their incalculable wealth of raw materials, and the forests of Siberia," he added in a September 1936 speech, "and if the unending wheat-fields of the Ukraine lay within Germany, our country would swim in plenty."[109] This simple theme, expansion to

102. On the connection between Weimar's liberal foreign policy and liberal Weimar society, Peter Krüger, *Die Aussenpolitik der Republik von Weimar* (Darmstadt, 1985), esp. 247–52, 552; on its collapse, Lee and Michalka, *German Foreign Policy*, chap. 4.

103. Hiden and Farquharson, *Explaining Hitler's Germany*, 115, call this the "consensus" view.

104. Gerhard Weinberg, *The Foreign Policy of Hitler's Germany: Diplomatic Revolution in Europe, 1933–36*, 2 vols. (Chicago, 1970), 1:3; Rich, *Hitler's War Aims*, xxxiii–iv; J. Sydney Jones, *Hitler in Vienna, 1907–1913* (New York, 1983), 158–62; Geoffrey Stoakes, *Hitler and the Quest for World Dominion* (Leamington Spa, N.H., 1986), 38, 50–51, 63.

105. Jones, *Hitler in Vienna*, 170, citing Adolf Hitler, *Mein Kampf* (Boston, 1942), 56–57.

106. Eberhard Jäckel, *Hitler's Weltanschauung* (Middletown, Conn., 1972), 119–21.

107. Smith, *Ideological Origins*, chaps. 4 and 5; Weinberg, *Foreign Policy*; Hiden and Farquharson, *Explaining Hitler's Germany*, 116–23, 150; Klaus Hildebrand, *The Foreign Policy of the Third Reich* (Berkeley, Calif., 1973).

108. Quoted in Berenice Carroll, *Design for Total War: Arms and Economics in the Third Reich* (The Hague, 1968), 97.

109. Ibid., 104.

achieve self-sufficiency in a predatory world, dominated his foreign policy thinking, writing, speeches, and actions from the 1920s through the Hossbach memorandum of 1937 and into the war itself.[110]

This contrasted with Stresemann's goal of creating a free trade zone in Central and Eastern Europe, in which Russia would without conquest play the role of a natural resource hinterland to Germany's industrial core. Such an arrangement provoked the opposition of protectionist German farmers as a recapitulation of Caprivi's policy of opening German borders to cheap East European grain. Hitler's plans for direct military conquest of the East European hinterland fit better the farmers' folkish concept of simply taking the land needed for agricultural colonization.[111]

Woodruff Smith's recent work *The Ideological Origins of Nazi Imperialism* contends that such notions of economic autarky through conquest of Eastern Europe represented a conflation of the two pre-1914 schools of expansionist thought—the folkish emigrationist tradition with its interest in agricultural colonization in the East, and the *Weltpolitik* tradition with its emphasis on economic rationality and great power competition.[112] Smith and other historians trace the percolation of these ideologies through the pulp press of the 1920s and show how various pan-German writers, including the "geopolitician" Haushofer, developed this synthesis.[113] In particular, the Pan-German League served both before and after World War I as, in Eckart Kehr's phrase, an "ideological holding company, which delivered intellectual armaments to other pressure groups," including the Nazis in the early 1920s.[114] Hitler was an avid reader of this literature, which gave shape to his earlier prejudices, while in prison working on *Mein Kampf*.[115] Hitler's own version of these ideas, therefore, can be understood in part as ideological blowback from the strategic mythmaking of the Wilhelmine era.[116]

Hitler's strategic ideas also recapitulated many of the features of the Wilhelmine big stick view of international politics, including social Darwinism, paper tiger images of opponents, and bandwagon assump-

110. Adolf Hitler, *Hitler's Secret Book* (New York, 1961), 97–100; Smith, *Ideological Origins*, 209–20; Carr, *Arms, Autarky and Aggression*, 71–72; Weinberg, *Foreign Policy*, 1:6, 12; Carroll, *Design for Total War*, 104.

111. Smith, *Ideological Origins*, 200–203.

112. Ibid., 209–11 and passim.

113. Stoakes, *Hitler and the Quest for World Dominion*, presents a detailed reconstruction of the connections between Hitler's thinking and pan-German and geopolitical thought in the pre– and post–World War I periods, esp. 30–32, 50–51, 63, 154, 159–60.

114. Quoted in ibid., 33.

115. Smith, *Ideological Origins*, 240.

116. Fritz Fischer speaks of a "continuity of illusions" between the expansionist aims of the Treaty of Brest Litovsk and Hitler's *Lebensraum* idea. Hiden and Farquharson, *Explaining Hitler's Germany*, 116, citing Fischer, *Bündnis der Eliten* (Düsseldorf, 1979), 93–94.

tions. Hitler's racial notions always hinged on the paper tiger image. Slavs, especially under Bolshevism, were an immense barbaric threat, yet their inherent inferiority made them easy pickings.[117] Moreover, when Hitler determined that he had to attack the United States, a similar paper tiger image was quickly conjured up.[118]

Like his Wilhelmine predecessors, Hitler contended that German military predominance would ultimately force Britain to become his ally.[119] Even Tirpitz's apparently discredited notion of the risk fleet made a comeback in the 1930s as an explanation for how the nascent Luftwaffe could induce friendship with Britain. Chamberlain's guarantee of Poland did not shake such big stick beliefs. Hitler expected that the German attack on Poland would cause Chamberlain's government to fall, so that he would have no opportunity to carry it out.[120] When Chamberlain's replacement, Winston Churchill, turned out to be an even stauncher foe, Hitler asserted that Churchill's days were numbered too: "Churchill is a man with an out-of-date political idea—that of the European balance of power. . . . When Singapore falls, Churchill will fall, too."[121]

No matter what Britain did, Hitler kept thinking along these lines. If beating France would not convince Britain of the need to ally with Germany, he reasoned, then beating the Soviet Union surely would.[122] Despite experience to the contrary, the same logic would work on a larger scale, Hitler asserted, "forcing England to the ground quickly and thereby keeping the United States out of the war."[123]

On the eve of attacking Poland, Hitler used the whole panoply of myths of empire—paper tiger imagery, bandwagon and domino theories—to explain his strategy to the Italians: "Any sign of yielding would, in view of the Slav mentality, be just the thing to cause an outburst of Polish insolence. Any yielding would therefore not strengthen the position as a whole, but would generally be interpreted by other countries as a sign of weakness. . . . The best means of restraining [the Western democracies] from taking action was to move swiftly against Poland.[124]

117. Jäckel, *Hitler's Weltanschauung*, 54–55; Hildebrand, *Foreign Policy* 105–20.
118. Weinberg, *Foreign Policy*, 1:21–22.
119. Rich, *Hitler's War Aims*, 157–64.
120. Weinberg, *Foreign Policy*, 2:629.
121. Adolf Hitler, *Hitler's Table Talk, 1941–1944* (London, 1953), 202.
122. Smith, *Ideological Origins*, 251–52; also Hiden and Farquharson, *Explaining Hitler's Germany*, 119–21.
123. Quoted in David Dallin, *Soviet Russia and the Far East* (New Haven, Conn., 1948), 161.
124. Memorandum by an official of the German Foreign Ministry's Secretariat, "Record of the Conversation between the Führer and Count Ciano," 13 August 1939, in *Documents on German Foreign Policy, 1918–1945*, ser. D, vol. 7 (Washington, D.C., 1956), 54. Thanks to Randall Schweller for this and some other citations on Hitler's bandwagon ideas.

[94]

Hitler did entertain the possibility that his opponents might sometimes engage in balancing behavior, but only when this did not threaten the core of his expansionist schemes. A partial balancing element in Hitler's thinking, for example, was the "lesson" he drew from World War I that Britain would balance against *colonial* expansionists. Consequently, he reasoned, as long as German aims stayed focused on the Continent, Britain would stand aside.[125] This suggests that Hitler, as might be predicted by a pattern of ideological or motivated psychological bias, would see only those balancing tendencies that did not threaten his plans.

COGNITIVE BIASES: THE LESSONS OF 1870?

The most obvious cognitive explanation for German aggressiveness would be the putative lessons of 1870. According to the mythology propounded by subsequent nationalists, Bismarck was "the diplomat of blood and iron, who used his sword to cut the tangles of politics on the battlefield."[126] Together with Field Marshal Helmuth von Moltke, practitioner of the strategy of rapid battles of encirclement and annihilation, Bismarck established the German Reich on glorious—and fierce—foundations as a result of the military victories over Austria in 1866 and France in 1870. Since we know that lessons rooted in such formative events often have unwarranted staying power, it seems possible that the subsequent belligerence of German statesmen and soldiers stems from the engrained recollection of these salient events.[127]

One problem with this tale is that subsequent disciples were so much more heavy-handed than the originals. What really happened was that nationalists made over the past in order to fulfill their need for glorious precedents for belligerence. As I have argued, Bismarck's diplomacy was in fact quite patient. Bismarck typically made sure that the opponent bore the onus of aggression, and he avoided falling into a minority coalition. The slash-and-burn Bismarck was not a real historical figure, but a mythical ex post facto creation of so-called patriotic societies in the 1890s, which erected Bismarck statues across Germany to call attention to the alleged contrast between Bismarck's ruthless brilliance and the debility of his successors.[128] Likewise, the real Moltke and Clausewitz were highly attuned to the advantages of

---

125. Jäckel, *Hitler's Weltanschauung*, 41.
126. General Alfred von Schlieffen, quoted in Snyder, *Ideology*, 133.
127. Jervis, *Perception*, chaps. 4–6.
128. Isabel Hull, "Prussian Dynastic Ritual and the End of Monarchy," 13–42, in Carole Fink, Isabel Hull, and MacGregor Knox, eds., *German Nationalism and the European Response, 1890–1945* (Norman, Okla., 1985), 24.

defensive military strategies, whereas the mythical Moltke and Clausewitz created by subsequent German militarists insisted that every war had to be total, decisive, and offensive.[129]

Even if the alleged lessons of 1870 might plausibly explain 1914, one would think that the disasters of the First World War would have kicked the alleged lessons of 1870 out of the German operational code for good. In fact, the lessons of 1914–18 were never learned properly, because German elites and historians systematically misrepresented Germany's role in causing the war and the reasons for its defeat. Traditional German elites in academia and the foreign ministry mounted a systematic, self-conscious campaign to whitewash the past and to intimidate objective historians.[130] Cognitive theory offers a fundamentally unsound view of the process by which Germans learned lessons from their own history.

Cognitive explanations for some of the Germans' strategic misperceptions cannot be excluded out of hand, however. For example, during the first Moroccan crisis, Bülow felt sure that Maurice Rouvier understood Bülow's reputational stake in the outcome, though Bülow did not see Rouvier's.[131] This double standard might be purely cognitive, due to Bülow's inability to put himself in Rouvier's shoes, but it might also be motivational, triggered by Bülow's need to perceive or argue for the feasibility of the policy to which he was politically committed.[132] Likewise, when German propagandists preached that Germans should be more like Britons in their unity, discipline, and civic-mindedness, this might reflect the well-known cognitive tendency to see others as more centralized and purposeful than they really are, but it might also reflect such public relations aims as overselling the threat and portraying socialists as unpatriotic.[133]

Overall, German strategic beliefs smack too much of rationalization to have a purely cognitive explanation. As I argued above, all too often strategic mythmakers twisted logic and ignored facts in justifying their pet programs, which often had an organizational or political motive behind them. Even the so-called lessons of formative events emerged through a process that was political and ideological, not strictly cognitive.

129. Snyder, *Ideology*, chaps. 4 and 5.

130. Holger Herwig, "Clio Deceived: Patriotic Self-Censorship in Germany after the Great War," *International Security* 12 (Fall 1987): 5–44. Sugarcoating the historical record is a major theme of Van Evera, "Causes of War."

131. Gooch, *Before the War*, 1:252, Bulow to Radolin, 4 May 1904; juxtapose this with Anderson, *First Moroccan Crisis*, 221.

132. Kaufmann, "Deterrence and Rationality," chap. 4, confirms the role of motivational biases in German perceptions during the first Moroccan crisis and also presents evidence on the effect of some cognitive biases.

133. Kennedy, *Antagonism*, 372.

DOMESTIC POLITICS: LOGROLLING AND MYTHMAKING

The most powerful explanation for German expansionism, and the one that has gained the greatest support from historians, focuses on the domestic political consequences of Germany's late industrialization. In this view, Germany's pattern of late but rapid development caused the simultaneous accumulation of extremely diverse social groups, unable to compromise their narrowly defined interests, which for some included militarism and imperialism. These groups could reconcile their conflicting interests only by logrolling, which gave each interest what it wanted most, and by mythmaking, which obscured the overextended consequences produced by this practice of logrolling. Since militarist and imperial interests were among those being logrolled, the process allowed those interests to run unchecked.

Within this general line of argument, it is worth distinguishing among three variants: one stresses the substantive interests of the individual groups, another stresses the political process by which those interests were integrated, and a third stresses the consequences of the ideological justification of the preferred policies of groups and coalitions. Some authors have emphasized one of these more than the others. In my view all three are necessary for an explanation that is logically and empirically satisfying.

The Pattern of Late Industrialization

The pattern of early textile industrialization, as exemplified by the experience of Great Britain, featured the gradual development of small-scale industry financed by the relatively mobile capital of traditional agricultural elites. Its social concomitants were the convergence of agricultural and commercial interests, the organizational diffusion of economic power, the mobility of economic investments, and the completion of a bourgeois-liberal political transformation before the development of a politically strong labor movement.[134] The pattern of late development, as exemplified by Germany, is the opposite on all counts.[135] It was characterized by the comparatively abrupt development of large-scale heavy industry, centrally financed by bank capital and

---

134. I say "concomitants" here because some of the factors listed may be seen as causes rather than consequences of early development.

135. This draws on Alexander Gerschenkron, *Economic Backwardness in Historical Perspective* (Cambridge, Mass., 1962); Barrington Moore, *Social Origins of Dictatorship and Democracy* (Boston, 1967); and Jeff Frieden, *Debt, Development, and Democracy: Modern Political Economy and Latin America, 1965–1985* (Princeton, N.J., 1991), on the political consequences of the mobility and immobility of capital.

[97]

organized into cartels that used their political and market power to protect their huge sunk investments.[136] The relatively poor landed elite, whose immobile "capital" was largely bound up in a politically repressed agricultural labor force, was not a significant investor in this industrial transformation.[137] Its social concomitants were the divergence of agricultural and commercial interests, the organizational concentration of economic power, the immobility of investments and consequently of interests, and the emergence of mass political movements without the prior completion of a bourgeois-liberal political transformation.[138]

This pattern had decisive consequences for the power and interests of the key actors, for the process by which conflicting interests were integrated, and for the opportunity to use ideology as a political weapon. Junker landowners, still enjoying a privileged position in the state and military bureaucracy and in Prussian electoral law, had an overwhelming incentive to use that political power to inflate the price of grain—their immobile asset—through protective tariffs, regardless of the economic or diplomatic cost to the rest of society. The military used its high degree of operational autonomy from civilian ministers and parliamentarians to pursue the usual inclinations of unconstrained military organizations: apolitical, offensive strategies for decisive victory, again regardless of the diplomatic cost.[139] Cartelized heavy industry used its market power, high-level political access, and political subsidies to mass groups to promote industrial protectionism and the building of a fleet while blocking a liberal political alliance between labor and export industry.[140]

136. Cartelization and industrial concentration, which Gerschenkron and others show was an inherent property of late industrialization, was further promoted as a way to protect price and profit levels during the post-1873 depression. On the cartelization of German industry, see Steven Webb, "Tariffs, Cartels, Technology, and Growth in the German Steel Industry," *Journal of Economic History* 40 (June 1980): 309–30; Wehler, *German Empire*, 41; Erich Maschke, "Outline of the History of German Cartels from 1873 to 1914," in F. Crouzet, ed., *Essays in European Economic History, 1789–1914* (New York, 1969), 226–58, esp. 227; Garst, "Capitalism," chap. 6.

137. Hanna Schissler, "The Junkers," in Moeller, *Peasants and Lords*, 24–51.

138. The classic works in this genre are by Thorstein Veblen, Hans Rosenberg, Ralf Dahrendorf, Eckart Kehr, and Hans-Ulrich Wehler. Geoff Eley and David Blackbourn have offered a critique of the Kehr-Wehler school that is convincing in some of its details but overall fails to advance an alternative paradigm. My own argument below attempts to incorporate many of the Eley-Blackbourn arguments into Wehler's basic framework. Their main empirical works are Geoff Eley, *Reshaping the German Right: Radical Nationalism and Political Change after Bismarck* (New Haven, Conn., 1980), and David Blackbourn, *Class, Religion and Local Politics in Wilhelmine Germany* (New Haven, Conn., 1980).

139. Snyder, *Ideology*; Gerhard Ritter, *The Schlieffen Plan* (New York, 1958); and on the offensive preferences of military organizations, Barry Posen, *The Sources of Military Doctrine* (Ithaca, N.Y., 1984), and Van Evera, "Causes of War."

140. Garst, "Capitalism," chap. 8, discusses the failure of the labor-export alliance. For

These group interests promoted policies that led to Germany's diplo-matic encirclement: Junkers got grain tariffs that antagonized Russia; the navy and heavy industry got a fleet that antagonized Britain; and the army got an offensive war plan that ensured that virtually all of Europe would be ranged among Germany's enemies. Thus three key elite groups had the motive and the opportunity to advance policies that embroiled Germany simultaneously with all of Europe's major powers.

Elite and Mass Coalition Politics

Individually, none of these elite interests was powerful enough to successfully assert its parochial policy agenda against the broader national interest. For example, even the Junkers suffered a setback on grain tariffs when in the Caprivi period they were temporarily without effective political allies. The army could adopt any operational strategy it preferred, but it depended on a majority in the Reichstag to vote for the troops to implement it. What made these interests politically effective was the way the political system integrated conflicting forces, creating alliances that made possible the adoption of these groups' parochial agendas.

In a system characterized by powerful groups with narrow interests, the natural solution is to integrate those interests by logrolling, giving each group what it wants most. Bismarck, Bülow, and Bethmann all gravitated to this solution to the problem of coalition making in Wilhelmine politics. Each relied primarily on the imperialist-protectionist marriage of iron and rye as the core of the ruling coalition.[141] Bismarck, however, enjoyed a stronger position as a unitary broker for coalition arrangements and so was able to reject some of the more reckless ideas of the groups whose interests he logrolled. When the army pressed for a preventive war against Russia in 1887, for example, Bismarck barred it, arguing that accepting the onus of being the aggressor would play into the diplomatic hands of Germany's opponents.[142] But subsequent chancellors were the captives of their coalitions and lacked the strength to turn back such demands.

---

a good example of Ruhr coal's using its market power to wreck the Reichstag's support for the labor-export alliance, see Bernd Weisbrod, "Economic Power and Political Stability Reconsidered: Heavy Industry in Weimar Germany," *Social History* 4 (1979): 241–63, esp. 257, on the illegal 1928 lockout. Also James, *German Slump*, 9–10; Abraham, *Collapse of the Weimar Republic*, 6–7.

141. Eckart Kehr, *Economic Interest, Militarism, and Foreign Policy* (Berkeley, Calif., 1977), 22–49; Wehler, *German Empire*, 94–99; Dirk Stegmann, *Die Erben Bismarcks* (Cologne, 1970), 352–408.

142. Snyder, *Ideology*, 128.

Though elite logrolling is a crucial part of the explanation for German overexpansion, it remains insufficient on two counts. Were the problem merely one of horse trading between a handful of relatively compact elite interests, the overextended foreign policy that resulted from the logrolling should have been reversed once the elites realized the policy was leading toward disaster. That is, at least some of the elite groups should have recalculated their interests and decided that the pursuit of parochialism at the cost of an unpromising war was not even in their own narrow self-interest. Rational choice theory makes it clear that a small number of compact groups should be able to solve this kind of collective goods problem by agreeing on new coalition terms that do not involve such disastrous collective costs.[143] Even if a gamble on war was worth it to the Junkers or the military, who might have faced poor coalition prospects in a reformed system, a labor-export coalition should have looked increasingly attractive to many bourgeois and middle-class groups as an alternative to the doomed formula of iron, rye, and encirclement.[144] Consequently, it seems necessary to supplement elite logrolling with mass politics and ideology to explain why this did not happen.

Iron and rye coexisted uneasily in their alliance, since many of their interests were strongly opposed.[145] Industry needed to tax agriculture to pay for the arms race its policies had provoked. Conversely, retaliation against agricultural tariffs stifled industrial exports. As a consequence, the marriage of iron and rye occasionally came unglued—for example, during the Caprivi interlude and again following the agrarians' refusal in 1909 to be taxed for the fleet.[146]

Because of the constant jockeying for advantage within the iron and rye coalition and the threat that it might break down, both agriculture and industry had an incentive to mobilize mass support against the other. Thus Caprivi's free-trade policies helped to trigger rural discontent, which was mobilized in agrarian leagues that reinforced Junker economic interests.[147] Likewise, agrarian resistance to the fleet led the navy and the industrialists to organize patriotic leagues, which were effective in getting out the vote in the 1907 "Hottentot election," for example.[148]

143. Russell Hardin, *Collective Action* (Baltimore, 1982), on k-groups.

144. Beverly Heckart, *From Bassermann to Bebel: The Grand Bloc's Quest for Reform in the Kaiserreich, 1900–1914* (New Haven, Conn., 1974), 208 and passim.

145. Geoff Eley, "Sammlungspolitik, Social Imperialism and the Navy Law of 1898," *Militärgeschichtliche Mitteilungen* 15 (1974): 29–64, reprinted in Geoff Eley, *From Unification to Nazism* (Boston, 1986), chap. 5.

146. Wehler, *German Empire*, 141–42; Kennedy, *Antagonism*, 348.

147. Puhle, "Lords and Peasants," 81–109, and Moeller, "Introduction," in Moeller, *Peasants and Lords*, 1–23.

148. Crothers, *German Elections*, chap. 3; Eley, *Reshaping*, chap. 8 and passim; Wehler,

Not only interest groups but also coalition leaders needed to mobilize mass support to strengthen them against centrifugal tendencies. Bismarck, for example, sought to recruit and empower middle-class progressives, whose support for his program of German national unity strengthened his hand against Catholic, Junker, and South German particularism.[149] Similarly, Caprivi removed legal restrictions on socialists and Catholics in order to recruit mass allies against the agrarians.[150] Even later, after the rise of the Social Democratic electorate, Bethmann favored the risky tactic of franchise reform for Prussian elections, in the hope that a progressive majority might balance Junker influence.[151]

Coalition leaders who pursued this strategy were like the sorcerer's apprentice.[152] While universal suffrage and Reichstag control over some taxation may have helped Bismarck in the early period of his alliance with the progressives, it later became part of the problem when Bismarck switched to the more elitist iron and rye coalition, socialist vote totals increased, small-town voters' deference to National Liberal dignitaries declined, and mass groups asserted their own parochial agendas against the elites who had hoped to manage them.[153] On balance, parochial elites like the Junkers or the navy had more success in mobilizing a mass following than did the coalition leaders, thus reinforcing rather than counteracting the cartelized pattern of German politics.

Coalition managers often resorted to superficial prestige strategies, such as seeking dramatic foreign policy successes in crisis showdowns to improve their governments' popularity. Johannes Miquel, who tried to reestablish the coalition of iron and rye at the turn of the century, hoped that "successes in foreign policy would make a good impression in the Reichstag debates, and political divisions would thus be moderated."[154] Bülow similarly argued that "the way to win popular support for the monarchy was to revive the 'national idea'."[155] But as the Moroccan crises of 1905 and 1911 show, belligerent crisis diplomacy

German Empire, part 3; Roger Chickering, *We Men Who Feel Most German: A Cultural Study of the Pan-German League, 1886–1914* (Boston, 1984), 227 and passim.

149. David Blackbourn and Geoff Eley, *The Peculiarities of German History* (New York, 1984), 145–46; David Blackbourn, "Progress and Piety: Liberals, Catholics and the State in Bismarck's Germany," in David Blackbourn, *Populists and Patricians* (London, 1987), chap. 7, 143–67.

150. J. Alden Nichols, *The Year of the Three Kaisers: Bismarck and the German Succession, 1887–88* (Urbana, Ill., 1987).

151. Jarausch, *Enigmatic Chancellor*, 106.

152. Blackbourn, *Populists*, chap. 1.

153. In addition to the various works by Eley and Blackbourn, see Stanley Suval, *Electoral Politics in Wilhelmine Germany* (Chapel Hill, N.C., 1985).

154. Geiss, *German Foreign Policy*, 78; Rohl, *Germany without Bismarck*, 250.

155. Geiss, *German Foreign Policy*, 78; Rohl, *Germany without Bismarck*, 130.

rarely worked, so the prestige strategy usually backfired in domestic politics: it simply showed up the social imperialist chancellors as weaklings. For these reasons, in the post-Bismarck years political decision making decreasingly followed the unitary pattern and increasingly followed the cartelized pattern.

Ideological Politics

Recruiting mass groups complicated the elite logrolling process. Decreasing the compactness of the logrolling groups made it more cumbersome for the conservative elites to terminate the vote trading arrangement if it became counterproductive. But this was not simply a problem of rational collective decision making by large groups. The additional problem was that many participants in the logrolling had fully internalized the myths of empire and consequently were unable to recognize that the big stick policies were failing. This was especially true of the Protestant, urban, upwardly mobile professionals, who voted for the fleet for ideological reasons. They joined the Navy League and Pan-German League, responded to imperialist appeals and threat inflation in the election of 1907, and were appalled by what they saw as the criminally weak stance of the German government during the second Moroccan crisis.[156]

These groups were ideological voters in two senses. First, they were attracted to national and imperial themes not because they had a direct material interest in the implementation of such policies, but because nationalist *ideas* tended to discredit those strata that hindered the emergence of modern middle-class social institutions: the sectional and anti-modern Junker, the sectarian Catholic, and the Social Democratic class enemy. The navy, in particular, was favored by these people as the embodiment of modern technology and—in contrast to the narrowly Prussian army—bourgeois German nationalism.[157] As time passed, these arriviste professionals and intellectuals found that they could even use nationalist themes against their erstwhile patrons, local National Liberal dignitaries, who could be attacked for being insufficiently resolute in standing up for German national interests.[158]

Second, they were ideological voters in the sense that they were consumers of an imperialist and navalist strategic ideology that was

156. This and the following points are discussed by Chickering, *We Men Who Feel Most German*, 261–66 on Morocco, and Eley, *Reshaping*, chaps. 4, 5, and 10.

157. Steinberg, *Yesterday's Deterrent*, 27–28, 37–43, 203; Wehler, *German Empire*, 137; Kennedy, *Antagonism*, 340–41.

158. Chickering, *We Men Who Feel Most German*, 114; Eley, *Reshaping*, 322–24 on the reaction to the Moroccan crisis of 1911.

prepared for and sold to them by conservative elites. The Navy League, for example, was largely the creation of Tirpitz's propaganda and organizational skills, backed by industrialist money to prime the pump.[159] Some of the early mass colonial leagues that advocated emigrationist programs seem to have been relatively spontaneous, but those that were oriented more toward economic imperialism and *Weltpolitik* typically had industrial backing. Once established, these organizations were often self-sustaining, but without the initial elite role it is unclear how successful such enterprises would have been.[160] Catholic rank and file were relatively immune to propaganda for the fleet, and the Center party voted against credits for the war in South-West Africa, breaking up Bülow's first coalition and setting the stage for the 1907 Hottentot election. But even the Catholics were responsive to propaganda about the encircling Entente, which obscured Germany's role in provoking its own isolation.[161]

Just as conservative elites structured the terms of vote trading with mass groups like the Center party, so too they structured the initial terms of ideological debate with mass radical nationalists. From an early stage in the development of Bismarck's preunification coalition strategy, he made it clear that the nationalist strain in bourgeois ideology, focused on creating a unified national market, had a political future, whereas its social and political reformist strain did not.[162] Likewise, Bülow's strategy of rejecting free trade and reform, reconstituting the marriage of iron and rye, and appeasing bourgeois interests with a naval law circumscribed the political possibilities for middle-class up-and-comers. In this environment, to be progressive was to be for the

159. Chickering, *We Men Who Feel Most German*, 60–61, 66.
160. For a variety of viewpoints and evidence bearing on these issues see Eley, *Reshaping*, chaps. 1–3; Smith, *Ideological Origins*, 34–37, 62; Chickering, *We Men Who Feel Most German*, 66, 227; Smith, *German Colonial Empire*, 121–25; Rohl, *Germany without Bismarck*, 229–58, esp. 234, 246–58; Richard Owen, "Military-Industrial Relations: Krupp and the Imperial Navy Office," in Richard J. Evans, *Society and Politics in Wilhelmine Germany* (London, 1978), 73–77; Kennedy, *Antagonism*, 258, 383. Blackbourn's conclusion, in *Populists*, 217, is that mass radical movements started the demagogy, and the elites spurred on this development, which they saw as both a threat and an opportunity. But in my view Blackbourn presents no clear evidence that masses rather than elites initiated the practice of imperialist, militarist, and nationalist demagogy.
161. Crothers, *German Elections*; Heckart, *From Bassermann to Bebel*, 52, 69–71; Ellen Evans, *The German Center Party, 1870–1933* (Carbondale, Ill., 1981), 163. Though the Junkers also spun out competing, folkish ideologies as part of their work in the Agrarian League, agricultural protectionist organizations, in contrast to middle-class navalist groups, are now believed to have rested largely on the mutual interests of the small and large growers. Thus James C. Hunt, "Peasants, Grain Tariffs, and Meat Quotas: Imperial German Protectionism Reexamined," *Central European History* 7 (December 1974): 311–31, has supplanted Alexander Gerschenkron, *Bread and Democracy in Germany* (1943; Ithaca, N.Y., 1989), on this point.
162. Blackbourn and Eley, *Peculiarities*, 145–46; Blackbourn, *Populists*, 143–67.

fleet and *Weltpolitik*. Even "liberal" intellectuals like Max Weber touted the fleet as part of a package of social imperialist reform, aimed at undermining Junker resistance to political liberalization and economic rationalization.[163]

This propaganda spewed forth by officials, respected liberal intellectuals, and industry-backed movements significantly affected the plausibility of competing arguments in the political arena. Before the development of Tirpitz's risk theory and the sales campaign based on it, fleet bills were unpopular in the nation at large and ran into crippling resistance in the Reichstag. The navy was seen as nickling and diming the taxpayers to death, buying an incoherent mix of cruisers and battleships with no clear strategic purpose. But once the elite public relations machine developed an attractive, though fundamentally spurious, strategic concept and threw its advertising resources behind it, popular resistance turned into popular enthusiasm. In Hamburg, for example, the Anglophile foreign-trading elite was initially fearful that the fleet would lead to war with England; but when Tirpitz explained that the fleet would bring them the commercial fruits of victory without even having to fight, they became supporters.[164]

Though the elites helped shape mass preferences, they found they could not limit the mass passions they had unleashed, especially when newly emerging elite groups found they could use nationalist arguments to flog the more cautious old elites.[165] This happened not only in small-town politics, but also within the General Staff itself, where bourgeois officers like Erich Ludendorff and Wilhelm Groener successfully criticized Junker superiors who argued that expanding the officer corps to meet the growing Russian threat would jeopardize its aristocratic purity.[166]

Increasingly, the sorcerer's apprentice felt overwhelmed by the monster he had helped create. Tirpitz's finely calibrated strategy vis-à-vis England and the Reichstag, never pushing for too much at any one time so as to jeopardize the whole game, came into conflict with the less patient demands of the Navy League, yet at the same time Tirpitz continued to depend on the league for his political clout with increasingly skeptical chancellors.[167] Kiderlen, whipping up mass passions as

---

163. Chickering, *We Men Who Feel Most German*, 145–46; Smith, *Ideological Origins*, 62.

164. Kitchen, *Political Economy*, 238. More generally, Steinberg, Kehr, and Eley present evidence of the persuasiveness of this propaganda.

165. Geoff Eley, "The Wilhelmine Right," in Evans, *Society and Politics*, 125–28; Chickering, *We Men Who Feel Most German*, 63, 213, 255.

166. Jack Snyder, "Civil-Military Relations and the Cult of the Offensive, 1914 and 1984," in Steven Miller, ed., *Military Strategy and the Origins of the First World War* (Princeton, N.J., 1985), 124–25.

167. Eley, *Reshaping*, 260–79.

a bargaining ploy during the second Morocco crisis, then found it difficult to make concessions, which radical nationalists would denounce as a sellout, owing to the way he himself had posed the issue.[168] Moreover, government parties failed to achieve a working majority in the 1912 election because Bethmann refused to run a chauvinist campaign, which he felt would ruin his chances of reining in naval expenditures.[169] Thus the old elites came to depend on uncontrollable, true believing radical nationalists for protection against socialist electoral victories. This explains, then, why the elite coalition of iron and rye found it impossible to retreat from an imperialist, logrolled platform even when its continuation seems to jeopardize the interests of the logrollers themselves.

Nazi Ideology: Unhinged from Politics?

Ideology must play an even more central role in explaining Nazi expansionism. Domestic political explanations that do not rely on ideology are unsatisfying. Elite logrolling, for example, played little role. Junkers, industrialists, and the military helped kill the Weimar Republic, but they did not in any way set the tone for Nazi foreign policy. Indeed, Hitler had to complete the subjugation of these groups before he could go on the warpath in the late 1930s.[170]

A mass logrolling argument is somewhat more plausible, though still not fully convincing. In this view the Nazis won power as a general protest movement, breaking the Weimar social stalemate by promising incompatible payoffs to every group in Weimar society: labor, industry, farmers, clerks, artisans.[171] Facing by the late 1930s the limits of economic recovery in an insufficiently large autarkic economy, Hitler saw conquest as the only alternative to a politically unacceptable decision to cut consumption.[172] Though this argument has gained more support than one might imagine, it nonetheless founders on the fact that Hitler *did* cut consumption without suffering political repercussions, and that he did it quite consciously in order to redirect resources into military production. In short, Hitler caused the foreign exchange crisis and the personal consumption crisis in order to gather the wherewithal to pursue a policy of conquest, not the other way around.[173] Thus it is

---

168. Blackbourn, *Populists*, 233; Smith, *Ideological Origins*, 136.

169. Jarausch, *Enigmatic Chancellor*, 90.

170. Hiden and Farquharson, *Explaining Hitler's Germany*, chap. 3; Ian Kershaw, *The Nazi Dictatorship* (London, 1985), chaps. 3 and 4.

171. James, *German Slump*, 354; Rich, *Hitler's War Aims*, xxxvii.

172. T. W. Mason, "Labour in the Third Reich," *Past and Present* 33 (April 1966), 112–41; James, *German Slump*, 419; Kershaw, *Nazi Dictatorship*, 121.

173. Kershaw, *Nazi Dictatorship*, 55.

hard to show a clear link between mass coalition politics and Hitler's expansionist strategy.

A related argument, also unsatisfying, stresses the alleged ideological prerequisites of Nazi electoral success. In this view the Weimar Republic was much like the Wilhelmine polity, Balkanized into myriad mass and elite groups that defined their interests narrowly. Stable coalitions were hard to form in this environment for many of the same reasons that Wilhelmine coalitions were riven with dissension. Though the Junkers were no longer major players, small farmers picked up their baton. Moreover, the onset of the depression made reconciling interests by normal electoral competition for the median voter still more difficult. American loans under the Dawes and Young plans in the 1920s had temporarily funded social welfare expenditures that dampened Germany's interest group struggles by underwriting a labor-export coalition. But when the flow of capital and trade dried up with the depression, zero-sum cartel politics reemerged.[174]

The Nazis were the one party to understand, in this view, that a successful appeal had to be national, cutting across the rhetoric of parochial interest yet at the same time offering a vision that would give all the groups what they wanted most.[175] The nationalistic *Lebensraum* doctrine seemed to offer such a vision, promising hard-pressed farmers the chimerical payoff of settlement colonies in the conquered lands, while offering industry expanded markets and resources under predictable political control. Synthesizing various strands of thought from the Wilhelmine and early Weimar radical nationalist repertoire, Hitler used these arguments in his speeches and writings as part of Nazism's global appeal.[176]

The problem with this view is that Hitler soft-pedaled his *Lebensraum* theme in the crucial years when the Nazis were winning huge electoral successes. His second book, where much of his imperialist thought is most clearly articulated, remained unpublished, because its extremism and belligerence were feared to be off-putting to the mass electorate and to big business. The theme of *Lebensraum* was dropped from Hitler's speeches in 1930.[177] In the early 1930s, moreover, his state-

174. McNeil, *American Money and the Weimar Republic*, chaps. 6–8 and the conclusion; Garst, "Capitalism and Liberal Democracy"; Weisbrod, "Economic Power," 243; Lee and Michalka, *German Foreign Policy*, 155.

175. Juan Linz, "Political Space and Fascism as a Late-comer," in Stein Larsen et al., eds., *Who Were the Fascists?* (Bergen, 1980), 153–91, esp. 154, argues that Nazi nationalism was a "catchall" device for unifying a stalemated society.

176. Smith, *Ideological Origins*, esp. 236–37, 240–41; James, *German Slump*, 354.

177. Eberhard Jäckel, *Hitler in History* (Hanover, N.H., 1984), 21, 34. MacGregor Knox, "After the Cold War: Notes of a Pessimist," paper delivered at a conference on the Long Peace (University of Rochester, October 1990), however, shows that Hitler made bellicose statements on other themes as late as 1930.

ments were ambivalent about the goal of autarky, so they can hardly have been used as a crucial ideological tenet to win elections.[178] Indeed, works on Hitler's electoral appeal rarely mention his foreign policy platform; if they do mention it, they deny that his visions of *Lebensraum* won him converts.[179]

It seems likely that Hitler's expansionist ideas helped him win the loyalty of the hard core of his nationalist supporters.[180] Even after 1930s, when Hitler was trying to broaden his base of support, his acceptance of traditional colonial thinking helped him seem "respectable" in the eyes of the elites who dominated the Colonial Society.[181] Overall, however, there is little support for the argument that Hitler's expansionist ideas directly helped him win broad electoral support and thus use nationalist appeals to overcome the social stalemate.

The most convincing explanation for Hitler's expansionist ideas, consequently, is that Hitler and the Nazis were true believing victims of the stew of strategic myths that the Wilhelmine and wartime radical right concocted and over time spiced up. Smith, for example, concludes that Hitler had been "politically socialized to accept the tenets of *Lebensraum* uncritically."[182] These tenets, he contends, had "been thoroughly legitimated in the course of their political employment during the previous two or three generations."[183] Moreover, they were not delegitimated despite the debacle of World War I, in part because setting the record straight would not have served the interests of the elite groups that maintained a strong grip on public discourse throughout the 1920s.[184]

This is a domestic explanation for Nazi expansionism in several senses. First, Nazi imperial myths grew up as a consequence of the peculiar political environment of Wilhelmine Germany. Second, the political environment in Weimar allowed these myths to survive, since established elites found it inconvenient to allow open discussion of the causes and consequences of Wilhelmine expansionism. Third, these

178. Smith, *Ideological Origins*, 244–45; Henry A. Turner, "Hitler's Secret Pamphlet for Industrialists, 1927," *Journal of Modern History* 40 (September 1968): 351; J. Heyl, "Hitler's Economic Thought: A Reappraisal," *Central European History* 6 (March 1973): 83–96. For a contrasting view, see John Hiden, "National Socialism and Foreign Policy, 1919–33," in Peter Stachura, ed., *The Nazi Machtergreifung* (London, 1983), 156–58; Carroll, *Design for Total War*, passim.

179. Ian Kershaw, "Ideology, Propaganda, and the Rise of the Nazi Party," in Stachura, *Nazi Machtergreifung*, 167; Jäckel, *Hitler's Weltanschauung*, 121.

180. Smith, *Ideological Origins*, 241. On the distinction between core and potential followership, Linz, "Political Space," 157.

181. Smith, *Ideological Origins*, 249.

182. Smith, *Ideological Origins*, 240, citing Klaus Hildebrand, *Vom Reich zum Weltreich* (Munich, 1969), 70–75.

183. Smith, *Ideological Origins*, 234.

184. Herwig, "Clio Deceived."

myths were an important part of Hitler's appeal to his core followers.[185] Imperial myths did not play a major role in broadening the Nazis' appeal to the wider electorate after 1930, however, or in the domestic politics of the National Socialist regime after 1933. Rather, they lived on independently, part of the ideological baggage that middle-class nationalists brought with them from earlier political battles.[186]

CONCLUSIONS

German overexpansion, rationalized by big stick strategic assumptions, is best explained as a result of the ideological blowback from the domestic political struggles characteristic of a late-developing society. German aggressiveness was not compelled by Germany's position in the international system; indeed, Germany's behavior was often wildly mismatched with the true incentives of the prevailing international order. Nor can Germany's big stick diplomacy be ascribed to the apparent lessons of the Reich's founding through "blood and iron" in 1870. Those lessons were transformed beyond recognition by the salesmen of militarism and radical nationalism. Moreover, double standards and logical contortions in German strategic assumptions suggest that they were more ideological than cognitive in nature.

Domestic explanations for German overexpansion must look not only at the interests of groups, but also at the process by which those interests were reconciled and at the unintended ideological consequences of the strategic myths used to promote those interests. The power and of interests separate groups are necessary but not sufficient to explain why Wilhelmine and Nazi foreign policy got so out of hand. German expansion in those periods was more extreme than any elite interest group individually desired. The most recent wave of historiography, for example, has pointed out that the Junkers wanted protectionism, not war and empire.[187] Tirpitz consistently counseled against war, because he knew better than anyone else how unready the fleet actually was.[188] Only 12 percent of Krupp's steel production in 1912–13 went to naval orders.[189] And the most militant elements in nationalist spectrum, middle-class professionals in the various patriotic leagues, had no direct material interest at all in militarist or expansionist

185. Jäckel, *Hitler in History*, 21.
186. Blackbourn, *Populists*, 219; Chickering, *We Men Who Feel Most German*, 6–8; Smith, *Ideological Origins*, 168, 205–6.
187. This is a central theme in the works of Eley, Blackbourn, and Moeller.
188. Fischer, *War of Illusions*, 162, 163, 169.
189. Owen, "Krupp," in Evans, *Society and Politics*, 83.

policies. Consequently, a domestic explanation that looked only at the power and interests of the separate groups would underpredict expansionism.

For the Wilhelmine period, the logrolling process goes further toward explaining the overexpansionist outcome. The combination of several weak imperial or militarist interests gave each of them the power to implement its parochial program and together created Germany's overcommitted, multienemy posture. Overexpansion was less prevalent under Bismarck because the logrolling was held in check by a strong broker, who vetoed the most extreme schemes for preventive war and colonial overextension. But because of the explosion of mass political participation after 1890 and the increasingly intransigent role played by economically doomed Junker landowners, Wilhelmine chancellors lost power compared with elite interest groups and their mass allies. In this situation, politics approximated the cartelized ideal type, and as predicted, strategic mythmaking and overextension mushroomed.

Weimar democracy also produced foreign policy outcomes that fit the predictions of the coalition politics theory. Electoral democracy empowered diffuse interests favoring free trade and cooperative, low-cost foreign policies. This outcome might be explained in part, however, by Germany's military weakness under the limitations of the Versailles Treaty.[190]

The Nazi era was a period of rule by a single dictator, during which expansion and strategic mythology ran amuck. The coalition politics theory makes only loose predictions in such cases, since the political system presents few constraints, for good or ill, on the whims of the dictator. In Hitler's case, his strategic views were decisively shaped by ideological blowback from Wilhelmine and wartime strategic propaganda aimed at radical nationalist mass groups. In short, the coalition politics theory provides a good explanation for all four periods between 1870 and 1945, including periods of greater and lesser German expansionism, but it does so only if long-term ideological consequences of domestic political struggles are part of the picture.

Germany's position in the international system was by itself a poor predictor of its foreign policy, but changes in the international environment frequently did affect German policy through their impact on German coalition politics and strategic mythmaking. For example, decreases in the world price of grain helped create the protectionist marriage of iron and rye in 1879 and helped scuttle the Caprivi reforms in the early 1890s. The encirclement of Germany in the years before

---

190. On competing views of Weimar foreign policy, Hans Gatzke, "Gustav Stresemann: A Bibliographical Article," *Journal of Modern History* 36 (March 1964): 1–13.

1914, a real change in the international setting, albeit provoked by Germany's own policy, gave the military and the radical nationalists ammunition with which to hype the foreign threat.[191] Finally, the collapse of international markets and credits dealt a death blow to the Weimar labor-export coalition.

It would be wrong to conclude from this that the link between domestic coalitions and foreign policy is simply spurious, in the sense that the international environment dictated both an optimal foreign policy and also an optimal domestic coalition to carry it out. Otto Hintze, for example, contended that the character of Prussia's military-bureaucratic state was a necessary adaptation to its vulnerable position in Central Europe.[192] Whether or not Hintze is correct about the origins of Prussia's state structure, it would be hard to argue that the late Wilhelmine ramshackle, acephalous, out of control political system was an optimal adaptation to anything. Nor was its self-defeating foreign policy. Nonetheless, within the range of choice circumscribed by preexisting social structures and state institutions, international events did influence which coalitions and policies might emerge at any given time.

This raises the question of policy prescriptions. Given the ability of the international environment to affect domestic political outcomes, how might one state try to influence another's coalition making or mythmaking in a more benign direction? One possibility is to behave in ways that directly discredit the opponent's big stick, paper tiger, and bandwagon myths.

Recently, for example, some scholars have argued that Germany went to war in August 1914 largely because its leaders believed the myth that Britain would not fight, and that the war might have been prevented had Britain made clearer deterrent threats.[193] Others suggest that Germany fought largely because its leaders believed the opposite myth: that the Entente had Germany encircled, that war was inevitable, and that it had better start sooner rather than later. Consequently, the war might have been prevented had the Entente members found a way to reassure Germany about their consideration for its basic national security requirements.[194]

My own view is that both myths were simultaneously operative and that together they constituted a double whammy whereby deterrent

191. Snyder, *Ideology*, 107.

192. Gilbert, *Historical Essays of Otto Hintze*, chap. 5.

193. Sean Lynn-Jones, "Detente and Deterrence: Anglo-German Relations, 1911–1914," *International Security* 11 (Fall 1986): 121–50; works cited by John Orme.

194. Richard Ned Lebow, *Between Peace and War* (Baltimore, 1981), chap. 5, and his other works cited above.

moves provoked conflict by tightening the perceived encirclement while appeasement provoked aggression by lowering its perceived risks. Thus both myths had to be discredited simultaneously in order to escape from this catch 22. To do this, the Entente members needed to convince Germany that they would fight if *and only if* Germany initiated the conflict. In principle this could have been achieved through a system of explicitly conditional defensive alliances, such as Bismarck achieved in the 1870s and 1880s, and through more defensive force postures. Geographical factors would have made it difficult to implement such a scheme perfectly, but surely the highly offensive force postures and virtually unconditional alliances of 1914 could have been improved on.[195] If so, it would have been harder to convince swing voters in the German political equation, like the Center party, of Germany's blameless role in the arms race.

In addition to directly discrediting an opponent's strategic myths, one might also try to change the incentives that influence its domestic coalition making, which is the root of those myths. Several times in the German story, external economic challenges slanted the incentives away from free trade, reformist coalitions and toward coalitions for autarky and expansion. Indeed, American decision makers learned this lesson after 1945 and consciously pursued a free-trade policy in part for this reason.

In sum, German overexpansion and self-encirclement were caused by a logrolling process controlled by the cartelized elites characteristic of a late-developing society, and also by the strategic ideologies that were the by-product of this coalition making. Though the international system hardly dictated German foreign policy, it did affect it, often for the worse, by discrediting anti-imperial groups and arguments. This means that even though the sources of aggression may be rooted primarily in pathological domestic structures, other states are not powerless to influence the virulence those pathologies attain.

---

195. On whether such a scheme was feasible, given the need for either Russia or France to have offensive forces to defend the other against German attack, see Van Evera, "Offense, Defense, and Strategy: When Is Offense Best?" paper delivered to the annual meeting of the American Political Science Association, Chicago, 1987; and the dialogue between Jack Snyder and Scott Sagan, "Correspondence: The Origins of Offense and the Consequences of Counterforce," *International Security* 11 (Winter 1986): 187–98.

[4]

Japan's Bid for
Autarky

Japan's attack on Pearl Harbor marks one of the most extreme examples of imperial overexpansion in the industrial age. A Japanese colonel, returning from a fact-finding mission to the United States in August 1941, reported to the chief of the army's General Staff that the United States commanded twenty times the steel production capacity of Japan, five times its capacity to produce aircraft, and ten times its overall war production potential. The chief of staff commended him for an excellent report, burned it, and had the author fired.[1] Moreover, a cabinet Planning Board study pointed out that plans to rectify Japan's resource deficit through conquest were not feasible, since they depended on importing huge amounts of war matériel from Japan's enemies. The author of this report was also fired, and the Planning Board was packed with analysts who would provide the right answers.[2]

Japanese overexpansion was remarkable not only for the sheer magnitude of the opposing forces it provoked, but for Japan's inability to learn to retrench from its mistakes in the 1930s. When the war in China in the 1930s threatened to ruin Japan's economy and stimulated the hostility of several great powers, the Japanese concluded that the solution was further expansion to cut off China's sources of supply and

To simplify locating works cited in the notes, the names of Japanese authors are given in Western order, with the surname last. Names of other Japanese persons referred to in the text and notes are given in Japanese order.

1. Kimitada Miwa, "Japanese Images of War with the United States," in Akira Iriye, ed., *Mutual Images: Essays in American-Japanese Relations* (Cambridge, Mass., 1975), 125–27. For the actual figures, see Paul Kennedy, *The Rise and Fall of the Great Powers* (New York, 1987), chap. 6.

2. Michael A. Barnhart, *Japan Prepares for Total War: The Search for Economic Security, 1919–1941* (Ithaca, N.Y., 1987), 170–71, 240.

conquer the resources needed to defend against the hostile encirclement. Finally, when the United States used an oil embargo to compel them to abandon this strategy, the Japanese again learned backward, concluding that the route to strategic solvency was not retrenchment but a preventive strike against an enemy whose war-making capacity was not vulnerable to preemption.

The Japanese case supports four main conclusions about the causes of overexpansion. First, the Japanese rationalized their self-defeating strategy through the usual combination of strategic myths: the paper tiger image, bandwagon theories, the turbulent frontier illusion, window logic, and the like. Some of the subtler, if equally self-deluding, Japanese argued that this course of expansion could be achieved by a strategy of offensive détente, which held that hostile opponents would fail to resist Japan's grab for an autarkic empire as long as the bid was implemented through controlled pressure, fig leaf concessions, and gradual, salami-slicing tactics.

Second, Japan's bid for empire and autarky was not a rational strategic gamble. Though the country was hard pressed by economic competitors in the 1930s, its lot in the international political economy was far from hopeless, and its exports rebounded from the depression better than those of most states. Alleged military threats to Japanese security, such as the buildup of the Soviet army in the Far East, were almost entirely reactions to Japan's own provocations. Objective international conditions sometimes played into the hands of the salesmen of militarist ideology, but they did not dictate Japan's imperialist binge or make it in any way rational.

Third, Japanese overexpansion and the strategic concepts that rationalized it are best explained as an outgrowth of Japan's domestic institutions and its route to modernity. Like Germany, Japan was a late, abrupt developer, modernized "from above" by traditional elites, with the military playing a central role. The overexpansion of the late 1930s was due to logrolling between the army and navy elites and to blowback from their self-serving imperial ideologies.

Fourth, Japan was most prone to overexpansion when its political system was most cartelized, and less prone when it was more unitary or more democratic. At first the *genro* oligarchy, the founding fathers of the Meiji restoration's revolution from above, served as a relatively unitary elite with a broad national perspective, checking overexpansion in the long-run interests of the Japanese state. In the 1920s the emergence of democratic political institutions partially took the place of the waning *genro* oligarchs as a check on the military's imperialist inclinations. By the 1930s, however, Japan's nascent democracy had collapsed, and policy was dominated by military cartels, whose logrolling led to open-ended expansion in pursuit of the chimerical goal of autarky.

Trends in Overexpansion: The Decline of Learning

From the Meiji restoration in 1868 until 1945, all Japanese governments were expansionist. Before the 1930s, however, Japan's expansionist enterprises were limited and, in the face of negative feedback, reversible. The Meiji leaders colonized Korea and Taiwan, fought a predatory war with China and a preventive one with Russia, and tried to impose onerous peace conditions on China that isolated Japan in the face of opposition from the great powers.[3] On the other hand, the majority of the Meiji leadership turned down proposals for a premature expedition to Korea on the grounds that Japan was still too weak, that the cost would derail domestic reforms, and that it would provoke the hostility of the European powers.[4] They practiced close cost-benefit calculations of their colonial enterprises. Despite jingoistic public and military pressures, the *genro* scaled back their demands on China in the face of British opposition and more generally came to understand the need for self-restraint to maintain the essential British alliance.[5] They were, moreover, primarily defensively motivated in their war with Russia, and they successfully conciliated Russia after the war.[6] In short, they were expansionists with limited aims, who learned well about the balancing character of the system.

Japan was also moderately expansionist in the "Taisho" period, named for the emperor who reigned from 1912 to 1926, but referring especially to the relatively liberal democratic 1920s. The leaders and strategists of Taisho Japan sought to gain a dominant position in China under the guise of cooperating with America's open door policy by making token concessions to China's interest in economic development.[7] The Japanese used more direct military methods in occupying part of

3. W. G. Beasley, *Japanese Imperialism, 1894–1945* (Oxford, 1987), chaps. 4–7, esp. p. 43.

4. W. G. Beasley, *The Meiji Restoration* (Stanford, Calif., 1972), 375.

5. Beasley, *Japanese Imperialism*, 55–58, 71; Marius Jansen, "Japanese Imperialism: Late Meiji Perspectives," in Ramon Myers and Mark Peattie, *The Japanese Colonial Empire, 1895–1945* (Princeton, N.J., 1984), 67; Ian Nish, *The Anglo-Japanese Alliance* (London, 1966).

6. Shumpei Okamoto, *The Japanese Oligarchy and the Russo-Japanese War* (New York, 1970), chap. 3; Beasley, *Japanese Imperialism*, 78–79; Ian Nish, *Alliance in Decline: A Study of Anglo-Japanese Relations, 1908–23* (London, 1972); Marius Jansen, "Modernization and Foreign Policy in Meiji Japan," in Robert E. Ward, *Political Development in Modern Japan* (Princeton, N.J., 1968), 184–85.

7. Akira Iriye, *After Imperialism* (New York, 1978), esp. 301–2.

Siberia in the aftermath of the Russian Revolution, though the size and extent of the operation reflected out-of-control decisions by military commanders.[8] Overall, however, clear limits were placed on the ends and means of expansion in the Taisho period: Japan pulled out of its quagmire in Siberia, made the concessions necessary to conclude the Washington Naval Treaty, played a patient game in China, and thereby gained the good graces of its Anglo-Saxon trading partners. The Seiyukai party, led by Premier (and former army general) Tanaka Giichi, suffered electoral defeat for his failure to rein in army assassinations, provocations, and intrigues in Manchuria.[9]

After the Kwantung army occupied Manchuria on its own initiative in 1931, however, self-correction no longer occurred as a result of overextension. Some voices, even within the military and the navy, warned about the dangers of a quagmire in China and the risks of provoking a war with America, but henceforth the solution would be not retrenchment, but further expansion and preventive aggression. A main task of this chapter is to explain why the previous pattern of successful learning in response to negative feedback operated in reverse after 1931.

Some scholars such as Miles Kahler and Charles Kupchan argue that the main turning point toward an overexpansionist grand strategy came in 1937, not 1931.[10] Indeed, until about 1937, when Japan embarked on large-scale, open-ended warfare against the Nationalists in China, the costs of Japan's imperial strategy did not outweigh its benefits. The military costs of conquering and occupying Manchuria had been low. At the same time, under the short-term Keynesian stimulus of the imperialists' plans for forced-draft development of heavy industry in Japan and Manchuria, the economy boomed. Only after 1937 did the costs of the strategy of autarkic empire outweigh the benefits, owing to the military quagmire in China and the cannibalizing of the light industrial, export-oriented sector of the economy.

In this sense scholars who point to 1937 as the turning point are correct. In a larger sense, however, the crucial step down the path to imperial overexpansion was taken with the occupation of Manchuria in 1931. As Kupchan himself correctly shows, the decision to occupy Manchuria was driven by one overriding objective: to use its resources and its potential for economic development to contribute to Japanese self-sufficiency and economic autarky in a future war against the Soviet

8. Beasley, *Japanese Imperialism*, 160; James W. Morley, *The Japanese Thrust into Siberia, 1918* (New York, 1957).

9. Beasley, *Japanese Imperialism*, 161, 187–88; Nish, *Alliance in Decline*, 373.

10. Miles Kahler, "External Ambition and Economic Performance," *World Politics* 40 (July 1988): 419–51; and Charles Kupchan, *The Vulnerability of Empire* (forthcoming).

Union, Britain, and the United States.[11] Of course Manchuria by itself was hardly sufficient to provide autarky in resources to the Japanese empire. Judged by the Japanese leaders' own standard, the occupation of Manchuria made sense only as a first step on a much more ambitious road of conquest. The conquest of Manchuria by itself was too little to achieve autarky, yet too much to maintain Japan's good diplomatic relations with the trading partners on which it was economically and strategically dependent.

Admittedly, most Japanese expansionists did not foresee that the occupation of Manchuria in 1931 was only the first step toward the conquest of all of East Asia and a war with the United States. But the logic of the goal of autarky pulled inexorably in that direction. Within three years it was clear that Manchuria by itself was not enough and that northern China would have to be incorporated too.[12] In this broader sense, the key turning point toward overexpansion came in 1931. The decisions of 1937 were driven by principles that had been embraced earlier.

THE INTERNATIONAL SYSTEM: IS MILITARISM A SPURIOUS CAUSE?

One might argue that Japan's expansionism—even its reckless, self-defeating overexpansion after 1937—can be explained largely by its especially vulnerable position in the international system. This view need not deny that Japanese decision making was riddled with militarist values and myths. Rather, it could contend that Japanese expansionist policies abroad and the domination of militarist circles at home were both caused by international pressures. In this view, militarism correlates with expansionism but does not cause it. Both are effects of the underlying cause, international conditions.[13]

Thus, if Meiji Japan was ruled by a military elite and developed militaristic institutions and ideas, this was because external pressure on Japan channeled political development in this direction. In this view Commodore Perry's Black Ships played the same role for Japan as encirclement in Central Europe played for Otto Hintze's Prussia.[14] Moreover, Japanese foreign policy and domestic arrangements were least militarized during the Taisho period, when the international

11. Kupchan, *Vulnerability*, Japan chapter.
12. Barnhart, *Japan Prepares*, 39.
13. There is no extended, systematic statement of this argument, but some related points can be found in James Crowley, *Japan's Quest for Autonomy* (Princeton, N.J., 1966), xv–xvii, 389, 391, 395; and Gordon Mark Berger, *Parties out of Power in Japan, 1931–1941* (Princeton, N.J., 1977), 353.
14. Beasley, *Meiji*, 11.

environment was most hospitable to liberal policies and institutions. World War I created a huge demand for exports, strengthening Japanese trading interests and showing Japan that free trade, not military expansion, paid off.[15] Relatively favorable international conditions continued through the 1920s, and as long as they lasted Japan played along with the Open Door policy in China while trying to cheat at the edges. But as soon as the world depression and its attendant protectionism created unfavorable conditions for liberal policies, Japan's relatively liberal Taisho institutions gave way to rampant militarism.[16] In these circumstances, the militaristic nationalists just turned Marxist analysis toward imperialist conclusions: the loss of Chinese and American markets was causing a crisis of overproduction in Japan's consumer export sectors, and the solution was the military conquest of markets and the forced-draft development of heavy industry.[17]

That Japan was a "late developer" also favored Japanese imperialism, not so much because it created a perverse set of domestic actors as because it affected Japan's international position.[18] A relatively backward state was at a disadvantage in Open Door competition with the United States, as demonstrated by America's use of its financial power to shift the China trade away from Japan during the depression. Consequently, Japan had an incentive to carve out an exclusive economic zone through conquest.[19] Also, Miles Kahler has argued that Germany and Japan, as late developers, were especially well situated to use the creation of a military-industrial-imperial complex as a Keynesian stimulus to development.[20]

Ultimately, however, these arguments for the rationality—indeed, the necessity—of Japan's expansionism are unpersuasive. While it is true that Japan's aggressiveness correlates in a loose way with the incentives created by the international system, at any given point Japan always behaved too aggressively for its own good. For example, the

15. William Lockwood, *Economic Development of Japan* (Princeton, N.J., 1954), 117; Sharon Minichiello, *Retreat from Reform: Patterns of Political Behavior in Interwar Japan* (Honolulu, 1984), 52.

16. Berger, *Parties*, 29, 34–39.

17. Seki Hiroharu, "The Manchurian Incident, 1931," in James Morley, *Japan Erupts: The London Naval Conference and the Manchurian Incident, 1928–1932* (New York, 1984), 180–81.

18. The young Konoe Fumimaro published an article in 1918 arguing that the status quo orientation of the Versailles system disadvantaged resource-poor "latecomers" like Japan. See Yoshitake Oka, *Konoe Fumimaro: A Political Biography* (Tokyo, 1983), 13.

19. Beasley, *Japanese Imperialism*, 71, 188–90. Conversely, Shidehara argued that Japan could win the Open Door competition against the Western powers owing to its lower wages and transport costs. Sadako Ogata, *Defiance in Manchuria: The Making of Japanese Foreign Policy, 1931–1932* (Berkeley, Calif., 1964), 8.

20. Kahler, "External Ambition," 451.

costly, pointless occupation of Siberia, already a product of an uncontrolled military, dates from the Taisho period. Most important, the conquest of an autarkic empire made no sense as a response to the setbacks Japan suffered during the depression of the 1930s, both because the need for it was insufficient and because the means to achieve it were hopelessly inadequate. Almost any other policy would have been better, given a rational appraisal of Japan's position in the international political economy and the balance of power system.

Economically, Japan adjusted well to the depression and to other powers' restrictions on Japanese exports. In part this was due to Keynesian stimulus, though this came more from the forced-draft creation of a heavy industrial base than from military outlays per se.[21] But Japan was also unique among the great powers in the success of its export recovery in the early and mid-1930s. Japan had an advantage as an exporter of cheap consumer goods in a depressed period when demand for such goods was strong.[22] Japan also had an advantage in its ability to repress wages.[23]

The declining rural living standard is one of the factors that allegedly necessitated imperial expansion. In fact, imperial expansion was a significant cause of this decline, since cheap rice from Korea and Taiwan significantly depressed farm profits in Japan. Indeed, the agricultural depression had set in already by 1925, though the world recession of 1929 made it worse.[24]

By the mid-1930s Japan's export revival was so successful that other states were increasing their tariffs barriers to counteract Japanese "dumping."[25] Nonetheless, this retaliation did not pose a grave threat to Japan's "trading state" strategy, in the view of the standard work on the subject, which concludes that "the root of Japanese imperialism is certainly not to be found in economic causes."[26] Rather, Japan's economic problems in the late 1930s were almost entirely caused by the

21. G. C. Allen, *A Short Economic History of Modern Japan*, 4th ed. (New York, 1981), chaps. 9 and 10; Kahler, "External Ambition," 419–51.

22. Kazushi Ohkawa and Henry Rosovsky, "A Century of Japanese Economic Growth," in William W. Lockwood, ed., *The State and Economic Enterprise in Japan* (Princeton, N.J., 1965), 82.

23. John G. Roberts, *Mitsui* (New York, 1973), 204–9.

24. Alan Gleason, "Economic Growth and Consumption in Japan," in Lockwood, *State and Economic Enterprise*, 419–20; Kahler, "External Ambition," 438; Peattie, "Introduction," in Myers and Peattie, *Japanese Colonial Empire*, 30; Hugh Patrick, "The Economic Muddle of the 1920s," in James Morley, ed., *Dilemmas of Growth in Prewar Japan* (Princeton, N.J., 1971), 215.

25. Takafusa Nakamura, *Economic Growth in Prewar Japan* (New Haven, Conn., 1983), 254–55.

26. Allen, *Short Economic History*, 164–65. Kahler relies upon this work for key elements of his argument. For a relevant theory, see Richard Rosecrance, *The Rise of the Trading State* (New York, 1986).

conscious shift from a trading-state strategy to a strategy of autarky and imperialism. The Japanese pattern after 1936 is similar to the Nazi experience in the same period.

By 1936 Keynesian stimulus and export recovery had basically solved Japan's economic adjustment to the depression. At that point the pursuit of military aggression in China and an arms buildup at home placed severe strain on an otherwise healthy economy. The mobilization of the economy for war after 1937 produced domestic inflation, wiped out Japan's foreign exchange, dried up loans from Washington, and starved the consumer and export sectors of funds.[27] "Konoe's summer gamble [of 1937]—ending the [China] incident with one immediate blow and paying for the effort later—had failed," says Michael Barnhart. "Japan's import requirements had skyrocketed as the war dragged on, just as the gamble was strangling its export industries."[28] By 1939 the cabinet Planning Board was begging for imperial retrenchment and a switch to a less ambitious war plan versus Russia in order to shift investment into light industrial export sectors. By fall 1941, the failure to adopt the Planning Board's strategy led to a situation where increases in steel for naval construction had to come at the army's expense, since the rest of the economy had already been cannibalized.[29]

In short, Japan's grab for autarky was economically unnecessary—indeed, it was a source of economic difficulties.[30] Beyond this, it was also impossible. In December 1937 the Planning Board pointed out, in Michael Barnhart's paraphrase, that "even if Japan occupied all of China and Southeast Asia, it would still find itself unable to wage a long war without relying on Anglo-American resources."[31] Moreover, Ishiwara's goals for the development of steel production in Manchuria were never met, in part owing to a lack of Western technical inputs.[32]

The counterproductive nature of Japanese imperialism was hardly unforeseeable. In fact, a variety of voices within the military, in high political circles, and in the public debate pointed out most of the

27. Barnhart, *Japan Prepares*, 91, 95–96, 102; Allen, *Short Economic History*, 147. Kahler, "External Ambition," 440, acknowledges this.

28. Barnhart, *Japan Prepares*, 103.

29. Ibid., 137–39, 256–57.

30. It is true, however, that despite these problems the economy as a whole, and especially its heavy industrial sector, continued to grow at a fast rate. Using 1929 as a baseline of 100 units of industrial production, production equaled 150.2 in 1936 and 182.5 in 1939. This growth occurred despite foreign exchange imbalances, bottlenecks, inflation, and other "signs of strain" after 1937. Jerome B. Cohen, *Japan's Economy in War and Reconstruction* (Minneapolis, 1949), 3, 9.

31. Barnhart, *Japan Prepares*, 104. For Admiral Yamamoto Isoroku's identical assessment, see Hiroyuki Agawa, *The Reluctant Admiral: Yamamoto and the Imperial Navy* (Tokyo, 1979), 188–89. On the limited economic benefits derived from the occupation of North China, see Cohen, *Japan's Economy*, 44–45.

32. Beasley, *Japanese Imperialism*, 216–17.

pitfalls: the stimulation of Chinese nationalism, the balancing responses of the great powers, the irrelevance of Korea to Japanese defense, the lack of oil tankers, and the like. Often these critiques came from the navy, which was always on the lookout for arguments to use against the army's resource-eating projects.[33] Typically they were advanced from a Realist perspective. Indeed, they argued that imperialism was the idealist position. "War is not a struggle between the just and the unjust," asserted Saito Takeo, a Japanese Diet member. "It is an out-and-out power struggle." Precisely for this reason, "the nation must cease questing after noble-sounding dreams and face realities"—the reality of Japanese weakness.[34]

Thus, though the degree of Japanese aggressiveness did correlate with the intensity of international competition in the economic and security spheres, it would be completely wrong to say that Japanese imperialism was simply a rational grab for autarky, compelled by the necessities of survival in international anarchy. Even James Crowley, who recognizes the role of international circumstances in shaping Japanese policy, acknowledges that the war with China was "inspired by an imperial ideology which was not circumscribed by careful or even credible strategic calculations."[35]

STRATEGIC CONCEPTS: PAPER TIGERS AND THE DOUBLE WHAMMY

Japanese militarists believed in the full range of imperial myths: paper tiger images, the bandwagon, and all the rest. These strategic views subjected the United States and other powers to a double whammy: their deterrent actions were read as confirming their predatory nature, and thus Japan's need to expand to achieve a more defensible perimeter, whereas their conciliatory actions were read as indicating their laxity in opposing Japanese expansion. Japanese expansionists' hostility toward the bearers of objective information demonstrates that these strategic concepts were ideological justifications for a predetermined program, not mere "beliefs." This interpretation is

33. Arthur Marder, *Old Friends, New Enemies: The Royal Navy and the Imperial Japanese Navy, Strategic Illusions, 1936–1941* (Oxford, 1981), 249; Seki, "Manchurian Incident," 179; Crowley, *Japan's Quest,* 141; Taichiro Mitani, "Changes in Japan's International Position and the Response of Japanese Intellectuals," in Dorothy Borg and Shumpei Okamoto, *Pearl Harbor as History: Japanese-American Relations, 1931–1941* (New York, 1973), 582–84; Jansen, "Japanese Imperialism," 65–68, citing F. G. Notehelfer, *Kotoku Shusui: Portrait of a Japanese Radical* (Cambridge, 1971), 82 ff.

34. James Crowley, "A New Asian Order: Some Notes on Prewar Japanese Nationalism," in Bernard Silberman and H. D. Harootunian, *Japan in Crisis: Essays on Taisho Democracy* (Princeton, N.J., 1974), 282–83.

35. Crowley, *Japan's Quest,* 378.

also supported by the high correlation between strategic arguments and the bureaucratic or political needs of the person making the argument. After 1931, strategic "perception" became largely autistic.

Paper Tiger Images

Japanese expansionists portrayed their adversaries as alternately aggressive and passive, conveniently melding this dual image into a unified justification for expansion and a proposal for how it could be safely achieved in the face of superior opposition. At the most general level, the strategic cliché of the Meiji era and later eras was that the Western powers were "ravenous wolves" that had used gunboat diplomacy to force unequal treaties on Japan.[36] The Washington Naval Treaties, argued the head of the Japanese navy, were mere fig leaves covering an inevitable American expansion into the Western Pacific, driven by the inherent properties of capitalist materialism.[37] In the view of Colonel Ishiwara Kanji, who masterminded the occupation of Manchuria, Japan had to expand to an autarkic resource base as preparation for an inevitable world war against American expansionism.[38] Noncapitalist materialism was seen to produce similar effects: the operations sections of the Army's General Staff considered war with the Soviet Union to be a historical inevitability.[39]

Western strength made a defensive strategy unavailing against the expected onslaught. To be capable of self-defense against the West, Japan had to emulate Britain, a small island that had aggregated great military power through cumulative conquests.[40] Because the West was so strong and insatiably aggressive, Japan had to expand to defend itself.

But if the Western powers were really so strong and aggressive, why would they not simply snuff out Japan's incipient moves toward empire? Here a new—some might say contradictory—element is added to the image. Though the pundits of the Kwantung army saw America's "open door" policy as just an excuse to bar Japanese influence from China, they concluded that American materialists, who were always "calculating economic interests," would ultimately decide that maintaining good economic relations with Japan was more important than trade with China. To sweeten the pot, they added, America might be offered

---

36. Jansen, "Japanese Imperialism," 62.
37. Sadao Asada, "The Japanese Navy and the United States," in Borg and Okamoto, *Pearl Harbor as History*, 234–35.
38. Mark Peattie, *Ishiwara Kanji and Japan's Confrontation with the West* (Princeton, N.J., 1975); Barnhart, *Japan Prepares*, chaps. 1–5.
39. Crowley, *Japan's Quest*, 111.
40. Jansen, "Japanese Imperialism," 63.

investment opportunities in a Japanese-dominated Manchuria.[41] Likewise, the Japanese army thought the United States would probably not impose economic sanctions in response to the conquest of Indochina "if we proceed with great caution."[42]

And if so-called caution failed to keep America napping, then deterrence would surely work. Foreign Minister Matsuoka Yosuke expected the Tripartite Pact with Germany and Italy to promote isolationism in the United States.[43] Military analysts doubted that the United States would embargo oil shipments, reasoning that the Americans would surely realize that this would trigger a Japanese attack and consequently America would be deterred from toying with such a trip wire.[44]

But whenever America showed signs of resisting Japanese expansion, the opposite aspect of the dual image was invoked. For example, in response to Japanese aggression in China, Secretary of State Henry Stimson announced that the United States would fortify Guam and the Philippines, in violation of the Washington Conference treaties. The Japanese navy merely took this opportunity to stress the uselessness of naval arms control, while the press argued more broadly that this showed the utter irreconcilability of Japanese and American goals.[45] Later, American bomber deployments in the Philippines simply confirmed American aggressiveness and gave Japanese militarists an argument for preventive action to take them out.[46]

When the Japanese army eventually became convinced that the United States would fight any Japanese attempt to gain control over indispensable Indonesian oil resources, it conjured up another facet of the paper tiger image to reconcile this perception with its irreversible course of expansion. America would fight, but a sharp rap would make it collapse, bringing an early end to the war. In this calculation the Japanese counted on the spiritual hollowness of America's materialist society, America's small economic stake in East Asia, the demoralizing effect of German victories on public opinion, and the divisive impact of trade unions, Communists, German and Italian fifth columns, "anti-Roosevelt elements," blacks, and isolationist Republicans.[47]

Some might contend that the United States did in fact behave like a paper tiger during much of this period, making fierce noises condemning Japanese aggression, but doing little to stop Japan's advance. But the

41. Ogata, *Defiance*, 166–67.
42. Scott D. Sagan, "Deterrence and Decision: An Historical Critique of Modern Deterrence Theory" (Ph.D. diss., Harvard University, 1983), 224.
43. Sagan, "Deterrence," 187.
44. Asada, "Japanese Navy," 254.
45. Crowley, *Japan's Quest*, 165.
46. Sagan, "Deterrence," 288–93.
47. The U.S. military agreed with some of this analysis. Sagan, "Deterrence," 282–85.

Japanese also held to a paper tiger view of the Soviet Union, which mounted a systematic arms buildup in its Far Eastern provinces in reaction to the Japanese occupation of Manchuria.[48] General Nagata Tetsuzan, for example, argued that the Russians were a powerful, aggressive adversary with whom conflict was inevitable, yet he thought it would be possible to avoid friction with them while Japan conquered the resource base in China that was necessary to deal with the Russian threat on a more equal footing.[49]

Either conciliatory or deterrent actions would fit with one facet or another of the paper tiger image and thus "confirm" the logic that justified aggressive Japanese strategies. This reasoning is clear in the Japanese navy's four conditions that would necessitate the initiation of war: a U.S. embargo; a large reinforcement of the Philippines; U.S. use of British bases to pressure Japan; and its opposite, a rift between Britain and the United States, allowing Japan to attack colonial possessions without fear of American involvement.[50] Historian Robert Butow comments that "what the members of the Japanese government did thereafter, perhaps more inadvertently than by design, was to create the very conditions in the Far East which the army and navy had already said would require Japan to go to war."[51] What Butow does not note is that if Japan pressed the issue, almost any Anglo-American response—or lack of response—would have created at least one of the four conditions.

Balancing and Bandwagoning

The handmaiden of the paper tiger image was the assumption that Japanese expansion would not provoke a balancing reaction from Japan's victims and their great-power allies. One argument offered was that Japan and her allies were too strong to resist. For example, Army Chief of Staff Sugiyama Gen argued that, since Germany was beating the Soviet Union, the United States would not go to war over French Indochina.[52] Likewise, argued the army's General Staff, Japan's alliance with Germany would deter the United States from freezing Japan's assets or attacking in response to a move on the Dutch East Indies.[53] A

48. Hata Ikuhiko, "The Japanese-Soviet Confrontation, 1935–1939," in James Morley, ed., *Deterrent Diplomacy: Japan, Germany, and the USSR, 1935–1940* (New York, 1976), 131–32; Kupchan, *Vulnerability*.

49. Barnhart, *Japan Prepares*, 34.

50. Marder, *Old Friends*, 134–35.

51. Robert J. C. Butow, *Tojo and the Coming of the War* (Stanford, Calif., 1961), 203.

52. Nobutaka Ike, *Japan's Decision for War: Records of the 1941 Policy Conferences* (Stanford, Calif., 1967), 88.

53. Crowley, "A New Asian Order," 285; see also Marder, *Old Friends*, 129; Hosoya Chihiro, "The Tripartite Pact, 1939–1940," in Morley, *Deterrent Diplomacy*, 183.

second argument was that a decisive fait accompli like the occupation of Shanghai could be followed by a moderate diplomatic settlement, defusing immediate resistance but accumulating a series of salami-slice victories in the long run.[54] Likewise, a 1936 cabinet meeting resolved that the Japanese advance in the South Seas should be done "gradually and peacefully," lest it "stimulate the powers concerned and fail to efface their apprehension about our empire."[55]

The most systematic attempt to explain how Japan might expand without provoking opposition was worked out by Ishiwara Kanji. His strategy was to use the resources of Manchuria and North China to develop Japan's heavy industry and build up the army in the first of two five-year plans. During this time, China would be appeased by trading territorial concessions in North China for favorable economic arrangements, and the Kuomintang would be penetrated by Japanese military advisers. The United States would be lulled by Japan's scrupulous adherence to the naval arms agreements, but then in the second five-year plan, Japan would break out of the naval constraints in a flat-out arms race. The balancing reaction of Japan's foes thus could be delayed by intimidating Russia, buying off Chiang Kai-shek, lulling America, and then sprinting to the acquisition of the autarkic base that Japan needed for an attritional struggle against the United States.[56]

In the event, blocking resistance developed far too early on every front. Between 1932 and 1936, the Soviet Union increased its Far Eastern force from four to fourteen divisions, whereas the overextended Kwantung army could deploy only three against them.[57] By July 1937 Chiang apparently decided to go all out in case the Japanese renewed their salami tactics, forcing them to pay the price of a major war if they insisted on keeping up the pressure. Ishiwara, seeing that his timetable required five more years of peacetime access to North China's resources, argued against the premature mobilization of the Japanese economy and army for a major military effort, but Sugiyama, then army minister, pushed the measure through.[58] Later the Dutch East Indies similarly foiled Japanese hopes to gain access to Indonesian oil through intimidation, without having to fire a shot. Batavia, rather than turning on the spigot to fill the tanks of the Japanese vessels that might attack them, cut the quota that Japan could purchase.[59]

All the historians who have looked at Ishiwara's strategy are struck

---

54. Crowley, *Japan's Quest*, 167, 337.
55. Ibid., 296.
56. Ibid., 282–85, 298–99; Barnhart, *Japan Prepares*, 77–81; Peattie, *Ishiwara*, 71–80.
57. Barnhart, *Japan Prepares*, 42.
58. Crowley, *Japan's Quest*, 345; Barnhart, *Japan Prepares*, 85–87.
59. Barnhart, *Japan Prepares*, 207; more generally, Crowley, *Japan's Quest*, 279–80.

by what they term its "fundamental inconsistency"—that Japan would have to conquer the vast resources needed to make her a power of global rank without thereby provoking the resistance of the Russians, the British, the Americans, or even the Chinese, who were to be the most immediate victims.[60] Another biographer states that Ishiwara himself understood that "the very political and military policies in Asia by which Japan might best prepare for war with the United States would themselves invite war with that country."[61] Thus, saying that Ishiwara disbelieved in the workings of the balance of power would be misleading. Rather, it seems more likely that he started with the unalterable goal of a centralized, self-sufficient Japanese empire geared for total war, realized that the logic of world politics worked against achieving it, and then concocted a scenario that would maximize its slim chances. On its face, this is the logic of ideology or motivated bias, not rationality or cognitive belief.

Windows

Once it became clear that opponents were beginning to balance against Japanese expansionism rather than being lulled by minimal Japanese self-restraint, there were strong pressures to attack before the forces of resistance were fully mobilized. Indeed, the need to exploit closing windows of opportunity and forestall power shifts is a constant theme in the argument of Japanese militarists. Meiji imperialists feared that the Europeans' head start in the race for colonies would mean not an "open door" in China, but a "closing door" for economic empire throughout East Asia.[62] Japan's 1904 surprise attack on Russia was both preemptive, in the sense of gaining a tactical first-strike advantage, and preventive, in the sense of forestalling the power shift that the completion of the trans-Siberian railroad would make possible. The incipient rise of Chinese nationalism made the Japanese, from 1927, resolved to forestall the Kuomintang in Manchuria.[63] In the 1930s, however, window logic cut both ways. In 1932, for example, the Japanese felt an incentive for preventive action against the Soviet buildup in the Far East, but they also believed the development of Manchuria as a industrial resource had to precede military action.[64] But after 1939 all the incentives, some real and some rather fantastic, worked in favor of exploiting the window of opportunity created by

60. Crowley, *Japan's Quest*, 280; Barnhart, *Japan Prepares*, 49.
61. Peattie, *Ishiwara*, 80.
62. Jansen, "Modernization," 179–80.
63. Crowley, *Japan's Quest*, 32.
64. Ogata, *Defiance*, 168.

the European war. Germany's offensive either defeated or tied down all the European colonial powers that stood between Japan and the resources of Southeast Asia. It also stimulated fears that Germany might somehow grab Indonesian oil first if a tardy Japan "missed the bus."[65]

What constituted a sufficient incentive for preventive attack was colored by domestic windows as well. Part of the argument for exploiting the window opened by Germany's conquests was that it had contributed to a climate of Japanese public opinion that was highly favorable to expansion but possibly transitory.[66] Likewise, an officer on the navy's operations staff argued that preventive action had to be taken to forestall increased American naval construction, noting that otherwise it would be difficult to control restless officers.[67] Primed by such domestic considerations to accept the logic of windows, Admiral Nagano Osami, on the day *before* the freezing of Japanese assets by the United States, said that there was "no choice left but to break the iron fetters strangling Japan."[68]

Cumulative Gains and Losses

The samurai who pushed through the Meiji restoration held typical military conceptions about the domino theory, the cumulativity of victories and defeats, and expansion as a prerequisite for self-defense. A prominent nationalist fanatic wrote, for example, that "if the sun is not ascending, it is descending." Consequently Japan must conquer Korea, Manchuria, and Russia's Kamchatka peninsula or else be conquered itself.[69] General Yamagata Aritomo, the senior oligarch who did so much to maintain the militarist character of the Meiji revolution from above, likewise argued that forward defense on the Asian continent was essential to maintaining Japanese security, though this was more asserted than analyzed. What is clear, however, is that the conquest of Korea was argued entirely in terms of security through expansion, not on grounds of economic benefit.[70]

Mechanisms by which gains and losses would allegedly snowball varied. Ishiwara stressed the cumulativeness of physical resources. Manchuria and Mongolia, for example, would help establish the industrial and resource base needed to support further conquests. In this

---

65. Marder, *Old Friends*, 124–25; Ike, *Japan's Decision*, 3.
66. Marder, *Old Friends*, 124–25.
67. Asada, "Japanese Navy," 251–52.
68. Ibid. 253–54.
69. Beasley, *Meiji*, 147–48, quoting Yoshida Shoin.
70. Beasley, *Japanese Imperialism*, 45–46, 77.

way, said Ishiwara, "war can maintain war."[71] Others cited domino effects on reputation. Tojo, for example, argued that a Japanese pullout from China would make the United States "more arrogant and over-bearing" and "would not be in keeping with the dignity of the army."[72] China specialists in the army's intelligence section insisted that "if we were to reveal carelessly a cordial feeling toward China, this would inevitably encourage the Chinese to become more presumptuous."[73] Another factor was the assumption of offensive advantage in military operations, which typically presupposed big first-strike advantages and led to the neglect of defensive weaponry like antiaircraft artillery.[74]

Such assumptions led the Japanese to try to solve security problems on the "turbulent frontier" of their empire through expansion.[75] For example, Premier Tanaka, formerly the vice-chief of the army's General Staff, thought it would enhance Japan's security to conquer a "buffer" against the Soviet threat, which would include the Soviet maritime provinces.[76] Similarly, the army thought the best way out of the quagmire in China was to invade Indochina and nearby southern ports, through which Chiang received 80 percent of his imported supplies.[77] Ishiwara usually argued that gains from conquest would cumulate in China, but when his industrialization timetable told him further advances were premature, he warned that "it will be what Spain was for Napoleon, an endless bog."[78] More commonly, however, Ishiwara and other Japanese militarists exaggerated the benefits, proba-bility of success, and cumulativeness of imperial endeavors while underestimating their costs.[79] "If Japan mobilizes," a China specialist in the intelligence section of the General Staff said in 1937, "we won't even have to debark onto the continent" to get the Chinese to accept Japanese terms.[80]

Strategic Concepts as Ideology and Manipulation

Japanese strategic analysis was utterly corrupted by the bureaucratic purposes it was designed to serve. There is a cornucopia of direct evidence that Japanese militarists consciously and systematically skewed

71. Seki, "Manchurian Incident," 148–49; Beasley, *Japanese Imperialism*, 182.
72. Sagan, "Deterrence," 264, citing Marder, *Old Friends*, 179; see also Ike, *Japan's Decision*, 140, 152.
73. Crowley, *Japan's Quest*, 213.
74. Marder, *Old Friends*, 323.
75. Peattie, "Introduction," 8.
76. Ogata, *Defiance*, 11.
77. Barnhart, *Japan Prepares*, 153.
78. Ibid., 89.
79. Ibid., 84.
80. Ibid., 85.

their analysis to support their preference for aggression.[81] Younger, militant naval staff officers, for example, conspired to keep information about shortages of manpower and matériel from more dovish senior commanders, falsifying such calculations as oil stockpiles to make a decision for war seem more feasible. Prewar oil supply analyses cooked the books by ignoring the inevitable increase in consumption in wartime and the wartime attrition of crude tankers. Moreover, when planners in the mobilization section told the operational section that something was impossible, they were told that their job was only to determine how, not whether, to implement an attack.[82] No study at all was done of the physical requirements needed to carry out the seizure of Indonesia called for in an authoritatitive 1940 policy document.[83]

In another example, military attachés posted in London and Berlin sought to deflate the militarists' assumption that German air raids were demoralizing the British, who would easily collapse under the weight of a German invasion, spreading defeatism to the United States as well. These attachés reported that such an invasion was impossible and was not being planned. Though backed up by the intelligence chief in Tokyo, the attachés were dismissed out of hand by the chief of the naval operations section, a notable hawk, on the grounds that they were obviously brainwashed.[84] Also ignored were attachés in Washington who warned about America's two-ocean strategy and the likelihood of an oil embargo.[85]

Changes in strategic "perceptions" were often directly caused by changes in policy preferences rather than the other way around. For example, top navy officials believed that an alliance with Germany would touch off a spiral of hostility with the United States, leading to a war that the Japanese would surely lose. But once it was clear that the army was intent on concluding the alliance at all costs, the navy accepted the army's arguments that the alliance would deter the United States. The reason for the change in "perceptions," Admiral Nagano explained, was that an army-navy clash, possibly leading to a coup d'état or a civil war, would be worse than a war with the United States: "We could not go through such a hell."[86] At the same time, the

---

81. For an excellent survey of this evidence, see Kupchan, *Vulnerability*.

82. Marder, *Old Friends*, 167–68, 255; Asada, "Japanese Navy," 257; H. P. Willmott, *Empires in the Balance: Japanese and Allied Pacific Strategies to April 1942* (Annapolis, Md., 1982), 68–74.

83. Tsunoda Jun, "The Navy's Role," in James Morley, *The Fateful Choice: Japan's Advance into Southeast Asia, 1939–1941* (New York, 1980), 249; and more generally, Mushakoji Kinhide, "The Structure of Japanese-American Relations in the 1930s," in Borg and Okamoto, *Pearl Harbor*, 596.

84. Marder, *Old Friends*, 125–26n.50, 261–62n.37, 335.

85. Higher-level naval authorities nonetheless expected stiff American resistance to Japan's southern advance. Asada, "Japanese Navy," 253–54.

86. Marder, *Old Friends*, 124–25, 178, quotation on 254.

navy hushed up its candid view that victory in a war with the United States was impossible, since that would undermine its principal rationale and its claim on scarce resources.[87]

All this underwent a brief reversal in early 1941, when the army chief of staff cooled toward the strategy of a southern advance, owing to an increase in his fear of Soviet military action. At this time he began to accept the navy's arguments against the southern advance, including the view that Britain and the United States were indivisible. In other words, when the army wanted to attack, it insisted that the United States would not respond to attacks on European possessions, but when it preferred not to attack for extraneous reasons, it agreed that the United States would respond.[88]

Exceptions to the usual pattern of strategic mythmaking also help prove the rule. For example, though Japanese militarists usually argued the advantages of the offense, they were happy to argue for the advantages of the defense when that served their organizational purposes. The Japanese navy accepted the argument that a fleet only 70 percent the size of America's would ensure Japan's security, given the logistic disadvantages of projecting power across the Pacific. Like Tirpitz's risk fleet calculus, this figure allowed plenty of room for naval building but also set a goal that was low enough to seem affordable in the eyes of the army and the civilians.[89]

Finally, and most important, many historians and commentators have remarked on the logical convolutions in basic Japanese strategic thinking, which seem transparently designed to justify aggression. Akira Iriye, for example, comments on the circular reasoning of the Japanese: "The policy of the southern advance would make conflict with the United States inevitable; since war was bound to occur, Japan should advance southward to prepare for the conflict."[90] Stephen Van Evera sees similar contradictions:

> Japanese leaders believed that the United States was so aggressive Japan had to prepare to meet her aggression by imperial expansion; but that the same United States was so meek that she would not fight seriously in the Pacific after a Japanese attack. They also believed that industrial strength was so decisive in modern war that Japanese security required an autarkic industrial empire; but also that Japan could gain this empire through war against a U.S. with ten times Japan's industrial capacity. These notions were inconsistent with one another, but consistent with the organizational interests of the Japanese military establishment. Each notion contributed to larger organizationally self-serving ideas: that Japan faced serious security problems,

87. Asada, "Japanese Navy," 249; Barnhart, *Japan Prepares*, 212.
88. Barnhart, *Japan Prepares*, 199, 210–11.
89. Crowley, *Japan's Quest*, 25, 46.
90. Akira Iriye, *Across the Pacific* (New York, 1967), 208.

which could be solved by offensive miltary operations. Thus each notion promoted the size and autonomy of the military, or followed from other ideas which did this.[91]

In sum, the character of Japanese strategic concepts suggests prima facie that they were the result of ideological and organizational manipulation, not the outcome or rational processes or merely cognitive distortions. This conclusion is strongly supported by direct evidence that Japanese strategists supressed inconvenient facts and consciously slanted their calculations to support their own preferences. Despite these manipulations, some historians contend that the cognitive impact of compelling formative experiences shaped much of the biased thinking of Japan's fact-flouting, logic-bending militarists.

COGNITIVE BIASES: EMULATING THE WEST, THE BUSHIDO CODE?

A variety of cognitive explanations might be advanced for Japanese overexpansion, but none of them is particularly persuasive. Perhaps the best is that a series of formative lessons taught the Japanese modernizing elite that international politics is at bottom a zero-sum military competition in which aggressive tactics pay off and cooperation does not. These lessons were taught, it is said, by Japan's observation of the fate of China and India at the hands of the West, Japan's own formative experiences with American and British gunboat diplomacy, Japan's successes in its own aggressive wars of 1895 and 1904–6, and the economic depression associated with the failure of Shidehara's cooperative diplomacy of the 1920s.[92]

This point is valid, but it is counterbalanced by all the lessons of an opposite nature that Japan might have learned: the lesson of 1895 that the fruits of aggression are taken away when it provokes a balancing coalition; the repeated lesson that assassination of foreign opponents only steels their successors to firmer resistance; the lesson of "no land wars in Asia" that might have been drawn from the quagmire in Siberia; the lesson from 1931 that the seizure of mainland buffer zones stimulates a Soviet arms race. Usually, however, militarists invented rationalizations to avoid drawing these conclusions. When the great powers prevented Japan from gaining the full fruits of its military victories in China in 1895 and at the end of World War I, Japanese

---

91. Stephen Van Evera, "Causes of War" (Ph.D. diss., University of California at Berkeley, 1984), 394.
92. Beasley, *Meiji*, 41; Peter Duus, "Economic Dimensions of Meiji Imperialism," in Myers and Peattie, *Japanese Colonial Empire*, 143; Crowley, *Japan's Quest*, 169.

militarists echoed the cliché that German militarists had long been repeating: "Our soldiers are very skillful, but our diplomats are very poor."[93]

Recently, two biographers of Ishiwara Kanji have cited the apparent influence of Germany's experience in World War I on the development of his Ludendorff-like views on total war.[94] It is undoubtedly true that the Ludendorff model helped crystallize Ishiwara's own ideas, but this begs the question of why he would pick that model. Surely the real lesson of German policy in their losing struggle was that middle-sized powers with limited resource bases simply could not expect to defeat an overwhelming, encircling coalition, provoked by their aggressive policies, no matter how technically expert their military and no matter how fully their economy was mobilized for war. Why then did Ishiwara and other Japanese militarists read the lesson backward, and why did it have such a profound effect on their thinking? Cognitive theory would certainly not expect the lessons from another power's travails to have a formative impact. Robert Jervis states that one's own experiences are the vivid ones that have a deep and lasting impact.[95] But organizational and ideological theories can easily explain Ishiwara's attraction to militarist theorists and practitioners like Moltke and Ludendorff. It also explains why Ishiwara was attracted to Leopold von Ranke's views on the *Primat der Aussenpolitik*, the notion that a country's domestic affairs had to be arranged to meet the requirements of international competition. As one historian of Japanese imperialism has remarked, "Ranke's belief that the dictates of foreign policy determine a country's domestic policy [is] a doctrine most convenient to empire builders."[96]

Another explanation, which some might label cognitive, is that a belligerent, zero-sum approach to politics was deeply rooted in the Bushido code of the samurai and permeated traditional Japanese culture.[97] Thus, the Pacific war was simply a Kurosawa epic in modern battle gear. Although this view cannot be completely rejected, several objections can be raised. First, such an argument is at least as much institutional and ideological as it is cognitive. The Bushido code obvi-

---

93. Yale Maxon, *Control of Japanese Foreign Policy: A Study of Civil-Military Rivalry, 1930–1945* (1957; Westport, Conn., 1973), 29. On the repeated, counterproductive assassinations, Roberts, *Mitsui*, 155, 266.

94. Barnhart, *Japan Prepares*, 31–32; Peattie, *Ishiwara*, 27–31.

95. Robert Jervis, *Perception and Misperception in International Politics* (Princeton, N.J., 1976), 262–69.

96. Lewis Gann, "Western and Japanese Colonialism: Some Preliminary Comparisons," in Myers and Peattie, *Japanese Colonial Empire*, 504–5.

97. Ramon Myers, "Post World War II Japanese Historiography of Japan's Former Colonial Empire," in Myers and Peattie, *Japanese Colonial Empire*, 458–59, discusses the "militaristic-feudal ruling elite."

ously served as the legitimating ideology of a military ruling elite, not just a "belief system."[98] Moreover, it leaves unexplained huge variations in Japanese strategic thinking over time and across groups.

For example, there was little fighting for the samurai to do in the Tokugawa period, before Japan was opened to the outside world, and many of them went soft and unmilitary. When Commodore Perry's fleet appeared, there was a wide range of opinion about whether to appease, reject, or exploit the foreigners' demands for free trade. In these debates, strategic preferences often correlated with social position. The Tokugawa government urged temporizing appeasement as a way of minimizing change and hanging on to their privileges. The impoverished lower samurai urged radical social changes as a means of fighting off the foreigners more effectively while enhancing their own status. Elites from provinces that had a lead in incorporating Western ways, such as Choshu and Satsuma, urged opening Japan in order to gain access to Western military and economic know-how, arguing also that they themselves, not the Tokugawa government in Tokyo, should be in charge of implementing such a strategy.[99] Peasants, meanwhile, had so little sense of Japanese nationalism that Yamagata and the modernizing Japanese leadership decided on a conscious policy to promote it.

Moreover, a cultural hypothesis fails to explain the major differences in foreign policy between the militarists, on one hand, and Shidehara and his relatively moderate big business supporters on the other.[100] If Japanese overexpansion rested in some measure on the samurai cultural traditions, it is clear that the Japanese military was the main repository of the belligerent version of those traditions.

Finally, some militarist perceptions might be explained not in terms of formative lessons and culture-based operational codes, but by common biases in information processing. For example, the captain who insisted that the United States would never embargo oil because Washington must know this would constitute a trip wire for a Japanese attack could be seen as suffering from the common tendency to assume that others know what we know and see things through the same lens as we do.[101] Conceivably, other examples of militarist myopia might

98. Robert Bellah, *Tokugawa Religion: The Values of Pre-industrial Japan* (Glencoe, Ill., 1957), chap. 4.

99. Beasley, *Meiji*, 118–20 and passim, presents evidence to this effect and also adds many nuances and qualifiers. In general Beasley contends that the character of the Meiji regime was affected both by pressure from the international environment and by tensions in the preexisting Japanese class structure, though his primary stress is on the former. See also Ellen Kay Trimberger, *Revolution from Above* (New Brunswick, N.J., 1978), 69, 81.

100. Beasley, *Japanese Imperialism*, 51–52, 78–79, 97, 168–69.

101. Asada, "Japanese Navy," 254; Jervis, *Perception*, chap. 5.

also have cognitive explanations of this type. But why should the Japanese military be especially prone to such misperceptions? One cognitive explanation might be that the Japanese army leaders' peculiar ignorance about the West led them to fall back on cognitive shortcuts and rules of thumb to guide their information processing. This might help to explain why the more cosmopolitan navy was less prone to wild expansionism than the more insular army. Of all naval officers with the rank of captain or higher, 50 percent had served abroad, usually in Britain or the United States, and most of them read American and British books.[102] On the other hand, the army's China specialists were the most belligerent and least accurate prognosticators about the prospects for Chinese resistance. Commander Ishikawa Shingo, who played a pernicious role in turning the Japanese navy toward a more militant policy, had traveled widely in Europe, America, and Southeast Asia and prided himself on being better informed "than any specialist in the Foreign Ministry."[103]

In summary, cognitive explanations are generally weak because they fail to explain why lessons were learned selectively, because they fail to explain most variations in strategic thinking over time and across groups, and because some of them can be subsumed under institutional or ideological explanations.

DOMESTIC POLITICS: MILITARISM AND POLITICAL DEVELOPMENT

Japan's pattern of late development, though not a carbon copy of Germany's, echoes several familiar themes. The Meiji restoration was a "revolution from above" that modernized Japanese society, economy, and military technology based on an elite alliance of the army, navy, local landlords, and state-supported business interests.[104] This constellation of power, presided over by a handful of founding fathers known as the *genro*, led to imperial overexpansion by roughly the same paths as did the similar constellation of power in the German case.

First, it conferred considerable power and autonomy on military organizations, which had an interest in imperial enterprises that further enhanced their claims on resources, autonomy, and prestige. Second, the *genro* oligarchs, like the founders of the German Reich, failed to replicate themselves and gradually lost power to organizations, interest groups, and mass political groupings that were strengthened

102. Marder, *Old Friends*, 289–90.
103. Asada, "Japanese Navy," 257; Marder, *Old Friends*, 131–33.
104. For citations, Beasley, *Meiji*, 7–8.

by the very modernization the oligarchs had promoted. As a result, army and navy elites decreasingly acted as far-sighted custodians of the national interest and increasingly became especially powerful, but parochial, logrollers. Third, when military interests were challenged by the rise of a more democratic polity in the 1920s, young military radicals were able to draw on the military's traditional autonomy, ideological capital, and broad penetration of elite and mass society to force through a pseudopopulist, imperialist alternative. As in Germany, militarists were able to align with upwardly mobile civilian "progressives," who sought to use social imperialism as a distinctive appeal to advance their fortunes against both the old oligarchy and mass democratic forces. While differing in details and emphasis, imperial Japan general-ly recapitulates the German pattern of powerful expansionist interest groups, whose influence is exacerbated by coalition-making dynamics and by the need to use a radical nationalist message to compete ideologically in the mass political marketplace.

The Pattern of Late Development

There exists a considerable literature comparing and contrasting Germany and Japan as exemplars of the "late" pattern of economic and political development.[105] In economic structure, some of the noted parallels include a large government role in mobilizing and allocating investment, centralized financial institutions, relatively low levels of mass consumption, and economic concentration in the hands of a few giant cartels.[106] But a key difference relevant to an analysis of imperial-ism is that, until the 1930s, the activities of *zaibatsu* cartels were focused in banking and trade, not heavy industry. Heavy industrial cartels oriented toward military production emerged as dominant economic units only *after* the militarists embarked on a strategy of industrial autarky and imperial expansion. Earlier cartels tended to have mixed interests in imperialism, profiting from Japanese colonialism and mili-tary provisioning, but also profiting from free trade with the developed West.[107]

In political structure, one difference was that the *genro* oligarchs dispossessed the landed *daimyo* elite, whereas landed Junkers remained

---

105. Beasley, *Japanese Imperialism*, 5–10; David Landes, "Japan and Europe: Contrasts in Industrialization," in Lockwood, *State*, 172–82.

106. Kazushi Ohkawa and Henry Rosovsky, "A Century of Japanese Economic Growth," in Lockwood, *State*, 51–52.

107. Nakamura, *Economic Growth*, 194, 210; Kozo Yamamura, "The Japanese Economy, 1911–1930: Concentration, Conflicts, and Crises," in Silberman and Harootunian, *Japan in Crisis*, 314–15; Roberts, *Mitsui*.

as a major support and personnel cadre for the post-1870 Reich.[108] But the upshot of this for imperial overexpansion and militarism is unclear. Though the *daimyo* were gone, local landlords played an important role as part of the ruling coalition of military, *zaibatsu*, and conservative political parties that managed democracy in the Taisho period much as the coalition of iron and rye had done in Wilhelmine Germany. In a system where apportionment was skewed to favor rural areas, landlords used their local domination to deliver conservative votes in exchange for pork barrel payoffs. This helped to maintain the social power of the military and other conservative elites despite the Taisho trend toward mass democracy.[109] Indeed, if the *daimyo* had survived as a powerful political force like the Junkers, there might have been less imperialism, since an even stronger landed elite would not have put up with having colonial rice depress prices on Japan's domestic market.

In general, the immobility of industrial and agricultural capital, which played a key role in explaining the cartelization of German politics, was not the central problem in the Japanese case. Rather, the main problem was the immobility of the organizational capital of the army and the navy.[110] A constitutional decision, forced through in 1878 by Yamagata to protect the military from what he saw as the necessary rise of parliamentary institutions, emulated the German model of making the military answerable only to the emperor except in budgetary matters.[111] This arrangement, especially in the context of conservative elite logrolling, gave the military considerable discretion in defining the boundaries placed on its activities abroad. Through its highly independent activities in Siberia and later in Manchuria, the army could use the tactics of fait accompli to create a market for its own highly specialized services.[112]

Above all, Japan's pattern of late development allowed the emergence of powerful military cartels.[113] A powerful, unitary elite might have contained the growth of military particularism. Conversely, a fully

108. Trimberger, *Revolution*, 34–36; Theda Skocpol, *States and Social Revolutions* (Cambridge, 1979), 101.

109. Peter Duus, *Party Rivalry and Political Change in Taisho Japan* (Cambridge, Mass., 1968), 32–33, 137–39, 152, 192, 196, 241; Robert Scalapino, "Elections and Political Modernization in Prewar Japan," in Ward, *Political Development*, 270.

110. Jansen, "Modernization and Foreign Policy in Meiji Japan," in Ward, *Political Development*, 188.

111. Maxon, *Control*, 22–23.

112. Beasley, *Japanese Imperialism*, 36; Kent Calder, "Japanese Foreign Economic Policy Formation: Explaining the Reactive State," *World Politics* 40 (July 1988): 517–78, at 529.

113. On the unfettered role of parochial interest groups in this period, see R. P. G. Steven, "Hybrid Constitution in Prewar Japan," *Journal of Japanese Studies* 3 (Winter 1977): 183–216.

institutionalized democracy might have kept militarism in check.[114] Indeed, the opening battle in the war to establish Taisho parliamentary democracy was the Diet's rejection in 1913 of a bill to expand the army.[115] But the considerable autonomy granted to the military by Yamagata's constitutional arrangements gave the military plenty of instruments to fight back with.

This was true even in the Taisho period. For example, the Japanese army sought to use the Bolshevik revolution as an opportunity to pursue its expansionist program on the Asian mainland. As the coalition politics theory would predict, the army's interventionist plans were resisted by unitary forces in the polity (the *genro*) and democratic forces (the leadership of the Seiyukai party). Saionji Kinmochi, the last surviving *genro*, tried in the late 1920s to gain automatic transfer of power to the party winning an electoral majority. One of his main objects in this was to ensure that Japan would maintain its Western-oriented liberal diplomacy.[116] The army counteracted this resistance, however, through faits accomplis in the field and through alliances with the navy, foreign ministry bureaucrats, and the powerful political-military clique from Choshu province. Only when military ventures, like the occupation of Siberia, had become obvious quagmires was the military-bureaucratic cartel reined in.[117]

Over time, the forces of restraint grew even weaker. The *genro* were swamped by the very growth of capitalist pluralism and parliamentary democracy they themselves had set in motion.[118] Moreover, the basically conservative economic and party elites that managed politics in the 1920s were only loosely committed to their alliance with mass democratic forces. When international conditions for free trade and liberal democracy turned unfavorable, many "Taisho democrats" were easily recruited for the radical nationalist alternative offered by the young military officers.[119]

In short, though Japan's pattern of late development was not identical to Germany's, it was similar in those key respects that made its politics vulnerable to the influence of military interests, cartelized

114. For relevant arguments, see Taichiro Mitani, "The Establishment of Party Cabinets, 1898–1932," in Peter Duus, ed., *The Cambridge History of Japan*, vol. 6, *The Twentieth Century* (Cambridge, 1988), 55–96, esp. 76.

115. Crowley, *Japan's Quest*, 13–15.

116. Saionji forced the collapse of the Tanaka government after the Chang Tso-lin affair. Lesley Connors, *The Emperor's Adviser: Saionji Kinmochi and Pre-war Japanese Politics* (London, 1987), 102, 107, 117–19.

117. Morley, *Japan's Thrust*, 50–58, 139–42, 146, 270–71, 291, 312–13.

118. Scalapino, "Elections," 273; see also Duus, *Party Rivalry*, 242–51; Beasley, *Japanese Imperialism*, 254.

119. I will discuss this in greater detail below.

politics, and the organization of mass political participation from above through social imperialist appeals.

Military Power and Interests

Military interests in imperialism can be divided into narrowly organizational and more broadly political conceptions. Instruments for achieving the military's ends can likewise be divided into the orthodox bureaucratic and the unorthodox social imperialist. Military generations and factions tended to divide along these lines. Both contributed to the power of the military, and the factional splits among them and the navy contributed to the uncontrolled character of Japanese expansionism.

The militarist expansionism of the older generation in the army was guided by an aggressive strategy of self-defense against a purported Soviet threat. The organizational logic of this stance was straightforward threat inflation and offense mongering as a rationale for large, expensive military forces. "Fear of the Soviet Union was 'necessary' for the Army, which had built up its forces on the basis of a possible war with Russia," says historian Sadako Ogata.[120] Three generals from the province of Choshu—Yamagata, Terauchi, and Tanaka—placed a high priority on parrying this alleged threat both in their military capacities and as leading political figures and premiers in the Meiji and Taisho periods.[121]

By the mid-1930s the main figure spearheading this traditional faction was Araki Sadao, who stressed the immediate Russian threat and the short-run strategic necessity of forward defense in northeast Asia. Araki was installed as war minister with the task of gaining control over the more radical faction of Nagata, Ishiwara, and Suzuki Teichi, who spoke for younger officers interested in economic reform within a much expanded China-centered empire. Whereas Araki was convinced that 1936 was the year of maximum danger for a Soviet attack, the Young Turks wanted to focus on developing China's resources first, in order to end what they saw as party and *zaibatsu* hegemony at home, and to create a planned economy geared toward total war. Only when that process was completed did they foresee war with the Soviet Union and the United States.[122]

At one level, these younger military radicals were merely seeking a narrow organizational goal—autonomy from political interference—in a

---

120. Ogata, *Defiance*, 168.
121. Maxon, *Control*, 20; Marius Jansen, "Introduction," in Morley, *Japan Erupts*, 124.
122. Crowley, *Japan's Quest*, 203–6, 246–48; Ogata, *Defiance*, 138. Barnhart, *Japan Prepares*, 58–59, notes that Americans like Joseph Grew knew about these cleavages.

particularly audacious way. Thus Ishiwara used his position on the staff of the Kwantung army to engineer the conquest of Manchuria, which he and his coconspirators set out to run as their very own industrial economy producing for their own military needs. Ishiwara's target for Manchurian steel production was half of that of Japan as a whole.[123] In this sense the radical militarists' plans for autarky for the Japanese empire were really plans for autarky for the Japanese army.[124]

But this scheme was linked to a broader political appeal. The Kwantung army touted its plans to make Manchukuo a state socialist "paradise" where the social evils of capitalism, communism, and electoral democracy would all be avoided by an efficient military administration acting on behalf of Japan's true, traditional values.[125]

Both the traditionalist and Young Turk military factions, despite their somewhat different programs, agreed that imperialism was a good way to provide the military with a prestigious social task. A caricature of this motive was Saigo Takamori's suggestion in 1873 that unemployed samurai be used in an invasion of Korea largely to keep them off the streets. The proposal was turned down by the *genro*, but just barely.[126] Half a century later Saigo was a hero among younger officers, but even the more traditional war minister, General Minami Iwao, told the premier that the army was indignant at civilian attempts to rein in military operations in Manchuria, which were tantamount to declaring the army useless.[127] The sentiment was similar to that of 1873, but by this time the military was virtually able to act on its own.

Both factions also were frustrated by the political and diplomatic developments of the late 1920s. On the narrow organizational level, the army was frustrated by a cut of four divisions in the force structure after the liquidation of the occupation of Siberia and by denial of permission to occupy Manchuria.[128] In 1928 the army insisted that its role in the assassination of the Chinese warlord of Manchuria was a strictly internal matter, a stance that led to the fall of the relatively

123. Beasley, *Japanese Imperialism*, 213–14.
124. Ogata, *Defiance*, 184–85; Barrington Moore, *Social Origins of Dictatorship and Democracy* (Boston, 1967), 303.
125. Ogata, *Defiance*, 184–85; Crowley, *Japan's Quest*, 95; Takashi Ito, "The Role of Right Wing Organizations in Japan," in Borg and Okamoto, *Pearl Harbor*, 497–502. In this way the Kwantung army sought to implement by fait accompli an ideological program similar to that of the terrorists and assassins in radical nationalist movements, who promised to smash liberal democracy and capitalism, protect Japan's peasants and workers, and then go on to civilize Asia.
126. Trimberger, *Revolution*, 30; Grace Fox, *Britain and Japan, 1858–1883* (Oxford, 1969), 280–81.
127. Maxon, *Control*, 84; Trimberger, *Revolution*, 130, citing Ben-Ami Shillony, *Revolt in Japan* (Princeton, N.J., 1973), 67.
128. Shuichi Kato, "Taisho Democracy as the Pre-stage for Japanese Militarism," in Silberman and Harootunian, *Japan in Crisis*, 233.

pro-military Tanaka of the Seiyukai party and his replacement with Shidehara Kijuro and the more liberal Minseito party.[129] The navy was similarly outraged by the London Naval Treaty of 1930, which it insisted violated the constitutional principle that the armed forces were answerable only to the emperor.[130] Military fears of Minseito budget cuts were exacerbated by Japan's decision to participate in the 1931 Geneva disarmament talks.[131]

More fundamental than grievances about specific policies were military objections to the whole tenor of Taisho Japan's bourgeois, democratic society. The military saw itself as the repository of Japan's true traditions, holding out against the debasement represented by liberalism, urbanization, pacifism, popular disrespect for soldiering, and *zaibatsu* manipulation of political parties.[132] It also saw the agricultural depression as a threat to the army's traditional base of mass support in the countryside.[133] Moreover, despite the social problems of the late 1920s, parliamentary democracy seems to have been setting in more firmly by the elections of 1928 and 1930. Previously, out-of-power parties had always fared poorly at the polls, because of government manipulation of the electoral process. But in 1928 the nonincumbent Minseito was barely defeated, and by 1930 it won with a significant majority on the heels of the Seiyukai's imperial embarrassments. Moreover, in the fashion described by Anthony Downs's theory of democratic party competition, the two major parties competed for the middle of the voting spectrum and between them garnered over 90 percent of the vote.[134] It is no wonder the military thought it was on a slippery slope toward real civilian control.

Against this backdrop, the program of reformist imperialists like Ishiwara and Suzuki must be seen as an attempt to head off such a development by offering an alternative social vision of comparable scale. These officers were no longer thinking in terms of military or even geopolitical strategy toward other great powers. Rather, they were thinking about the survival of military values in Japanese society, as well as the kinds of ideology and institutions that could ensure it. No doubt there was some sincerity in their notion of saving the

---

129. Ogata, *Defiance*, 16; Beasley, *Japanese Imperialism*, 187–88.

130. Kato, "Taisho Democracy," 233; Tatsuo Kobayashi, "The London Naval Treaty, 1930," in Morley, *Japan Erupts*, 11–118.

131. Crowley, *Japan's Quest*, 106.

132. Crowley, *Japan's Quest*, 86–87; Jansen, "Introduction," in Morley, *Japan Erupts*, 130; Beasley, *Japanese Imperialism*, 11.

133. Kato, "Taisho Democracy," 233; Maxon, *Control*, 73; Barnhart, *Japan Prepares*, 64–65.

134. Scalapino, "Elections," 276–77; Duus, *Party Rivalry*, 29, on the center-seeking character of politics in the two-party system.

depression-buffeted Japanese peasant, since many of the younger officers came from peasant stock themselves.[135] Still, it is hard to see the reformers' plans to turn Japan into an industrial autarky as truly aimed at helping the peasants. Just as colonialism had hurt agriculture in the 1920s, so the investment priorities of the 1930s kept agriculture the most depressed sector of the economy.[136] Above all, the military reformers' army colors show through.

This ideology of social imperialism, sold through tactics of persuasion and intimidation, was quite effective and helps account for the successful overthrow of Taisho democracy.[137] Among the more orthodox persuasive tactics were the use of the prestige of specialized information and expertise. For example, the London Naval Treaty of 1930 initially received favorable commentary in the Japanese press, and the returning negotiators were welcomed back as heroes. The navy's resistance to the treaty was dismissed as special pleading, and the public was warned not to be taken in by the navy's abuse of its monopoly of technical knowledge in arguing against the agreement. But the navy mounted an overwhelming counterattack through the press, through public speeches around the country by active duty and retired officers, and through popular navy leagues and ultranationalist societies. In the face of this, pro-treaty voices increasingly exercised prudent self-censorship, and the tide of public opinion began to turn against the treaty.[138] Seiyukai party politicians chose to ride this wave into office, asserting, for example, that the navy's criticism of the London treaty must be valid, since they were the experts.[139]

Both persuasion and coercion were used in selling the army's Manchurian campaign. As early as 1920, Nagata Tetsuzan, one of the principal figures in the "total war" faction, set as a central goal the creation of a favorable climate of opinion within the Japanese public and army for a military solution in Manchuria.[140] By 1931 it had become official General Staff policy to develop "a general understanding within Japan and abroad of the necessity to use force in Manchuria."[141] Pamphlets disseminated paper tiger and bandwagon concepts, supporting the need for a military buildup and the creation of an autarkic imperial base through slanted strategic analysis.[142]

135. Trimberger, *Revolution*, 128–30; Gann, "Western and Japanese Colonialism," 508.
136. Kurt Steiner, "Popular Political ?articipation and Political Development in Japan: The Rural Level," in Ward, *Political Development*, 238–39.
137. Berger, *Parties*, 81–82.
138. Tatsuji Takeuchi, *War and Diplomacy in the Japanese Empire* (Garden City, N.Y., 1935), 303–4; Kobayashi, "London Naval Treaty," 57–59; Kupchan, *Vulnerability*.
139. Kobayashi, "London Naval Treaty," 81.
140. Seki, "Manchurian Incident," 162.
141. Crowley, *Japan's Quest*, 113.
142. Ibid., 225; also 207–9.

Despite this, initial press commentary on the occupation of Manchuria was mixed, including some calls for a tightening of control over military operations by the civilian cabinet. The army fought criticism by withholding accurate information about what was happening in Manchuria, by arguing that its actions were required to protect the security and prosperity of the Japanese homeland, and ultimately by forbidding criticism in the press.[143]

Public opinion, fed a diet of slanted interpretations of the fait accompli in Manchuria, generally backed the army's plans. In the 1932 election and thereafter, the Seiyukai used a pro-imperialist platform, increasingly similar to the positions of the military radicals, to turn out the Minseito, whose liberal policies seemed to offer only hardship in the face of depression conditions.[144] From this point on, however, the elections did not matter, since governments were no longer being formed based on parliamentary results.[145]

Other unorthodox techniques of persuasion included threatened coups d'état in Japan itself and the assassination of political rivals. The tendency in recent scholarship is to minimize the effect of intimidation of politicians and naval figures through the threat of assassination. These authors contend that assassination was the tool of unsuccessful extremist sects, that responsible military authorities of neither faction sanctioned it, that perpetrators were punished, and that there is little evidence that assassination targets changed their policies because of this danger.[146] Although this work may be a useful corrective to the view that the threat of physical violence alone explains the army's political domination in the 1930s, it surely goes too far in the other direction. Admiral Yamamoto stated that opposition to the army would get him killed or possibly trigger a civil war.[147] Admiral Yoshida suffered a nervous breakdown because of pressure from the army, which he ultimately did not resist.[148] Admiral Yonai's relatively moderate government was forced out of office by an army coup threat, linked to the demand to sign a treaty with the Nazis.[149] Tojo's main qualification for the job of premier was that only he could control the army.[150]

143. Takeuchi, *War and Diplomacy*, 346–47, 362–66; Richard H. Mitchell, *Censorship in Imperial Japan* (Princeton, N.J., 1983), 255–58; for background, Richard H. Mitchell, *Thought Control in Prewar Japan* (Ithaca, N.Y., 1976), esp. 82–83, 283–84, 341.

144. Scalapino, "Elections," 279–80; Crowley, *Japan's Quest*, 126, 171.

145. Berger, *Parties*, 80.

146. Ben-Ami Shillony, "Myth and Reality in Japan of the 1930s," in W. G. Beasley, ed., *Modern Japan* (Berkeley, Calif., 1975), 81–89; Crowley, *Japan's Quest*, 133–34, 173–74.

147. Agawa, *Reluctant Admirals*, 192.

148. Marder, *Old Friends*, 115.

149. Butow, *Tojo*, 139.

150. Ibid., 288–302. Barnhart, *Japan Prepares*, 254, states that "anticipating army revolt if [navy minister] Oikawa were tapped [for the premiership] and then refused to make a firm decision for war, [lord keeper of the privy seal] Kido favored Tojo's appointment."

Machine guns were deployed around the naval ministry, but apparently caving in on policy disputes was thought a better strategy for self-defense.[151]

In short, far more than in Germany's case, a powerful explanation for Japanese overexpansion is the straightforward hijacking of the state by a concentrated militarist interest group. Still, in understanding both the army's power and its motives, it is necessary to place them in the context of the broader political system. The army's motives, especially those of the "total war" faction, were not simply to inflate the foreign threat as a means of keeping budgets high or to find employment on foreign battlefields. Rather, the military was engaged in a systematic effort to combat emerging democratic trends that threatened the long-run position of military values and institutions in Japanese society. The doctrine and strategy of autarkic imperialism was an essential element in that struggle.

The army's success in this endeavor was also a function of its broader political context. The terms of the Meiji restoration had given the army considerable autonomy, which could be used to pursue its own agenda outside civilian control. Moreover, the constellation of other conservative political forces that dominated late Meiji and Taisho politics—the navy, landowners, *zaibatsu*, and conservative political parties—lacked an overwhelming interest in fighting to defend Taisho democracy and Shidehara diplomacy. International and domestic conditions unfavorable to liberal policies made it just as attractive for most of these interests to acquiesce to the military's authoritarian, imperial rule, no matter what qualms they had about its extremism.[152]

Coalition Making and Logrolling

As I argued in chapter 2, there are two conceptual problems with single-interest, "hijacking" theories of overexpansion. The first problem is how relatively narrow interests can attain enough power to force through their parochial agenda. The previous section explained how this was possible for the army in the Japanese case. The second problem is why such an interest group, once it attains sufficient power to force through its agenda, would persist in a policy that seems calculated to ruin a country in which it has such a preponderant stake.

Prince Higashikuni might also have kept the military in line, but it was thought imprudent to risk associating a member of the royal family with the outbreak of war.

151. Marder, *Old Friends*, 101.

152. "A growing segment of party and non-party elite groups subscribed to the military definition of the problems Japan confronted abroad, and to military prescriptions for the resolution of those problems," says Berger, *Parties*, 81. On the mixed interests of the *zaibatsu*, see Roberts, *Mitsui*, 134–35, 198, 263–64; Beasley, *Japanese Imperialism*, 39.

A simple answer in the Japanese case might be that by 1936 the military was riding a tiger and could not safely dismount. In this view, the army and navy could escape from the China situation only by handing power back to the civilian parties, since their right to rule hinged on the imperial program they had embarked on. As Barnhart notes, if the navy's "leaders found war with America unacceptable, they had to confess that their fleet was worthless."[153] Arguably, the same logic held for the army. Thus, no matter how unpromising the prospects for military conquest, the domestic consequences of retrenchment would always be worse for the military elite. Although this answer may be satisfactory, the dynamics of coalition making provides an interesting supplementary explanation.[154]

At several junctures the militarists themselves foresaw the coming disaster. Some of them might have decided to pull back had it been up to them alone. The navy, most obviously, would never have pushed matters to the point of war with the United States except for its interaction with the army. Whenever possible, the navy aligned itself with moderates in the foreign ministry in order to restrain the army's China policy.[155] The navy was also reluctant to sanction the advance into Southeast Asia, even though its own roles, missions, and budgets would be enhanced by preparations for these operations.[156]

But the navy was finally driven to drop its resistance to this move, believing that only by agreeing to the southern advance could they head off a war with Russia that they saw as strategically senseless and disastrous for the navy's claims on scarce resources.[157] Admirals increasingly took the attitude that a naval war against overwhelming opposition, including that from the United States, was inevitable, and that announcing it to be unwinnable would simply give the army an excuse to take away resources that would be desperately needed for the struggle. As early as 1934, Admiral Suetsugu Nobumasa stated that "even [war with the United States] is acceptable if it will get us a budget."[158] Eventually, even moderate admirals accepted such reasoning. "It's an impossible state of affairs," said Yamamoto in fall 1940. "The one thing the navy must do now is see that it gets everything that it considers necessary in making proper preparations."[159]

153. Michael Barnhart, "Autarky and International Law: Japan's Attempt to Achieve Self-Sufficiency and the Origins of the Pacific War" (Ph.D. diss., Harvard University, 1980), 121.
154. Deborah Welch Larson, "Foreign Policy Decisions as Bureaucratic 'Resultants': Japanese Decision-Making, 1940–1941" (Stanford University, unpublished MS., 1975), argues that Japanese policy was the outcome of bureaucratic compromises.
155. Crowley, *Japan's Quest*, 223.
156. Barnhart, *Japan Prepares*, 269.
157. Ibid., 266.
158. Ibid., 39.
159. Agawa, *Reluctant Admiral*, 192.

Likewise, "total war" officers like Ishiwara were not in favor of expanded military operations in China after the 1937 provocation at the Marco Polo Bridge. They saw it as premature, jeopardizing their industrial development plans, and possibly unnecessary, since their hope had initially been to "Finlandize" China without onerous military operations.[160] In light of these considerations, Ishiwara urged ending the war through negotiations.

More traditional military figures and the civilian prime minister, Konoe Fumimaro, however, insisted on gambling on a quick, decisive military victory.[161] In part this decision might have been spurred by unwarranted optimism in military intelligence, but the main reason for it was Konoe's reckless strategy for fashioning a new political coalition that would restore civilian control over the military. Konoe's plan was to use mobilization for war as an excuse to push through a radical centralization of the economy in civilian bureaucratic hands and to form a mass party to support this new form of organization. In essence, he gambled on co-opting the program of the "total war" faction of the army, seeing it through to a successful conclusion under civilian auspices.[162] Again in 1938, Konoe tried using a victory in China to promote a "new political system" in Japan, a development driven by the domestic necessity to gain control over the military.[163]

Konoe's recklessness was not primarily inspired by devil-may-care illusions about the ease of conquest. In fact, he contrasted the failures suffered by Wilhelmine Germany, whose policy had provoked the resistance of the whole world, to the successes enjoyed by Japan in 1905, when a flexible and self-restrained policy had kept the enemy diplomatically isolated. "In present-day Japan, even those who advocate the most uncompromising foreign policy probably would not claim that it is desirable to wage a war which gyrates enemies throughout the world."[164] Rather, Konoe's policy was driven by the domestic necessity to regain control over a set of highly autonomous military factions, no one of which could exercise the unified, rational control needed to keep policy coherent.

Typically, cabinet policy-making in the 1930s worked by logrolling various army and navy concerns, producing "compromises [that] often led to makeshift and inconsistent national policies."[165] The develop-

160. Barnhart, *Japan Prepares*, 18.
161. Ibid., 104–5.
162. Berger, *Parties*, 79, 154–56, 265; Crowley, *Japan's Quest*, 361–62; Barnhart, *Japan Prepares*, 94, 106.
163. Berger, *Parties*, 231–37.
164. Crowley, *Japan's Quest*, 244, quoting remarks of July 1936.
165. Berger, *Parties*, 81, also 6–7; more generally, Crowley, *Japan's Quest*, 179–80; Barnhart, *Japan Prepares*, 36–38.

ment of cabinet documents laying out grand strategy directly reflects the contradictions inherent in this logrolling process. In October 1932, for example, a policy study reflecting army priorities proposed a three-point program, featuring the economic development of Manchukuo, the political decentralization of China, and naval arms control, to avoid provoking Britain and America. The navy, however, balked at the naval arms control provisions, insisting that Japan should aim to break out of the London Treaty when it came up for revision in 1936. The army, in turn, added language to the effect that the abrogation of the naval treaties would accelerate the formation of resistance to Japanese encroachments on China, requiring accelerated Japanese preparations for a military solution by 1936.[166] Likewise, the "Fundamental Principles" study of 1936 authorized the army to prepare for a war against the Soviet Union to be fought simultaneously with a naval war against the United States, while imports of strategic matériel continued unimpeded.[167]

These were straightforward logrolls, in which each of the participants prevailed on the one issue that mattered most to that organization. Arguably, either of the two services could have crafted a feasible, not too overextended strategy separately, but by logrolling their separate projects, they put Japan hopelessly into red ink. In this sense the logrolling dynamic was essential to explaining the overcommitted outcome.

Konoe's contribution to Japanese overextension was not a matter of simple logrolling. Though he co-opted many of the policy planks of the separate militarist factions, he did not do this to rule through a permanent policy of logrolled payoffs. Rather, he hoped to devise a creative synthesis under his own control, which in the long run would end the need for logrolling military interests. This was a coalition making dynamic that contributed to imperial overextension, but unlike logrolling its outcome cannot be simply reduced to the sum of the vote traders' concentrated interests. Indeed, this tactic occasionally required Konoe to take imperial gambles that were even more reckless than some of the military factions themselves advocated.

Civilian Elements of the Imperialist Coalition

Konoe's role points out the need to assess the part that nonmilitary groups may have played in making the imperialist coalition of the 1930s. Scholars have mentioned two civilian groups in this regard. First are the government bureaucrats. Like the military, they saw their

166. Crowley, *Japan's Quest*, 193–95.
167. Barnhart, *Japan Prepares*, 45. For other examples see Larson, "Foreign Policy Decisions," 30, 60, citing Herbert Feis, *The Road to Pearl Harbor* (Princeton, N.J., 1950), 86–87; and Butow, *Tojo*, 275.

power ebbing during the rise of Taisho democracy. Cabinets increasingly were dominated by party politicians rather than bureaucrats. If bureaucrats were to play a decisive political role, they would have to take part in party politics. Insider maneuvering among the *genro*, provincial cliques, military, and *zaibatsu* no longer sufficed. But after the Manchurian crisis of 1931, the demise of party-dominated cabinets gave bureaucrats a chance to wield unhampered administrative power. To some of them, therefore, an alignment with modernizing elements in the military to create a highly centralized bureaucratic apparatus that would place the Japanese economy on a rationalized war footing seemed attractive.[168] As Gordon Berger's recent study argues, "the military and bureaucratic elites were able to persuade many of their counterparts in other elites and much of the populace that Japan had entered a period of national crisis in her foreign and domestic affairs, which required an application of military and bureaucratic expertise the parties could not provide."[169]

The second civilian group comprised young, progressive intellectuals—journalists, professors, politicians. During the Taisho period, these reformers advanced a systematic critique of the failure of the old-style bureaucrats, *genro*, and provincial cliques to foster social justice and economic growth. To meet the challenge of the advanced democracies in a way consistent with traditional Japanese values, they argued, the old elites would have to make way for a new, reformist elite (themselves), that could tap the latent energies of the Japanese people.[170]

These young progressives came in two main varieties during the Taisho period—pro-Parliament democrats and authoritarian nationalists. Both criticized the old elites and sought a leading role for their own ideas in the name of the welfare of the masses. But beyond that, they parted company. Parliamentary democrats tended to be closer to the working class and more favorably inclined toward Shidehara's diplomacy and Wilsonian international principles. Authoritarian nationalists tended to be closer to military and bureaucratic modernizers and disdainful of Wilsonian hypocrisy. They sold reform in part as a way to head off the threat of working-class power, not to speed its arrival.[171]

But even the more nationalist of these Taisho civilian intellectuals fell

168. Robert Spaulding, "The Bureaucracy as a Political Force, 1920–1945," in Morley, *Dilemmas*, 33–80; Berger, *Parties*, 67–74; Duus, *Party Rivalry*, 42–82.

169. Berger, *Parties*, 32; and on Konoe, 79, 113–15, 265.

170. Minichiello, *Retreat*, introduction and chap. 1. For their antecedents in the late Meiji period, see Carol Gluck, *Japan's Modern Myths: Ideology in the Late Meiji Period* (Princeton, N.J., 1985). Note the parallel to the opportunistic, upwardly mobile German imperialists discussed in chapter 3.

171. Minichiello, *Retreat*, 18, 49, 52, passim; Oka, *Konoe*, 11.

far short of the military in their penchant for armed interventionism. For example, Nagai Ryutaro, later a major figure in militarist cabinets, worked satisfactorily as a key deputy in Shidehara's foreign ministry. Though irritated by sanctimonious, racist Anglo-Saxon imperialism, Nagai generally accepted the necessity for naval arms control and Shidehara's view that Japan should expand its influence through economic means.[172]

Thus progressive intellectuals were divided on the issue of a militant Japanese foreign policy, and even the more nationalist among them fell short of the military in their penchant for armed force. Once military faits accomplis made Taisho democracy and Shidehara diplomacy dead letters in any event, however, some progressive intellectuals like Nagai did not hesitate to take a role in forging the new political order. Both ideals and opportunism led them toward collaboration with army progressives of the Ishiwara variety.[173]

Whether this means that civilian progressives were a major independent force in the imperialist coalition is another matter. Figures like Nagai and Konoe prospered politically in the 1930s in large part because they were convenient as popular, respectable front men for the military.[174] Antimilitarist progressive intellectuals were forced into the political periphery, as Cassandra-like Minseito Diet members.[175] Civilian "reformers" who shared the military's approach to national renewal flourished in this environment; civilian proponents of a more democratic program of reform were pushed aside or repressed.[176]

As I argued above, sometimes the progressive civilians exacerbated Japanese expansionism, trying to outmilitary the military and thus regain civilian control. As Konoe told the last remaining *genro*, Saionji Kinmochi, civilians could regain power only by meeting the national problems that were pushing the military into politics.[177] And frequently this meant adopting the military's policies.

Usually, however, Konoe and Saionji acted as a brake on the military's expansionist schemes, albeit ineffectually. Though Ishiwara was less warlike than Konoe in the China Incident, War Minister Sugiyama was more warlike, insisting on policies that Konoe felt would embroil Japan directly with America and Britain.[178] There was little Konoe could do to

172. Minichiello, *Retreat*, 78, 81.
173. Ibid., chap. 5.
174. Oka, *Konoe*, 27–28, 47; Minichiello, *Retreat*, 111.
175. Minichiello, *Retreat*, 109, contrasts the fate of Nagai, whose career prospered in league with the military, and Saito Takao, his former collaborator in the 1924 battle for universal suffrage, whose career foundered on opposition to military rule.
176. Ibid., 5, 111.
177. Oka, *Konoe*, 32.
178. Ibid., 54.

directly overrule Sugiyama. One of Konoe's attempts to negotiate with Chiang Kai-shek was derailed when the military arrested his diplomatic emissary![179] Eventually Konoe succeeded in ousting Sugiyama as war minister, but his replacement, General Itagaki Seishiro, whom Konoe chose because he was reputed to favor an early settlement of the Sino-Japanese conflict, quickly fell under the sway of his more militant subordinates.[180] Saionji's strategy, equally ineffectual, was simply to avoid provoking a direct confrontation with the military in the hope that a return to Shidehara diplomacy could be effected when the military somehow calmed down.[181]

In summary, civilians played a peripheral role in Japan's imperialist coalition of the 1930s. Some collaborated in the implementation of the military's plans; some participated in order to act as a modest braking mechanism; others were pushed aside. Their significance was not in the role they played in support of imperial expansion, but in their failure to play a strong role in opposing it. All of the main civilian groups—bureaucrats, intellectuals, and *zaibatsu*—were divided or ambivalent about the demise of Taisho democracy and the rise of imperial authoritarian rule. None had decisive interests in opposing the drift toward militarist adventurism.

Ideological Politics and Conceptual Blowback

Another explanation for why the logrollers failed to retreat from the precipice is that years of strategic mythmaking had so skewed Japanese perceptions that a clear-sighted appraisal of alternatives had become impossible. One way this myopia may have arisen was that elites confused each other about the costs and risks of various alternatives by systematically falsifying or withholding information. As I noted above, crucial calculations on the logistics of the southern advance were either falsfied or not done; accurate appraisals of the situation in Europe and America were suppressed; Young Turks withheld information from higher military authorities.[182] The foreign minister was apparently not informed that the war would begin with an attack on American territory at Pearl Harbor, so he had no opportunity to point out that this would undermine the prospect that America would become reconciled to Japanese expansion after a short war.[183] In another instance,

179. Ibid., 57; also 55.
180. Ibid., 73–75.
181. Ibid., 31; also Connors, *Emperor's Adviser*, chaps. 6 and 7.
182. For other examples, see Ike, *Japan's Decision*, 188–90.
183. Scott Sagan, "The Origins of the Pacific War," *Journal of Interdisciplinary History* 18 (Spring 1988): 916–17.

the army exaggerated the extent of the foreign military aid going to Chiang Kai-shek via Indochina in order to explain their inability to defeat him; as a consequence, the strategic value of the southern advance was overrated.[184]

Strategic falsifications were difficult to reverse without a loss of personal or organizational credibility. The navy in particular argued itself into a corner, contending that prospects for a war against the Anglo-Americans were good as long as the Soviets were not involved. These assertions trapped them into having to accept the southern advance, putting them on the slippery slope toward a war with America that they knew would be virtually unwinnable.[185] As Navy Minister Oikawa privately admitted in the fall of 1941, "If we were to say that we were not able to carry out operations against the United States, it would have meant that we had been lying to the Emperor."[186]

On the other hand, it seems unlikely that Tojo was unaware that the navy had exaggerated its self-confidence for reasons of bureaucratic politics.[187] Tojo, Konoe, and others had frank conversations about Japan's slim prospects in a long war with the United States.[188] Indeed, blowback from strategic mythmaking may have been most devastating not in making the Japanese confident about their chances of victory, but in making it impossible for them to conceive of a successful policy of retrenchment. Because Tojo believed the United States was out to dominate the entire Far East, he assumed that any concessions would lead America to increase its demands.[189]

Ideological blowback among the broader public had a less obvious role in decisions to gamble on war in 1941. Japanese leaders were much less influenced by radical mass opinion than Wilhelmine leaders had been in 1914, for example. Nonetheless, a policy of appeasement and retrenchment at that point would surely have discredited the military leadership that had for years trumpeted a policy of war and expansion. Social imperialism had been part of the military's standard operating procedure for decades, beginning with Saigo's 1873 plan to invade Korea, "a far-reaching scheme, which will divert abroad the attention of those who desire civil strife," as Saigo himself described it.[190] Ishiwara Kanji put forward a variation on this notion in May 1931, arguing that success in war was a prerequisite for reform, since it

184. Ikuhiko Hata, "Continental Expansion, 1905–1941," in Duus, *Cambridge History*, 6:308–9.
185. Barnhart, *Japan Prepares*, 211.
186. Marder, *Old Friends*, 177.
187. Larson, "Foreign Policy Decisions," 61; Butow, *Tojo*, 281–83.
188. Barnhart, *Japan Prepares*, 252.
189. Sagan, "Origins," 911–12.
190. Beasley, *Meiji*, 373.

"arouses and unites the public" under martial law.[191] Even the *genro* had found that retreating from imperialist rhetoric was not easy when the public decried the compromise peace after the Russo-Japanese War.[192] After three decades of accelerating mass political participation, military social imperialists might have found a retreat from the brink even harder to explain.[193]

CONCLUSIONS

Japanese overexpansion, rationalized by the usual repertoire of imperial myths, is best explained as a consequence of Japan's path to modernity, which gave the military a dominant role among Japanese interest groups and truncated the development of democratic forces that might have kept militarism in check. As predicted by the coalition politics theory, Japanese overexpansion was least egregious when Japanese politics were most unitary, under the Meiji *genro*, and when they were most democratic, in the Taisho period. Overexpansion was greatest when political decision making was reduced to logrolling among concentrated military cartels in the 1930s.

Some of Japan's imperial excesses can be explained simply as a result of the army's highjacking the state to its own ends. This perspective is insufficiently illuminating on its own, however. First, the military's interest in expansionism was spurred to a significant degree by the need to concoct a political ideology of autarkic empire as an antidote to the relative liberalism of Shidehara diplomacy and Taisho democracy. Second, logrolling led the army and navy into strategic overcommitments that were far more acute than either would have chosen separately. Konoe's attempts to regain civilian control by outimperializing the military were another pernicious effect of the coalition-making process. Finally, ideological blowback, the entrapment of Japanese elites in their own strategic deceptions, may have also played an important role.

Realist and cognitive theories hardly provide satisfactory alternative explanations. "Formative" lessons were shaped more by the social position of the persons drawing conclusions than by the events themselves. International pressures also provide an unsatisfactory explanation, since forces discrediting the Shidehara approach should have been more than outweighed by forces working against militaristic

---

191. Ogata, *Defiance*, 48–49.
192. Jansen, "Introduction," 185.
193. Saburo Ienaga, *The Pacific War, 1931–1945* (New York, 1978), chap. 2, documents the militarist and imperialist indoctrination to which the Japanese public had been subjected during the 1930s.

alternatives. Setting aside Japan's domestic pathologies, Japan could easily have solved its international economic and security problems in the middle and late 1930s through imperial retrenchment and a return to Shidehara diplomacy. Indeed, in March 1937 Ambassador Joseph Grew saw the Hayashi/Sato government as an attempt to do just that.[194] This attempt failed not primarily for international reasons, but because it contradicted the interests and ideas of Japan's dominant militarist elites. Thus it would be wrong to say that reckless imperialism was compelled by Japan's position in the international system.

Nonetheless, it is true that international events interacted with Japanese domestic structure in ways that favored militarist solutions. Western gunboat diplomacy helped ensure that the Meiji reforms would take on a military caste. At the end of the 1920s, depression and protectionism helped kill Taisho democracy. This outcome raises the question of how other powers might have acted differently to avoid triggering a militaristic Japanese reaction.

In the American State Department, Grew and Stanley Hornbeck debated in the late 1930s the tactics of how to do this. Grew argued that "moderates" in Japan could be helped by avoiding the imposition of American economic sanctions, whereas Hornbeck argued that American retreats would only increase the likelihood of war by proving that the militarists were right.[195] Late in the game, it is possible that no tactical combination would have worked, for intellectual and political reasons. Intellectually, once the paper tiger image was well established, the double whammy was in operation: any American policy or its opposite could be taken as a reason to expand. Politically, as Barnhart notes, attempts to use cleverly targeted threats and concessions to play on army-navy rivalry might simply have triggered an army coup d'état.[196]

A strategy with a greater probability of success would have had to be preventive. At the outset of the depression, keeping open American markets for Japanese silk and refraining from using American loans to steal Japan's share of the China market would have improved Shidehara's chances of staying in power. This insight, of course, was reflected in

194. Barnhart, *Japan Prepares*, 118.
195. Barnhart, *Japan Prepares*, 176–77; Irvine Anderson, *The Standard-Vacuum Company and United States East Asian Policy, 1933–1941* (Princeton, N.J., 1975), 121–22; Waldo Heinrichs, *American Ambassador: Joseph Grew* (Boston, 1966), 264–67.
196. Barnhart, *Japan Prepares*, 264–65. Conceivably, American acceptance of Japan's proposal to withdraw from Indochina in exchange for a free hand in China might have averted war, but this would have meant sacrificing a strategically useful ally to get an unsecured promise of good behavior in the future. Waldo Heinrichs, *Threshold of War* (New York, 1988), 154–59, 207–11. See also the discussion of options for compromising with the United States at the 6 September 1941, Imperial Conference in Ike, *Japan's Decision*, 135–36.

America's post-1945 foreign economic strategy. A stronger military deterrent would in this case probably have been counterproductive, since a deterrent force would have been indistinguishable from a capability for conquest. Any American naval and land forces that could have physically barred Japan from conquest on the Asian mainland would by their nature have left the Japanese home islands utterly vulnerable to blockade, if not invasion. In the long run, this presumably would have served only to feed the arguments of proponents of expansion and autarky.

In sum, domestic pathologies associated with late development put Japan on a path toward militarism and imperialism, a trajectory that was reinforced, though not dictated, by international circumstances and the policies of the other great powers.

[5]

Social Imperialism in
Victorian Britain

The grand strategy of Great Britain contrasts starkly with those of Germany and Japan. With the latter two, the puzzle is why they pursued hyperaggressive expansionism that led to their encirclement and conquest by the other great powers. In the British case the puzzle is for the most part the opposite. As Paul Kennedy has put it, "Why did the British Empire last so long?"[1] How did Britain manage to stay on the winning side in two world wars, while retaining its imperial holdings, decades after the relative decline of its industrial base?

Kennedy's answer is that Britain pursued a strategy opposite to Germany's and Japan's. That is, Britain divided its rivals through a strategy of selective appeasement.[2] As the Foreign Office's Eyre Crowe understood but his German contemporaries did not, Britain maintained its naval hegemony because it usually avoided threatening several great powers at the same time.[3] Moreover, British colonial administrators were usually forced to be cost conscious, paying for self-defense out of their own revenues and muting local resistance by means of indirect or collaborative rule.[4]

Occasionally Britain's grand strategists deviated from these principles of selective appeasement and self-financing, but when they drifted toward overextension, corrective measures were usually taken rather quickly. In the 1850s, for example, Prime Minister Palmerston flirted with the possibility of expanding the Crimean War into a global

1. Paul Kennedy, *Strategy and Diplomacy, 1870–1945* (London, 1984), chap. 8.
2. Ibid., chaps. 1 and 8.
3. Paul Kennedy, *The Rise and Fall of British Naval Mastery* (London, 1976), 157–58. Crowe was the author of a famous 1907 memorandum on the balance of power, reprinted in G. P. Gooch and Harold Temperley, *British Documents on the Origins of the War, 1898–1914,* vol. 3 (London, 1928).
4. Kennedy, *Strategy and Diplomacy,* 206–12.

struggle to permanently smash Russian power and establish British hegemony by direct force of arms, but he was turned back by more prudent cabinet colleagues.[5] Likewise, the "scramble for Africa" in the 1890s involved Britain in a costly land war in South Africa, provoked the enmity of every other major European power, and consequently undermined British naval dominance. As a result, British statesmen entered into a series of conciliatory ententes with their colonial opponents to reestablish their strategic position.[6] This chapter presents three central arguments about this pattern of limited overexpansion followed by sensible retrenchment.

First, overexpansion correlated with periods of imperial mythmaking, but relatively free public discourse on grand strategy helped keep imperial excesses in check. Imperialists like Palmerston, Benjamin Disraeli, and Joseph Chamberlain resorted to the full panoply of arguments for security through expansion: paper tiger images, bandwagon and domino theories, El Dorado myths, and the like. In contrast to the experience of Germany and Japan, however, anti-imperial arguments were also prominently articulated by figures like Richard Cobden, William Gladstone, and J. A. Hobson. Under the close intellectual scrutiny of open debate, most important statesmen avoided taking extreme positions on the spectrum of strategic ideology, and their stances shifted over time in response to new evidence.

Second, Britain's strategic thinking was on the whole more clear-eyed than that of Germany and Japan because of differences in Britain's domestic political structure. Britain's pattern of early industrialization and early democratization worked against development of the kind of narrowly self-interested imperialist cartels that logrolled to produce overexpansion in Germany and Japan. The role of English landowners in capitalizing small-scale industry created a commercial-agricultural elite with diffuse interests and mobile capital, capable of taking the long view on most strategic and economic issues. This oligarchy, which dominated the British cabinet well into the twentieth century, injected a unitary element into British politics, acting as a check "from above" on imperialist cartels and coalition makers. At the same time, the democratic element in the British political structure acted for the most part as a moderating force, keeping the oscillations between Gladstone and Disraeli, for example, within a relatively narrow range.[7]

5. Winfried Baumgart, *The Peace of Paris 1856* (Santa Barbara, Calif., 1981), 17.

6. George W. Monger, *The End of Isolation: British Foreign Policy, 1900–1907* (London, 1963), esp. 114; C. C. Eldridge, *Victorian Imperialism* (Atlantic Highlands, N.J., 1978), 211, 215; A. P. Thornton, *The Imperial Idea and Its Enemies* (London, 1966), 109–11.

7. The latter argument is advanced by Michael Doyle, *Empires* (Ithaca, N.Y., 1986), 296.

Third, domestic structure can also explain those periods when Britain teetered on the brink of strategic overextension—periods when the Victorian political system was most cartelized and thus most resembled Wilhelmine Germany. Most notably, this happened at two points in Victorian Britain's cycle of industrial development: during Britain's most rapid social and economic changes in the middle of the nineteenth century, and at the beginning of its relative industrial decline in the 1890s.[8]

In making these points, I will focus disproportionately on the period of Palmerston's social imperialism before and during the Crimean War. I chose this focus for several reasons. First, the Palmerston period is a hard case for the coalition politics theory. It shows that domestic forces can explain not only the obvious cases of German and Japanese overexpansion, but also interludes of overexpansion in cases where domestic political pathologies are more subtle and transitory. If the theory of coalition politics can explain the nuances of imperial strategy better than Realist and cognitive theories even when coalition effects are comparatively weak, this will demonstrate its explanatory power and broad applicability especially well. Though the main lesson of the British and American "early developer" cases is their difference from the German and Japanese "late developer" pattern, an important secondary lesson is that coalition dynamics can produce a lesser brand of overexpansion even in these more moderate cases. Treating the Palmerston period in some detail will help to establish this point.

Second, the Palmerston period highlights the effects of industrialization on social structure and strategic ideology and thus helps validate the timing and character of a state's industrialization as a worthy theoretical point of departure. Third, the analysis of Palmerston's social imperialism is original in many respects and consequently requires a fairly detailed treatment of a relatively short period to substantiate the argument. Finally, from the standpoint of contemporary American readers, the cautionary tale of an essentially moderate imperial power occasionally flirting with overexpansion may provide salutary lessons.

8. This would be at stages two and four of the product cycle. See James Kurth, "The Political Consequences of the Product Cycle," *International Organization* 33 (Winter 1979): 1–34. Charles Kupchan, *The Vulnerability of Empire* (forthcoming), documents a third period of imperial overextension in the 1930s. Charles Bright, "Class Interest and State Policy in the British Response to Hitler," in Carole Fink, Isabel Hull, and MacGregor Knox, eds., *German Nationalism and the European Response, 1890–1945* (Norman, Okla., 1985), 207–46, esp. 238, notes that this was a period of increasing dependency of British investment and trade on the formal empire. James Neidpath, *The Singapore Naval Base* (Oxford, 1981), chronicles the lobbying of military bureaucracies for the maintenance of imperial commitments. Thus an interest group or cartelization explanation for this period of overextension seems plausible, though I do not attempt to develop one here.

PALMERSTON'S BID FOR HEGEMONY

The decades between 1830 and 1860 witnessed "an extraordinary assertion of British power in relation to every state on the Asian mainland," in the words of a recent student of the Anglo-Russian Great Game. "By 1860 the British had fought and defeated the Russians, the Chinese, the Egyptians, the Persians, the Afghans, the Burmese, the Baluchis of Sind, and the Sikhs. . . . They had forced on Russia and China, the only other great powers in Asia, treaties which limited their rulers' freedom of action in humiliating fashion. In terms of power politics it was an impressive record."[9]

Much of this expansion and war making was quite rational: its costs were fairly low, and its economic benefits were often high. Precisely in these years, rapid industrialization was making imperial expansion necessary and possible for Britain. Industrialization increased the gap between Britain's power and that of other states, making conquest easier at the same time as it created a need to exploit the nation's industrial innovations on a larger, more efficient scale. Partially excluded by protective tariffs from European markets, British manufactures, notably textiles, had to be marketed to Asian customers in order to maintain the industrial boom and to pay for imported food for a rising urban population. By midcentury, India and the Ottoman empire, including Egypt and the Danube area, were each buying more textiles from Manchester than was Europe.[10] At the same time, the opening up of Danube grain export markets exerted downward pressure on food prices in Britain, which was importing one-fourth of its bread grains by 1851.[11]

It is difficult to disagree with those economic historians who judge that military force was necessary to open—and keep open—most of these Asian import and export markets.[12] India's own textile industry had been so competitive in the 1790s that Manchester demanded tariff

9. David Gillard, *The Struggle for Asia, 1828–1914* (London, 1977), 43.

10. Arthur Redford, *Manchester Merchants and Foreign Trade, 1794–1858* (Manchester, 1934), 199, app. B; P. J. Cain and A. G. Hopkins, "The Political Economy of British Expansion Overseas, 1750–1914," *Economic History Review*, ser. 2, 33 (November 1980): 463–90, esp. 478; D. A. Farnie, *The English Cotton Industry and the World Market, 1815–1896* (Oxford, 1979); Albert H. Imlah, *Economic Elements in the Pax Britannica* (Cambridge, Mass., 1958); Malcolm Yapp, *Strategies of British India* (Oxford, 1980), 3.

11. Asa Briggs, *Victorian People*, rev. ed. (Chicago, 1970), 21. By 1851, Ottoman grain exports to Britain equaled those of Russia. For background, see Vernon John Puryear, *International Economics and Diplomacy in the Near East, 1834–1853* (Hamden, Conn., 1969), esp. 127–30. See also David Urquhart, *Turkey and Its Resources* (London, 1833).

12. Cain and Hopkins, "Political Economy," 479. Paul Kennedy, *The Realities behind Diplomacy* (London, 1981), 19, says that "the economic arm and the fighting arm of the country were now mutually supporting organs of a grand strategy predicated upon commercial expansion, colonial exploitation, domestic stability, and insular security."

protection against imports of Indian cotton goods.[13] Though technological change made Manchester more competitive by the 1840s, the Indians, like the continental Europeans, could have raised protectionist barriers against British textiles had India retained its political sovereignty. Likewise in China, Britain used gunboat diplomacy to keep the door open to opium imports from India, by which Calcutta earned the funds to pay for British textiles and for Indian defense.[14] British military power also kept Turkey and the Danube out of the hands of protectionist Russia and, as a quid pro quo for defending the Turkish sultan against his rebellious Egyptian vassal, broke down nontariff barriers to expanded trade.[15] Lord Palmerston was characteristically succinct in stating the problem and the cure: "The rivalship of European manufactures is fast excluding our productions from the markets of Europe, and we must unremittingly endeavour to find in other parts of the world new vents for the produce of our industry. The world is large enough . . . to afford a demand for all we can manufacture; but it is the business of the Government to open and to secure the roads for the merchant."[16]

British assessments of the advisability of imperial expansion normally paid close attention to the balance of economic costs and benefits. Influenced by the principles of utilitarian political economists, "who demanded the application of the measuring-rod of utility in all matters connected with government and public finance,"[17] the British government sought to ensure that the costs of empire were not disproportionate to the benefits.

Some conquests had no direct economic payoff but were justified as measures to secure the communications and frontiers of the real economic assets like India. Although some of these defense-in-depth operations seem in retrospect to be of dubious necessity, in general British imperial expansion in this period met rational cost-benefit criteria.[18]

13. Redford, *Manchester Merchants*, 109–10.

14. D. K. Fieldhouse, *Economics and Empire* (London, 1973), 212–15; Michael Greenberg, *British Trade and the Opening of China, 1800–42* (Cambridge, 1951); G. S. Graham, *Great Britain and the Indian Ocean, 1810–50: A Study in Maritime Enterprise* (Oxford, 1967), 294–305.

15. Vernon John Puryear, *England, Russia, and the Straits Question* (1931; Hamden, Conn., 1965).

16. Charles Webster, *The Foreign Policy of Lord Palmerston, 1830–1841* (New York, 1969), 2:750–51, quoting Foreign Minister Palmerston's letter to Lord Auckland, 22 January 1841.

17. J. B. Conacher, *The Aberdeen Coalition, 1852–1855* (Cambridge, 1968), 59. For example, Richard Cobden argued against increasing the naval budget by showing that naval patrols in certain waters cost more than the value of the trade they protected. Christopher J. Bartlett, *Great Britain and Sea Power, 1815–1853* (Oxford, 1963), 261.

18. For example, Yapp, *Strategies*, 335, 341–43, shows the bogus nature of arguments justifying the invasion of Afghanistan in 1838 as a cost-effective security strategy.

For example, India was required to pay for the bulk of its immediate defense needs out of internal resources. Likewise, a navy sufficient to provide global command of the sea was a bargain at £7 million a year, compared with Manchester's £54 million textile export market.[19]

The Crimean War, however, was not cheap at £70 million, compared with an annual state budget that rarely exceeded £50 million in the preceding years. The siege of Sebastopol was especially costly given the tenuous connection between this military operation and any enduring imperial benefits.[20] Nonetheless, war expenses did not noticeably drain the British economy, which was entering its most prosperous decades. Half of the expense was covered immediately through a supplementary income tax: William Gladstone, the chancellor of the exchequer, held that making people pay war expenses on a current account basis and not through long-term loans "is a salutary and wholesome check, making them feel what they are about, and making them measure the cost of the benefit upon which they may calculate."[21]

Part of what is to be explained about British imperialism, then, is how the British were able to avoid the temptations of overexpansion: why, unlike some other imperial powers, they were able to extricate themselves from quagmires on the "turbulent frontier"; how they maintained sufficient restraint to avoid provoking a balancing coalition; and what made them relatively good learners about the location of the cost-benefit equilibrium.

This, however, is only part of the picture. Recent historians have argued that during the Crimean War Palmerston came very close to discarding that sense of proportion in grand strategy, embarking on a quixotic world war to dismember the Russian empire, and seeking to establish global British hegemony on its ruins.

To the Brink of Unlimited War?

The "usual view" of the Crimean War portrays it as a limited conflict intended to contain Russian expansion into an area threatening the security of India, to preserve the balance of power in Europe, and to

19. Bartlett, *Great Britain*, 339; Kennedy, *Rise and Fall*, 172; Redford, *Manchester Merchants*, app. B. Between 1830 and 1850, cotton provided about 45 percent of Britain's exports. Between 1840 and 1860, the cotton textile industry accounted for 10 percent of national income (7 percent of value added, once the value of the imported raw cotton is deducted). Farnie, *English Cotton Industry*, 9–11, 24, 91.

20. These war expenditures might be judged in part against the value of trade with the Danube area, which the war helped to secure. This trade never amounted to more than a few million pounds a year. Puryear, *England*, 118–23; P. J. Cain, *Economic Foundations of British Overseas Expansion* (London, 1980), 32.

21. Olive Anderson, *A Liberal State at War* (New York, 1967), 195, 201; Conacher, *Aberdeen Coalition*, 59.

maintain that balance through a new, liberal Concert of Europe based on the Anglo-French alliance.[22] Moreover, all the main actors in the 1853 Russo-Turkish crisis have been portrayed as basically risk averse and limited in their aims. In this traditional view, the confrontation escalated out of control owing to a tangle of misperceptions and diplomatic mistakes, dubbed "bluffs and blunders" in the historical literature.[23]

In particular, Prime Minister Aberdeen's conciliatory stance toward Russia, coupled with tensions in the Anglo-French relationship, led Tsar Nicholas to think he could safely occupy Ottoman provinces along the lower Danube, holding them as a lever to extract Turkish acceptance of Russia's predominant position in the region.[24] Britain found it difficult to design a measured response, owing to divisions within the cabinet, an enflamed public opinion, and a Turkish ally who saw a golden opportunity to drag Britain into a war on Constantinople's behalf.[25]

Once the war was under way, military victories were needed to satisfy the aroused public and, later, to justify the sunk costs of the campaign. Since Russia voluntarily withdrew from the Danube principalities to appease Austria, the original object of the war was achieved even before British and French armies arrived.[26] Britain and France consequently decided to aim their attack at the Crimean peninsula and the Sebastopol naval base there. Though it was far from clear that the strategic and diplomatic benefits of this operation outweighed its costs, it was felt that the allied armies could not just stand on the defensive, doing nothing while a peace was negotiated on the basis of the status quo ante. Domestic political expectations of victories, as well as the need to punish the aggressor to deter future attempts, demanded more active measures.[27] Once Sebastopol fell, there had been enough of a victory to satisfy the home front and enough punishment to teach Russia a lesson. The way was thus clear for an agreement curtailing Russian naval power in the Black Sea and forcing the renunciation of Russian aims in the Balkans and against Turkey.

---

22. Paul Schroeder, *Austria, Great Britain, and the Crimean War* (Ithaca, 1972), 400; Gavin Burns Henderson, *Crimean War Diplomacy* (Glasgow, 1947), 11.

23. Ann Pottinger Saab, *The Origins of the Crimean Alliance* (Charlottesville, Va., 1977), 155–57; Saab's introduction to Baumgart, *Peace of Paris*, ix–xiv.

24. John Shelton Curtiss, *Russia's Crimean War* (Durham, N.C., 1979), 62–63; Saab, *Origins*, 13, 52; A. M. Zaionchkovskii, *Vostochnaia Voina* (Saint Petersburg, 1908–13), 357–58, 603–4.

25. Saab, *Origins*, 157; Conacher, *Aberdeen Coalition*, chaps. 7–11.

26. Richard Smoke, *War: Controlling Escalation* (Cambridge, Mass., 1977), 151.

27. Norman Rich, *Why the Crimean War?* (Hanover, N.H., 1985), 172–73; G. P. Gooch, *The Later Correspondence of Lord John Russell* (London, 1925), 2:199, 27 March 1855; Conacher, *Aberdeen Coalition*, 441, quoting Palmerston: "Small results will not do after our great exertions."

Britain and France were unable in the long run to enforce this agreement, which extended their influence beyond the equilibrium point between their power and Russia's.[28] Russia took advantage of the Franco-Prussian War of 1870–71 to renounce the naval clauses of the treaty, and in 1877–78 it mounted another military campaign to roll back Turkey in the Balkans.[29] But taking a more positive view of the accomplishments of the Crimean War from the British standpoint, the conflict did temporarily weaken Russia—or at least demonstrate its inherent weakness—so that the political liberalization of Europe could go forward without the threat of Russian intervention along the lines of 1848.[30]

This traditional account of the Crimean War as a limited defense of the balance of power, complicated by "bluffs and blunders," is not so much wrong as incomplete. A recent wave of historical research has argued that this interpretation underestimates the extent to which key British leaders, in particular Lord Palmerston, seized on the Russo-Turkish crisis of 1853 as an opportunity to overturn the world balance of power, in hopes of ushering in a period of British global hegemony and shoring up a pseudoliberal status quo at home.[31]

Although this view remains controversial, the evidence in support of it is extensive. As early as the 1830s, Foreign Secretary Palmerston had entertained the idea of a decisive war as the solution to Russian geopolitical competition. "The fact is that Russia is a great humbug," he wrote to his brother in 1835, "and that if England were fairly to go to work with her, we should throw her back half a century in one campaign."[32] Though neither Palmerston nor Britain's other leaders actively sought a hegemonic war in 1853, once the war was on Palmerston immediately began to urge ambitious war aims. In a

---

28. Cobden had foreseen during the abortive 1855 peace talks that Russia could not be trusted to adhere to its promise to forgo a Black Sea fleet and that in the long run Britain and France would lack the power or will to enforce it. Nicholas C. Edsall, *Richard Cobden, Independent Radical* (Cambridge, Mass., 1986), 278.

29. A. J. P. Taylor, *The Struggle for Mastery in Europe, 1848–1918* (1954; London, 1971), 215, 228–54.

30. Kingsley Martin, *The Triumph of Lord Palmerston* (1924; London, 1963), 27.

31. These domestic arguments are not fully developed, however. For example, Saab, in her introduction to Baumgart, *Peace of Paris*, xiv, says that "Baumgart reveals some leanings towards the 'primacy of domestic politics school.'" Richard Shannon, *The Crisis of Imperialism, 1865–1915* (London, 1974), also stresses the domestic connection, though he treats only the postwar period. Schroeder, *Austria*, 11–12, 32–33, 119–21, 246–48, discusses the domestic setting of British policy during the Crimean War. Taylor, *Struggle for Mastery*, 59–61, is an earlier work that anticipates some of the revisionist arguments.

32. H. L. Bulwer, *Life of Henry John Temple, Viscount Palmerston* (London, 1871–74), 3:5, reproduces Palmerston's letter of 10 March 1835, also quoted in Harold N. Ingle, *Nesselrode and the Russian Rapprochement with Britain, 1836–1844* (Berkeley, Calif., 1976), 116.

memorandum circulated to other cabinet members in March 1854, Palmerston described his "beau ideal of the result of the war." He envisioned Russian territorial concessions in the Baltic to Sweden and Prussia; the creation of an independent Poland; the cession of the Crimea, Circassia (on the eastern shore of the Black Sea), and Georgia to Turkey; and Austrian control of the Danube principalities.[33]

A year later Palmerston, now prime minister, warned that "Russia has not yet been beat enough to make peace possible.... We shall find all our steadiness and skill required to avoid being drawn into a peace which would disappoint the just expectations of the country, and leave unaccomplished the real objects of the war."[34] In particular, Palmerston wrote to his brother that he foresaw "a danger of peace" after the fall of Sebastopol.[35] Far greater defeats would have to be imposed on Russia to weaken it sufficiently and to establish a *cordon sanitaire* to bar future expansion.[36]

After Sebastopol actually fell, Russia became more accommodating and France threatened to conclude a separate peace on moderate terms. Palmerston, agreeing with Foreign Secretary Clarendon that the war would have to be continued for another year to secure the desired "fresh territorial arrangements," suggested to the cabinet that Britain might have to fight on without France.[37] Palmerston informed the French that "the English nation would be delighted with a good peace which would assure the objects of the war; but rather than be dragged into signing a peace with inadequate terms, she would prefer to continue the war with no other allies than Turkey, and she feels wholly able to sustain the burden."[38]

This was not mere braggadocio. Palmerston took an active interest in preparations for expanding the war into the Baltic theater, chiding British naval authorities for their ambivalent assessment of the chances of destroying and capturing Russia's Kronstadt naval base through naval gunfire and amphibious landings.[39] To implement this expansion

---

33. Palmerston wrote: "Such results it is true could be accomplished only by a combination of Sweden, Prussia and Austria, with England, France, and Turkey, and such results presuppose great defeats of Russia. But such results are not impossible and should not be wholly discarded from our thoughts." Gooch, *Later Correspondence of Lord John Russell*, 2:160–61. Lansdowne's reaction was to decline comment on such hypothetical notions. Aberdeen saw this as a plan for a thirty years' war. Donald Southgate, *"The Most English Minister"* (New York, 1966), 346.

34. Southgate, *Most English Minister*, 384.

35. Baumgart, *Peace of Paris*, 14.

36. Ibid., 13, 14; Rich, *Why the Crimean War?* 158–60, 172–74.

37. Baumgart, *Peace of Paris*, 14, 32; Lytton Strachey and Roger Fulford, eds., *The Greville Memoirs* (London, 1938), vii, 170. The cabinet rejected Palmerston's proposal.

38. Southgate, *Most English Minister*, 385.

39. British Museum Add. MS. 48579, 122. Palmerston, for example, forwarded an

of the conflict, preparations were made to construct 150 steam gunboats.[40] Clarendon characterized these measures as "preparations such as there has been no instance of before in the history of this country."[41]

One historian has recently concluded that "if Palmerston had had the power of a Russian tsar, he undoubtedly would have opted for war" to be continued on a broader scale throughout 1856.[42] "I suspect," opined one of Palmerston's contemporaries, "Palmerston would wish the war to glide imperceptibly into a war of nationalities, as it is called, but would not like to profess it openly now."[43] In expanding the war, he might have received strong backing from the press and "public opinion," as expressed, for example, in the London *Times*' view that the fall of Sebastopol was merely "a preliminary operation."[44] By the latter stages of the war, newspapers in the industrial cities of the Midlands were proclaiming that the "war will probably give us a better route to India via Syria and Mesopotamia. All Asia lies before us."[45]

The revisionists' account further contends that Palmerston's wider war would have had disastrous consequences, harming Britain's geopolitical position through overextension. They point out, for example, that Napoleon III apparently hoped to use a "war of nationalities" against Russia as an opportunity for France to expand in the Rhineland, using Prussia's allegedly pro-Russian policy as an excuse for attacking it.[46] Thus, excessively diminishing one of Britain's foes might only strengthen another excessively. Moreover, the more Russia was reduced, the more likely it was that allies would drop out of Britain's

---

unencouraging memo from the Admiralty to the war minister, remarking, "I should hope that our gun boats would be more than a match for those of the Russians, and if our floating batteries are really shot proof, as is said, they will surely give us an advantage over everything Russian," including shore batteries.

40. Baumgart, *Peace of Paris*, 7. James Phinney Baxter, *The Introduction of the Ironclad Warship* (Cambridge, Mass., 1933), 72–73, 76, describes plans in the fall of 1854 to build forty gunboats, floating batteries, and other armored vessels for use in the campaign of 1855, noting also the expectation that Kronstadt and Sebastopol would both fall under their barrage.

41. In Parliament on 31 January 1856, quoted in Herbert Maxwell, ed., *Life and Letters of the Fourth Earl of Clarendon* (London, 1913), 2:116.

42. Baumgart, *Peace of Paris*, 33.

43. Ibid., 82n.49; Strachey and Fulford, *Greville Memoirs*, 7:173, 6 December 1855.

44. Baumgart, *Peace of Paris*, 31; Briggs, *Victorian People*, chap. 3.

45. Briggs, *Victorian People*, 66, quoting the Sheffield and Rotherham *Independent*, January 1855.

46. Baumgart, *Peace of Paris*, 17. Austen Henry Layard, "The Results and Prospects of the War," *Quarterly Review* 195 (December 1855): 279–80, seems almost to welcome a French war with Prussia and Austria, who "will have to pay the penalty which history teaches us has been inflicted upon those nations which have not had the wisdom or the courage to throw the weight of their strength and influence boldly into the scale when called upon to engage in a war of principles."

camp and adhere to Russia's. If Palmerston were to pursue the dismemberment of Russia, America showed signs of throwing its weight into the scales against Britain.[47]

In the revisionist view, only "checks and balances" in the British cabinet prevented Palmerston from exploiting jingoistic public opinion in pursuit of a disastrous, almost Wilhelmine grasping for world power.[48] Not only Gladstone but even the usually sympathetic Clarendon complained that an unrealistic Palmerston "is perpetually making new maps of Europe, but that is mere child's play unless he can adapt his means to his ends, and I am sure that Austria, without whom we can achieve no great inland things, will never assist us in the dismemberment of Russia or the resuscitation of Poland."[49]

What needs to be examined, consequently, is, first, how much of Britain's outward imperial thrust can be explained as a rational response to the real incentives and dangers of the international environment; second, what explains those imperial excesses that cannot be explained in rational terms; and third, how Britain learned to pull back from those excesses.

Palmerston as Realist: A Policy of Containment?

A Realist defense of Palmerston's grand strategy would argue that much of Britain's expansion in this period directly paid for itself in economic terms and that the rest was necessary to contain the expansion of Russian power, which threatened important British economic assets and the general balance of power. Indeed, Palmerston's private and diplomatic correspondence argued in these terms. Toward the end of the Crimean War, for example, he reminded Clarendon that "whatever the conditions of the peace may be, the Russian government will set to work the moment peace is concluded to . . . redeem by encroachments on the weak the position and power which she will have lost by the assaults of the strong, and that by endeavoring to bar her up on all sides as well and as much as we can, we are taking the best means of avoiding future collisions."[50]

---

47. Baumgart, *Peace of Paris*, 17; Frank A. Golder, "Russo-American Relations during the Crimean War," *American Historical Review* 31 (April 1926): 462–76; Alan Dowty, *The Limits of American Isolation: The United States and the Crimean War* (New York, 1971), 71. Clarendon recognized that if Britain sought a decisive victory against Russia, "we should have had all Europe against us at once and the United States soon." E. D. Steele, "Palmerston's Foreign Policy and Foreign Secretaries, 1855–1865," in Keith Wilson, ed., *British Foreign Secretaries and Foreign Policy* (London, 1987), 66.

48. Baumgart, *Peace of Paris*, 33.

49. Gooch, *Later Correspondence*, 2:164, Clarendon to Russell, 7 May 1854.

50. British Museum Add. MS. 48579, 73–74, to Clarendon, 25 September 1855.

Thus a treaty linking Britain with Sweden would be "part of a long line of circumvallation to confine the future extension of Russia even if the events of the war should not enable us to drive her outposts in, at any part of her present circumference."[51] Likewise, the liberation of the Black Sea littoral was part of this strategy of containment through rollback: "Georgia and Circassia taken away would be a better security than a large money payment. . . . If you take away from her those advanced posts no money can enable her to regain them except by war, which the loss of them disables her from waging with the same advantage."[52] Settling for more limited aims "would be only like turning a burglar out of your house, to break in again at a more fitting opportunity."[53]

Seen in this light, Palmerston was simply trying to achieve a marginally better containment perimeter. In November 1855, for example, Palmerston told Clarendon that Russia "expects that next year Cronstadt will be destroyed and Petersburg menaced and possibly Finland invaded . . . and that she will be out of Georgia and Circassia."[54] To avoid this outcome, Russia might be willing to agree to acceptable terms, such as the elimination of her Black Sea fleet and bases. Still, "this may or may not be."[55] If so, the credible threat to continue the war would be diplomatically useful; if not, Britain would have to continue the war and actually accomplish what Russia then only feared.

In fact, the most recent study of Russian policy points out that Tsar Nicholas wanted peace in 1856 for precisely the reasons that made Palmerston reluctant to end the war: another year of combat would surely ruin the army, navy, and treasury and might lead to the loss of many of Russia's peripheral territories.[56] Thus even Palmerston's relatively ambitious aims were not on their face unattainable. Moreover, when he realized that French and Austrian support for a wider war could not be obtained, his correspondence with Clarendon reveals his gradual acceptance of a less than ideal peace.[57] As Palmerston admitted to his antiwar cabinet colleague Gladstone, "If by a stroke of the wand I could effect in the map of the world changes which I could wish, I am

51. Ibid.; see also Rich, *Why the Crimean War?* 158.
52. British Museum Add. MS. 48579, 79, to Clarendon, 9 October 1855.
53. To Russell, 26 May 1854, quoted in Rich, *Why the Crimean War*, 109. Note the same argument and imagery in Samuel Huntington, "Conventional Deterrence and Conventional Retaliation in Europe," *International Security* 8 (Winter 1983–84): 32–56.
54. Kronstadt was Russia's Baltic fleet base near Saint Petersburg. British Museum Add. MS. 48579, 82–83, 23 November 1855.
55. Ibid.
56. John Shelton Curtiss, *Russia's Crimean War* (Durham, N.C., 1979), 499–501.
57. Add. MS. 48580, 8–11, 28 and 29 February 1856.

sure that I could make arrangements far more conducive than some of the present ones to the Peace of Nations [and] the Progress of Civilization . . . , but I am not so destitute of common sense as not to be able to compare ends and means."[58] In short, it was characteristic of Palmerston to talk big but act within limits.[59] Realists might contend that he was aggressive and ambitious in pursuit of the containment of Russia but not insensitive to cost and feasibility.

Nonetheless, this is far from the whole story. Though Palmerston's strategic conceptions were not as reckless as the revisionists sometimes portray them, they often fit geopolitical reality poorly, exaggerating the advantages of a policy of security through expansion. Palmerston and other proponents of aggressive containment of Russia based their policy on an exaggerated paper tiger image, erroneous domino theories, and unwarranted assumptions of offensive advantage. Not only were these ideas largely incorrect, but their contorted logic suggests they were justifications for a policy that had been adopted on other grounds. To refute the view that Britain's aggressive strategy of containment was simply a Realist response to international conditions, I will describe the strategic beliefs of Palmerston and other participants in Britain's debates on grand strategy, pointing out where their views distorted actual conditions and where their logic smacks of rationalization.

THE SPECTRUM OF STRATEGIC IDEOLOGIES

Interventionists like Palmerston vied with anti-interventionists like Richard Cobden for the domination of early Victorian discourse on grand strategy. Those at the interventionist pole of the debate, notably an influential group of articulate Near East and South Asia specialists, invoked all the familiar rationales in making their case. Palmerston's strategic pronouncements were usually quite similar to those of this group, though his behavior was more pragmatic and complex than his terse strategic obiter dicta suggest. Their noninterventionist opponents ranged from free-trade ideologues on the left, like Cobden and John Bright, to Tories like Lord Aberdeen, who believed that conciliatory policies toward all the great powers would help recreate a legitimist Concert of Europe and dampen the pan-European movement for revolutionary political change. The strategic conceptions of the anti-interventionists provide a mirror image of the usual imperial myths.

58. Herbert F. C. Bell, *Lord Palmerston* (Hamden, Conn., 1966), 2:114, to Gladstone, 6 February 1855.
59. Kenneth Bourne and Roger Bullen have suggested to me that Baumgart's evidence must be evaluated in this light. Interviews, December 1986.

They held a prickly hedgehog image of the adversary and believed in balancing and quagmire theories.

The strategic arguments advanced by both the interventionists and their opponents were fundamentally ideological in character. Again and again, participants in early and mid-Victorian strategic debates cooked their arguments to rationalize predetermined conclusions, often to further a domestic political agenda. These rationalizations took on a life of their own as target groups came to believe the strategic propaganda and as strategic mythology became the necessary political basis for governing coalitions.

The Ideology of Aggressive Containment

The case for an assertive British strategy in the Near East and South Asia was put most coherently and effectively by a closely cooperating group of regional experts, most notably John McNeill, David Urquhart, and George de Lacy Evans in the 1830s and Austen Henry Layard during the Crimean War.[60] Their ideas are of interest not only because their tightly argued views conveniently mark one pole in the debate, but also because of their great impact on public opinion. Spurred by Russia's expansion in Central Asia, its wars of encroachment on Persia and Turkey in the late 1820s, and the 1833 Russo-Turkish Treaty of Unkiar Skelessi, which seemed to ratify Russian political dominance at Constantinople, these articulate regional specialists systematically set out to convince the British public, Parliament, and cabinet of the need for an offensive strategy of containment in the Near East. Attracting attention through a series of dramatic pamphlets and magazine articles, they were transformed overnight from impoverished civil servants at the outskirts of the empire to esteemed members of Parliament, diplomats, and protégés of the powerful.[61]

Cobden believed that Urquhart's propaganda had had a huge impact on public opinion, claiming that "one active mind has during the last two years materially influenced the tone of several of the newspapers and incessantly roused public opinion, through every accessible channel of the periodical press against Russia."[62] Urquhart's press cam-

60. Kenneth Bourne, *Palmerston: The Early Years, 1784–1841* (New York, 1982), 561.

61. Evans began writing because he needed the money. See Edward M. Spiers, *Radical General: Sir George de Lacy Evans* (Manchester, 1983), 16–18, 65. McNeill's first book was written with the express purpose of launching his political and diplomatic career. Palmerston, one of the ostensible targets of the book for being too soft on the Russians, helped set up introductions for McNeill's political bid. Florence Macalister, ed., *Memoir of the Rt. Hon. Sir John McNeill* (London, 1910), 175, 178. See also Gordon Waterfield, *Layard of Nineveh* (London, 1963), 91, 228, 233–34, 239; Yapp, *Strategies*, 202.

62. Edward Hughes, *The Development of Cobden's Economic Doctrines and His Methods of Propaganda* (Manchester, 1938), 1.

paign, said a later historian, led to an "otherwise inexplicable increase of attacks upon Russia" in the British Parliament and press.[63] One cabinet member concluded that Urquhart's threat-inflating propaganda was so widely accepted that "Even [Prime Minister] Melbourne himself seemed to think Russia might possibly send a fleet into the Channel and sweep our seas."[64] Palmerston thought Urquhart's pamphlets so important—and so extreme and inconvenient—that he arranged to send him on a diplomatic mission to Turkey just to get him out of England.[65]

Despite the obvious prominence of the Near East experts in the strategic debate of the 1830s, their arguments did not immediately carry the day. They received a mixed evaluation in the press and were adopted only selectively into Palmerston's own geopolitical thinking.[66] Palmerston's assertive but more subtle approach to containing Russian expansion was seen as pusillanimous by the expert publicists.[67]

Thus the greatest impact of the writings of the 1830s was not on immediate public policy decisions. Rather, its achievement was to make Russophobia and domino theorizing common and respectable elements in public discourse—in their milder forms, almost conventional wisdom by the 1850s. Layard, receiving an enthusiastic reception for his strategic arguments for an aggressive prosecution of the Crimean War, reaped what Urquhart, Evans, and McNeill had sown twenty years before.[68] And Palmerston could, whenever he found it convenient, draw on the reservoir of Russophobia that these writings had helped create.

The Russophobes' strategic ideology was a carefully crafted propaganda platform, aimed at developing rationalizations for a policy of aggressive containment. Both the internal character of the arguments and direct evidence of the authors' propagandistic intent suggest that the policy preference came first and the universally used strategic arguments were then brought out to justify it.

Russia as paper tiger. In the Russophobes' propaganda, notes one historian, "Russia, as becomes a villain, is diabolic, clever, yet some-

---

63. John Howes Gleason, *The Genesis of Russophobia in Great Britain* (1950; New York, 1972), 183; David Ross, *Opinions of the European Press on the Eastern Question* (London, 1836), ix, 133.

64. John Cam Hobhouse, *Recollections of a Long Life*, vol. 5 (New York, 1968), 39, diary entry for 17 June 1835; S. Maccoby, *English Radicalism* (London, 1935), 369.

65. Bourne, *Palmerston*, 562–63.

66. Yapp, *Strategies*, 202.

67. Ross, *Opinions*, xii; Richard Shannon, "David Urquhart and the Foreign Affairs Committees," in Patricia Hollis, ed., *Pressure from Without in Early Victorian England* (London, 1974), 239–61.

68. Gleason, *Genesis*, 277.

how easy to defeat by courage and a fleet."[69] Russia is portrayed as a unitary, rational actor with unlimited aims of conquest, but fortunately averse to risk and weak if stopped soon enough.[70]

Russia had succeeded in self-aggrandizement only because other powers had not stood firm against it, they argued. "With the exception of Napoleon himself, Russia has effected more conquests than all the European states together in modern times, yet her aggressions never have produced a coalition against her," say McNeill and Urquhart. "Her victims have been left without sympathy or support."[71] This is because Russia's diplomats bide their time and have "never pushed her successes in the East so far as to involve her in a contest with any of the great powers in Europe."[72] As American Cold War theorists of the "Bolshevik operation code" would put it, Russia "pushes to the limit" but "knows when to stop."[73] Moreover, the Russians understand that Britain's motives are strictly defensive, so in implementing a stalwart containment policy, Britain need not exercise any self-restraint to reassure them.[74]

Given this image of an implacable but risk averse expansionist foe, the obvious prescription is to stand firm. Here the argument of McNeill and Urquhart is uncannily like Thomas Schelling's application of the game of "Chicken" to nuclear diplomacy and like Kurt Riezler's brinkmanship theory. "Let us grant both [England and Russia] dread war equally," they postulate; "whichever country, therefore, makes an advance, or establishes a point, will secure the advantage of the other's dread of the . . . consequences. But Russia alone understands how those steps are to be made, and therefore this dread is turned solely to her account."[75] Like Schelling's Stalin or Khrushchev in the Berlin crises, Tsar Nicholas manipulates to his advantage the "last clear chance" to avoid disaster. An irrevocable commitment to stand firm is, for Britain or for America, the winning countermove.

Completing the paper tiger image, Russia is not just a risk averse

69. Martin, *Triumph*, 46.

70. John McNeill, *Progress and Present Position of Russia* (1936; London, 1954), preface to 3d ed., vi; John McNeill and David Urquhart, "The Diplomacy of Russia," *British and Foreign Review*, no. 1 (1835): 102–33, reprinted in Ross, *Opinions* (authorship of unsigned article as attributed by *Wellesley Index to Victorian Periodicals*, 3:77); Gleason, *Genesis*, 174.

71. McNeill and Urquhart, "Diplomacy," in Ross, *Opinions*, 347.

72. McNeill, *Progress*, preface to 3d ed., vi, 92–93.

73. Alexander George, "The Operational Code," in Erik Hoffmann and Frederick Fleron, *Conduct of Soviet Foreign Policy* (New York, 1980), 165–90, citing Nathan Leites, *A Study of Bolshevism* (Glencoe, Ill., 1953).

74. "No one accuses England of aggressive designs," say McNeill and Urquhart. "Why does she, therefore, parade her pacific dispositions, if not to excite the ambition of others?" "Diplomacy," in Ross, *Opinions*, 382.

75. Ibid., 388.

expansionist but also "more formidable in offensive than defensive warfare" and "less invulnerable in reality than in appearance" as long as Britain takes the offensive.[76] The reason for this approach is that the possession of Turkey and the Straits would "multiply the internal strength of Russia" through "the acquisition of the richest empire, of the most important position on the face of the earth, and of rendering available the military and financial resources hitherto expended in observing [i.e, guarding] large and extensive acquisitions which henceforward will be invulnerable."[77] But Russia knows that it is too weak to take Constantinople unless invited to do so by the European powers. This—and not any compunction about overturning the status quo—explains why Russia did not try to seize Constantinople when in 1829 "her troops were encamped on the Bosporus."[78] In short, like a proper paper tiger, "Russia is yet so weak, that she may be easily, very easily curbed; but will become, if not curbed, too powerful to be opposed."[79]

Subsequent historians and contemporary observers have noted that the view of Russia as strong in offense but weak in defense was the reverse of the truth. Lacking good ground transportation, a modern fleet, and a full treasury, Russia found it difficult to sustain the projection of military power over long distances. Slow to mobilize its forces, it could not capitalize on first-strike advantages. Seizing Constantinople would not change this, since Russia's offensive limitations were socioeconomic, not geographical.[80] Yet reports by British diplomats and military attachés who pointed out these facts were not publicly distributed or, if they were, had been altered to present more alarmist estimates.[81]

The domino theory. Along with the paper tiger image went the Russophobes' view of the tightly interconnected, domino character of the international system. They contended that if Russian expansion was allowed to make any more progress in the Near East or Central Asia, the result would be the loss of India, a major European war, and probably Russian hegemony in Eurasia.[82] For material and psychological reasons, victories in this region would tend to be cumulative and decisive in the hegemonic contest between Britain and Russia. Arguing for a maximal view of Britain's aims in the coming war against Russia,

76. George de Lacy Evans, *On the Designs of Russia* (London, 1828), 17.
77. McNeill and Urquhart, "Diplomacy," in Ross, *Opinions*, 349.
78. Ibid., 386.
79. Ibid., 365–66.
80. Curtiss, *Russia's Crimean War*, 35–36; Bartlett, *Great Britain*, 93–95, 103–5, 119.
81. Gleason, *Genesis*, 111–12, 278; Bartlett, *Great Britain*, 106; Bourne, *Palmerston*, 565.
82. McNeill, *Progress*, 96; Evans, *Designs of Russia*, passim.

Layard asked in 1853, "Are we prepared to take possession of Asia Minor, Mesopotamia, Syria, and Egypt, or can we allow them to pass into the hands of Russia and France? For we must do one or the other."[83]

The Russophobes believed that bandwagon psychology could be a potent offensive weapon for either Russia or Britain, depending on who exploited it more aggressively. Russia could invade Afghanistan to trigger revolts in British India and a pro-Russian bandwagon in neutral Persia.[84] To preempt this danger, the Russophobes argued that Britain should harness bandwagon psychology to its own ends, promoting a war of nationalities. In this scheme Britain would use its fleet to attack Russia's commerce, naval bases, and capital city, at the same time issuing a call for revolt by Finns, Poles, and other captive nationalities against their Russian masters.[85] The material and financial costs of such a war for world hegemony should be no worry, they argued: Rome's and Mohammed's victories had pyramided from a small initial investment, and so would Britain's.[86]

Though the Russophobes generally assume an offensive bandwagon psychology, sometimes they argue the reverse when their argument requires it. Urquhart, for example, is at pains to prove it is feasible to prop up Turkey as a bulwark against Russia. This requires showing that Turkey can defend itself against its rebellious Egyptian subjects, led by Mohammed Ali and his son Ibrahim. In this case Urquhart is pleased to argue in favor of effective guerrilla resistance against outside intervention.[87] In fact, local resistance to Egyptian occupation of Syria and Lebanon did work as Urquhart predicted, but then it also worked that way in Afghanistan, which neither the Russophobes nor Palmerston were inclined to foresee.[88]

The Thermopylae corollary. Accompanying the domino theme in their argument was its Thermopylae corollary.[89] For Urquhart the Caucasus was an "impassable barrier," easily defended if aid was given to the noble Circassian tribesmen; but once past that point, Russian expansion would ride an unstoppable wave.[90] For McNeill, the control of

83. Waterfield, *Layard*, 240; see also Gleason, *Genesis*, 174–75; Urquhart, *Turkey*, 220 ff.; Ross, *Opinions*, vii; McNeill, *Progress*, 107–8; Evans, *Designs of Russia*, 104–5.

84. McNeill, *Progress*, 104–9; see also Ross, *Opinions*, xi.

85. Evans, *Designs of Russia*, 167–200, esp. 188, 199.

86. Ibid., 220.

87. Urquhart, *Turkey*, 234.

88. Harold Temperley, *England and the Near East: The Crimea* (1936; Hamden, Conn., 1964), 118; Yapp, *Strategies*, 210.

89. I discuss the Thermopylae concept in chapter 1.

90. Gleason, *Genesis*, 179–80.

Constantinople was the "point beyond which force and violence are no longer necessary" for Russia, because her geopolitical position would become so strong that hegemony would be possible through the mere hint of force. Fortunately Turkey was not collapsing, according to "those who have observed her most nearly," and would not collapse if Britain acted forcefully in its defense.[91]

The clearest case of a falsified Thermopylae argument was the propaganda campaign in the 1830s in favor of a forward defense of India by invading Afghanistan. McNeill and other Russophobe area specialists invoked their supposed expertise to claim that such an expedition to keep Russia at bay would be cheap and effective and would forestall the need for spending millions of pounds on security forces inside India. The unsuccessful Afghan War of 1838–42 showed that the Russophobes' calculations were completely wrong and that earlier estimates by London and Calcutta government experts had been correct. Ironically, the Great Indian Mutiny of 1857 came not when Russian power was threatening, but when it was prostrate.[92]

The El Dorado theme. The Russophobes portrayed Turkey's territory as a potential El Dorado that could tip the global balance of power if Russia were to develop and exploit its resources ruthlessly. The vast forests of Asia Minor could be used to build a Russian fleet at one-third the cost of ship construction at Toulon. Greek sailors and the iron, copper, and cordage available on the Black Sea littoral would give Russia naval "supremacy in the Mediterranean."[93] Likewise for England, commercial opportunities in Turkey, the Danube, Persia, and even Circassia and Turkestan were portrayed as virtually limitless.[94]

The closing window of opportunity. Many of the arguments above were consistent with a policy of unyielding containment and mutual stalemate, but the Russophobes wanted more than that. Britain could not just let Russia bide its time until a propitious moment to seize the Straits occurred, they argued. Rather, it must face the need for a preventive war to roll back Russian influence. "The result of a war in the East at this moment would break Russia to pieces," said McNeill and Urquhart. "So disproportionate is the relative strength of the

91. Ibid., 183; McNeill, *Progress,* 96. Contradicting himself, he also says that the collapse of Turkey would lead to a European war.

92. Yapp, *Strategies,* 125–27, 282–85, 335, 341–43, 380; Macalister, *Memoir,* 209, 257–58; Spiers, *Radical General,* 26–27.

93. Evans, *Designs of Russia,* 12–16, 127–29, 151; Ross, *Opinions,* 276–77.

94. Gleason, *Genesis,* 180; McNeill, *Progress,* 95; Urquhart, *Turkey,* passim. On the Indus and in Turkestan, British agents argued that all good things go together—trade, defense, and uplift of the locals. Yapp, *Strategies,* 199–201, 208–9, 381, 401–2.

parties, that Russia must submit to any terms that England may dictate, whenever she places Russia between the two alternatives—her terms or war."[95] "There are worse evils than war, and, if it must be encountered, it is better by far to face it at once than to patch up a hollow, and perhaps not very creditable, truce, with the prospect of having war forced upon us a year or two hence, in circumstances, probably, less advantageous to us, and more advantageous to Russia. Turkey is still erect and stout of heart," but an interminable state of war preparation would over time weaken it.[96]

This strand in the argument, relatively muted in the propaganda of the 1830s, became central during the Crimean War. As Palmerston averred in dispatches and Layard argued in Parliament and in the periodical press, it was not enough to stalemate Russia's current attempt to expand. "Until [Russia's] pride is really humbled, the contest must be carried on." Amphibious operations in the Baltic were necessary to "inflict serious damage" on Russia and "compel her to yield to our demands." Russia must be the first to propose its own capitulation, because "he who first anxiously offers the terms of accommodation is presumed to be the weakest." If Britain was even slightly forthcoming, Russia would not admit the irrevocable nature of its defeat and would try again at the first favorable moment.[97]

Thus, sometimes it was convenient to argue that Russia was risk averse and easy to deter. This was the case at the early stage of the propaganda battle, when the task was to convince the audience that a forward strategy of containment would be cheap and risk free. But sometimes it was convenient to argue that Russia was extremely difficult to deter. This was the case during the war, when the task was to justify in defensive terms the additional costs of fighting for broader, more expansionist war aims.

The propagandist character of the arguments. In short, the strategic picture painted by Russophobe writers conveniently provided every conceivable rationalization for aggressive British expansion in Eurasia at Russia's expense. In particular, national security was highlighted as the main justification for expansion. If Britain did not send the fleet into the Black Sea and the infantry into Afghanistan, India would be lost, and before long it would be Ireland's turn.[98]

The irony of this argument is that it is so theoretical, so driven by a bandwagon image of the international system and by the general point

95. McNeill and Urquhart, "Diplomacy," in Ross, *Opinions*, 385.
96. McNeill, *Progress*, preface to 3d ed., ix–x.
97. Layard, "Results and Prospects," 254–55, 286.
98. Evans, *Designs of Russia*, 12.

the authors want to prove, yet it was propounded by writers who staked their credibility on their knowledge of the particularities of the Near East.[99] In making their case, they constantly attempted to trade on their monopoly of detailed information about the region that Russia threatened, yet it was the critics of the Russophobes who actually had a better eye for local variety and detail.

British government analyses, for example, pointed out that the Russophobes' calculation that Russia could invade India via the Persian town of Herat ignored logistics and that the supposed million-man Russian army was a myth.[100] Colonel Evans's response was that civilian critics could know nothing of military matters and that their views were "entirely Russian in spirit."[101] McNeill, a cooler character and better informed, tried to salvage the argument by admitting the logistic difficulties of a large-scale Russian invasion, but stressing instead the arguments about bandwagon psychology, which were harder to refute conclusively.[102]

If the Russophobes' writings have a schematic, argument-driven character, that is not because they lacked detailed knowledge of the region. McNeill in particular had spent many years there. Palmerston judged him by "far the ablest man we have ever had in Persia."[103] If McNeill's publications pass off cartoonlike domino theories as regional expertise, his private correspondence shows far more complex views, including an understanding of the dynamics of quagmires on an empire's turbulent frontier.[104] McNeill's publications reflect the general thrust of his real thinking but reduce it to a simple line of argument, with all facts pointing to the same conclusion for maximum public relations impact.

These experts' published arguments should be viewed above all as ideology. Urquhart's correspondence reveals an explicit preoccupation with the tactics of inflating minor incidents to incite public opinion against Russia and thus tie the government's hands.[105] The group of propagandists, moreover, exercised close control over the content of their collective message. For example, they lauded Evans for launching the opening salvo exposing the Russian threat, but they criticized him for overstating Turkish weakness on the tactical grounds that portraying the situation as hopeless was as dangerous as underestimating the threat. To construct an ideal argument, they understood that the

99. McNeill, *Progress*, 96; Ross, *Opinions*, 284, 296.
100. Yapp, *Strategies*, 202–4; Spiers, *Radical General*, 23–24, 216.
101. Spiers, *Radical General*, 24–25.
102. Ross, *Opinions*, 167–74.
103. Yapp, *Strategies*, 134.
104. McNeill, *Memoirs*, 92.
105. Gleason, *Genesis*, 187.

domino theory had to be complemented by the Thermopylae myth: though the cost of not acting would be huge, the cost of acting decisively would be small.[106]

Often scholars are obsessed with finding out what public figures "really" believed, as distinct from what they said in public for tactical reasons. In this case, however, the caricatured domino theories that the Russophobes purveyed in print and in parliamentary debates were more significant than what they "really" believed. The "real" strategic ideas of the regional experts had some small, direct influence on government policy and on Palmerston's geopolitical worldview. But their published arguments had much greater importance, through their effect on the conventional wisdom of the generation that provided the social base for Palmerston's social imperialism.

Palmerston's Strategic Beliefs

Palmerston's strategic pronouncements were similar to those of the Russophobes, though less extreme and tempered in practice by an understanding of the need for self-restraint until an opponent had been diplomatically isolated. Paper tiger, domino, and Thermopylae themes pervade his geopolitical concepts, but especially interesting is the role of liberal ideology in his approach to grand strategy.

Character of the opponent. Palmerston, like the Russophobes, saw Russia as risk averse but as having unlimited aims. "The moderation of the Czar . . . reassures me poorly," he said of Russian salami-slicing tactics in 1848–49. "From moderation to moderation he might finish, if one let him have his way, by invading the entire world."[107] Consequently Russia had to be opposed, but this could be done without great risk. "Russia will go as far as she can without war with England," he wrote McNeill in 1838 regarding the threat of a Russian invasion of India via Afghanistan, "but her system of aggrandizement is founded on the principle of encroachment and not war with equal or superior powers and whenever she finds such a war likely to be the result of further encroachment, she will stop for the moment, and wait for a more favorable opportunity."[108]

With such an enemy, standing firm—and especially talking loudly— provides the surest guarantee of keeping the peace. "Russia has

---

106. Ross, *Opinions*, vii–ix; McNeill and Urquhart, "Diplomacy," in Ross, *Opinions*, 365–66.

107. Saab, *Origins*, 8.

108. Yapp, *Strategies*, 278–79; see also Rich, *Why the Crimean War?* 61.

advanced because nobody observed, watched, and understood what she was doing," Foreign Secretary Palmerston explained to Prime Minister Melbourne in 1835. "Expose her plans and you half defeat them. Raise public opinion against her and you double her difficulties. I am all for making a clatter against her. Depend upon it, that is the best way to save you from the necessity of making war against her."[109] Conversely, Palmerston typically held that appeasement would lead to war, whether with France in 1840 or with Russia in 1853, when he held that talk of "peace at any price" had misled the tsar.[110]

Underlying Palmerston's belief in the effectiveness of threats was his "consciousness of strength, this feeling of natural power," which could not fail to impress other states as long as Britain demonstrated the will to use its great capabilities.[111] But despite Palmerston's confidence in British power, he acted decisively only after manipulating the Concert of Europe to isolate his opponent. Even when he thought Britain was strong enough to prevail in a one-on-one fight, he realized that reckless action might provoke opposition from third parties.[112] Only when Britain's opponents had isolated themselves by supporting aggression against Turkey did Palmerston drop his self-restraint. Thus Palmerston forced an isolated France to abandon its Egyptian ally, Mohammed Ali, in his war against the Turks in 1840; he compelled an isolated Russia to accept British dominance in the Turkish Straits in 1841; and he relentlessly pursued the war against an isolated Russia in 1854–55.[113]

In this sense Palmerston understood that balancing behavior was the norm in international politics. But unlike idealized versions of the Concert of Europe propounded by modern political scientists, Palmerston's image of the Concert had little room for reciprocal obligations of self-restraint in the long-run maintenance of the system. Though restrained if a balancing coalition might form against him in the short run, when an enemy was down Palmerston took advantage of that vulnerability. He consciously exploited Russian setbacks in the Caucasus in 1838 to push for a revision of the Straits Convention, noting that "you should always deal with a Bully when he has just had his nose pulled."[114] After humiliating France in the Mohammed Ali crisis of 1840, Palmerston refused to make facing-saving gestures because he wanted to show France that good relations with Britain could be

109. Webster, *Foreign Policy*, 2:563.

110. Roger Bullen, *Palmerston, Guizot and the Collapse of the Entente Cordiale* (London, 1974), 31; Conacher, *Aberdeen Coalition*, 159.

111. Louis Fagan, *The Reform Club* (London, 1887), 89; see also Bullen, *Palmerston*, 32; Bourne, *Palmerston*, 576; Temperley, *England*, 114.

112. Webster, *Foreign Policy*, 2:599.

113. Ibid., vol. 2, chap. 8; Bourne, *Palmerston*, chap. 11.

114. Gleason, *Genesis*, 231.

maintained only on British terms.[115] In short, Palmerston's notion of a stable Concert was not one featuring internalized norms of reciprocal self-restraint, but one in which the other powers accepted British primacy.

Though this big stick diplomacy was sometimes effective, it often proved counterproductive. Russian pressure on the Turkish Straits and India was, in the view of today's historians, often spurred by a sense of vulnerability to British encroachment.[116] Similarly, the Crimean War itself was triggered in part by Tsar Nicholas's fear of the bandwagon consequences of the loss of Russian prestige owing to France's successful coercion of the Turks in 1852.[117] Thus big stick diplomacy helped create the problem it was intended to avert.

Palmerston was moderate, however, compared with the Russophobe area specialists. They saw a single enemy, whereas Palmerston answered Urquhart's attacks with the assertion that England had only "eternal interests," not "perpetual enemies" or "eternal allies."[118] Palmerston thought McNeill's 1836 pamphlet *Progress and Present Position of Russia in the East* so extreme that it would ruin McNeill's effectiveness in his diplomatic post in Persia. McNeill agreed to publish anonymously. Still, Palmerston defended to Melbourne his use of extremist Russophobes in the diplomatic service, admitting "their faults and weaknesses" but insisting that Russia could not be counteracted "unless we employ agents who meet the unsleeping activity of hers, with something like equivalent zeal."[119]

Domino theory. Notwithstanding his greater caution, Palmerston shared with the Russophobes whose services he enlisted a domino theory of international politics. Small states standing alone are insufficient buffers: "Afghanistan must be ours or Russia's."[120] Resources are cumulative: giving Syria to Mohammed Ali will strengthen, not satiate him, and its loss will weaken the Turks.[121] Palmerston likewise sees Russia

115. Webster, *Foreign Policy*, 2:724.

116. Bartlett, *Great Britain*, 93; Puryear, *England*, 25n.55; 30–31nn.68–69; Philip Mosley, *Russian Diplomacy and the Opening of the Eastern Question in 1838 and 1839* (Cambridge, Mass., 1934), 40; Gillard, *Struggle for Asia*, 65.

117. Curtiss, *Russia's Crimean War*, 84; Gillard, *Struggle for Asia*, 80.

118. Jasper Ridley, *Lord Palmerston* (London, 1970), 334, in response to Urquhart's censure motion in 1848.

119. Bourne, *Palmerston*, 562, September 1835. Palmerston soon became less tolerant toward Urquhart, who arranged for a British trading vessel, the *Vixen*, to violate Russian customs restrictions on the eastern shore of the Black Sea, leading as Urquhart apparently calculated to the *Vixen's* seizure and offering a pretext for an outburst of emotional Russophobia in Britain. Bourne, *Palmerston*, 564; Gleason, *Genesis*, chap. 7.

120. Bourne, *Palmerston*, 560.

121. Henry H. Dodwell, *The Founder of Modern Egypt* (1931; Cambridge, 1967), 117, quoting a statement of 4 February 1833.

as weak if it stands on the defensive, but if Russia were to conquer the resources of Turkey, it would become a "colossus, . . . exercising a dominant control over Germany," achieving naval superiority in the Mediterranean, and sweeping British trade from the Levant.[122] Even the most far-flung geopolitical positions are tightly interconnected: "We are defending Turkey in the Basque Provinces" by resisting the growth of Russian influence in Spain.[123] Commitments are highly interdependent, and actions on small questions set precedents for big ones:

> It must perpetually happen that the particular object or interest, to defend which a country stands out to resist an aggressive war, may in its separate and intrinsic value not be worth the expenses that must be incurred to defend it. But any nation which were to act upon the principle of yielding to every demand made upon it, if each separate demand could be shown not to involve directly and immediately a vital interest, would at no distant period find itself progressively stripped of the means of defending its vital interests, when those interests came at last to be attacked.[124]

Thermopylae corollary. Palmerston believed in the domino theory in both its material and its psychological versions; he also believed in its Thermopylae corollary. Forward defense of a key position was always cheaper than strategic retrenchment, he argued. In his strategic assessments, such key positions proliferated indiscriminately. "Diarbekir [on the upper Tigris], one of the places which Russia proposes Mehemet Ali to occupy, is the central key of the whole of Asia Minor."[125] The Oxus River in Turkestan is likewise considered a key point of forward defense: a Russian attack on India will not be prevented by "staying at home to receive the visit."[126]

In general, Palmerston contended that only small efforts would be needed to forestall big consequences. "If England allows and acquiesces in the assertion of independence by Mehemet Ali," Palmerston warned Melbourne in May 1838, "she seals the doom of Turkey, and hands over the Dardanelles to Russia." To prevent this, "naval aid is all we need afford."[127] Consequently, isolationism is false economy. Palmerston poked fun at the cost consciousness of the Manchester anti-interventionists:

> If this country were threatened with an immediate invasion likely to end in its conquest, [John Bright] would sit down, take a piece of paper, and would

---

122. Bell, *Lord Palmerston*, 2:131.
123. Webster, *Foreign Policy*, 2:604–5, January 1837.
124. Bullen, *Palmerston*, 56, Palmerston to Russell, September 1840.
125. Temperley, *England*, 93, quoting Palmerston, July 1839.
126. Webster, *Foreign Policy*, 2:739, 741.
127. Bourne, *Palmerston*, 568–69. The latter statement, at least, turned out to be true.

put on one side of the account the contributions which his Government would require from him for the defence of the liberty and independence of the country, and he would put on the other the probable contributions which the general of the invading army might levy upon Manchester, and if he found that, on balancing the account, it would be cheaper to be conquered than to be laid under contribution for defence, he would give his vote against going to war.[128]

But Palmerston understood that cost effectiveness arguments were important, and he consistently used the domino and Thermopylae themes to rebut Manchester-type objections.[129]

Strategic beliefs as rationalizations. Like the arguments of the Russophobes, the image of the international environment that Palmerston articulated smacks of a debater's brief for aggressive expansion disguised as a requirement of national security. The images of the enemy, of the material and psychological dynamics of the system, and even of the Concert of Europe seem to line up all too systematically as rationalizations for an aggressive policy. Anomalies in Palmerston's beliefs reinforce this impression. For example, he normally depicts non-European states as power vacuums, ripe for exploitation and conquest, yet this will not do for Turkey, which must be seen as at least strong enough to be salvageable. Consequently he complains that ignorant people think of Turkey in terms of misleading metaphors—a crumbling building, a sapless tree, the sick man of Europe. In fact Turkey is regenerating, and besides, "No empire is likely to fall to pieces if left to itself."[130] In Persia and Afghanistan, Palmerston fears that Russia will invade and then use local troops to swell its armies, but in Turkey he warns that if the sultan invites in Russian troops for protection against Mohammed Ali, his own subjects will revolt.[131] The additional irony is that Palmerston prefers the Turks to the Egyptians as a bulwark against Russia because the Turks are weaker and hence more malleable.[132]

There are other oddities, if not downright contradictions, in Palmerston's statements and rationalizations, all serving to justify aggressive expansion. As for the Russophobes, Russia can be either easy or hard to deter, depending on the argument needed at the moment. Similarly, France, Russia, and Egypt are easily cowed because Britain is materially so overwhelmingly strong, yet small reputational or material re-

---

128. Bell, *Lord Palmerston*, 2:103–4, in Parliament, 1854.
129. For other examples, Southgate, *Most English Minister*, 138–40.
130. Kenneth Bourne, *The Foreign Policy of Victorian England, 1830–1902* (Oxford, 1970), 233–35.
131. British Museum, Add. MS. 48492, 37, Palmerston to Ponsonby, 9 August 1833.
132. Temperley, *England*, 93.

verses will jeopardize Britain's global power position in its entirety. At one moment an offensive bridgehead at Constantinople is needed to deter Russian attacks on vulnerable India; at the next moment Constantinople is the alleged weak spot that must be defended by offensive thrusts from India.[133] Finally, even as Russia lies prostrate at the end of the Crimean War in 1856, Palmerston is invoking the Russian threat to justify thrashing the Persians at Herat.[134]

It is difficult to distinguish debater's points from sincere beliefs in Palmerston's geopolitical statements. The bombast of his public speeches and anonymous newspaper articles is almost matched by the hawkish aphorisms that enliven his private letters and diplomatic memoranda. Even in the latter forums, however, he often seems to be taking a tactical stance—trying, for example, to stiffen the spine of a conciliatory diplomat. He lacked confidants to whom he could fully explain his true thinking. Still, that his actions were normally more prudent than his rhetoric, whether public or private, suggests that he may have understood the requirements of balance of power diplomacy reasonably well. Even the big stick rhetoric was normally trained on small powers—and on great powers only when they were at a disadvantage.

But if Palmerston himself could distinguish between rhetoric and reality, many of his supporters could not, and sometimes he felt constrained to act on his rhetoric. Palmerston's letters to Britain's peace negotiators continually remind them that "the eyes and thoughts of all England are fixed on this negotiation" and constantly try to stiffen them against concessions.[135] One reason for this prodding is geopolitical: "If the war goes on the results of another campaign will enable us, this time twelvemonth, to obtain from Russia much better conditions than those which we are now willing to accept." A second reason, no less emphasized, is a domestic political one: "The British nation is unanimous [in its willingness to fight on] for I cannot reckon Bright, Cobden & Co. for anything, and even if we the government were not kept straight by a sense of our public duty, the strong feeling which prevails throughout the country would make it infeasible for us to [stop fighting]."[136] To a negotiator's offer to accept the blame for a compromise peace, Palmerston replies that there are those in "the House of Parliament and the nation whose appetite for victims would not be so easily satiated, and who would have stomach for a cabinet in addition to a Minister Plenipotentiary."[137] Thus Palmerston faced a

---

133. Yapp, *Strategies*, 291; also 202, 587.
134. Gillard, *Struggle for Asia*, 96–97; Yapp, *Strategies*, 288, 294–95.
135. Add. MS. 48580, to Clarendon, 24 February 1856.
136. Add. MS. 48579, 101, to Ambassador Seymour, 24 January 1856.
137. Ibid., 103.

milder version of the "sorcerer's apprentice" problem that had confronted the social imperialists of Wilhelmine Germany.

Geopolitics and Liberalism in a Unified Ideology

The best way to understand Palmerston's geopolitical thinking is to place it in the context of his views on the role of ideology in foreign— and domestic—affairs. Palmerston believed that the main historical force shaping his era was the conflict between revolution and reaction. Both these poles were evils, the latter largely because it played into the hands of the former. To prevent the triumph of either, an activist policy in support of mildly reforming constitutional government was neces- sary at home and abroad. Through a strategy of controlled concessions and liberal symbolism, moderate reformers could be split off from revolutionaries and used by enlightened aristocrats as allies in the fight against both the Left and the Right. In a career-making 1829 speech on civil strife in Portugal, Palmerston first articulated in public the views that would guide his policy for the next forty years:

> There are two great parties in Europe; one which endeavours to bear sway by the force of public opinion; another which endeavours to bear sway by the force of physical control; and the judgment almost unanimous of Europe, assigns the latter as the present connexion of England.
> The principle on which the system of this party is founded is, in my view, fundamentally erroneous. There is in nature no moving power but mind, all else is passive and inert; in human affairs this power is opinion; in political affairs it is public opinion; and he who can grasp this power, with it will subdue the fleshly arm of physical strength . . . those statesmen who know how to avail themselves of the passions, and the interests, and the opinions of mankind, are able to gain an ascendancy, and to exercise a sway over human affairs far out of all proportion greater than belong to the power and resources of the state over which they preside; while those, on the other hand, who seek to check improvement, to cherish abuses, to crush opinions, and to prohibit the human race from thinking, whatever may be the apparent power which they wield, will find their weapon snap short in their hand.[138]

Inflexible reactionaries like Wellington and Metternich were hastening the collapse of the established order, both at home and abroad. Irresistible new forces in politics had to be shaped, not repressed, Palmerston argued. Divide and conquer was the main means for achieving this: "*Divide et impera* should be the maxim of government in

138. Bourne, *Palmerston*, 298–99.

these times. Separate by reasonable concessions the moderate from the exaggerated, content the former by fair concessions and get them to assist in resisting the insatiable demands of the latter."[139]

Palmerston's private letters seem not much different from his public speeches in extolling the tactical advantages of an ideologically liberal foreign policy.[140] Even the public speeches frankly admitted the social imperialist aspects of his vision: "If the nation is overflowing with so much pugnacity," he warned in his Catholic Emancipation speech of 1829, "let us vent it on any and every other nation of the earth, let us not exercise a suicidal fury on ourselves."[141]

In short, Palmerston was utterly frank about the tactical nature of his support for a liberal foreign policy.[142] He told public and private audiences alike that his main interest in liberalism was as part of a strategy to maintain the old order by dividing its enemies and co-opting into it a new, energetic class. He said quite openly that his game was to seem as liberal as possible, especially in foreign affairs, while making the fewest possible concessions to the forces of change in domestic affairs. Thus Palmerston worked against Whig cabinet colleagues to minimize the extent of electoral reform bills, while defying their ban on receiving the popular Hungarian revolutionary, Lajos Kossuth.[143]

Palmerston saw the war between constitutional liberalism, on the one hand, and revolution and reaction, on the other, as a tightly interconnected, global process. Because this was a battle of ideas as well as military force, dominolike contagion was an ever present possibility. Given the clustering of revolutionary epidemics in the years 1830 and 1848, this view was common and well founded.[144] Palmerston hoped to use this bandwagon effect to win victories for England abroad and to mobilize political support for himself at home.[145]

In short, Palmerston's strategic ideology was composed of two mutu-

139. Kennedy, *Realities*, 39.
140. Bourne, *Palmerston*, 249, 314.
141. Bell, *Lord Palmerston*, 1:79.
142. Webster, *Foreign Policy*, 1:81, says that Palmerston was "sincere" in tailoring his policy to the enthusiasms of the middle-class radicals, but only in the sense that "this attitude was based on practical considerations rather than on any philosophical outlook"— namely, the need to avoid the "explosion" that would occur if middle-class demands were completely stonewalled.
143. Bell, *Lord Palmerston*, 2:44–45.
144. Leslie Mitchell, *Holland House* (London, 1980), chap. 11.
145. Palmerston claimed, for example, that the Western "free states" should "be on the advance" in the struggle against the Eastern "arbitrary governments," and thus "all the smaller planets of Europe will have a natural tendency to gravitate toward our system." Webster, *Foreign Policy*, 1:390. On Palmerston's domestic gain from this, see Clarendon to John Russell after Palmerston's Don Pacifico speech. Gooch, *Later Correspondence*, 2:78–79, 1 July 1850.

ally reinforcing strands: a prudently aggressive conception of geopolitics and a prudently interventionist liberalism. Both saw Britain as enjoying exceptional strength in international competition. Both saw flux and the bandwagon, rather than equilibrium, as the law of international life. The geopolitical strand seemed to grow out of Palmerston's Tory roots and his maiden parlimentary speech in 1808 in defense of a preventive surprise attack on the Danish fleet. It provided a rationale for expansion that appealed to a Tory constituency, the party that had gained power from the Whigs on a platform of realpolitik nationalism during the wars of the French Revolution. The liberal strand appeared at the time of Byronic infatuation with Greek and Polish independence and just before the French revolution of 1830 and England's Great Reform Bill of 1832. It appealed to radicals, who felt that "we were fighting abroad upon the same principle as we were fighting against boroughmongers at home," and to the liberal Foxite branch of the Whig aristocracy, whose political ideology ever since the Glorious Revolution of 1688 had rested on support for liberal principles at home and abroad as the only guarantee against monarchical usurpation.[146]

Liberal principles established only a loose constraint on Palmerston's policy, however, since liberal rhetoric could justify virtually any action and its opposite. Palmerston called support for reactionary Turkey a "liberal" policy, on the grounds that the Turks had given Kossuth sanctuary from the Austrians and had acceded to a British free-trade treaty.[147] It is ironic that Palmerston argued against underrating Turkey's potential for reform while opposing further electoral reform in Britain on the grounds that additional voters would be "necessarily low in the scale of Intelligence and political knowledge."[148] Moreover, when cost effectiveness arguments were weak, malleable ideological appeals could substitute for them. For example, in answer to Cobden's statistics showing that a war for Turkey would cost more than the stakes were worth, Palmerston grandly claimed that the British always "went to war for the liberties of Europe and not for the purpose of gaining so much per cent on our exports."[149]

At the most fundamental level, Palmerston's policy was driven neither by his geopolitical maxims nor by liberal rhetoric, but by his social imperial strategy. Palmerston saw international conflict as an opportunity to harness liberal energies to a task other than social change at home. Whigs who dissented from Palmerston's belligerent foreign policy, like Lord Holland, disagreed primarily because they

---

146. Gleason, *Genesis*, 119, 126; Mitchell, *Holland House*, chaps. 2, 3, 8, and 10.
147. Martin, *Triumph*, 162–63, 198.
148. Conacher, *Aberdeen Coalition*, 292.
149. Martin, *Triumph*, 123.

thought that foreign wars tended to justify domestic repression by Tories and the Crown. Thus differences in domestic political notions seem to have been driving the superficial differences in geopolitical or ideological perceptions of the Eastern Question.

If Palmerston's geopolitical and ideological arguments against Holland, Cobden, and other anti-interventionists were tactics in support of a larger social agenda, the same can be said of Cobden's arguments, which lined up just as predictably on the opposite side.

The Ideology of Anti-imperialism

Cobden offered the clearest, most consistent argument against imperial expansion, but other political figures, ranging across the political spectrum from ultra-Tory to Whig aristocrat, presented similar critiques. Though the rhetorical style varied, the predictable list of anti-imperial arguments was always well represented: Russia is weak in offense, strong in defense; dominoes do not cascade; war is caused more often by conflict spirals than by deterrence failures. For these anti-imperialist ideologues, like their imperialist opponents, what came first was a general social ideology; specific geopolitical arguments were rationalizations pulled in the wake of the ideology.

Cobden. Richard Cobden was a successful self-made Manchester cotton merchant. A good deal of the financial backing for Cobden's Anti–Corn Law League, the pressure group that helped force the repeal of grain tariffs in 1846, came from Midlands industrialists. They wanted to repeal the Corn Laws so that other countries could earn foreign exchange with which to buy more Manchester textiles. Another motive was to secure cheaper food for industrial workers, so that wages could be reduced.[150]

Though Cobden cooperated with these industrialists in the Anti–Corn Law campaign, he conceived a social philosophy that expressed the interests and outlook of his class at a much higher level. Sometimes, as in Cobden's opposition to the 1850 loan for a Russian military buildup, this brought him into conflict with the short-run profit motive. Overall, however, his ideology provided a coherent justification for some of the dearest interests of the new manufacturing class—free trade, cheap government, and a weakening of the aristocracy's political monopoly. The final element, international peace, did not flow directly from the class's economic or political interests, but it fit nicely with the moralistic, evangelical background that was disproportionately represented

150. William D. Grampp, *The Manchester School of Economics* (Stanford, Calif., 1960), 108–10; also 117.

in the industrialist class.[151] Above all, it provided a broadly appealing universalist veneer that helped sell the rest of the self-interested package.

The outline of Cobden's ideology closely anticipated the later arguments of Joseph Schumpeter. Colonies and a bloated military establishment, according to Cobden, are "costly appendages of aristocratic life." "The battle plain is the harvest field of the aristocracy, watered with the blood of the people." Indeed, the whole balance of power concept is the concoction of militarist aristocrats.[152] Imperialism only increases the national debt, which feeds aristocratic bureaucrats in the army, church, and civil service and justifies agricultural tariffs to service the debt, again feeding the landowning aristocracy and stifling productive commerce.[153] Imperial victories were defeats in disguise, since they inflated the prestige of the parasitical aristocracy and thus helped squelch reform: "Let John Bull have a great military triumph, and we shall have to take off our hats as we pass the Horse Guards for the rest of our lives."[154] Military victories, morever, had no commercial value: "Cheapness, and not the cannon and the sword, is the weapon through which alone we possess and can hope to defend our commerce."[155]

Cobden was proud that in his ideology "all good things pull together."[156] Nowadays social psychologists might call this an irrational bias for consistency.[157] Another interpretation is that Cobden, as both the operational head and the chief ideologist of the free trade movement, had an acute sense of how to package ideas in a way that would sell. Cobden's own testimony provides evidence for this view. In written instructions to propagandists and orators of the Anti–Corn Law League, he reminded them, "Don't let the enemy make it be believed that this is a mere manufacturers' or cotton spinners' question."[158] Instead, arguments should be couched in terms that played on the moral feelings of the audience.[159] He believed that the free-trade movement

151. John Bright was a Quaker, for example, though Cobden himself was Anglican. Briggs, *Victorian People*, 120–21.

152. Peter Cain, "Capitalism, War and Internationalism in the Thought of Richard Cobden," *British Journal of International Studies* 5 (October 1979): 229–47, quotations at 233, 236.

153. Ibid., 236.

154. Letter to Bright, 1 October 1854; John Morley, *The Life of Richard Cobden*, abridged ed. (London, n.d.), 311–12.

155. Briggs, *Victorian People*, 214.

156. Quoted in Patricia Hollis, "Pressure from Without: An Introduction," in Hollis, *Pressure*, 7.

157. Robert Jervis, *Perception and Misperception in International Politics* (Princeton, N.J., 1976), chap. 4.

158. Grampp, *Manchester School*, 111.

159. Hollis, "Pressure," 10–11.

had been successful largely because it had been put over as a "national issue" rather than as one group's interest contending with another's. In carrying out that public relations strategy, equating peace and free trade had played a considerable role.[160]

Ironically, because Cobden's larger ideology sometimes ran counter to the short-run interests of the manufacturers, for that audience he and Bright had to reverse propaganda tactics. "How inventive some of them were in thinking of economic reasons to justify their non-economic or even anti-economic purposes," muses one historian.[161] In urging Manchester manufacturers to contribute to the broader social reform platform of the League, Cobden used basically the same argument for limited reform as Palmerston did: "Let us invest part of our property, in order to save the rest from confiscation."[162] Naturally, the amount of reform desired by the wealthy bourgeoisie and their middle-class allies was greater than the reform that Whig aristocrats could tolerate, but Cobden was not an unmitigated democrat. He opposed legislation to regulate working conditions in factories and resisted the extension of the electoral franchise in the 1850s.[163]

Yet Cobden was not consistently calculating and opportunist. The peace issue seems to have been a—perhaps *the*—genuine core value to which he stayed true even when it hurt him with most of his industrialist and middle-class backers. He stuck to his opposition to the Crimean War, for example, even at the cost of his parliamentary seat. Thaddeus Delane, editor of the London *Times*, remarked with some slight exaggeration that "Cobden and Bright would be our ministers now but for their principle of 'Peace at all price.'"[164]

Cobden's geopolitical arguments were deduced from his more general worldview, sometimes producing powerful insights, but sometimes running roughshod over obviously contradictory facts. Russia, Cobden argued, was economically too weak to be a threat, and if it industrialized it would become more pacific. Further expansion would be difficult for Russia, owing to the financial and logistical weaknesses inherent in its economic backwardness. Only trade and innovation would increase Russia's power—not conquest. Without the economic resources to maintain a first-class navy, Constantinople would be a "splendid prison" for the tsar's empire, not a springboard for conquest.[165]

Palmerston thought Cobden was trying to have both sides of the argument in his characterizations of Russia: "At one moment he tells us

160. Grampp, *Manchester School*, 96–97, 100–101; also, 84–85.
161. Ibid., 1–2.
162. Morley, *Cobden*, 74.
163. Cain, "Cobden," 245–46.
164. Briggs, *Victorian People*, 218, in 1855.
165. Gleason, *Genesis*, 184–85, 234; Cain, "Cobden," 236.

[185]

that Russia is so weak that she could be crumpled up like a sheet of brown paper. . . . At another moment he declares that war with Russia would be ruin to England."[166] Palmerston, the great purveyor of paper tiger images of the enemy, was faulting Cobden for engaging in the identical, but reversed, rhetorical ploy.

In fact, Cobden's view was that Russia was weak in offense but strong in defense—a basically accurate assessment.[167] But this in itself did not answer Urquhart's argument that the expansion of the perimeter of Russian protectionism would hurt British trade in the growing Near Eastern market. For Cobden the ideologue, "all good things must go together," and for Cobden the debater and the interpreter of Manchester's interests, Urquhart's point could not go unanswered. Cobden the pamphleteer consequently wound up arguing that Russian domination of Turkey would actually be an advantage to British trade, since it would raise Turkey's cultural level and value as a market, which Britain would capture for its superior manufactures despite Russian political hegemony.[168] Similar faith that market forces could overcome political constraints led Cobden to see British rule in India as a needless expense, assuming that the benefits of trade could be gotten regardless of the political arrangements.[169]

In support of this view, Cobden pointed to the failure of Napoleon's continental system, which he claimed, in contrast to more recent historians, had only trivially affected British trade with Europe. From this he concluded by analogy that "Russian violence cannot destroy or even sensibly injure our trade." Britain's success in trade comes from "cheapness," not military power, and the only threat to it is "greater cheapness of the manufactures of another country."[170] Along the same lines, Cobden argued that Wellington's pointless "descent upon the [Iberian] Peninsula was made after Nelson had at the battle of Trafalgar destroyed Napoleon's power at sea. From that moment we were as safe from molestation in our island home, as if we had inhabited another planet."[171]

In short, Cobden's geopolitical arguments—whether sound or exaggerated—support the ideological message that all good things go together. The laws of political economy make Britain so favorably

---

166. *Hansard Parliamentary Debates*, 3d ser., 29:1806, 16 August 1853.

167. Curtiss, *Russia's Crimean War*, 35–36.

168. Cain, "Cobden," 236; Louis Mallet, ed., *The Political Writings of Richard Cobden* (London, 1878), 103–8.

169. Morley, *Cobden*, 333–34; see also Eric Stokes, *English Utilitarians and India* (Oxford, 1959), 43.

170. Cain, "Cobden," 236–37; Eli F. Heckscher, *The Continental System* (Gloucester, Mass., 1964), 324–63.

171. Letter to Bright, 1 October 1854, Morley, *Cobden*, 311–12.

situated that it can "afford to be moral" (read noninterventionist) in its foreign policy.[172] France has a predilection for men on horseback because of its experience with foreign aggression,[173] but because Britain is utterly secure, it can get rid of its own parasitical military-aristocratic overlords and pursue a line of fiscal retrenchment. These were all arguments that Cobden believed in, but they were also a coherent ideological package that he thought he could sell to the Manchester industrialists and to the country at large.

Noninterventionist Whigs. Another source of noninterventionist geopolitical arguments came from the more liberal Whig aristocrats, trying to replace the centrist Melbourne-Palmerston coalition with a bloc of Cobdenite radicals and Foxite Whigs. These argued geopolitical points similar to Cobden's, but of course omitting the anti-aristocratic overlay. For example, Lord Durham, envoy to Saint Petersburg in 1835 and a perennial loose cannon on the Whigs' radical fringe, provided detailed reports showing the weakness of the Russian fleet and demonstrating that Russia's power "is solely of the defensive kind." Even Palmerston was impressed by this analysis, perhaps because at this stage he needed arguments to contain out of control Russophobes like Urquhart even more than he needed grist for the social imperialism mill.[174]

Noninterventionist Tories. Finally, noninterventionist views were also expressed on the right of Britain's political spectrum. The Tory politician Lord Stanley confided to his diary at the outset of the Crimean War that there were numerous back-bench country gentlemen who "object to fight where England has nothing to gain: and who in their hearts agree with Cobden."[175] Like Stanley, Lord Aberdeen was one of the front-bench Tories whose geopolitical views reflected this mentality. Disliking foreign adventures and believing that a conservative Concert would best preserve the political order of Europe, Aberdeen held to a spiral theory of international conflict. Thus he was inclined to appease both France and Russia, and he disagreed with Palmerston at almost every turn. For example, as foreign secretary in the mid-1840s, Aberdeen thought defense budget increases would ruin Britain's relations with France. Palmerston thought a superior British squadron in the Mediterranean would make the French more friendly, but Aberdeen believed

---

172. Morley, *Cobden*, 47.
173. Edsall, *Cobden*, 261.
174. Webster, *Foreign Policy*, 2:564–66; Gleason, *Genesis*, 167, 173; Chester New, *Lord Durham* (London, 1968).
175. Edsall, *Cobden*, 272–73; see also Donald Southgate, "From Disraeli to Law," in Donald Southgate, ed., *The Conservatives* (London, 1977), 141.

the opposite, citing French pride.[176] Likewise, Aberdeen denied that marginal setbacks in peripheral areas would snowball. "It is idle," he contended, "to maintain that the balance of power in Europe can in any degree depend on the preservation of one Governor of Egypt more than another."[177]

Thus most of the main participants in Britain's strategic debates in the early Victorian era articulated highly ideological images of the opponent and the international system. Palmerston and the Russophobes used all the standard myths of empire to justify an interventionist strategy; Cobden exploited every possible argument to prove the opposite. But whether interventionist or noninterventionist, the arguments of both sides were similar in their fact-crunching consistency. The rhetoric on each side of the debate portrayed a world in which all geopolitical, economic, and moral considerations supported a particular approach to grand strategy. Much of this debate appeared to be about questions of realpolitik, but in fact it was largely driven by the broader social ideologies of the participants or by their tactics in domestic politics.

COGNITIVE EXPLANATIONS

Strictly cognitive explanations for arguments about security through expansion fare no better than Realist explanations. In principle, pressure toward cognitive consistency might account for the tendency of "all good things to go together" in strategic belief systems, whether Cobden's or Urquhart's. Similarly, many features of the Russophobes' image of Russia could be explained in terms of typical cognitive errors in making assessments about others: for example, the tendency to see others as purposeful, centralized, hyperrational, innately inclined toward aggression, and conciliatory only when coerced. Likewise, the perceptions of Russophobe Near East experts could be explained in terms of a professionally narrow focus of attention, leading them to exaggerate the importance of their region or its attractiveness as a target.[178] Yet direct evidence of propagandistic intent suggests that the root cause of argumentative overkill or stereotyped views of the Russian threat was ideological expediency, not a cognitive need for consistency or selective attention.

176. Bartlett, *Great Britain*, 3, 160–66; Gleason, *Genesis*, 273.

177. George Hamilton Gordon, Fourth Earl of Aberdeen, *Selections from the Correspondence of the Earl of Aberdeen*, vol. 3, (privately printed), Aberdeen to Princess Lieven, 12 December 1840, p. 182a; reprinted in E. Jones Parry, ed., *The Correspondence of Lord Aberdeen and Princess Lieven, 1832–1854*, vol. 1 (London, 1938), 156.

178. For the relevant hypotheses, see Jervis, *Perception*, chaps. 4, 8, and 9.

[188]

Strictly cognitive "lessons of history" also offer flawed explanations. On its face, it seems possible that British leaders overgeneralized from their successful uses of force in this period and came to think of themselves as omnipotent. Force often worked, so they kept using it until experience proved otherwise. But when force failed, interventionists avoided drawing generalized lessons from those experiences. For example, the setback in Afghanistan in 1838–42 changed British policy in Afghanistan for a time, but Palmerston applied no lessons from this experience to questions of containment elsewhere on the Russian periphery.

Since our own era seems to have been dominated by the Munich analogy and lessons about Hitler, it is natural to ask whether the Napoleon analogy played a similar role in Palmerstonian Britain. Palmerston did once call Tsar Nicholas the "new Napoleon," and Palmerston's role as a junior Tory minister during the Napoleonic struggle could conceivably have imbued him with a heightened sense of the need to be timely in cutting potential hegemons down to size.[179] But other political figures drew radically different lessons from the Napoleonic struggles. Aberdeen learned that a legitimist Concert was needed to forestall future outbreaks of revolutionary passion and that maintaining this system required some appeasement of Russian and French national ambitions.[180] Holland learned that any foreign military intervention could be used by Tories and the Crown as an excuse to undercut "liberty" at home and thus the political position of the Whigs. Cobden learned that market forces prevail over political attempts to ban trade. Lessons drawn from the Napoleonic struggle were thus not strictly cognitive, but were powerfully mediated by social position, ideology, or other factors.

Cognitive explanations are also undermined in that the people with the most information about regional security problems—the area specialists—were the most biased in their assessments. Cognitive theory would expect that people with the least information should be the most biased, since they would have a greater need to use oversimplified rules of thumb in processing information. For all these reasons, strictly cognitive interpretations of British strategic conceptions are fundamentally unsatisfactory.

DOMESTIC COALITION POLITICS

The best explanation for Palmerston's strategic ideology focuses on its role in governing Britain during its most rapid phase of industriali-

179. Bourne, *Palmerston*, 64, 82.
180. J. B. Conacher, *The Peelites and the Party System, 1846–52* (Hamden, Conn., 1972), 84; see also David Wetzel, *The Crimean War: A Diplomatic History* (New York, 1985), 66.

zation in the middle of the nineteenth century. At this juncture, which has been called the "age of equipoise," rapid economic change left a wide range of premodern and modern social groups simultaneously occupying the political stage. The need to reconcile these diverse interests during the transition to modernity made the task of governing extremely difficult.[181] Just as Wilhelmine elites resorted to social imperialism to manage their analogous problem after the 1890s, Palmerston used an ideology of pseudoliberal expansion abroad to redirect the middle class away from its concern with reform at home. This approach allowed him to stand astride the deadlocked political system, using his popularity with reformers in foreign policy to stay in power without enacting domestic reforms.

In Germany the game of social imperialism had to last forever, since the elites' cartelized interests put them permanently at odds with democratic reform. In Britain, however, the game bought the time necessary for adjustment to modernity. Britain's landed elites, with their relatively diffuse interests and mobile capital, were eventually able to accept that free trade and further democratic reform did not fundamentally jeopardize their social or economic position. With Palmerston's death in 1867, the use of social imperialism to straddle irreconcilable interests gave way to a more modern democratic system of two parties competing for mass majorities by trying to co-opt the middle of the political spectrum. This gave median voters the power to express opposition to costly imperial overextension, as in Gladstone's successful anti-imperial electoral campaign of 1880. As the astute Salisbury remarked, "Though the feeling against Russia is strong, it no where rises to the Income-tax point."[182]

The Pattern of Early Industrialization

Britain's early textile industrialization had a two-edged effect on the development of a logrolled social imperial coalition. On one hand, compared with Germany's late industrialization, Britain's early industrialization produced—and reflected—a social structure in which aristocratic and bourgeois interests were not so sharply divided. Textile industrialization in Britain began as a small-scale, decentralized process, capitalized in large part by the commercialization of agriculture. The development of the woolens industry, in particular, benefited

181. W. L. Burn, *The Age of Equipoise* (London, 1964); Gary W. Cox, *The Efficient Secret: The Cabinet and the Development of Political Parties in Victorian England* (Cambridge, 1987), 32–36.
182. Marvin Swartz, *The Politics of British Foreign Policy in the Era of Gladstone and Disraeli* (New York, 1985), 67, quoting remarks of October 1877.

agriculturalist and entrepreneur alike. Moreover, landed aristocrats accumulated substantial investments in strictly commercial ventures. In Jane Austen's novels, the financial fortunes of the provincial baronet rise and fall not with the price of corn but with the fate of his investments in the Indies. As Prime Minister Robert Peel put it, "Agricultural prosperity. . . is interwoven with manufacturing prosperity and depends on it more than on the Corn Laws."[183] Thus, after 1688 Parliament grew in strength as an institution representing the joint interests of a relatively unified agricultural-commercial elite.[184]

Consequently, in comparison with Wilhelmine Germany the British sociopolitical system had moderate characteristics on several key dimensions that affect imperial logrolling and the development of strategic ideology. The economic interests of elite groups tended to be relatively diversified, and those of aristocratic and commercial-industrial groups overlapped. A strong central authority was provided by the extremely wealthy, commercialized aristocratic families that supplied cadres for the cabinet. All important groups had a stake in economic sectors with a promising future. Finally, bourgeois groups were gradually mobilized into the political process. All these factors made it possible for the various elite groups to reach acceptable, value-integrating compromises based on long-run encompassing interests, in contrast to the Germans' logrolling among narrow, often doomed, sociopolitical constituencies.[185]

On the other hand, Britain's rapid industrialization during the first half of the nineteenth century did cause a pileup of diverse social groups, leaving monarchs and landed aristocrats on the same historical stage with laissez faire entrepreneurs and a radical workers' movement. Group interests in the England of 1848, ranging from Whig aristocrat to Lancashire cotton manufacturer to Chartist factory operative, were somewhat less diverse than those in the Germany of 1898, ranging from Junker to Krupp to Social Democrat. Nevertheless, the resulting social divisions remained difficult to compose through value-integrating compromise. At the elite level, large-scale cotton industrialization exacerbated whatever gap remained between aristocratic agriculturalists and bourgeois entrepreneurs, since calico mills used foreign fiber and had an interest in importing cheap foreign food for their work

183. Norman Gash, "From the Origins to Sir Robert Peel," in Southgate, *Conservatives*, 96.
184. Alexander Gerschenkron, *Economic Backwardness in Historical Perspective* (Cambridge, 1962); Barrington Moore, *Social Origins of Dictatorship and Democracy* (Boston, 1967), chap. 1; Peter Katzenstein, *Between Power and Plenty* (Madison, Wis., 1978), 324–26; W. O. Aydelotte, "The Business Interests of the Gentry in the Parliament of 1841–47," in G. Kitson Clark, *The Making of Victorian England*, 2d ed. (New York, 1969), 290–305.
185. See chapter 3 above.

force. Though buffered by its commercial holdings, the aristocratic landowning and governing class had some reason to feel uncertain about the future and to resist economic, social, and political changes that powerful new social groups were demanding.[186]

Coalition Politics in the "Age of Equipoise"

Between the First and Second Reform Acts of 1832 and 1867, there was an "age of equipoise" between the old oligarchical political system and the emerging two-party mass electoral system. Social, political, and economic patterns combined elements of the old and the new. Food imports were cheap after the repeal of the Corn Laws in 1846, but land was hard for nonaristocrats to buy. Religious Dissenters could study at Oxford and Cambridge but could not administer the universities.[187] Politically, reform efforts focused on marginal questions of administrative efficiency, leaving intact the system of restricted suffrage and open balloting, heavily skewed to favor the rich and the rural.[188]

This limited franchise produced a chronic political stalemate in Parliament, with Protectionist Tory landlords numerically balancing radical and Irish members. Moderately reformist Whigs and "Peelite" Tories, the free-trading disciples of Robert Peel, could neither form stable coalitions with these extremes nor govern alone. Especially after the repeal of the Corn Laws in 1846, which produced an irrevocable split between Peelite and Protectionist Tories, this division created a situation of weak, short-lived coalitions or minority governments. A typical stalemate was that of 1852, when the Protectionists commanded 292 votes, the radicals 160, the Irish 50, the Whigs 130, and the Peelites 30.[189] Whigs, Peelites, and radicals tended to cooperate on free trade and administrative reforms, but most Whigs and Peelites balked at further electoral reform. Whigs trusted few of the radical leaders enough to offer them cabinet posts, and the radicals themselves, like

186. For background, see W. D. Rubinstein, "Wealth, Elites, and Class Structure of Modern Britain," *Past and Present* 76 (August 1977): 112–13.

187. Burn, *Age of Equipoise*, 327.

188. D. C. Moore, "The Other Face of Reform," *Victorian Studies* 5 (September 1961): 31–32, has argued that the curtailment of pocket boroughs and the separation of urban from county districts after 1832 helped the landed aristocracy at the expense of the central government. He traces the origins of the reform spirit back *before* the July 1830 revolution in France, showing that populist reform demands came both from radicals and from back-bench ultra-Tories, country gentlemen who want to decentralize political power as a means of reducing taxation (pp. 8–9). For Palmerston's efforts to turn the reform bill of 1832 into a more conservative document, see Bourne, *Palmerston*, 514.

189. Maccoby, *English Radicalism*, 435–36; see also Martin, *Triumph*, 75; Lucy Brown, *The Board of Trade and the Free Trade Movement* (Oxford, 1958), 57–60.

Cobden, generally thought that accepting official but powerless posts would undercut their ability to exert "pressure from without."[190]

Since free trade prohibited a Whig-Protectionist alignment, center-left and center-right coalitions were both impossible during this age of equipoise. As the Peelite leader James Graham wrote to the Whig leader John Russell in July 1852, "I see plainly the materials for overthrowing a Government, none on which the foundation can be laid for building up a powerful one."[191] Coalitions therefore had to cobble together ad hoc majorities issue by issue. Palmerston, for example, wrote Lord John Russell that the Irish radical leader Daniel O'Connell "will be a great difficulty for us. To act with him will often be impossible; to break openly with him would be hurtful." But still, "nine times out of ten he will support us."[192] Nonetheless, ad hoc arrangements could not remove the fundamental problem of a political spectrum that was too broad and too divided. "What will Sir Robert Peel do on the Corn Law?" Russell mused to his Whig colleague Lansdowne in November 1841. "If he does a good deal, the Squires will say with some reason that they have been betrayed, and if he produces some small measure, the attack from the manufacturing community will be sharp."[193]

One solution to the impasse would have been to enlarge the franchise, swamping the Protectionists with middle-class votes and paving the way for an unassailable Whig-radical coalition. This strategy of co-optation was the typical Whig solution and the one Russell normally favored.[194] The Corn Law issue had shown that appeasement could demobilize and co-opt the radical middle classes. Cobden himself made this pitch to Russell in February 1846, promising to dismantle the Anti–Corn Law League if repeal was effected immediately: "The protectionist landlords—the political landowners—will surely weigh the cost to themselves of keeping the League alive, flushed with victory, and with nothing else to do but concentrate all their efforts upon the Counties. They will purchase the possession of their wretched rag of protection for three years by the loss of half their political influence."[195]

But more conservative Whigs like Lansdowne and Palmerston felt that further electoral reform would mean sliding too far down the slippery slope. Russell's answer to Lansdowne's objections in 1849

190. Spiers, *Radical General*, 122.
191. Gooch, *Later Correspondence*, 2:105; more generally, Donald Southgate, *The Passing of the Whigs, 1832–1886* (London, 1962), 290–91.
192. Gooch, *Later Correspondence*, 1:47, on coalition tactics in October 1841.
193. Ibid., 1:50.
194. Maccoby, *English Radicalism*, 437, on Russell's 1852 reform bill as an attempt to prolong Whig rule by expanding the electorate at Tory expense.
195. Gooch, *Later Correspondence*, 1:107.

shows rather plainly that his aim in pursuing electoral reform was to elect more middle-class liberals, but it is unclear how he meant to control them: "If indeed the object were to please the radicals, and not offend the protectionists, that would be hopeless; but to add largely to the number of voters, with increased strength to the constitution and in such a manner that the radicals must support the plan, is not I think a desperate task."[196]

At this same juncture, shortly after the continental revolutions and Chartist revolts of 1848, Palmerston feared even an election under the 1832 franchise, not to mention one under an even more populist electoral scheme.

> In the present temper of the country, and in the present state of Europe, [an election would be] a misfortune. All kinds of questions would be set afloat, both political and commercial. Pledges would be required in many places in favor of [the secret] Ballot, Extension of Suffrage, and other matters of that kind. The farmers all over the country would vote for Protectionist candidates. What would happen in Ireland I cannot say, but a General Election would not be a convenient thing there, in its progress or result. In this country the new returns would probably give strength to the two extremes, to the Protectionists and to the Radicals, and the Whigs would be the sufferers.[197]

Social Imperialism and Palmerston's Coalition Strategy

Given that the later Gladstonian solution of a ruling liberal coalition was premature in the 1850s, the natural tactic for governing during the impasse was to logroll—to give each of the main interests what it wanted most, regardless of the incoherence of the overall policy. On its face, this seems to be the secret of Palmerston's political success. He simply logrolled an expansionist foreign policy, which was popular with the liberal business and middle classes, and a halt to domestic political reform, which the Tory landowners wanted. As Lord Derby, the Protectionist leader, put it in 1857, Palmerston "has been a Conservative minister working with Radical tools, and keeping up a show of Liberalism in his foreign policy, which nine in ten of the House of Commons care nothing about."[198] In the phrase of a recent historian, "Palmerston acted as a checkmate" on domestic reform, aligning his Whig-Peelite cabinet with intransigent Tories on domestic questions and with radical imperialists on foreign issues. "So long as he remained

196. Ibid., 1:197, September 1849.
197. Ibid., 1:194, Palmerston to Russell, April 1849.
198. Robert Stewart, *The Foundation of the Conservative Party, 1830–1867* (London, 1978), 311.

a force no other forces were either strong enough or sufficiently motivated to free the board for maneuvers. . . . Palmerston enabled the parliament of the 1832 franchise to talk liberally without actually putting their opinions to the test."[199]

Calling Palmerston a logrolling broker grossly understates his tactical achievement, however. Through the propagation of a liberal imperial ideology, Palmerston played a major role in creating a strong liberal constituency for imperialism. In the early 1840s many middle-class liberals had been Cobdenite anti-imperialists, leading the attack in Parliament on British overextension in the Afghan War.[200] But by the eve of the Crimean War Palmerston's strategic ideology had convinced radical elements in his coalition that foreign expansion would be a vehicle for reform, not an alternative to it.

The chief critic of Palmerston's overextended policy in the first Afghan War was the radical J. A. Roebuck, later Parliament's loudest voice in favor of the vigorous prosecution of the Crimean War. In both instances, Roebuck's main aim was to publicize the incompetence of the establishment as a pretext for promoting reform. In the Cobdenite heyday of the early 1840s, Roebuck found it expedient to do this by attacking the fundamental misconceptions of imperialist policy. But after Palmerston's ascendancy it seemed expedient to laud the goals of the policy while assaulting the aristocratic, charge-of-the-light-brigade incompetents implementing the policy.[201] One way to oust a class opponent is the Cobden approach: denigrate his function; another is to show that your class can carry out that function better. As the newspaper of Roebuck's Sheffield constituency put it, "All Asia lies before us," but to seize it we must push through a "radical change" in "our whole system of administration."[202] Thus, just as in Wilhelmine Germany, radical middle-class nationalists tried to force their way into a share of state power by linking incompetence in foreign expansion and the unfitness of the old elite to govern.[203]

The irony, of course, is that Palmerston used middle-class imperialism to block social and policial reforms. Some imperialist radicals like Austin Henry Layard were co-opted with offers of government jobs,

199. Shannon, *Crisis of Imperialism*, 20–22. For similar analysis, see Briggs, *Victorian People*, 35.

200. On middle-class radical opinion, Robert Eadon Leader, *Life and Letters of John Arthur Roebuck* (London, 1897); Southgate, *Passing*, 75; Briggs, *Victorian People*, 64; Eldridge, *Victorian Imperialism*, 81–82. For some typical parliamentary debates, see *Hansard*, 3d ser., 39:1093–1113, 14 December 1837; *Hansard*, 3d ser., 67:138, 1 March 1843.

201. Yapp, *Strategies*, 454–55; Briggs, *Victorian People*, chap. 3; Anderson, *Liberal State at War*.

202. Briggs, *Victorian People*, 66, quoting the Sheffield and Rotherham *Independent*, January 1855.

203. See Anderson, *Liberal State at War*.

but a real opening up of the political system had to wait for Gladstone's center-left anti-imperialist coalition.[204] Cobden was one of the few radicals who understood what was being done to them, taking as the slogan for his unsuccessful 1857 electoral campaign: "Palmerston for ever, no reform, and a Chinese war."[205] Palmerston not only managed the logrolling of interests, but also influenced how middle-class radicals perceived their interests and manipulated their expectations of the side benefits that imperial logrolling might bring.

Preparing the strategic ideology. Palmerston had been pursuing a strategy of liberal social imperialism since the end of the 1820s, as reflected, for example, in his 1829 remarks about venting class hatreds abroad. The liberal imperial ideology required time to take root, however, and needed a dramatic catalyst to realign British politics. The 1833 crisis over Russia's one-sided treaty with Turkey came too soon to serve as that catalyst. Neither Palmerston nor the public was ideologically prepared for it. The Russophobe propagandists had only begun to beat their drum. And until late 1832, Palmerston's own view of the Eastern Question still reflected George Canning's approach of cooperating with Russia against Turkey to establish an independent Greece, a good "liberal" policy.[206]

An 1840 showdown with France and Egypt was another partial step toward preparing Palmerston's social imperialist strategy. Palmerston overrode his Whig colleagues in insisting on using military force to defeat an Egyptian invasion of Turkish-held Syria, while relying on Britain's naval superiority to deter France from intervening on behalf of its Egyptian ally.[207] This crisis was not an ideal catalyst for a social imperial realignment of British politics, since France was too liberal an enemy to arouse the hatred of liberal British opinion.[208] Nonetheless, the easy victory was popular and demonstrated the Whig government's political reliance on Palmerston's foreign policy successes.[209] Moreover, in light of Palmerston's penetration of the daily press, it would have been dangerous for Palmerston's Francophile cabinet colleagues to confront him publicly on this issue.[210]

Palmerston followed up this victory over the French and their Foxite Whig allies with a gratuitous attack on French atrocities in Algeria,

204. Waterfield, *Layard*, 261–62; Southgate, *Most English Minister*, 363.
205. George F. Bartle, *Sir John Bowring and the "Arrow" War in China* (Manchester, 1961), 308.
206. Webster, *Foreign Policy*, vol. 1, chap. 4; Bourne, *Palmerston*.
207. Bourne, *Palmerston*, 593, July 1840.
208. Briggs, *Victorian People*, 54.
209. Bourne, *Palmerston*, 607.
210. Ibid., 508, 600, 603, 605, 611, 614.

which Palmerston sought to give the widest possible media exposure.[211] This bid to use a new style of demagogy to free himself from political dependence on his Whig colleagues went for naught in the short run, when the Whigs lost the general election. Back in the Foreign Office after repeal of the Corn Laws split the Tory party in 1846, however, Palmerston used the same tactics, appealing to middle-class opinion over the heads of his cabinet colleagues through a calculated policy of vocal support for liberal causes abroad.[212]

The revolutions of 1848. Palmerston's return to office was soon followed by a revolutionary tide in Europe, which presented both dangers and opportunities for his policy. On one hand, there was danger of a spillover of revolutionary ideas from the Continent into British politics. But on the other hand, it presented the possibility that Britain might be able to shape these new political energies toward the creation of a Pax Britannica abroad and the perpetuation of a social stalemate at home. Seizing the opportunity to exert diplomatic pressure against Austria and Russia in support of national independence and constitutionalism, Palmerston used the theme of liberal imperialism more and more openly in the late 1840s to gain a personal political following among middle-class radicals and entrepreneurs.[213]

At the same time, Palmerston played skillfully on the readiness of the middle class for an elitist reform program, rather than a populist one, after the repeal of the Corn Laws and the Chartist disturbances and European revolutions of 1848. The Corn Law issue had been the popular engine that drove the whole anti-imperialist platform. Anti-imperialism was in itself a weak ideology without the tie to the Anti–Corn Law issue and League, which disbanded in 1846, as Cobden had promised Russell it would. Repeal took away the upper middle class's most powerful reason to align with lower middle and working classes in an antiestablishment mass-mobilizing movement. At the same time, 1848 gave propertied liberals some second thoughts about the political risks of a populist coalition. The smug Crystal Palace era had arrived.[214]

Don Pacifico. Palmerston knew just how to articulate the aspirations and attitudes of middle-class "radical" opinion at this juncture—and

211. Ridley, *Lord Palmerston*, 280–81, interprets this speech as domestic political manipulation.

212. This is Bourne's interpretation; see also Wetzel, *Crimean War*, 60–61.

213. See Palmerston's remarks to the Reform Club in 1850, quoted in Fagan, *Reform Club*, 88.

214. Briggs, *Victorian People*, 49, 87–88; Burn, *Age of Equipoise*, 60; Michael Bentley, *Politics without Democracy* (London, 1984), 146.

how to link it to an imperial rather than a reforming agenda. His opportunity came through a diplomatic crisis following Palmerston's use of naval coercion to extract compensation for dubious debts owed by the Greek government to one Don David Pacifico, a Portuguese born in Gibraltar and thus a British citizen. This high-handed move brought censure from the European Concert and in particular was exploited by Napoleon in a manner costly to British prestige. After being raked over the coals in the House of Commons by Cobdenites, Peelites, and protectionist Tories as well, Palmerston turned this comic opera into a personal triumph by explaining that the slighting of the rights of a single Englishman anywhere on the globe could not be allowed to go unchallenged. Just as the status of *Civis Romanus* had brought unquestioned rights and immunities throughout the civilized world to citizens of that earlier empire, so too the citizen of the British Empire had earned the right to exact unquestioned respect in the present day. Alone among European peoples, the Briton had demonstrated in 1848 that "liberty is compatible with order" when "every class of society accepts with cheerfulness" its lot in life and "every individual . . . strives to raise himself."[215]

Almost every diarist of the era recorded that Palmerston's was "the most effective and extraordinary speech I ever heard in my life."[216] Overnight Palmerston became a middle-class icon, surviving a vote of no confidence on the strength of a newspaper and letter-writing campaign. His strongest support came from radicals like Roebuck and Thomas Anstey, who not long before had been trying to impeach him.[217] Among those parliamentarians who had voted for the secret ballot in 1850, an acid test of radicalism, 105 voted with Palmerston and Roebuck on this confidence motion, 7 against.[218]

Also working in Palmerston's favor was the fact that a defeat on the confidence motion would have placed the Russell government in jeopardy, risking the formation of a protectionist government. Consequently, opponents of Palmerston's gunboat diplomacy, like Peel, were reluctant to speak out against it.[219] This factor also helped gain the support of the liberal press in manufacturing centers like Leeds, which otherwise had at least mild reservations about gunboat diplomacy.[220]

The catalytic crisis of 1853. Despite the *Civis Romanus* triumph, it still took Russia's overplaying its hand in the Turkish crisis of 1853 and the

215. Ridley, *Lord Palmerston*, 387.
216. This reaction from Hobhouse, *Recollections*, 6:257–58, was echoed by friends and foes alike. Bell, *Lord Palmerston*, 2:27–28.
217. Ridley, *Lord Palmerston*, 388.
218. My own tabulation from division lists.
219. Gordon, *Aberdeen Correspondence*, 8:309, 346–48.
220. *Leeds Mercury*, 22 June 1850, p. 4.

sinking of Turkey's squadron at Sinope to let Palmerston ride to power on the patriotic tide. As home secretary in Aberdeen's Whig-Peelite cabinet, Palmerston was not the day-to-day manager of the developing crisis. Through Russophobe speeches and articles and through subtle pressure on cabinet deliberations, however, he intimidated the cabinet into a firmer policy than it might otherwise have adopted.[221] Other cabinet members were sensitive to the implicit danger that a weak policy would cause him to resign, take his case to the people, and overturn the ministry.[222] As Aberdeen told the queen: "The situation of Lord Palmerston is peculiar. Unless he should continue to be a cordial Member of Your Majesty's Government, he may very easily become the leader of the Opposition. . . . He has more than once, recently, been thwarted in his endeavour to press a warlike policy upon the Cabinet."[223]

To preempt such a defection, Foreign Secretary Clarendon included Palmerston in the crisis deliberations from the start and was careful not to be outflanked on the hawkish side.[224] Throughout the crisis, Clarendon kept one eye on Palmerston and the other on public opinion. For example, Clarendon, Aberdeen, and Graham thought Stratford Canning too bellicose as ambassador to Turkey, but they refrained from removing him because the public success of Palmerston's attack on Cobden made it suicidal to seem too weak.[225] Likewise, Clarendon advised Aberdeen to send the fleet to the Straits as "the least measure that will satisfy public opinion and save the Government from shame hereafter, if, as I firmly believe, the Russian hordes pour into Turkey from every side. It may do us some good to ourselves, which should not be our last consideration."[226]

In all this, fear of public opinion and fear of the Russians were closely intermingled: "We can't press the Turks too hard about [accepting the compromise Vienna] Note,—first because public opinion at home would be against it, and second because, if we did, they would certainly refuse and say they would fight single handed. We should still have to help them, because otherwise Russia would be established

---

221. Bell, *Lord Palmerston*, 2:90–92; Martin, *Triumph*, chaps. 3–7; Rich, *Why the Crimean War?* 63–64.

222. This fear affected policy during the war too. George Douglas, Eighth Duke of Argyll, *Autobiography and Memoirs* (New York, 1906), 1:489–94, presents the view that the cabinet was letting war policy drift owing to fear of public opinion and of each other. "We are shy of each other because we do not know each other's views," says Argyll in the fall of 1854. See also Conacher, *Aberdeen Coalition*, 440–41.

223. Gordon, *Aberdeen Correspondence*, 10:220, 10 September 1853.

224. Maxwell, *Clarendon*, 2:8.

225. J. L. Herkless, "Stratford, the Cabinet and the Outbreak of the Crimean War," *Historical Journal* 18 (September 1975): 500, citing Strachey and Fulford, *Greville Memoirs*, 7:30–31, on Palmerston's August 1853 parliamentary speech.

226. Martin, *Triumph*, 106.

at Constantinople in a twelvemonth."[227] One suspects that domestic politics may have weighed more heavily on Clarendon than geopolitics, however, given his distaste for "all these disputes about nothing and this miserable rivalry for useless influence" in peripheral regions.[228]

Russell's support for a firm policy may have been influenced by similar considerations. From the beginning of the Whig-Peelite coalition government, Russell had been angling to replace Aberdeen as its head. Seeing that Aberdeen was vulnerable for appearing too pacific in the Turkish crisis, Russell told Aberdeen that "unless he was in my place, he could not remain a member of the Government," as Aberdeen reported to Graham in October 1853. Looking for "some ground of difference," Russell "is more warlike than ever."[229]

If a hard line on the Eastern Question could be used offensively against Aberdeen, it also served as protection against Palmerston. For offensive ammunition, Russell counted on his electoral reform proposal to force Palmerston to resign on unpopular grounds. The essence of this strategy, as well as its risks, comes through in Russell's 10 December letter to Aberdeen:

> If Palmerston should resolve to separate himself from us, another grave question arises. Can we hope to bring the Reform measure to a successful issue? I have reflected much on this, and my conclusion is that provided the Government stands well with the country on other topics [i.e., the Turkish crisis] we should carry our Bill in all its main and essential provisions. But here arises a further question. How shall we stand on Eastern affairs? And here I cannot but feel that an increased weight of responsibility would rest upon me, if I had to encounter Palmerston as a critic, instead of having him by me as a colleague.[230]

Palmerston did threaten to resign over the reform issue, but he still got the better of Russell when the press played it as a veiled protest against Aberdeen's "weak" policy toward Russia.[231] "Palmerston has

227. Herkless, "Stratford," 501, quoting Clarendon, 12 September 1853; Maxwell, *Clarendon*, 2:20.

228. Matthew S. Anderson, *The Eastern Question, 1774–1923* (New York, 1966), 129, citing F. Wellesley, *The Paris Embassy during the Second Empire* (London, 1928), 26. On the influence of public opinion on Clarendon's policy, Conacher, *Aberdeen Coalition*, 151, 184, 199–200, 240.

229. Gordon, *Aberdeen Correspondence*, 10:263; also 237, 275, 278, 288. Russell also had strategic arguments, such as the domino theory, to offer in support of a firm stance. "If we do not stop the Russians on the Danube, we shall have to stop them on the Indus," he asserted. Though Russell's strategic beliefs were in general hawkish enough that this policy preference was not out of character, his threat to resign if the Turks were pushed to accept the Vienna Note makes little sense as strategy but a lot of sense in terms of public opinion and cabinet politics. Conacher, *Aberdeen Coalition*, 182–83.

230. Gordon, *Aberdeen Correspondence*, 10:394–95, Russell to Aberdeen, 10 December 1853; also Bell, *Lord Palmerston*, 2:94.

231. Bell, *Lord Palmerston*, 2:100; Conacher, *Aberdeen Coalition*, 222.

stolen a march by combining the Eastern Question with Reform. I am at a loss what to do," admitted Aberdeen to Graham. "Truly he is a great artist." Russell, outmaneuvered by his own tactic, saw Palmerston as "wishing to go to war to stave off reform," a characterization that Aberdeen thought "perfectly true."[232]

As a result of this incident, the not implausible belief arose that if only Palmerston had been in control from the start, pursuing a policy of forceful deterrence, the Russians would have backed down before the crisis got out of control. Consequently, when radical protests over the incompetent prosecution of the war brought down Aberdeen's Whig-Peelite coalition, it was not the radicals who took power, but Palmerston.[233]

Consolidating his position, Palmerston broke reformist critics like Cobden and Bright by fighting the general election of 1857 on the issue of his gunboat diplomacy in China. Gaining the largest majority since Melbourne's post–Reform Bill victory in 1832, Palmerston demonstrated that Parliament could be bullied through jingoistic appeals to public opinion.[234] As Cobden remarked, "the most warlike returns" came from the cities with broad suffrage, "the least warlike from the most aristocratic counties." In the words of historian Asa Briggs, "The Crimean War seemed to have reversed the direction of British politics."[235]

Mobilizing the masses against the Whigs. In carrying out these tactical manipulations, Palmerston was never guided by short-run political expediency. In fact, he was constantly taking stands that were disadvantageous in cabinet politics in the short run. As early as 1830, Palmerston saw that sticking to his "principles"—his long-run strategy of a liberal, interventionist foreign policy—would benefit him more than getting back into a Tory cabinet.[236] The aggressive policy toward France in 1840 endangered his position in the Francophile Whig cabinet. His audience with Kossuth in 1851, against royal wishes and cabinet orders, helped prepare the way for his removal as foreign minister.[237] But Palmerston understood that his political strategy hinged not on winning the favor of this or that ministry or faction, but on his

232. Gordon, *Aberdeen Correspondence*, 10:393–94, Aberdeen to Graham, 10 December 1853; Bell, *Lord Palmerston*, 2:97.

233. Southgate, *Most English Minister*, chap. 18.

234. Shannon, *Crisis of Imperialism*, 20; David Krein, *The Last Palmerston Government* (Ames, Iowa, 1978), 9; Stewart, *Foundation*, 311.

235. Briggs, *Victorian People*, 219.

236. Bourne, *Palmerston*, 313. As late as 1851–52 Palmerston discussed with Tory leaders the possiblity of his entering a Protectionist ministry.

237. Bell, *Lord Palmerston*, 2:44. But Palmerston also worked to discredit the radical Kossuth by exploring his connection to a scheme to store explosives in Britain, to be used for revolutionary purposes.

ability to build his reputation as a forceful agent of responsible liberal imperialism, which would allow him to create a coalition that would straddle normal party lines.[238] As I argued above, such a straddle was necessary to form a stable government in the stalemated conditions of the mid-Victorian equipoise. Palmerston, an insightful political entrepreneur, developed an effective long-run strategy for governing in these conditions through "liberal" imperialism.

This strategy had a self-reinforcing effect on Palmerston's political behavior. Because he aimed to operate across party lines, he was constantly in trouble with Whig ministers. This forced him to resort even more strongly to social imperialist tactics to maintain his personal position. From about 1846 onward, Palmerston and Russell were thus locked into competition to mobilize mass support against each other, with Palmerston relying on ploys like the Don Pacifico affair and Russell on the promise of a new reform bill.[239] As early as September 1848, Russell had agreed with the queen that Palmerston should be dropped from the cabinet, but this had to be delayed, since Russell also realized that his government could not survive without its most popular minister.[240]

This dynamic played a part in the terminal phase of the Crimean War, when Russell made a bid to regain his political standing as the proponent and negotiator of a compromise peace settlement. Aligned with the French, who were becoming eager to terminate an unprofitable venture, Russell might have been able to show the country the fruitlessness of Palmerston's whole war policy and in the process recapture a following as the politician who would reestablish political reform as the top priority. Understanding this, Palmerston had all the more incentive to continue the war to a dramatically successful conclusion, lest liberal imperialism lose some of its luster to the competing cause of liberal domestic reform. Palmerston successfully deployed his ideology of security through expansion in weathering a confidence vote in the Commons, leaving Russell and his French collaborator Edouard Drouyn as the ones who had to resign.[241]

Thus the strategy of social imperialism permitted Palmerston to achieve what Russell's strategy of electoral reform could not manage

238. Bullen, *Palmerston*, 56–57, gives an example of Palmerston's playing the diplomatic game to build his reputation, not to gain the object of the dispute.

239. I am indebted to Roger Bullen for discussion on this and the following points.

240. Southgate, *Passing*, 268–71; Bell, *Lord Palmerston*, 2:43, 50. Lieven and Aberdeen comment upon Palmerston's "isolated and menacing situation vis-à-vis his colleagues" as a result of his social imperialist policy. Parry, *Aberdeen-Lieven Correspondence*, 2:315, 317.

241. Rich, *Why the Crimean War?* 149, 155–56, provides background and suggests that Russell was consciously engaging in a political strategy of product differentiation against Palmerston. See also Gooch, *Later Correspondence*, 2:184–207; Henderson, *Crimean War Diplomacy*, 37–38, 41; Schroeder, *Austria*, 249–50.

during the mid-Victorian stalemate. It provided a means for mobilizing mass political support without overturning oligarchical rule and the old social order.[242] And consequently it allowed him to form a relatively stable government, acting as a sociopolitical "checkmate" for over a decade until his death in 1865, which broke the logjam and permitted such innovations as the Second Reform Act, competitive examinations for the civil service, free education, and church reform.[243]

Why Social Imperialism Was Persuasive

As I have argued, underlying social and political conditions were favorable for the success of social imperialist appeals. Social divisions, exacerbated by rapid industrialization, made it difficult to build stable coalitions on other foundations. Meanwhile, the extension of the franchise in 1832 created a group of middle-class voters with uncertain interests that propagandists competed to mobilize behind their programs. But why were the pro-imperialists more successful in this quest than their anti-imperialist opponents?

A simple but incorrect answer might be that middle-class voters objectively benefited from imperialism. It is certainly true that some large trading interests directly sought and profited from gunboat diplomacy to open up the China market, for example.[244] But comprehensive studies suggest that the main beneficiaries of empire were London financial interests, and that the tax burden may have made empire a net loss for the broad middle classes.[245] In the 1830s and 1840s many middle-class radicals could be found on both sides of the imperial issue. Even in the 1850s, radicals remained ambivalent toward empire and retained a latent ability to shift back to the anti-interventionist stance of 1843. Though the imperialist Roebuck was one of industrial Sheffield's representatives in 1853, the other was an opponent of involvement in the war.[246] After the Crimean War, Roebuck himself joined Cobden and Gladstone in condemning Palmerston for his crude coercion of China, claiming that the "honor of England had been desecrated by the proceedings at Canton."[247] Though Palmerston took

242. On Palmerston's domestic conservatism in the post-Crimea period, see Hollis, *Pressure*, 152; Southgate, *Passing*, 294.
243. Burn, *Age of Equipoise*, 319.
244. British Museum, Add. MS. 43668, 68, Bowring to Cobden, 22 February 1850; also John Bowring, *Autobiographical Recollections of Sir John Bowring* (London, 1877), 288–90; George F. Bartle, *Sir John Bowring and the Chinese and Siamese Commercial Treaties* (Manchester, 1962); Redford, *Manchester Merchants*, 120–22; Add. MS. 43667, 233, 16 December 1848.
245. Lance Davis and Robert Huttenback, *Mammon and the Pursuit of Empire: The Political Economy of British Imperialism, 1860–1912* (Cambridge, 1986); Cain and Hopkins, "Political Economy of British Expansion," 463–90.
246. Briggs, *Victorian People*, 66.
247. Leader, *Roebuck*, 264–65.

this issue to the public and gained a large electoral victory, the anti-interventionist side of the radical consciousness was not dead but merely dormant, waiting for Gladstone to revive it as one of the props of the Liberal party.

In short, the ambivalence of its interests in empire made the middle class open to persuasion in either direction. In a world of perfect information, this would have made such voters selective and usually moderate on imperial issues. But in a world of potent propaganda, it made them volatile and vulnerable to manipulation.

Palmerston and the Russophobes prevailed in mobilizing mass support for the Crimean War in part because they enjoyed significant advantages in organization and monopolies on information. One factor was the organizational collapse of Cobden's peace lobby, which had been built around the Anti–Corn Law League after the repeal of the Corn Laws in 1846. Once this fight was won, the middle class had less reason to use generalized foreign policy attacks to discredit the old elite.[248] As Roebuck accurately foresaw, "The lecturers, the printers, the patriots will cease to have a pretext for their union, their outcry, and *ergo*, for their pay, and thus an army of noisy people will suddenly be disbanded."[249]

Palmerston and the Russophobes mounted a more effective propaganda effort in the long run, in part because the proponents of imperial expansion seemed to have greater standing as expert authorities. People with "hands on" imperial experience tended to be agents, experts, diplomats, or soldiers who typically had a parochial interest in imperial activity.

An important example is Austen Henry Layard. A misfit in his downwardly mobile but proper middle-class family, Layard found adventure and fame as a self-taught archaeologist and the discoverer of ancient "Nineveh." Partly to get money for his excavations, he attached himself to Stratford Canning, then ambassador at Constantinople. He parlayed this connection and his world-famous book on Nineveh into a meteoric career in Parliament and the Foreign Office, where he was undersecretary in a short-lived government in 1851. Kept out of the Aberdeen coalition government by Peelite objections, Layard set about forcing his way back in. For that purpose, the Turkish crisis of 1853 was a godsend. Layard's apparent area expertise made him a natural rallying point for disaffected backbenchers on both sides of the House. His indictment of the weakness of the government's policy was

248. This was Cobden's own analysis. Conacher, *Peelites*, 146–47, 208; Edsall, *Cobden*, 288.
249. Leader, *Roebuck*, 167.

extremely effective, despite his gratuitous personal attacks on the mild Aberdeen.[250] "Knowledge is power," one colleague told him, "and in that respect, you are as regards Turkey second to none."[251]

Presumably Layard might have tried to use his expertise on the opposite side of the argument, ingratiating himself with Aberdeen by supporting a cautious policy. On its face, however, it seems a bad strategy to launch a political career on the argument that Turkey is not threatened and not important, and that therefore one's own expertise is not needed very much, aside from warning England to stay out. Of course, strictly cognitive biases might have led Layard and the other area experts to overrate the importance of their own region and to worry inordinately about threats to British influence there. But only motivated biases—or outright manipulation—can explain why Layard changed his mind on the possibility of Turkish reform after he started exploiting the issue for political gain. He found it embarrassing to have his own books quoted against him in parliamentary debate.[252]

Although the systematic bias of area experts was not lost on some of the shrewder newspaper editors, it was still difficult to overcome. For example, commenting on alleged dangers on India's turbulent north-western frontier in 1849, The Sheffield *Independent* remarked that "we hear only one side of the story" from military officers looking for glory and honors, who fail to understand that "extended empire is not always increased strength."[253]

This advantage was still more difficult to overcome when joined to Palmerston's own press juggernaut. Palmerston bought journalistic loyalty by providing consular appointments for journalists' sons and by supplying current, detailed information on diplomatic developments.[254] Thus monopoly powers of office were turned into superior organization and penetration of the press. Melbourne thought this crucial to Palmerston's success in the Levant crisis of 1840. If Palmerston "had not had as devoted an assistant as the *Morning Chronicle*," Melbourne believed, "he would hardly have been able to maintain his course or carry through his measures."[255]

The advantage of persistence also worked in the pro-imperialists' favor. Russophobe area experts were a self-renewing resource, and Palmerston was rarely out of office. In contrast, Cobden's most effec-

250. Waterfield, *Layard*, 91, 228, 233–34, 239.
251. British Museum, Add. MS. 38981.
252. Waterfield, *Layard*, 244.
253. Sheffield *Independent*, 10 March 1849.
254. Stephen Koss, *The Rise and Fall of the Political Press in England* (London, 1981), 72–80; Bourne, *Palmerston*, 474–91, 614–17, passim; Bullen, *Palmerston*, 29; Webster, *Foreign Policy*, 1:50.
255. Bourne, *Palmerston*, 617.

tive propaganda base was an ephemeral, single-issue organization. As a recent historian remarked, "Ten or fifteen years of propaganda for the Turkish reform movement and an even longer period of intermittent Russophobia had left their mark," producing a "stereotype built up in the public mind out of the dreams and visions of politicians and publicists such as Palmerston, Stratford de Redcliffe [Stratford Canning], and David Urquhart."[256]

Finally, some have argued that this particular period in European history was dominated not so much by the rising tide of the bourgeoisie as by the explosion of literacy, the penny press, university education, and a surplus of intellectuals. Editors and publicists used their distinctive weapon, ideas on the printed page, in a battle of self-assertion against each other and the old elites.[257] The effects of the penny press are often described in terms similar to the alleged effects of television in our own era. At any rate, it is clear that contemporaries believed the press had an extraordinary influence on literate opinion: "On almost all the great questions which have agitated the public mind during the last twenty years, the fiat of the *Leeds Mercury*, in the populous districts where it circulates, has generally been considered as satisfactory and decisive."[258] In short, imperial ideologists were able to have a large impact because of their apparent monopoly on expertise and effective organization, and because of the ambivalent interests of the audience.

Conclusion: Palmerston's Social Imperialism

Palmerstonian imperialist excesses were mostly a by-product of coalition politics and ideology, not a direct expression of the concentrated interests of a middle-class constituency. As with the German Navy League, most middle-class adherents had no pecuniary stake in the building of the fleet or in any empire that it would "protect." Rather, upwardly mobile middle-class groups sought to use this issue to gain access to political power, by outbidding the old elites on symbolic nationalist issues. Though pecuniary interests played a role for some British liberals, the most outspoken of them were often making tactical use of imperial arguments. They wanted to use the war as a lever for achieving administrative, if not necessarily electoral, reform. They did not consciously trade reform for empire. Rather, that outcome was the unwanted result of Palmerston's ability to use his patriotic stature and

256. Saab, *Origins*, 130.

257. Alan Sked, *Europe's Balance of Power, 1815–1848* (London, 1979), 175–79.

258. Donald Read, *Press and People* (London, 1961), 205; more generally, Kennedy, *Realities*, 51–59.

liberal imperial ideology to block reformist assaults on a conservative domestic policy.

Despite the apparent popularity of Palmerston's assertive foreign policy, there was no obvious preponderance of pro-imperialist sentiment in the body politic during these mid-Victorian years. Even at the height of the war fever after the Sinope incident, Clarendon could write, "I am convinced that within six weeks after the first shot was fired by England against Russia there would be mighty few partisans of war policy."[259] By the end of the war, the protectionist Tories were "passivist, economical, non-imperialist . . . , barely distinguishable from . . . Cobden and Bright."[260] The moral fervor of the radical left, now geared up for bashing Chinese, quickly turned toward isolationist abhorrence of complicity in Turkish atrocities after Palmerston's death. Even in the core of Palmerston's governing coalition, Gladstone and his group of former Peelite Tories wanted less imperialism and more reform.

But this potential anti-imperialist coalition was spread from the extreme left of the political spectrum to the extreme right. Gladstone, its natural leader, refused at this stage in his political evolution to align with either of the extremes, which were anathema to his basically moderate, technocratic sensibilities. As a politically isolated subordinate in Palmerston's cabinet, Gladstone constituted a check only on the more extreme expressions of Palmerston's foreign policy.[261] Palmerston, spanning the mid-Victorian political impasse, was able to use the Crimean War as a realigning issue to mobilize public support against splintered elite opponents and opponent-allies. From then on he was generally able to use the momentum of office to set the political agenda and choose the issues on which elections would be fought.

In explaining the origins of Palmerston's social imperialism, however, it is also important to remember its moderation compared with that of the late industrializing nations. The distinctive feature of Victorian imperialism was the ability to learn from its costly mistakes and pull back from the brink of serious overextension. In this Britain differed markedly from Germany and Japan, which reinforced failure because their cartelized and myth-ridden political systems suppressed learning. In contrast, Britain's "early industrializer" polity gave power to an elite oligarchy with relatively diffuse, encompassing interests and to a mass

259. To Stratford Canning, 8 October 1853, quoted in Herkless, "Stratford," 518. Schroeder, *Austria*, 413, comments: "Clarendon feared just as much that the public would find out what Britain's policy really was and repudiate it as he feared that public opinion would drive Britain into an unnecessary war."
260. Southgate, "From Disraeli to Law," 141.
261. Krein, *Last Palmerston Government*, 25; Conacher, *Aberdeen Coalition*, 389; Stewart, *Foundation*, 315–17.

electorate with an interest in keeping the tax burden of empire low. These groups had strong incentives to learn from negative feedback, and for the most part they did so effectively.

For example, at the point where Palmerston came very close to launching a social imperialist total war against Russia, cabinet moderates like Gladstone held him in check.[262] They continued to do so down through his parting debacle, a would-be intervention against Prussia over its annexation of Schleswig-Holstein.[263] Palmerston learned fairly quickly that he could benefit from jingoistic politics only if the costs were kept low. This was due above all to the residual strength of the relatively unified Whig oligarchy, with its comparatively long time horizon and encompassing interests. Though Palmerston's liberal imperial coalition had its advantages during the age of equipoise, other coalitions were not unthinkable and were preferable to high-cost imperial adventurism. Indeed, Gladstone used disgruntlement over the Schleswig-Holstein affair to launch his bid to establish the Liberal party as a reformist, anti-interventionist, mass-based political instrument.[264]

One could argue that Palmerstonian social imperialism actually played a positive role in the development of Britain's stable two-party democracy. Long-run structural forces, associated with the pattern of early industrialization, favored a democratic outcome, but Palmerston's pseudoliberal imperialism arguably bought time for a relatively smooth transition from oligarchic rule to the system of two umbrella parties, competing for the broadest popularity in the middle of the political spectrum.[265] The merger of the Whigs and radicals into a mass liberal party was still ahead in the early 1850s.[266] So was Benjamin Disraeli's later strategy of working-class Toryism, which attempted to redirect mass claims toward factory owners rather than landowners.[267] Booming industry, a higher standard of living, and high agricultural prices in the 1850s and 1860s were needed to reduce conflicts of interest across the political spectrum sufficiently to allow the passage of the Second Reform Bill and the safe arrival of modern politics.[268]

262. Baumgart, *Peace of Paris*, 32–33.
263. Lawrence Steefel, *The Schleswig-Holstein Question* (Cambridge, Mass., 1932), 171; W. E. Mosse, *The European Powers and the German Question, 1848–71* (1958; New York, 1969), 202–6; Krein, *Last Palmerston Government*, chaps. 11 and 12.
264. Krein, *Last Palmerston Government*, 165–66.
265. Hollis, *Pressure*, vii–viii; Shannon, *Crisis of Imperialism*, 47–48.
266. On the difficulties of achieving this as late as 1859, Southgate, *Passing*, 292–94.
267. Doyle, *Empires*, 275–94; also Charles Maier, "'Fictitious Bonds...of Wealth and Law': On the Theory and Practice of Interest Representation," in Suzanne Berger, *Organizing Interests in Western Europe: Pluralism, Corporatism, and the Transformation of Politics* (Cambridge, 1981), 51, on "the ritualistic debates between Disraeli and Gladstone."
268. J. B. Conacher, *The Emergence of British Parliamentary Democracy in the Nineteenth Century* (New York, 1971), argues that prosperity made the working class "responsible"

DENOUEMENT: VICTORIAN IMPERIALISM AFTER PALMERSTON

With Palmerston's death in 1865 and the passage of the Second Reform Bill in 1867, the use of social imperialism to bridge irreconcilable interests gave way to a system of two parties competing for mass majorities by trying to co-opt the middle of the political spectrum. This enhanced the power of the median voters, who expressed their natural antipathy to imperial overextension when it grew too costly—for example, in Gladstone's successful anti-imperialist electoral campaign in 1880.[269]

With the declining competitiveness of British manufactures in the 1890s, however, a significant bloc of voters acquired a plausible parochial interest in protectionism within an expanded empire.[270] This interest, championed by Joseph Chamberlain, formed an indispensable part of Salisbury's Conservative coalition of the 1890s, logrolling its electoral support in exchange for a central place in imperial policy.[271] As a result, Salisbury often found himself constrained to accept colonial policies that he knew were counterproductive, because he was politically dependent on Chamberlain's votes. This was at least partially true of the policies that led to the Boer War and the Fashoda crisis. Salisbury's proposed concessions, which would have headed off the Fashoda confrontation, died in the British cabinet for this reason.[272] "Chamberlain was at the height of his powers," says G. N. Sanderson, "and he flatly vetoed the proposal, complaining that Salisbury wanted 'to give away everything and get nothing.'"[273]

This coalition arrangement coincided with the development of all sorts of Salisbury-style balance of power justifications for the expansionist policy that Chamberlain wanted on economic and domestic political

---

(pp. 68–69) and that by the time of the Second Reform Bill, the working-class movement "had attained precisely that level of development at which it was safe to concede its enfranchisement and dangerous to withhold it," the opposite of the situation in 1848 (p. 115). After the Schleswig-Holstein crisis, Cobden and the Tory leader Stanley even found it possible to coordinate tactics in pursuit of anti-imperialist goals. Mosse, *European Powers*, 209.

269. Marvin Swartz, *The Politics of British Foreign Policy in the Era of Gladstone and Disraeli* (New York, 1985).

270. Cain and Hopkins, "Political Economy of British Expansion," 466, 485–86; Ronald Robinson, "Imperial Problems in British Politics, 1880–1895," in E. A. Benians, ed., *The Cambridge History of the British Empire* (Cambridge, 1959), 127–80, esp. 158.

271. Richard Jay, *Joseph Chamberlain* (Oxford, 1981), 194, 169, 188, 211–12, 285.

272. J. L. Garvin and J. Amery, *Life of Joseph Chamberlain*, 6 vols. (London, 1936–69), esp. 3:203, 213–14, 217–19, 232; also, 3:20, 220, 316.

273. G. N. Sanderson, *England, Europe and the Upper Nile* (Edinburgh, 1965), 320. For Boer examples, J. A. S. Grenville, *Lord Salisbury and Foreign Policy* (London, 1964), 264, 267; also Andrew N. Porter, *Origins of the South African War: Joseph Chamberlain and the Diplomacy of Imperialism, 1895–1899* (Manchester, 1980), 43.

grounds. Fantastic domino scenarios, linking the damming of the Upper Nile to the collapse of British power in India, date from this period.[274] At the same time, strategic polemics propagated by Chamberlain and his allies trapped not only Salisbury but even Chamberlain himself into pursuing an inflexible policy toward the Boers.[275]

These policies led to costly overextension in Africa and more generally to Britain's international isolation, euphemistically called "splendid isolation." Faced with the obvious failure of Chamberlain's strategy of protectionism and expansion, oligarchs and voters alike came to reject it.[276] Industrial decline created elites and voters with concentrated interests in expansion, thus making the political system more cartelized and prone to imperial coalition logrolling.

Given the underlying features of the early industrializer polity, however, these interests were far too weak to succeed in the face of clear evidence of the costs of overextension. London financial elites interested in preserving an open world economic order joined with consumers interested in preserving cheap food imports in defeating Chamberlain's schemes for an expanded empire behind a tariff wall.[277] Liberals favoring free trade and a limitation on imperial commitment won the 1906 election.

VICTORIAN IMPERIALISM: THEORETICAL IMPLICATIONS

Domestic political structure explains not only Britain's general ability to learn to retrench, but also the Victorians' two interludes of moderate overextension: Palmerston's social imperialism and the scramble for Africa. Overextension and strategic mythmaking occurred when the political system was most cartelized and politically stalemated. This happened first during the "equipoise" between traditional and modern society caused by rapid industrialization, and later when declining industrial sectors sought political remedies to protect their vested interests. In both periods, imperialist logrolling and strategic mythmaking helped create and manage heterogeneous coalitions to govern a

274. Ronald Robinson and John Gallagher, *Africa and the Victorians* (New York, 1961), 285–86.

275. This is a main theme of Porter, *Origins*, esp. 246, 260, 266–67, and H. C. G. Matthew, *The Liberal Imperialists* (London, 1973), 171–78. See also Grenville, *Lord Salisbury*, 264, 267; Thomas August, *The Selling of the Empire* (Westport, Conn., 1985), chaps. 2 and 3; A. N. Porter, "Sir Alfred Milner and the Press, 1897–1899," *Historical Journal* 16 (June 1973): 323–39; J. A. Hobson, *Imperialism* (Ann Arbor, Mich., 1965).

276. For background on "splendid isolation" and Chamberlain's policy as one variant of it, see Christopher Howard, *Splendid Isolation* (London, 1967), esp. 19.

277. D. C. M. Platt, *Finance, Trade, and Politics in British Foreign Policy, 1815–1914* (Oxford, 1968), 105–7; Bernard Semmel, *Imperialism and Social Reform* (Cambridge, Mass., 1960), 85; Peter Gourevitch, *Politics in Hard Times* (Ithaca, N.Y., 1986), 76–83.

deadlocked society. In sum, when Victorian society was most like Wilhelmine society, Victorian foreign policy was most like Wilhelmine foreign policy.

This finding has particular theoretical importance, because it shows that the domestic structure theory can explain overexpansion even in cases where coalition dynamics operate only weakly. In this sense Victorian Britain is a hard case, which establishes the broad applicability of the theory of coalition politics and strategic ideology. It suggests, for example, that its application might extend to the moderate overextension of democratic nations like the United States.

The British case is also noteworthy for the strong support it gives to coalition ideology theories against simpler interest group theories. In the German and Japanese cases, imperial policies and ideologies were sometimes rather closely tied to the interests and propagandizing of particular groups or bureaucracies. Palmerstonian social imperialism, however, was not a simple logroll of groups benefiting concretely from overexpansion. This makes it easier to see the independent effect of a coalition maker using imperial ideology to maintain power in a divided, stalemated polity.

Finally, even more strongly than the German and Japanese cases, the British case shows the role of international events as a trigger unleashing latent opportunities for social imperialism. Palmerston had been working for over two decades to establish a system of rule based on pseudoliberal imperialism for middle-class radicals and social stasis for aristocratic elites. But until Tsar Nicholas "made his day" by blundering into the Crimean crisis, it was not at all clear that Palmerston's formula would succeed. By acting in a way that seemingly discredited Palmerston's anti-imperialist opponents, the Russians turned the latent possibility of a social imperialist coalition into a reality. In the German and Japanese cases, the domestic forces working for self-destructive expansionism were so strong that they might have prevailed regardless of international conditions. The British case, where this seems not to be true, underscores the need for statesmen to assess carefully how ill-considered policies might unleash the fierce but dormant nationalist potential of other societies.

[6]

Soviet Politics and Strategic Learning

On a comparative scale, the Soviet Union's tendency toward overexpansion has been moderate. Through its aggressive behavior, the Soviet Union has occasionally provoked the formation of encircling great-power coalitions, and it has occasionally become overextended at the periphery. But each time, it has learned to retrench in the face of effective opposition.

Any theory of overexpansion should be able to explain periods of retrenchment as well as periods of self-encirclement. What needs to be explained about the Soviet case is (1) the lack of significant overexpansion before World War II, and Stalin's adoption of a hedgehog strategy of "socialism in one country"; (2) three periods of moderate overextension in 1947–50, 1958–62, and the late Brezhnev period; (3) the relative effectiveness with which the Soviets learned to retrench from these bouts of overextension and self-encirclement; and (4) the different character of Soviet strategic learning in the Gorbachev period.

Soviet strategic ideas and variations in them over time provide a useful starting point in explaining this pattern. The Soviets' moderate expansionism reflects the two-sided character of their strategic beliefs. On the one hand, the Soviet Union was born believing that security required expansion. Most early Bolsheviks held that the revolution in Russia would be truly secure only when socialism had replaced capitalism in the more advanced countries, and that Soviet policy should therefore promote socialism's spread. On the other hand, the Soviet Union's early leaders understood that if they exercised restraint in foreign policy, the capitalist powers would be more likely to focus their aggression on each other and leave the Soviet state alone.

The relative predominance of these two faces of Soviet strategic thinking has varied over time, and the Soviets' propensity to expand correlates with these variations. Stalin's prewar strategy was based on the image of a very hostile West, but he saw few opportunities to pursue this zero-sum competition through offensive action. Rather, he decided, the Soviet Union should emulate the prickly but defensive hedgehog. Stalin tried to avoid early embroilment in a conflict by building up a military deterrent and by avoiding provocations that could give the West a pretext for attacking.[1] As early as 1925 Stalin held the view that if war comes "we shall have to take action, but we shall be the last to do so in order to throw the decisive weight into the scales."[2]

In contrast, Stalin's belligerent policies in the Berlin crisis of 1948–49 and the Korean War seemed almost calculated to provoke the consolidation of NATO and the 250 percent increase in United States defense spending in 1950 alone.[3] As Winston Churchill asked, "Why have they deliberately acted for three long years so as to unite the free world against them?"[4] One reason was the emergence of Andrei Zhdanov's strategy of security through expansion: not only was the West perceived as unalterably hostile, but many offensive opportunities were seen for combating the West's aggressive plans.

Two more times, during Khrushchev's missile diplomacy and Brezhnev's Third World expansionism, aggressive Soviet actions unified the opposing camp, provoked it to intensify its military preparations, alienated neutrals and socialist allies, and wasted scarce Soviet economic resources. These episodes too were fueled by the emergence of an ideology of security through expansion: the notion that changes in the "correlation of forces" in favor of socialism would force the West to accept détente on Soviet terms.

After each of these periods of self-encirclement, the Soviets learned to retrench from their aggressive stance in order to demobilize the opposing forces their actions had conjured up. Discredited ideas of security through expansion were at least temporarily supplanted by the notion that Western hostility was contingent on Soviet provocations and that offensive opportunities were scarce. In the third of these episodes of retrenchment, Gorbachev and his supporters have learned

---

1. Even the exception proves the rule. Foreign Minister Maxim Litvinov's collective security policy can easily be explained as an attempt to lure France into a direct fight on Germany's border, while the Soviet Union would be buffered from significant involvement by the barrier of Polish territory. Telford Taylor, *Munich* (Garden City, N.Y., 1979), 452–56; Barry Posen, "Competing Images of the Soviet Union," *World Politics* 39 (July 1987): 579–604.

2. Louis Fischer, *Russia's Road from Peace to War* (New York, 1969), 304.

3. John Lewis Gaddis, *Strategies of Containment* (New York, 1982), 113.

4. Quoted in Marshall Shulman, *Stalin's Foreign Policy Reappraised* (Cambridge, Mass., 1963), 13.

deeper, more permanent lessons about the counterproductiveness of militancy and expansionism.

This pattern of strategic beliefs and behavior has been strongly influenced by the domestic political pattern associated with "late, late" industrialization.[5] On one hand, some of the political consequences of abrupt, "catch up" industrialization favored the development of conflict-causing strategic ideologies. The Soviet leadership had an incentive to exaggerate foreign threats in order to mobilize the Soviet population for the "revolution from above" and to justify the accompanying political repression. That social transformation also tended to concentrate power in the hands of a single dictator, leaving foreign policy hostage to his whims, for better or for worse. Finally, the pattern of late, late industrialization created a set of institutions—especially the militant party and the military-industrial complex—with vested interests in expansion and an arms race. After Stalin's death these institutions logrolled as self-interested imperial cartels.

On the other hand, late, late industrialization also created strong, unitary elites and institutions with the power to keep imperial logrolling in check. In particular, the Politburo served as a unitary oligarchy with relatively diffuse, encompassing interests. Though influenced by the parochial interests of institutional constituencies, its members' loyalties were largely to the Politburo itself and to the socialist system.[6] This provided some latitude for parochial strategies in foreign affairs, but the worst excesses of those strategies were kept in check by the Politburo's unitary, encompassing perspective.

These features of late, late development also help explain variations in Soviet strategy over time. The cautious yet threat exaggerating hedgehog strategy of the interwar period fit nicely with Stalin's need to mobilize his society for the revolution from above. Stalin's turn to a more offensive strategy in the late 1940s is more difficult to attribute to any simple domestic cause. In part it reflects the fluid international environment, in which offensive tactics seemed more plausible. In part it also reflects blowback from the militant ideas and institutions left over from the mobilization campaign of the 1930s, as well as the vagaries of an unchecked dictator. The strategies of "offensive détente" adopted by Khrushchev and Brezhnev have clear domestic origins: these internally inconsistent strategies were largely the product of logrolling among various Party, military-industrial, and intelligentsia groupings.

5. Alexander Gerschenkron, *Economic Backwardness in Historical Perspective* (Cambridge, Mass., 1962).
6. On the Politburo as its own constituency, see Harry Gelman, *The Brezhnev Politburo and the Decline of Detente* (Ithaca, N.Y., 1984), 52–55.

Periods of Soviet retrenchment before Gorbachev were mere interludes during which discredited imperial coalitions regrouped in a slightly modified way. This oscillation between expansion and retrenchment reflected the tension between the cartelized aspects of the post-Stalin political system, which promoted overexpansion, and the unitary Politburo elite with encompassing interests. Gorbachev went much further than previous retrenchers in attacking the institutional origins of ideologies of security through expansion and in creating a new political base that supported his more benign strategic ideology.[7] But if that political base should collapse, the "new thinking" in foreign policy is likely to erode, to be replaced by strategic concepts more in keeping with whatever domestic political order replaces glasnost and democratization.

RATIONAL ADAPTATION TO INTERNATIONAL CIRCUMSTANCES?

A number of American authorities on Soviet foreign policy have portrayed the Soviets as cool, calculating practitioners of realpolitik and as rationally responsive to the dictates of prevailing international conditions. Adam Ulam notes that as early as the winter of 1918, the Realist Lenin prevailed over the ideologues Trotsky and Bukharin in the decision to sign the Brest-Litovsk Treaty. Marshall Shulman shows that even before Stalin's death the Soviets were beginning to adapt rationally to evidence that the militant Berlin policy had been a debacle. Several commentators have asserted that more recent Soviet expansionism was a purely realpolitik endeavor, having more to do with the great power polices of the tsars than with the messianism of the Bolshevik revolution.[8]

No one, however, has tried to test systematically whether variations over time in Soviet grand strategy correlate with variations in the international circumstances the Soviet Union has faced.[9] Showing that the Soviets eventually adapted to clear evidence that their policy was counterproductive is hardly the same as showing that the policy was compelled by international exigencies in the first place. In this

7. This analysis is developed at greater length in Jack Snyder, "The Gorbachev Revolution: A Waning of Soviet Expansionism?" *International Security* 12 (Winter 1987–88): 93–131.

8. Adam Ulam, *Expansion and Coexistence* (New York, 1975), chap. 2; Shulman, *Stalin's Foreign Policy*, chaps. 1 and 11; other works cited in Richard Herrmann, *Perceptions and Behavior in Soviet Foreign Policy* (Pittsburgh, Pa., 1985), 13–18.

9. An exception is Herrmann, who does this only for the Brezhnev period. See also Scott Parrish, "Soviet Reactions to the Security Dilemma: The Sources of Soviet Encirclement, 1945–1950" (certificate essay, Columbia University, Harriman Institute, 1990).

section I will ask how closely Soviet policy has matched those exigencies. Overall, I find that considerations of realpolitik account rather poorly for at least two of the three expansionist periods of Soviet policy.

The international setting of Soviet foreign policy might be broken down for analytical purposes into endemic circumstances that characterize almost the whole Soviet period and variable circumstances that change with the character of the opponent, with current military technology, or with the international distribution of power.

Endemic Conditions

Three relatively constant features of the Soviet Union's position in the international system are its relative backwardness, its economic self-sufficiency, and its legacy as a revolutionary state.

Backwardness. Among the more enduring circumstances is Russia's relative backwardness. Throughout the Soviet period, Russia has faced potential enemies enjoying a larger, more sophisticated economic and technical warmaking potential. The exception is the eve of World War II, when the German and Russian economic bases were roughly equal in overall size, though the Germans enjoyed significant advantages in military organizational skills.[10] Objectively, Russia's endemic backwardness should have given Soviet grand strategists a strong incentive to adopt a variety of compensating countermeasures. These include appeasing opponents so as to play for time while catching up, remaining open to importing of technologies from more advanced economies, and seeking allies among the least threatening of the more advanced powers.

Thus, in principle, Soviet backwardness can easily explain periods when the Soviet Union was using détente to seek a breathing spell vis-à-vis potential enemies, to reduce ideological militancy to attract allies, and to encourage capital or technological imports. Indeed, Russian and Soviet diplomacy records many such periods. Stolypin's détente with Germany to buy time for reforms after the Russo-Japanese War, Stalin's cautious buck-passing diplomacy during the interwar period designed to buy the time needed for forced-draft industrialization, Stalin's adoption of the "popular front" strategy in the mid-1930s to make the Soviet Union more palatable as an ally of France, Malenkov's and Khrushchev's attempts to buy time after the Berlin and Korean debacles until the Soviet Union could field a nuclear deterrent, Khrushchev's eagerness for détente after the Cuban missile crisis, and

10. Paul Kennedy, *The Rise and Fall of the Great Powers* (New York, 1987), 332.

Gorbachev's attempt to use a peace campaign to head off the Strategic Defense Initiative—all conform to the general pattern of a backward state hoping to postpone a sharpening of international competition until it can catch up. Russia's endemic backwardness fits awkwardly, however, with more assertive periods of Soviet foreign policy.

Economic self-sufficiency. The Soviet economy comprises all the natural resources needed to sustain a long war in the face of an economic blockade. Whereas Germany and Japan had a plausible incentive to expand in order to achieve autarky, the Soviet Union had no such incentive, because it had already achieved it. Russia could safely play the hedgehog, even if it turned out that aggressors could not be deflected by Soviet appeasement and self-restraint.[11]

Though Russia can be basically self-sufficient in wartime, in peacetime its relative backwardness gives it an incentive for expanded trade and technology transfers with more advanced economies to help it catch up. As Gorbachev has recently been stressing, this economic incentive gives the Soviets a powerful reason to avoid projecting an aggressive image, which would make potential enemies reluctant to engage in trade. Thus both Russia's self-sufficiency in war and its incentives for trade in peacetime offer plausible explanations for periods when the Soviets have behaved with self-restraint.

A revolutionary state. For Realists like Kenneth Waltz, a state's position in the international system should not be affected by its domestic characteristics. Revolutionary or socialist states face the same constraints of the anarchic international system as do reactionary or capitalist ones, and consequently they should behave in broadly similar ways.[12] Some of Waltz's students, however, though Realists, have begun to explore the distinctive circumstances facing revolutionary states.[13] They find that social revolution often creates conditions that intensify the security dilemma, placing the security of the revolution at odds with that of surrounding status quo states. Social revolutions in one country raise the specter of similar revolutions in neighboring countries with similar social structures. Moreover, social revolutions often weaken the state in the short run but promise to strengthen it in

11. Jerry Hough, *Opening up the Soviet Economy* (Washington, D.C., 1988); Richard Day, *Leon Trotsky and the Politics of Economic Isolation* (Cambridge, 1973).

12. Kenneth Waltz, *Theory of International Politics* (Reading, Mass., 1979), chap. 2; Kenneth Waltz, *Man, the State, and War* (New York, 1959), chap. 5.

13. The following points are discussed by Stephen Walt, "The Foreign Policy of Revolutionary States," paper prepared for the annual meeting of the American Political Science Association, Chicago, September 1987; see also Stephen Van Evera, "Causes of War" (Ph.D. diss., University of California at Berkeley, 1984).

the long run, thus giving the status quo powers an incentive to snuff them out preventively. Finally, social revolutions create "fifth columns" in both the revolutionary and the status quo states. These inherently offensive tactical assets threaten the very survival of the opposing state, whether they are used for offensive or defensive motives. Thus the capitalist powers' backing of Russian Whites and the Bolsheviks' alliance with European Reds created a tight security dilemma for both sides, even though support for such fifth columns was in part defensively motivated.

Even beyond the early postrevolutionary years, the availability of "progressive" fifth columns in the capitalist camp has given the Soviet Union an endemic incentive to use offensive political tactics to gain advantages in a highly competitive relationship. In addition, fear of the advanced capitalists' ability to use economic penetration to foster fifth columns in Soviet society has placed sharp limits on the Soviets' willingness to pursue economically beneficial intergration into the world market. Consequently, aggressive policies abroad often look tactically attractive, while the appeasement needed to enhance trade opportunities often does not.

Variable Factors

I will group the variable aspects of the Soviet Union's position in the international environment under two categories: whether the opponent is unconditionally hostile, and whether the international situation creates offensive or defensive advantages. Incentives for offensive action might include an unstable political status quo in a key region, windows of opportunity, technological or geographical circumstances favoring the attacker, revolutionary situations favoring offensive political instruments, and the number of great powers in the balancing system. Overall, Soviet policy has correlated weakly with such realpolitik incentives, especially in those periods when it was most offensive.

The character of the opponent. If one's opponent is by nature implacably hostile and aggressive, offensive strategies may seem more attractive. The foe is already so malevolent that offensive tactics cannot provoke it further, and strictly defensive or accommodating tactics can do nothing to make it fundamentally more benign. Moreover, it may be so aggressive that the prospect of a bloody stalemate may not deter it. Conversely, if one's opponent is only conditionally aggressive, recognizably defensive strategies may help demobilize its hostility.[14] Logically, therefore,

14. For further discussion, see Robert Jervis, *Perception and Misperception in International Politics* (Princeton, N.J., 1976), chap. 3.

one might expect the Soviets to have risked overextension and overassertiveness toward their prewar fascist opponents while scrupulously avoiding it toward their postwar democratic adversaries.

The reverse was more nearly the case. Stalin bent over backward to avoid provoking the Japanese and the Nazis but then adopted a direct confrontational style against the easy-to-provoke Americans after the war. Conceivably this was because after the Marshall Plan the Soviets concluded that America was already resolved to do its worst. Yet Politburo member Andrei Zhdanov's keynote speech to the founding meeting of the Cominform, which was a response to the Marshall Plan, does not support this view. On that occasion he portrayed the West as far from fully mobilized for confrontation. Though he saw the imperialists as ready for a military showdown, they were unable to engineer it because the people in their countries wanted peace. "The warmongers fully realize," he reassured his audience, "that long ideological preparation is necessary before they can get their soldiers to fight the Soviet Union."[15] What he failed to consider was that a policy of direct confrontation would feed the anti-Soviet militancy of precisely those wavering democratic publics.

Throughout its history, Soviet strategy has been almost perfectly unsuited to the real character of its opponents. Stalin tried to accommodate an unappeasable opponent, Hitler, while the three postwar leaders each embarked on overconfrontational and overexpansionist projects against democratic adversaries whose publics might otherwise have lost the stomach for a serious arms race. Only Gorbachev has a grand strategy that is synchronized with the real character of his international opponents.

Unstable status quo. When the political status quo in a key region is ambiguous or fluid, great powers can easily conclude that their only viable strategic options are either expanding or accepting geopolitical losses. Trying to stabilize the status quo looks like building a defensive bulwark on quicksand. Thus when the status quo is unstable, the security dilemma is tight: policies that enhance one's own position necessarily jeopardize that of one's opponent. Under such conditions aggressiveness is at a premium, and errors of overextension should be common. Conversely, when the status quo is stable the security dilemma is weak, since both sides can remain secure by defending the status quo.[16]

15. Myron Rush, *The International Situation and Soviet Foreign Policy* (Columbus, Ohio, 1969), 134; also 138.

16. Robert Jervis, "Cooperation under the Security Dilemma," *World Politics* 30 (January 1978): 167–214.

This hypothesis is a satisfactory explanation only for the immediate post-1945 period. The collapse of German and Japanese power created a power vacuum at key locations in the heartland of the industrialized world. In Europe the political status quo was fluid both within and between important nation-states. One obvious solution was to establish a new status quo based on a division of Europe into spheres of influence along the frontier of the Soviet and Anglo-American occupation zones. As Stalin put it privately, "Everyone imposes his own [social] system as far as his army can reach. It cannot be otherwise."[17]

In retrospect, this looks like a stable basis for a political status quo, but several powerful factors worked to undermine it. This dividing line would have split Germany in two, and both the Soviets and the Americans were loath to bear the onus for a division that could give rise to a revanchist grudge on the part of the Germans.[18] The Soviets, moreover, did not want a divided Germany, since they hoped to extract reparations from the Ruhr industrial region in the Western sector. Other locations, such as Korea, entailed similar problems. The Turkish Straits, likewise, were a position of strategic importance to both sides where a reliable formula for shared control would be hard to devise. The status quo was further blurred by the existence of socialist fifth columns in key Western countries and of the West's potential economic leverage over Eastern Europe.

In these circumstances, offensive means were often attractive as instruments to achieve defensive gains—namely, Stalin's pressure on Turkey to gain a secure lock on the Straits, the strikes in France to derail the Marshall Plan, and the squeezing of Berlin to derail West German unification. Though all these policies had counterproductive effects that were foreseen by at least some Soviet figures, a Realist might nonetheless legitimately contend that they were at least plausible tactics in the face of a fluid status quo and tight security dilemma.[19]

This conclusion is reinforced by the difficulty both sides had in devising strategies that made defensive measures distinguishable from offensive ones. The Marshall Plan and West German currency reform were primarily defensive efforts aimed at shoring up fragile societies against economic chaos that could lead to a revolutionary situation, but the Soviets saw them creating a pole of economic attraction to lure away their East European clients. Likewise, the draconian communization of Eastern Europe, including the Czech coup, was largely a

17. Milovan Djilas, *Conversations with Stalin* (New York, 1962), 114.
18. Hannes Adomeit, *Soviet Risk-Taking and Crisis Behavior* (London, 1982), 130.
19. For contemporary Soviet critics, see Gavriel Ra'anan, *International Policy Formation in the USSR: Factional "Debates" during the Zhdanovschina* (Hamden, Conn., 1983), chap. 6; and Ronald L. Letteney, "Foreign Policy Factionalism under Stalin, 1949–1950" (Ph.D. diss., Johns Hopkins School of Advanced International Studies, 1971).

defensive move to consolidate the Eastern bloc in the face of the challenge of the Marshall Plan, but to the West it looked like communism on the march, preparing for revolutionary action throughout the Continent.[20]

In another example, in April 1945 French party chief Jacques Duclos wrote an article, instigated by Moscow, that condemned the American Communist party for having renounced the goal of forcible seizure of power. Duclos later revealed that the threat was intended as an oblique deterrent, to remind the West that Communist fifth columns could retaliate in the event of a separate peace with Germany and a reversal of alliances. The article, however, was seen in the West as an offensively motivated declaration of ideological war, not as a contingent deterrent threat.[21] This indistinguishability of offensive and defensive threats made for a tense, competitive détente in 1945–46. In 1947 Duclos's threats became the Cominform's deeds, which were likewise indistinguishable between offensive and defensive motives.

Though the fluid status quo seems a real incentive for offensive action in the late 1940s, by the late 1950s Khrushchev's claims that circumstances in Germany were highly unstable seems more like a rhetorical tactic aimed at rationalizing offensive action. In fact, by the mid-1950s the two Germanies were well integrated into the military and political structures of the opposing blocs. There were a few bones of contention, of course. The West refused de jure recognition of the German Democratic Republic; emigration across the uncontrolled border in Berlin was moderately high; integration into NATO meant movement toward de facto West German access to nuclear weapons. Nonetheless, Khrushchev does not seem to have been unduly exercised about these problems until they came to be a stumbling block in the path of détente with the West and a reorientation of Soviet budget priorities away from defense. When this occurred, in 1958, Khrushchev issued his Berlin ultimatum as a lever to compel progress in East-West détente and to show his Soviet colleagues that favorable political outcomes could be achieved without backbreaking defense expenditures.[22] To enhance the credibility of his "threat that leaves something to chance," as Thomas Schelling put it, Khrushchev purposely exaggerated the extent to which Berlin was an "abnormal situation" that could get out of control if nothing was done about it.[23] As the Berlin crisis of

20. William Taubman, *Stalin's American Policy* (New York, 1982), chap. 7.

21. Vojtech Mastny, *Russia's Road to the Cold War* (New York, 1979), 272.

22. The argument above is based on James Richter, "Action and Reaction in Soviet Foreign Policy" (Ph.D. diss., University of California at Berkeley, 1989), chap. 4.

23. For this argument and supporting evidence, see Hope Harrison, "Was Khrushchev a Student of Thomas Schelling? Khrushchev's Coercive Diplomacy in the 1958–1961 Berlin Crisis" (unpublished manuscript, Columbia University, Harriman Institute, 1987). See also Jack Schick, *The Berlin Crisis, 1958–1962* (Philadelphia, 1971), 102.

1961 showed, the division of Germany was by this time basically stable, despite Khrushchev's destabilizing rhetoric, which touched off a sharp acceleration in flight across the border. Unilateral defensive measures like the construction of the Berlin Wall were adequate to achieve Soviet security goals.

In short, the security dilemma caused by a fluid status quo plausibly explains Stalin's overaggressive, counterproductive policies in Europe in the late 1940s. But in later periods the alleged instability of the status quo seems more like a rationalization than a reason for Soviet overassertiveness.

Windows of opportunity. Russia is always catching up with its competitors but never quite makes it. This gives the nation a perpetual incentive to avoid overextension in the short run and to delay showdowns with adversaries indefinitely. These general incentives associated with backwardness plausibly explain periods of caution, but not periods of aggressive assertiveness in Soviet grand strategy. Nevertheless, it is not inconceivable that short-term fluctuations in the Soviet Union's relative power might create ephemeral "windows of opportunity" for offensive action. With the help of some unconvincing analytical contortions, Soviet periods of overextension under Stalin, Khrushchev, and Brezhnev might all be interpreted in this light.

In 1947 the Soviets feared that the Marshall Plan and the formation of a West German state, if successfully implemented, would create a powerful American spearhead in Europe, radically changing the balance of power there and threatening to attract Eastern Europe into the American sphere of influence. To forestall this adverse trend, Stalin had an incentive to use offensive instruments of coercion decisively in the short run, using the French Communist party to try to hinder implementation of the Marshall Plan and exploiting the anomalous geographic position of Berlin to roll back West German currency reform. With the benefit of hindsight, we now know that these offensive cards were hardly opportunities, fleeting or otherwise. Neither achieved its aim, and together with the attack on Korea and the Czech coup, they galvanized Western unity, spurred Western rearmament, and isolated Western Communist parties. Even at the time, French observers thought that militant resistance to the Marshall Plan would only increase its popularity.[24]

Khrushchev's missile diplomacy was likewise spurred by an apparent window of opportunity, owing to the Soviets' temporary advantage in intercontinental ballistic missile technology and Khrushchev's ability

24. Irwin Wall, *French Communism in the Era of Stalin* (Westport, Conn., 1983), chap. 3.

to inflate its strategic consequences through bluff and bluster. But this window was closed by 1961, before the Cuban missile crisis, when satellite reconaissance revealed that the missile gap actually favored the United States. Fleeting opportunity is at best a small part of this story.[25]

Brezhnev's Third World expansionism might also be explained as a result of the window of opportunity created by the anti-interventionist "post-Vietnam syndrome" in the United States and the collapse of the Portuguese empire. This argument needs close scrutiny, however. According to the canonical Soviet rationale of that period, increasing "realism" (read "passivity") in American foreign policy was supposed to be not a short-lived opportunity requiring pell-mell exploitation, but rather an open-ended, ever-deepening trend. Moreover, even after many Soviet commentators were arguing that the Vietnam syndrome was over, Soviet military interventions in the Third World continued.[26] Arkady Shevchenko reports that Central Committee foreign policy specialists, who had used the Vietnam syndrome to argue that intervention in Angola would be safe, were by 1977 arguing the opposite: a "new militancy" was required to counter the increasingly assertive, increasingly antidétente Carter policy. Imperialism doesn't change its spots, they now insisted, and it must be combated aggressively.[27]

Another problem for the opportunity explanation is that by the mid-1980s the Soviets were turning down opportunities to make inroads in former Portuguese colonies that they would have eagerly snapped up in the 1970s. The Soviets came to see helping "progressive" Mozambique fight against insurgent guerrillas as no opportunity at all, heeding Yuri Andropov's disgruntled warning that "it's one thing to proclaim socialism as a goal and another to build it."[28] The objective situation was about the same, but the Soviets' view of it had changed.

Overall, Russia's backwardness has given it a strong incentive not to provoke intensely competitive reactions from its technically and economically more advanced adversaries. This is only a little less true in the age of the Strategic Defense Initiative than it was under the Romanovs. When the Soviets have abandoned the strategy of playing for time and adopted instead a tactic of exploiting fleeting offensive opportunites, the costs and risks have for the most part strongly

---

25. Richter, "Action and Reaction," offers further criticism of the opportunity thesis.
26. Ted Hopf, "Soviet Inferences from Their Victories in the Periphery: Visions of Resistance or Cumulating Gains?" in Robert Jervis and Jack Snyder, eds., *Dominoes and Bandwagons: Strategic Beliefs and Great Power Competition in the Eurasian Rimland* (New York, 1991), 145–89.
27. Arkady Shevchenko, *Breaking with Moscow* (New York, 1985), 298.
28. Andropov speech to the Central Committee, *Pravda*, 16 June 1983, 1; *Current Digest of the Soviet Press* [hereafter *CDSP*] 35:8.

outweighed the benefits. Consequently, objective strategic incentives of this kind provide a weak explanation for periods of Soviet overextension.

Multipolarity and bipolarity. In a system of many powers, there may be an incentive to let other states bear the costs of containing an expansionist. Stalin played the diplomatic game appropriately to these circumstances in the 1930s, preferring if possible to let France and Britain bear the brunt of Nazi aggression. Only the unanticipated collapse of France ruined Stalin's chance to ride free on French defense or to intervene with "decisive weight" on the heels of a German pyrrhic victory. "Couldn't they put up any resistance at all?" complained the stunned dictator to his Politburo colleagues in the spring of 1940.[29] Though Stalin's strategy ultimately failed, it nonetheless had played adeptly on the structural incentive in favor of buck-passing in a multipolar system.[30]

Although multipolarity can plausibly explain the Soviets' cautious prewar diplomacy, bipolarity cannot be blamed for the occasional postwar periods of Soviet overassertiveness. It is occasionally claimed that in a system of two powers the characteristic error is aggressive overreaction to the peripheral expansionism of the adversary.[31] If so, this must stem from some psychological consequence of watching each other like hawks, not from the structural incentives of the situation, which point in quite the opposite direction. In bipolarity, the size of the two powers allows them to rely to a large extent on internal resources for their security. They depend less on allies, especially peripheral ones, than in multipolarity, so competition on the margins can be relatively lax.[32] Moreover, opportunistic expansionists have less reason to hope they will be able to overturn the balance in a bipolar system. In a multipolar system, there is always the outside chance that buck-passing powers can be defeated piecemeal, but in bipolarity the hard core of resistance will remain intact despite some peripheral victories.[33]

29. Nikita Khrushchev, *Khrushchev Remembers*, (Boston, 1970), 1:134. Isaac Deutscher says: "the major premiss of Stalin's policy, and his major blunder: he expected Britain and France to hold their ground for a long time." Stalin had also expected Poland to resist longer. Deutscher, *Stalin* (New York, 1949), 437, 441. On Stalin's similar strategy toward Japan, Jonathan Haslam, *Soviet Foreign Policy, 1930–33* (London, 1983), 75, 81.

30. Though multipolarity favors buck-passing when the defense is believed to be dominant, it favors tight, unconditional alliances when the offense is thought dominant. See Thomas J. Christensen and Jack Snyder, "Chain Gangs and Passed Bucks: Predicting Alliance Patterns in Multipolarity," *International Organization* 44 (Spring 1990): 137–68.

31. Waltz, *Theory of International Politics*, 171–72.

32. Ibid., 169, 207–9, makes this argument, which seems to contradict his contention about the link between bipolarity and overreaction. For further discussion, see Christensen and Snyder, "Chain Gangs," 142.

33. Aside from the fundamental problem that bipolarity does not predict and cannot structurally explain reckless overextension, there is the further problem that even a psychologized version of the hypothesis does not fit the evidence. If states in bipolarity

Communist and "progressive" allies abroad. One explanation for the Soviets' occasional counterproductive overassertiveness is that revolutionary forces abroad constitute a key competitive resource for both offensive and defensive purposes. In this view, sometimes the Soviets simply cannot refrain from using this potent offensive weapon in the service of urgent defensive goals, even at the risk of galvanizing an escalatory response. In other words, given the Soviets' comparative advantage in offensive instruments of coercion, objective circumstances may make it especially difficult for them to avoid overextension and counterproductive provocations.

Bolshevik thought assigns a central role to promoting revolutionary change in the Third World as a way to weaken imperialism, whether for offensive or defensive goals, by shrinking its base of economic exploitation. In a particularly colorful example, the Indian communist M. N. Roy argued at the end of the Russian civil war that a cost-effective way to defend the Bolshevik revolution against British intervention would be to send a Communist army to the northern frontier of India. This, he argued, would encourage an Indian uprising, thus depriving Britain of a crucial source of superprofits, sending the British economy into a tailspin, and touching off a social revolution in Britain itself. Ironically, this was an idea originally propounded by the Russian chauvinist General Skobelev in 1876, but it is a concept that has in its general form become a recurrent theme in Soviet grand strategic thinking, especially among Central Committee ideologues.[34] Shevchenko recounts a conversation with Vadim Zagladin, deputy chief of the Central Committee's International Department, who complained that "you Foreign Ministry people don't understand the power of Communist ideas in the world and the way to exploit them."[35]

This raises the question of just how valuable the offensive exploitation of world revolutionary forces has been in the East-West struggle

---

become overaggressive because they focus their attention single-mindedly on each other's transgressions and know that sole responsibility for stopping expansion lies with themselves, then we should find policy being driven by one-dimensional images of an implacable enemy whose appetite grows with the eating. This fits the Soviets' enemy image of the United States in the late 1940s but fails to account for the overassertiveness of Khrushchev and Brezhnev, who rationalized their too ambitious policies as much through images of the "realism" and decadence of the West as through images of its implacable enmity. See the section on strategic concepts below.

34. Robert Donaldson, *Soviet Policy toward India: Ideology and Strategy* (Cambridge, Mass., 1974), 6, on Roy; more generally, Richard Lowenthal, *Model or Ally?* (New York, 1977), 359–76.

35. Shevchenko, *Breaking with Moscow*, 190. For more such anecdotes, based on interviewing of Moscow's foreign policy elite in 1989, see Sally J. Onesti, "Portrait of a Generation: Soviet Interpretations of Soviet Foreign Policy and Detente, 1969–74," (Columbia University, Ph.D. diss., 1990), chap. 3.

for power and security. Objectively speaking, the strategic benefits of this weapon have been virtually nil, while the costs have been extremely high. Molotov was correct when he argued, as if tutored by Paul Kennedy and Kenneth Waltz, that Soviet security is based on Russia's internal military and industrial might. Efforts like Zhdanov's to capitalize on Communist fifth columns have been unsuccessful. The use of revolutionary ideological affinities to penetrate the Third World yielded a string of weak, fickle, and expensive allies, as current Soviet analysis itself admits.[36] The attempt to maintain centralized control over the world communist movement as an instrument serving Soviet state interests served only to exacerbate the split with China, creating a real geopolitical debit.[37]

The counterproductive aspects of playing the world revolutionary card have been foreseeable to many Soviets, including the ideologues who especially advocate this policy. Lenin himself expected a balancing response to Soviet assertiveness: "The more victorious we are, the more the capitalist exploiters learn to unite and the more determined their onslaught."[38] Zagladin has invoked this concept of Lenin's to explain what he revealingly calls imperialism's "counteroffensive" in the 1980s.[39] In short, Soviet overextension is poorly explained by the alleged need to capitalize on intrinsically offensive political instruments, which have proved to be of marginal value for offensive purposes and hugely counterproductive for defensive purposes.

Military technology and geography. Another questionable explanation for periods of Soviet offensive behavior and strategy rests on technological or geographical circumstances that allegedly placed a premium on the use of offensive tactics for both offensive and defensive goals. Stalin implicitly based his prewar diplomacy on the assumption that the defender enjoyed a military advantage, which justified his expectation that France would hold out against a German attack. In contrast, Russia's strategists in 1914 did not believe the defender enjoyed a great advantage, were skeptical that France could hold out alone against Germany, and consequently did not count on riding free on French defense. Though Stalin's view turned out to be too optimistic, it was widely shared at the time, owing to the apparent lessons of World War I.[40]

36. See sources cited in George Breslauer, "Ideology and Learning in Soviet Third World Policy," *World Politics* 39 (April 1987): 429–48.
37. Richard Lowenthal, *World Communism* (London, 1964); Stephen Walt, *The Origins of Alliances* (Ithaca, N.Y., 1987), 35–36.
38. Quoted in V. S. Semyonov, *Nations and Internationalism* (Moscow, 1979), 239.
39. V. Zagladin, "World Balance of Forces and the Development of International Relations," *International Affairs* (Moscow), 3 (March 1985): 74.
40. Christensen and Snyder, "Chain Gangs," 153–55, 157–59.

After the war, changes in the geopolitical setting seemed at least superficially to provide incentives for more offensive strategies and tactics, which helped to lure the Soviets into an overextended position. At the tactical level, for example, Khrushchev pointed out that "the American foot in Europe had a sore blister on it. That was West Berlin. Anytime we wanted to step on the Americans' foot and make them feel the pain, all we had to do was obstruct Western communications with the city."[41] Taking advantage of this vulnerability through offensive means was an enticing tactic in the service of defensive as well as offensive goals. At various times, squeezing Berlin was seen as a good way to forestall the formation of a revived, irredentist West Germany, to deter Germany from acquiring nuclear weapons, and to solve the problems of propaganda broadcasts and East German emigration.[42]

On a broader strategic level, Russia's postwar strategists feared that if America were allowed a bridgehead in Europe, the disparity in gross national product between the two powers would prove decisive in a long war in which American matériel could be transported to the European front. To prevent this, "the bridgehead on which American militarists count to concentrate and deploy their forces for land engagements will be liquidated" by "mighty air raids with the use of the newest means of armament" and "powerful offensive operations on a large scale with a high tempo of advance" by Soviet ground forces.[43] Mirroring the Schlieffen Plan, Soviet strategy counted on the offensive exploitation of an opportunity at the outset of a war to forestall a disadvantageous trend if the conflict became prolonged. Michael MccGwire has recently argued that this situational imperative drove the Soviet General Staff's quest in the Brezhnev era for conventional offensive capabilities to throw U.S. forces off the Eurasian land mass.[44]

Were it not for nuclear weapons, such situational incentives might satisfactorily explain the seemingly overambitious, offensive character of Soviet diplomatic and military strategy during much of the postwar period. But nuclear weapons reduce such incentives for offense to secondary considerations, providing instead a powerful strategic incentive to defend the status quo, not overturn it.

Why should this be so? Once both sides deploy large numbers of

41. Nikita Khrushchev, *Khrushchev Remembers: The Last Testament*, Bantam ed. (New York, 1976), 572.

42. Schick, *Berlin Crisis*.

43. Raymond Garthoff, *Soviet Strategy in the Nuclear Age* (New York, 1958), 136, citing Major General V. Khlopov, writing in a restricted circulation journal, *Voennaia Mysl'* 6 (June 1950): 75–76. U.S. war planning did in fact reflect this scenario.

44. Michael MccGwire, *Military Objectives in Soviet Foreign Policy* (Washington, D.C., 1987), chaps. 3 and 4.

invulnerable nuclear weapons, a large-scale confrontation for major stakes becomes a competition in risktaking, which will be won by the side that is better placed to tolerate the shared danger of escalation. In a confrontation of this kind, the defender of the status quo enjoys two major advantages: first, people are usually willing to run bigger risks to keep what they have than to acquire what they covet; second, the would-be attacker usually bears the onus of "the last clear chance" to avoid disastrous escalation. This motivational asymmetry makes deterrence easier than compellence.[45]

This puts strategies like squeezing Berlin and attacking America's Eurasian bridgeheads in a different perspective. Despite the Soviets' local superiority around Berlin, the United States cared enough about the city to make the onus of escalation weigh heavily on any Soviet decision to force a change in the status quo. Especially since the Soviets' most acute grievance could be solved by a defensive measure, building the Berlin Wall, the balance of motivation strongly favored the West. For similar reasons, the notion that the Soviets would have the resolve or the need to launch a decisive Soviet conventional offensive in Europe is even more problematic.[46]

This way of thinking about the political consequences of nuclear weapons is not entirely alien to the Soviet political leadership. Like Thomas Schelling, Khrushchev understood that under conditions of mutual societal vulnerability "the people with the strongest nerves will be the winners," but he did not fully grasp the asymmetrical advantages of the side defending the status quo.[47] This lesson from his own missile diplomacy was apparently not lost on his successors, who propounded the thesis that the improved correlation of military forces would promote progressive change, but only by deterring imperialist intervention to reverse it.

Rational risk acceptance. One final "rational actor" explanation must be addressed. In this view, the Soviets simply have a strong motivation to expand and therefore are willing to run moderate risks to their own security to do so.[48] Since the costs and risks incurred in periods of Soviet overextension were not excessive, Soviet strategy has always

45. Robert Jervis, "Why Nuclear Superiority Doesn't Matter," *Political Science Quarterly* 94 (Winter 1979–80): 617–33; Jack Snyder, "Science and Sovietology," *World Politics* 40 (January 1988): 181–87.

46. For a fuller critique of the paradoxes of the Soviets' conventional option, see Snyder, "Gorbachev Revolution," 123–24.

47. Mohamed Heikal, *Sphinx and Commissar* (London, 1978), 97–98.

48. Herrmann, *Perceptions*, 12–16, cites this literature. An interesting discussion placing the opportunism hypothesis in a domestic political context is Dennis Ross, "Risk Aversion in Soviet Decisionmaking," in Jiri Valenta and William Potter, *Soviet Decisionmaking for National Security* (London, 1984), 237–51.

been fully rational. Given Soviet goals and risk acceptance, it is contended that the Soviets have always behaved appropriately in light of objective international constraints and opportunities.

There are two problems with this view. The first is that, even if true, it begs the question. What causes this Soviet willingness to run security risks, even moderate ones, for the sake of expansion? If the necessities of security and power competition in international anarchy are not sufficient to explain it, then what is? To answer this, we are unavoidably thrust back into the realms of subjective beliefs and domestic politics.

The second problem is that the Soviets have *not* been cleared-eyed, rational evaluators of the costs and the risks their expansionist enterprises pose to Soviet security. As demonstrated in the previous section on strategic concepts, Soviet proponents of aggressive policies always argued that they were necessary to reduce security risks. Thus Zhdanov did not argue that fomenting strikes in France would provoke Western threats to Soviet security yet was worth the gamble for the sake of international revolution. Rather, he argued that militant action would derail the Marshall Plan, defend East European dominoes, and thus enhance Soviet security. Likewise, Khrushchev and Brezhnev argued that pushing for progressive change would enhance Soviet security by promoting favorable changes in the correlation of forces, which were needed to make détente irreversible. In short, Soviet expansionists were not clear-eyed, risk accepting opportunists. Rather, their arguments systematically swept the trade-off between security and expansion under the rug.

Net Evaluation of Realist Explanations

In summary, Soviet grand strategy has often been mismatched with objective situational incentives, especially in the postwar period. The three periods of overambitious assertiveness clashed directly with the implications of Soviet backwardness, the nuclear revolution, and the provokable character of the Soviets' democratic opponents. But there were some situational factors, especially the unstable postwar status quo in Europe, that did militate in favor of offensive strategies. On balance, Realism provides a good explanation for Stalin's buck-passing diplomacy of the 1930s and a fairly plausible explanation for his aggressive policies in Europe in the late 1940s. It explains less well Khrushchev's diplomatic overassertiveness and Brezhnev's imperial overextension.

To develop a better explanation for the Soviets' overextension and self-encirclement, it is necessary to look not only at the real incentives of their international position, but at what they believed those incentives were.

[229]

Soviet Strategic Concepts

Like British debates on grand strategy, Soviet strategic thinking has been diverse, with as many as four conceptually distinct schools of thought active at any given time and with considerable variation over time in the relative strength of the contending schools. For analytical convenience, these outlooks can be divided along two dimensions: first, whether imperialism's hostility toward socialism is conditional or unconditional, and second, whether offense is the best defense in international politics. This yields the four permutations shown in table 2.[49]

Molotov: Western hostility is unconditional; the defense has the advantage. Vyacheslav Molotov, as foreign minister in the mid-1950s, argued that Soviet efforts to relax tensions with the West would not lessen the imperialists' hostility but would only reduce vigilance within the socialist camp. He saw very few opportunities to exploit imperialist vulnerabilities through offensive action, however arguing against Khrushchev, for example, that the Third World and Yugoslavia were inextricably tied to the opposing camp. Attempts to woo them by reforming Russia's Stalinist image would only lead to unrest in Eastern Europe, he accurately predicted. Consequently the Soviet Union should adopt a hedgehog strategy of autarky, internal repression, and the forced-draft development of the country's military-industrial base.[50] Stalinists like Molotov and Lazar Kaganovich, weaned on Stalin's strategy of "socialism in one country," thus saw a militant defense as the best way to secure the revolution. As Stalin himself had put it, "Of course, the Fascists are not asleep. But it is to our advantage to let

Table 2. Soviet schools of thought on grand strategy

	Defense has the advantage	Offense has the advantage
Western hostility is unconditional	Molotov	Zhdanov
Western hostility is conditional	Malenkov, Gorbachev	Khrushchev, Brezhnev

49. These four strategies are a variation on the four images discussed in Franklyn Griffiths, "The Sources of American Conduct: Soviet Perspectives and Their Policy Implications," *International Security* 9 (Fall 1984): 3–50. The most important difference is that I split Griffiths's first image into two strategies, those of Molotov and of Zhdanov.

50. David J. Dallin, *Soviet Foreign Policy after Stalin* (Philadelphia, 1961), esp. 229, 332–33; Mohamed Heikal, *Sphinx and Commissar*, 90–92; Uri Ra'anan, *The USSR Arms the Third World* (Cambridge, Mass., 1969), chap. 4.

them attack first; that will rally the working class around the communists."[51]

Zhdanov: Western hostility is unconditional; offense has the advantage. Andrei Zhdanov represented a different brand of militancy. Like Molotov, he believed that Soviet concessions would not diminish the aggressiveness of the West, but he was distinctive in arguing that a political offensive was the best defense against imperialism's hostile onslaught. As part of his militant Cominform strategy, for example, Zhdanov promoted the use of violent strikes by Western Communist parties as a means to prevent the implementation of the Marshall Plan, which Zhdanov saw as the groundwork for an American policy of rollback in Eastern Europe.[52]

Malenkov: Western hostility is conditional; the defense has the advantage. Georgii Malenkov, in contrast, believed that Western aggressiveness could be defused by Soviet self-restraint and that defensive advantages dominated the international system. Malenkov's views dovetailed with the arguments of Eugene Varga, who contended that institutional changes in the American state during World War II had made it a stronger but less aggressive international competitor, more able to control the heedlessly aggressive impulses of the monopoly capitalists.[53] Malenkov argued that the imperialists had become realistic and sane enough to be deterred by a minimum atomic force, so that defense budgets could be safely cut and the heavy industrial priority reversed.[54] Moreover, he argued, Soviet political concessions in Europe would demobilize and split the West, leading to a new Rapallo. There is

51. E. H. Carr, *Twilight of the Comintern, 1930–1935* (New York, 1982), 27–28.

52. Ra'anan, *International Policy Formation,* esp. chap. 10. Werner Hahn, *Postwar Soviet Politics* (Ithaca, N.Y., 1982), sees Zhdanov as relatively moderate, especially in comparison with the Party militants who succeeded him, like Suslov. In fact, Zhdanov's constituencies did lead him to be "moderate" on some foreign and security issues at least some of the time—for example, limits on defense spending (to undercut Malenkov's heavy industrial base), opportunities for foreign trade (a Leningrad interest), communization of Eastern Europe by political (not police) methods. But the suggestion that Zhdanov was actually opposed to the Cominform policy that he implemented so vigorously is at odds with the memoirs of the European communists who lived through it. See Blair Ruble, *Leningrad: Shaping a Soviet City* (Berkeley, Calif., 1989), 30–32; Jerry Hough, "Debates about the Postwar World," in Susan J. Linz, *The Impact of World War II on the Soviet Union* (Totowa, N.J., 1985), 275; Eugenio Reale, *Avec Jacques Duclos au banc des accusés* (Paris, n.d.), 10–11 and passim. Zhdanov's Cominform speech is reprinted in Rush, *International Situation,* 124–39.

53. Ra'anan, *International Policy Formation,* chap. 6; Hough, "Debates," 268–74; Marshall Shulman, *Stalin's Foreign Policy Reappraised* (New York, 1969), 32–34, 111–17; Bruce Parrott, *Politics and Technology in the Soviet Union* (Cambridge, Mass., 1985), 82–91; Letteney, "Foreign Policy Factionalism," 61–62, 65.

54. Herbert Dinerstein, *War and the Soviet Union* (New York, 1959), chap. 4.

evidence that Malenkov warned on similar grounds against invading South Korea.[55]

Khrushchev and Brezhnev: Western hostility is conditional; offense has the advantage. Nikita Khrushchev and Leonid Brezhnev shared the Malenkov-Varga thesis that "realists" in the West made possible a relaxation of international tension, but they coupled this with a belief in offensive advantage in international politics. Imperialism could behave in a heedlessly aggressive manner, they believed, but prudent forces within the capitalist camp, especially the bourgeois state and public opinion, would restrain the most reckless of the monopoly capitalists. The influence of such realists could be strengthened by Soviet policy in two ways: first, Soviet efforts to shift the world correlation of forces, including the military balance, to the advantage of socialism would cause realists increasingly to shun the dangers of direct confrontation; second, projecting an image of restraint in the methods by which the Soviets pursued their expansionist goals would lull the West. These two elements would reinforce each other, according to Khrushchev and Brezhnev. The increased strength of the socialist camp would leave imperialism little choice but to accept détente on terms favorable to socialism. Détente in turn would weaken imperialism by hindering its counterrevolutionary interventions in the Third World. The success of the strategy would depend, in their view, on active measures to improve the Soviet position at the expense of the West, not simply on the passive acceptance of a stalemate or balance.[56] As Khrushchev put it: "Peace cannot be begged for. It can be safeguarded only by an active purposeful struggle."[57]

In terms of the categories laid out in chapter 2, Brezhnev, Khrushchev, and Zhdanov were bandwagon theorists who portrayed the opponent as a paper tiger. To paraphrase Zhdanov's speech to the Cominform in

55. Letteney, "Foreign Policy Factionalism," 330. Letteney also provides indirect but voluminous evidence that Malenkov and his allies criticized the 1948 Berlin policy as having justified the formation of NATO and the deployment of American nuclear forces within striking distance of the Soviet Union. See pp. 56, 77, 82–83, quoting *Izvestiia*, 12 February 1949; 19 March 1949; 22 July 1949. Zhdanov appointees ran Soviet policy in Germany until the lifting of the blockade in 1949, when they were replaced by Malenkov-Beria men. See Ann Phillips, *Soviet Policy toward East Germany Reconsidered: The Postwar Decade* (Westport, Conn., 1986), 34. Authors like Dunmore who portray Malenkov as a belligerent cold warrior during this period present virtually no evidence to support their view. It is likely, however, that Malenkov supported the military buildup at this time because it led to the return to power of his wartime heavy industry cronies. See Jeremy Azrael, *Managerial Power and Soviet Politics* (Cambridge, Mass., 1966), chap. 5. I am indebted to Dr. Azrael for a helpful discussion of these issues.

56. Griffiths, "Sources," 3–50, and Raymond Garthoff, *Detente and Confrontation* (Washington, D.C., 1985), 36–68, elaborate on and qualify these basic themes.

57. Quoted by Adomeit, *Soviet Risk-Taking*, 224.

1947, if the forces of socialism remained timid and passive, imperialism would topple Eastern Europe like a row of dominoes, whereas militant socialist action in Western Europe would derail the Marshall Plan and drive the American paper tiger back across the Atlantic with little difficulty.[58] Khrushchev and Brezhnev saw a similar dynamic at work, though they counted not on the sharp rap of militant action by the working class, but rather on the more gradual effects that a mixture of lulling and intimidation would have on the "realistic" American paper tigers and on bandwagoning Europeans, neutrals, and progressive forces in the Third World.

In contrast, Molotov and Malenkov were balance of power theorists who saw the Western states not as paper tigers, but as prickly hedgehogs. Molotov, at least in the mid-1950s, was merely pessimistic about the prospects of Soviet offensive tactics, whereas Malenkov took this insight a step further by arguing that aggressive, militant Soviet policies had provoked Western hostility to the danger point.

The relative strength of these four outlooks has varied over time. In terms of long-run secular trends, the hedgehog outlook dominated Soviet strategy before World War II; the Zhdanovite was preeminent in the early Cold War period, as was offensive détente in the Khrushchev and Brezhnev decades; and Malenkovite views gained a dominant position only under Gorbachev. In the postwar period, however, a cyclical trend is also apparent. Thus Malenkovite views at least temporarily gain in relative strength whenever more militant policies fail. Malenkov benefited from the discrediting of the militant line after the West's balancing reaction to the Berlin blockade and the Korean War. Khrushchev himself switched to a nonoffensive, Malenkovite approach to détente in 1963–64 after the failure of his missile diplomacy. Finally, Gorbachev's ability to implement a Malenkovite strategy of retrenchment to demobilize the encircling coalition has also benefited from the manifest failures of Brezhnev's SS-20 diplomacy in Europe and his support for unpopular socialist regimes throughout the Third World.[59]

COGNITIVE EXPLANATIONS: CORRECTING BOLSHEVIK MYOPIA?

Though the Soviets' strategy has often been at odds with the reality of their geopolitical situation, they nonetheless have typically explained their policy as a response to the current "character of the epoch" and the nature of advanced capitalism at the current stage of its "general

58. Reprinted in Rush, *International Situation*, 124–39.
59. Francis Fukuyama, "Patterns of Soviet Third World Policy," *Problems of Communism* 36 (September–October 1987): 1–13.

crisis."[60] A great deal of scholarly literature assumes that Soviet misperceptions of the international system stem from cognitive biases, rooted in the peculiarities of Bolshevism's Marxist-Leninist origins and formative revolutionary experiences. Such cognitive explanations, based on the purely intellectual staying power of formative impressions, are difficult to disentangle from explanations that stress the staying power of antiquated Soviet institutions and their ideological justifications.[61] Nonetheless, I will work from the assumption that the Bolshevik intellectual legacy has a life of its own and can be studied independent of its institutional base.

George Breslauer offers the most succinct statement of the cognitive explanation. Citing classic works on the "Bolshevik operational code" by Nathan Leites and Alexander George, Breslauer argues:

> The Leninist-Stalinist tradition shaped the original content of [the major] dimensions of Soviet foreign policy ideology. Leninist ideology included a commitment to "make the world safe for socialism," both by maintaining Soviet power in the U.S.S.R. and by providing varied sorts and degrees of assistance to radical and other "anti-imperialist" forces abroad. Thus it became the historical responsibility of the party leadership to reconcile these normative imperatives by seizing opportunities for expanding the anti-imperialist camp without jeopardizing the continuation of party power in the socialist homeland. . . .
>
> Empirical beliefs about the character of the contemporary era were also components of the Leninist heritage: that imperialism in this stage of its final crisis was diabolical and conspiratorial; that the struggle with the imperialist enemy was zero-sum in character; that imperialism would seek to inflict cumulative losses on socialism if given the opportunity; but that growing contradictions among imperialist forces and growing opposition to imperialist exploitation among the peoples of the Third World would frustrate imperialist efforts to turn back the clock of history.
>
> Finally, strategic prescriptions for the conduct of struggle on the international stage encouraged Soviet leaders to seize opportunities for advance only after careful calculation of costs, risks, and likely payoffs, but then to push to the limit of attainable, cumulative gains. At the same time, though, strategic prescriptions called for avoiding adventurism, for knowing when to stop, and for retreating before superior force.[62]

Though deeply rooted in the foreign policy mentality of the Soviet elite, these concepts underwent an important revision in 1956, says

60. Shulman, *Stalin's Foreign Policy*, 9 and passim; Griffiths, "Sources."
61. B. Thomas Trout, "Rhetoric Revisited: Political Legitimation and the Cold War," *International Studies Quarterly* 19 (September 1975): 251–84.
62. Breslauer, "Ideology and Learning," 431–32, drawing on Nathan Leites, *A Study of Bolshevism* (Glencoe, Ill., 1953); Alexander George, "The 'Operational Code': A Neglected Approach to the Study of Political Leaders and Decisionmaking," *International Studies Quarterly* 13 (June 1969): 190–222.

Breslauer, when Khrushchev learned that nuclear weapons had made war no longer "fatalistically inevitable" and that socialism might triumph peacefully because realists in the imperialist camp feared the consequences of war. Further development of these lessons was limited during the Brezhnev era, says Breslauer, reflecting the persistence of deep-seated cognitive predispositions. Under Gorbachev, however, the Soviets are back on the upward learning curve, shedding still more of the zero-sum ideological baggage of their Leninist-Stalinist intellectual heritage. From the cognitive viewpoint, this lesson was driven home by discouraging feedback from the expansionism of the 1970s.[63]

There are three main problems with this explanation. First, Leites's formulations of it are nonfalsifiable, since for any given situation they could explain any Soviet behavior and its opposite. The Bolshevik "pushes to the limit" but "knows when to stop," yet none of the operational code theorists have explained how he knows when to stop.[64] Such ambivalent and truistic strategic axioms hardly have much explanatory power.

To breathe life into this theory as an explanation for Soviet overexpansion, we would have to stipulate that, when in doubt, the Bolshevik leans toward offensive solutions to strategic problems. William Taubman, for example, implies that Stalin, Khrushchev, and Brezhnev have all acted according to a "double whammy" operation code, featuring what I would call a paper tiger image of the opponent— "antagonistic, powerful, and treacherous" yet at the same time "vulnerable, weak, and susceptible to Soviet manipulation." As a result, Stalin read any American action as confirming his belief in an assertive Soviet policy: conciliatory American moves were taken as invitations to press ahead, while American firmness was read as confirming the view that America was implacably hostile.[65]

But a reformulation of the Bolshevik operational code argument to stress its offensive bias would immediately run afoul of the second objection—that the political legacy of Lenin and Bolshevism was far too ambivalent to impart a systematically offensive bias to later foreign policy choices.

On one hand, Lenin and the Old Bolsheviks were quintessential realists. As such, they understood the dangers of gratuitously provocative or overextended strategies. Lenin condemned adventurism as an

63. Breslauer, "Ideology and Learning," 433–35, 438–41, and personal communication.

64. Breslauer, "Ideology and Learning," 432, and personal communication, acknowledges the difficulty of testing the operational code theory and so distances his own learning argument from the particular strategic prescriptions advanced in the operational code literature. For an excellent critique of the operational code literature, see James Goldgeier, "Soviet Leaders and International Crises" (Ph.D. diss., University of California at Berkeley, 1989), conclusions.

65. Taubman, Stalin's American Policy, 10, 234, 237–38, 243, 248–49.

"infantile disorder" and condoned tactical retreats and alliances with capitalist powers to ensure the survival of the Bolshevik revolution in a hostile international environment. He accepted the necessity for the Treaty of Brest-Litovsk on the grounds that the hope of a revolution in Germany was chimerical. He opposed M. N. Roy's plan to cause a social revolution in England by liberating India, backed the Rapallo détente with Weimar Germany, and in general approved a nonrevolutionary foreign policy as the necessary complement to the foreign trade requirements of the market-oriented New Economic Policy.[66]

Stalin's diplomacy in the 1920s and 1930s was similarly circumspect. If anything, he learned too well the operational code's axiom that, on the defensive, a Bolshevik must be wary of imperialist provocations, designed to create a pretext for attack. Stalin was so circumspect on these grounds that he virtually forbade the Red Army to shoot back at the outset of the German surprise attack in June 1941. This passive stance, and more generally Stalin's buck-passing strategy in the late 1930s, cannot be written off as simply the result of weakness. The Soviet Union was far stronger vis-à-vis Hitler than it was vis-à-vis the United States after the war, both in fact and in Stalin's own estimation, yet Stalin adopted a far more assertive strategy in the latter case.[67]

Yet the Leninist legacy also has its militant, offensive side. Lenin saw politics as a fight to the finish (the famous question of "Who will defeat whom?'), requiring decisive action to seize the intiative at the propitious moment. Lenin risked everything on a bid for revolution in October 1917 at a time when other Party leaders wanted to play it safe.[68] Likewise, in the counteroffensive against Poland in 1920, Lenin decided over Trotsky's objections to seize a risky opportunity to capture Warsaw.[69]

In short, Bolshevik political culture might be able to explain an offensive strategic belief system, but it could also explain its opposite.[70] Explanations of Soviet foreign policy based on the Leninist legacy are either nonfalsifiable, if they admit the ambivalence of that legacy, or erroneous, if they overemphasize those aspects of Bolshevik political culture that condone offensive strategies.

A third problem is that such explanations offer very poor predictions of the timing of offensive overextension. One would expect a great deal of assertiveness early in the Soviet experience, when revolutionary

66. The basic facts are covered in Ulam, *Expansion and Coexistence*, chaps. 2–4.
67. Taubman, *Stalin's American Policy*, 134–35.
68. Sheila Fitzpatrick, *The Russian Revolution* (New York, 1982), 54–55.
69. The attempt failed. Louis Fischer, *Russia's Road from Peace to War* (New York, 1969), 43.
70. Franklyn Griffiths, "Inner Tensions in the Soviet Approach to 'Disarmament,'" *International Journal* 22 (Autumn 1967): 593–617.

myopia should have been operating in full force. In fact, the war against Poland is the only clear example of overextension until the late 1940s. Most of Leites's illustrations of hard-nosed principles of Soviet diplomacy (e.g., "It pays to be rude") come from the post-1945 period. This theory also explains later developments poorly. Breslauer's periodization might lead us to expect a noticeable decline in Soviet aggressiveness after the intellectual innovations of 1956, yet Khrushchev's reckless missile diplomacy almost immediately followed this. Khrushchev thought differently about nuclear weapons than did Molotov, for example, but what he had "learned" was that in the nuclear era "the people with weak nerves will go to the wall."[71]

Finally, cognitive learning theorists take credit for evidence that fits not only their own theory, but other theories as well. Few would deny that Gorbachev's learning about Third World quagmires and NATO's balancing reactions to Soviet missile deployment was in one sense a cognitive adjustment to evidence that Brezhnev's grand strategy had clearly failed.[72] But Soviet leaders in earlier periods also had clear evidence that overaggressive Soviet diplomacy provokes balancing Western responses. And indeed, some Soviet leaders, like Malenkov and Aleksei Kosygin, appear to have read those lessons correctly. Thus the interesting question is not whether Soviet leaders have the intellectual wherewithal to learn about the realities of international politics, but whether those who learn such lessons can survive in Soviet domestic politics.[73]

DOMESTIC POLITICS: ATAVISMS OF THE REVOLUTION FROM ABOVE

The Soviet late, late pattern was like a flat-out version of German late industrialization: rapid, concentrated in large-scale heavy industry,

71. Heikal, *Sphinx and Commissar*, 97–98, quoting Khrushchev in a meeting with Nasser, July 1958. Breslauer accommodates Khrushchev's behavior to his theory by invoking the persistence of an ingrained optimism in Soviet political ideas.

72. Robert Legvold, "War, Weapons, and Soviet Foreign Policy," in Seweryn Bialer and Michael Mandelbaum, *Gorbachev's Russia and American Foreign Policy* (Boulder, Colo., 1988), 97–132; Robert Legvold, "Soviet Learning in the 1980s," in George Breslauer and Philip Tetlock, *Learning in U.S. and Soviet Foreign Policy* (Boulder, Colo., 1991).

73. George Breslauer offers an eclectic attempt to integrate cognitive and domestic-political explanations in "All Gorbachev's Men," *National Interest* (Summer 1988): 91–100. Other kinds of cognitive explanations, like those based on attribution theory and actor/observer differences, might plausibly explain some of the tension in Soviet-American relations since 1945. Garthoff's compendium of Soviet and American double standards in blame casting during the collapse of détente in the 1970s, *Detente and Confrontation*, is highly reminiscent of the hypotheses put forward in that literature. Nonetheless such a theory, which basically posits a constant bias in human perception, cannot by itself account for those variations over time in Soviet strategy that I seek to explain. Parrish, "Soviet Reactions to the Security Dilemma," argues that varying geopolitical conditions may either magnify or dampen the effects of attribution biases.

centrally financed, and shaped by state intervention.[74] But this difference in degree was so great that it constituted a difference in kind. To
carry out this revolution from above, old social groups had to be
broken up and political power concentrated in the hands of a unitary
"organizational weapon," to use Philip Selznick's term for the Communist party.[75] The resulting political and economic structures were so
centralized that, rather than being bases for interest group logrolling as
in the German case, they could be dominated from the unitary focal
point of the totalitarian dictator.

This concentration had a two-edged effect on strategic mythmaking
and overexpansion during the Stalin period. On one hand, it created a
strong, centralized power with an encompassing perspective to check
parochial interests. On the other hand, the mobilizing tasks of the
revolution from above created a domestic propaganda need to exaggerate threats from the international environment and gave Communist
party institutions a vested interest in such myths. Moreover, the
hyperconcentrated structure of power left Stalin unchecked by any
political counterweight, so that any strategic myths he personally
accepted would not undergo close scrutiny. As a result, Soviet
overexpansion, as in 1947–50, was not precluded by this unitary
political structure.

After the revolutionary stage of the industrial transformation was
completed, and after Stalin's death, the institutions and ideas it created
lived on for decades as atavisms. A hybrid system with both cartelized
and unitary elements developed, in which the Politburo oligarchy
managed and shaped the logrolling among various institutionally based
groups. In this system the military-industrial complex and the mobilizing "combat party" played key roles in the formation of domestic
political coalitions, driving foreign and security policies in a militant,
expansionist direction.[76]

Recently, however, Gorbachev and his allies have been attacking
these old institutions and ideas as self-serving holdovers from the
outmoded tasks of "extensive" economic development—that is, the
administrative mobilization of underutilized human and material resources. Instead, argue the reformers, the Soviet Union needs to break
the power of these old institutions and dogmas in order to create new
institutions that will better suit to the needs of "intensive" economic
development—that is, the efficient allocation of resources in response

74. Gerschenkron, *Economic Backwardness*, chap. 6.
75. See Philip Selznick, *The Organizational Weapon* (Glencoe, Ill., 1960); Philip Selznick,
Leadership in Administration (New York, 1957), 125.
76. On the emergence of militarized socialism, see Mark von Hagen, *Soldiers in the
Proletarian Dictatorship: The Red Army and the Soviet Socialist State, 1917–1930* (Ithaca, N.Y.,
1990).

to demand.[77] Given the nature of this task, they argue, these new institutional forms must allow a greater role for markets and grass roots political participation. By breaking the power of imperialist interests and by empowering constituencies favoring détente and participation in the world market, Gorbachev's domestic changes have contributed to the waning of Soviet militarism and expansionism.[78] But the long-term outcome of these changes in foreign policy will depend on the future evolution of Soviet domestic institutions.

Institutions and Ideas of the Revolution from Above

Stalinist institutions were marked by their origins in the attempts of an autocrat to whip his backward society to modernize in the face of foreign competition. In this process, international pressure provided both the motive and the opportunity to smash obsolete institutions and replace them with more efficient, centrally controlled ones.[79] "Old Russia . . . was ceaselessly beaten for her backwardness," Stalin warned at the height of the First Five-Year Plan. "We are fifty or a hundred years behind the advanced countries. We must make good this lag in ten years. Either we do it or they crush us."[80]

The tsars, too, had tried to spur revolutions from above for much the same reason. As Stalin explained, however, "none of the old classes . . . could solve the problem of overcoming the backwardness of the country."[81] Instead, they were barriers to the needed transformation. But all of these old urban and elite classes, including the old working class, had been swept away between 1917 and 1921 by the combination of war, revolution, foreign intervention, and civil war. The Bolsheviks were not yet strong enough in the early 1920s to break the peasantry and mobilize the material and labor surpluses needed for rapid industrialization. During the 1920s, however, they were able to forge a spearhead for completing the social transformation from the ranks of the new, tabula rasa working class, which was younger and less tainted with reformist trade unionism than the old working class had been.[82]

77. When I use the term institution, I mean not only bureaucratic organizations, but also established ways of organizing social relationships, such as the institution of central planning or of market.

78. Valerii Karabaev, "Our Debts," *Literaturnaia Gazeta*, 21 October 1987, 4, translated in Foreign Broadcast Information Service, *Daily Report* (Soviet Union), 29 October 1987.

79. In addition to Gerschenkron, for a state building perspective on the Bolshevik revolution, see Theda Skocpol, *States and Social Revolutions* (Cambridge, 1979).

80. Quoted in Deutscher, *Stalin*, 328.

81. Ibid., 321.

82. Sheila Fitzpatrick, "The Russian Revolution and Social Mobility," *Politics and Society* 13 (1984): 124–26. For another perspective, see John B. Hatch, "The 'Lenin Levy' and the Social Origins of Stalinism: Workers and the Communist Party in Moscow, 1921–1928," *Slavic Review* 48 (Winter 1989): 558–77.

This revolution had institutional and intellectual consequences. Institutionally, its implementation required a more militant mobilizing party, the strengthening of repressive police institutions, and a more centralized authoritarian economic structure to overcome bottlenecks and assert the priority of military-related heavy industrial production. Through upward mobility from the new working class, it also created by the late 1930s a politically dependent, hothouse technical elite— what Stalin called "a new Soviet intelligentsia, firmly linked with the people and ready en masse to give it true and faithful service."[83] This was the Brezhnev generation, for which the Great Purges cleared the way.

Intellectually, these institutions and personnel were motivated and tempered by the inculcation of an ideology of political combat and the exaggeration of internal and external threats. This approach mobilized energies when pecuniary rewards were lacking, justified repression, and legitimated the priority of resource allocations for the military-industrial complex. According to the definitive study of the enlistment of workers in the campaign to collectivize agriculture:

> The recruitment of the 25,000ers took place in the context of the First Five-Year Plan mobilization atmosphere. The leadership manipulated and played upon popular fear of military intervention and memories of civil war famine, rekindled by the war scare and the grain crisis of the late 1920s. The dominant motifs of the First Five-Year Plan revolution were military and the imagery was that of the Russian civil war. The working class was called upon to sacrifice for the good of the cause and the preservation of the nation. The state sought to deflect working class grievances away from systemic problems and toward the external and internal enemies—the kulak, the bourgeois specialist, the Nepman, and the political opposition [inside the Party]—all said to be in league with the agents of international imperialism.[84]

Though this paranoid, pressure cooker atmosphere was largely fomented from above by Stalin and his allies, recent studies have stressed that it was readily internalized and exploited by the upwardly mobile militants who were Stalin's shock troops. During the collectiv-

---

83. Speech to the March 1939 Party Congress, quoted in Sheila Fitzpatrick, "Stalin and the Making of a New Elite, 1928–1939," *Slavic Review* 38 (1979): 377–402.

84. Lynne Viola, *Best Sons of the Fatherland: Workers in the Vanguard of Collectivization* (New York, 1986), 37. For Stalin speeches clearly showing the manipulation of the 1927 war scare for factional and mobilizational purposes, see Jane Degras, *Soviet Documents of Foreign Policy*, vol. 2, *1925–1932* (London, 1952), 233–37, 301–2. While Stalin was trumpeting the threat in public, a briefing to the Politburo from Foreign Minister Chicherin argued flatly that the idea of an imminent danger of war was utter nonsense. See Michal Reiman, *Die Geburt des Stalinismus* (Frankfurt, 1979), 37; translated as *The Birth of Stalinism* (Bloomington, Ind., 1987).

ization campaign and the later purges, these young radicals exaggerated the threat of foreign subversion to push campaigns to extremes and to sweep away the older bureaucratic elite that was blocking their path to social advancement.[85]

Stalinist Atavisms and the Politics of Expansion

After the period of rapid social mobilization, these institutions and ideas lived on. As early as the late 1940s, the institutional instruments of mobilization were turning into self-interested cartels. The intellectual instruments were turning into tools for justifying these institutional interests, especially the role of orthodox ideology in shaping society, the allocative priority of the military-industrial complex, and petty interference by Party bureaucrats in day-to-day economic administration.

Foreign policy ideas played an important role in rationalizing and reconciling group interests. By the late 1940s, three of the four schools of thought in Soviet grand strategy discussed above had emerged, each supported by a distinctive constituency. Molotov's hedgehog strategy gained adherents among Stalin's old henchmen and the military-industrial complex. The Zhdanovite strategy appealed to party militants, while Malenkov sought adherents for a domestic and international relaxation of tensions among the intelligentsia. The fourth school of thought, offensive détente, resulted from the efforts of political entrepreneurs like Khrushchev and Brezhnev to form coalitions among the other three. It was this fourth school that held the reins of policy for most of the 1950s, 1960s, and 1970s. The preferences and power of individual interest groups are necessary, but not sufficient, to explain this outcome. Only by adding the dynamics of logrolling and strategic mythmaking by coalition leaders can Soviet overextension in this period be fully explained.

Molotov, the Military, and the Hedgehog Strategy

Molotov, at least by the time of Stalin's death, was promoting a strategy of "fortress Russia," shunning adventurism but stressing high levels of vigilance against socialism's enemies at home and abroad. Since Molotov's prestige and legitimacy hinged on being Stalin's chief lieutenant, especially in foreign affairs, his interests as well as his habits were served by his being the guardian of orthodoxy.

85. J. Arch Getty, *Origins of the Great Purges* (Cambridge, 1985). See also Lynne Viola, "The Campaign of the 25,000ers: A Study of the Collectivization of Soviet Agriculture, 1929–1931" (Ph.D. diss., Princeton University, 1984), 29, and Viola, *Best Sons*, 6, 25, 37, 62–64. For a debate on the new social history of the Stalin period, see Fitzpatrick, Stephen Cohen, and other commentators in *Russia Review* 45 (October 1986).

A more enduring constituency for this hedgehog strategy lay among the military-industrial interests. When Khrushchev moved to limit military spending and simultaneously to provoke foreign conflicts, for example, a powerful leader of the opposition was Frol Kozlov, whose political base was rooted in Leningrad's military-oriented economy.[86] In Kozlov's view, an outlook that became especially prominent in the Brezhnev era, the methodical development of Soviet military strength was the prerequisite for successful dealings with the West.

The professional military itself inclined to this view, which justified high levels of expenditure on military forces and the heavy industrial sectors that supplied them. The military also liked this strategy because it warned against foreign showdowns for which the military felt unprepared. Western scholarship on the "pacifist realism" of military professionals would expect such an outlook.[87] This view was prevalent under Khrushchev. During this period, the strategic ideology of the Soviet military stressed straightforward threat inflation, denying that there were any "realists" in the West who could be partners in arms control, or for that matter, who could be intimidated by Khrushchev's brinkmanship into accepting détente on Soviet terms.[88]

In the Brezhnev era, however, increased Soviet capabilities made the top brass much more willing to advocate military intervention abroad and to offer Soviet military power to deter American intervention against Soviet Third World clients.[89] For example, seeing off the Egyptian war minister at the Moscow airport on the eve of the June 1967 war, Marshal Andrei Grechko advised, "Stand up to them! The moment they attack you, or if the Americans make any move, you will find our troops at your side."[90] Later, during the war of attrition, when Kosygin was telling the Egyptians to "cool the situation" and avoid "anything that can be taken advantage of by the Israeli warmongers," Grechko was urging the opposite: "You should be more daring. . . . Why are you afraid? The Soviet navy in the Mediterranean is following the American

---

86. Ruble, *Leningrad*; Carl Linden, *Khrushchev and the Soviet Leadership* (Baltimore, 1966), 50–54 and passim; Sidney Ploss, *Conflict and Decision-Making in Soviet Russia* (Princeton, N.J., 1965), 216–34; Christer Jonsson, *Soviet Bargaining Behavior: The Nuclear Test Ban Case* (New York, 1979), 133–208; Michel Tatu, *Power in the Kremlin* (New York, 1970). Adomeit, *Soviet Risk-Taking*, 269–70, points out that Kozlov was apparently not a risk taker.

87. Samuel Huntington, *The Soldier and the State* (New York, 1957), 62–79, and Richard Betts, *Soldiers, Statesmen, and Cold War Crises* (Cambridge, Mass., 1977); and for qualifications to the argument, Van Evera, "Causes of War."

88. Jonsson, *Soviet Bargaining Behavior*, chaps. 11–13.

89. F. Stephen Larrabee, "Gorbachev and the Soviet Military," *Foreign Affairs* 66 (Summer 1988): 1002–26, esp. 1006; Celeste Wallander, "Third-World Conflict in Soviet Military Thought: Does the 'New Thinking' Grow Prematurely Grey?" *World Politics* 42 (October 1989): 31–63.

90. Heikal, *Sphinx and Commissar*, 28.

Sixth Fleet like a shadow. They can't do anything. If the Americans put their marines into Israel we are ready to land our troops in your territories. And then I should like to see who would win!"[91] Finally, in June 1972, Grechko told the Politburo in the presence of the Egyptian chief of staff that, contrary to the Soviets' policy up to that point of restraining the Arabs by limiting arms supplies, "Egypt must be supplied with the weapons to ensure victory."[92]

These anecdotes show not only that the Soviet military leadership came to abandon the hedgehog strategy for a more assertive stance, but that the military adopted arguments reminiscent of the logic of offensive détente, extended to provide a theory of escalation control in limited conflicts. Thus Soviet military capabilities would constrain American escalation even while a Soviet client used Soviet-supplied arms to achieve "victory" over an American ally. This logic was also applied in preparing for a limited conventional war in Europe. The Soviet army would strive for a decisive victory using conventional forces only, and realists in NATO would be deterred from retaliating with nuclear arms by the threat of Soviet escalation. Flush with increased capabilities, the Soviet military was weaned from the hedgehog strategy and co-opted into a coalition favoring the more assertive strategy of offensive détente.[93]

The military's interest in such a strategy is not difficult to imagine, since it posed a demanding task that would justify open-ended expenditures on conventional forces. But why was the military worth co-opting into a ruling coalition? The value of the military's support to a would-be coalition maker does not stem from fear that it would mount a coup against a leader it disliked. Rather, the military's power over policy stems from its virtual monopoly on information and analytical expertise in many aspects of national security debate.[94] Its value to a ruling coalition, and the political danger it poses to potential enemies, stems from the same source. The military can enhance the political credibility of leaders it favors by endorsing their national security strategies on technical grounds. On the same grounds, it can undercut the credibility of leaders it opposes. This power to persuade

91. Ibid., 194–95. This is corroborated in general terms by analysis of the Soviet press reported in Ilana Kass, *Soviet Involvement in the Middle East* (Boulder, Colo., 1978), and Dina Spechler, *Domestic Influences on Soviet Foreign Policy* (Washington, D.C., 1978).

92. Saad el-Shazly, *The Crossing of the Suez* (San Francisco, 1980), 161.

93. For this interpretation, Snyder, "Gorbachev Revolution," 123–24; for background, MccGwire, *Military Objectives*, chap. 4.

94. On the information monopoly, see Condoleezza Rice, "The Party, the Military, and Decision Authority in the Soviet Union," *World Politics* 40 (October 1987): 66–71; and Stephen Meyer, "Civilian and Military Influence in Managing the Arms Race in the U.S.S.R.," in Robert Art et al., *Reorganizing America's Defense* (Washington, D.C., 1985), 37–61.

cannot be used to dictate to a unified leadership, but it can be used to good effect when civilian leaders are jockeying against each other, as they were during much of the post-Stalin period.

Zhdanov, the Militant Party, and Progressive Change Abroad

The essence of the Zhdanovite strategy was the militant use of party instruments to promote "progessive" political change abroad. Its constituency was the Communist party bureaucracy and its orthodox ideologues, who needed a strategic ideology to use as a weapon in struggles against a competing faction led by Malenkov. As early as 1941, Malenkov was attempting to promote the professional interests of the new technical elite against meddling Party bureaucrats. He decried the "know-nothings" and "windbags" in the Party bureaucracy who exercised "petty tutelage" over industrial experts, rejected sound technical advice, and spouted empty quotations about "putting the pressure on."[95] The war greatly increased the autonomy of technical experts, so that by 1945 Stalin needed to use Zhdanov to promote a "Party revival" to redress the institutional balance of power.

Zhdanov used foreign policy ideas as a weapon in this struggle. He inflated the threat of ideological subversion from abroad to justify the priority of ideological orthodoxy at home. He argued for the thorough communization of Eastern Europe, including East Germany, relying heavily on the mobilizing skills of the Party to carry it out.[96] And he emphasized the strategic value of Communist fifth columns in the West.

Why did this militant, Zhdanovite view prevail in Soviet policy in the fall of 1947? Historians agree that the answer lies in Stalin's preferences rather than in the power of Zhdanov and his supporters.[97] Stalin may have backed Zhdanov's viewpoint after the adoption of the Marshall Plan because international conditions seemed to require such a militant approach. Some authors, however, suggest that Stalin had to inflate the foreign threat in this period to reassert social controls that had been relaxed during the war. This became especially pressing given the need to consolidate Soviet power in the newly conquered lands of Eastern Europe. The militant Zhdanovite "two camps" ideology was well suited to these tasks of domestic and imperial consolida-

95. William McCagg, *Stalin Embattled* (Detroit, 1978), 117 and passim.
96. Timothy Dunmore, *Soviet Politics, 1945–1953* (New York, 1984), 116–17; Radomir Luza, "Czechoslovakia between Democracy and Communism, 1945–1948," in Charles S. Maier, ed., *The Origins of the Cold War and Contemporary Europe* (New York, 1978), 73–106.
97. Ra'anan, *International Policy Formation*, 116.

tion, even if it was counterproductive as a strategy for dealing with the West.[98]

Upon Zhdanov's death in 1948, the heir to his strategy and position in the Central Committee Secretariat was Mikhail Suslov, who defended the Zhdanov line against Malenkov's criticism that it had served only to unify and militarize the West.[99] Until Suslov's own death in 1982, he served as the proponent of militant and ideologically orthodox means for promoting progressive change abroad and as the enforcer of the Party's corporate interests in domestic coalition making.[100]

Malenkov, the Intelligentsia, and the Relaxation of Tensions

Malenkov argued for a relaxation of tensions in Soviet policy at home and abroad, echoing Eugene Varga's arguments that the strengthened capitalist state was better able to control the aggressive monopoly capitalists. Consequently, the increasingly realistic imperialists could be deterred with a small nuclear force, whereas a more menacing military and diplomatic stance would only play into the hands of the military-industrial complex in the West.

Malenkov sought a constituency for these views among the urban middle class and the cultural and technical intelligentsia. The charges leveled by Zhdanovite inquisitors against Varga's book read like a sociological profile of Malenkov's would-be constituency: "technical" and "apolitical," suffering from "empiricism," "bourgeois objectivism," and a "non-party" outlook.[101] Malenkov's conception of international politics served the interests of the intelligentsia by removing the major justification for oppressive petty tutelage over them by party ideologues and bureaucrats, for the economic priorities that impoverished their living standard, and for a renewal of the purges.[102]

98. McCagg, Stalin Embattled, chaps. 11 and 12; Trout, "Rhetoric Revisited," 262–67. In addition, McCagg argues that Stalin maintained his own power in part by playing off his lieutenants and their institutional constituencies against each other. In promoting the "Party revival" as a counterweight to Malenkov and Beria, Stalin may have found it tactically expedient to support the militant Cominform strategy that the Zhdanovites preferred.

99. Letteney, "Foreign Policy Factionalism," 197, quoting a Suslov speech in Pravda, 29 November 1949; Shulman, Stalin's Foreign Policy, 118–20.

100. Roy Medvedev, All Stalin's Men (Garden City, N.Y., 1984), chap. 3; Shevchenko, Breaking with Moscow, 180, 190–91, 220, 262; Parrott, Politics and Technology, 193–98; Jan S. Adams, "Incremental Activism in Soviet Third World Policy: The Role of the International Department of the CPSU Central Committee," Slavic Review 48 (Winter 1984): 614–30; works cited above by Gelman, Tatu, Linden, and Ploss.

101. Franklyn Griffiths, "Images, Politics, and Learning in Soviet Behavior toward the United States" (Ph.D. diss., Columbia University, 1972), 40–41.

102. Boris Nicolaevsky, Power and the Soviet Elite (New York, 1965), chap. 3, esp. p. 153; Roger Pethybridge, A Key to Soviet Politics (London, 1962), 30–36.

This strategy failed, however, because the class that Malenkov hoped to recruit was subject to counterpressures: many members worked in the military-industrial complex, and many had benefited from Stalin's "Big Deal" with the new intelligentsia, receiving some of the minimal trappings of petty bourgeois status and life-style in exchange for absolute political loyalty to the orthodox regime.[103] Even a decade later, Kosygin still found that this stratum constituted an inadequate social base for a similar strategic ideology.[104]

The Khrushchev and Brezhnev Synthesis

The strategies articulated by Molotov, Zhdanov, and Malenkov were each associated with one of the key constituencies that formed around the institutions left over from the First Five-Year Plan. That is why each of them failed. None of these strategic ideologies had a sufficiently broad-based appeal to prevail in Soviet politics. Khrushchev and Brezhnev succeeded because they used the concept of offensive détente to achieve that broader synthesis.

In promoting offensive détente, Khrushchev and Brezhnev were acting as political entrepreneurs, cementing a broad political coalition with a strategic ideology that promised something for everyone: progressive change for Suslov and the ideologues; military modernization and enhanced national security for the military-industrial constituencies; détente and increased foreign trade for the cultural and technical intelligentsia. The problem was that this political formula worked at home but not abroad. In practice it led to overcommitted, contradictory policies that provoked the hostility of the West, revealing (as Gorbachev has put it) that its strategic vision was "a world of illusions."[105]

This process played itself out somewhat differently under Khrushchev and Brezhnev, reflecting the different political uses to which the two leaders put the strategy of offensive détente. In the early Khrushchev period, offensive détente was a strategic ideology that served to legitimate the outcome of political logrolling. This was also how Brezhnev used the strategy. But between 1958 and 1962 Khrushchev tried to make good on the promises of offensive détente in order to escape the

103. Vera Dunham, *In Stalin's Time: Middleclass Values in Soviet Fiction* (Cambridge, 1976).

104. Parrott, *Politics and Technology*, 182–86, 190, 197; Gelman, *Brezhnev Politburo*, 85 and passim; Heikal, *Sphinx and Commissar*, 194.

105. My interpretation closely parallels that of Richter, "Action and Reaction." Richter's dissertation, based on exhaustive research in primary source material, is in some respects an application to foreign policy of George Breslauer's authority-building argument, which inter alia showed how Soviet coalition making has led to overcommitted, "taut" policy platforms. George Breslauer, *Khrushchev and Brezhnev as Leaders* (London, 1982), esp. 288.

contraints of his logrolled coalition and, as a consequence, provoked the worst of the Cold War crises.

Khrushchev's version of the strategy of offensive détente hinged on nuclear technology and especially the intercontinental ballistic missile, which was to serve as a cheap cure-all, changing the correlation of forces and leading to détente with the West, a favorable political settlement in Europe, low-cost security, and the freeing of resources for a rise in Soviet living standards.[106] Such arguments were an attractive element in Khrushchev's political platform during the succession struggle.[107] They had the further advantage that they could not fully be tested until the ICBM was actually produced. By 1958 Khrushchev had his ICBM and was eager to move on to the next phase of his domestic game plan, capping military expenditures and increasing investment in chemicals and other sectors that would benefit agricultural and consumer production.[108] But the West refused to play its part in the script. Instead of becoming more "realistic," the Americans rejected pleas for a summit, refused to move toward recognition of the German Democratic Republic, and seemed headed toward the nuclearization of the Bundeswehr.[109]

Khrushchev sought to push on with his budgetary reversal despite this refusal, but several Politburo members balked. "Until the aggressive circles of the imperialist powers reject the policy of the arms race and preparations for a new war, we must still further strengthen the defenses of our country," said Suslov. This had been "the general line of our party... in the period 1954–1957," and implicitly it had been Khrushchev's personal pledge during the succession struggle. Thus Suslov called on Khrushchev to "honestly fulfill [the Party's] duties and promises before the Soviet people."[110] The Berlin crisis offered Khrushchev a way out of this impasse. Using it as a lever to gain a summit, the recognition of the GDR, and progress on the test ban, Khrushchev hoped to demonstrate that the correlation of forces had already changed enough to achieve détente on favorable terms, allowing

106. In addition to Richter, see Arnold Horelick and Myron Rush, *Strategic Power and Soviet Foreign Policy* (Chicago, 1966); Parrott, *Politics and Technology*, 131, 137, 158–63, 171–72; Heikal, *Sphinx and Commissar*, 97–98, 128–29.

107. As early as 1954, Khrushchev had used nuclear strategy as a successful political weapon against Malenkov, and in a passage from a speech that his colleagues excised from the *Pravda* version, Khrushchev bragged that "we were even quicker than the capitalist camp and invented the hydrogen bomb before they had it; we, the Party and the working class, we know the importance of this bomb." Wolfgang Leonhard, *The Kremlin without Stalin* (Westport, Conn., 1975), 88.

108. For minor qualifications, Breslauer, *Khrushchev and Brezhnev*, 67–71.

109. Schick, *The Berlin Crisis*.

110. *Pravda*, 12 March 1958. James Richter alerted me to this speech.

radical cuts in conventional forces and a leveling off of nuclear expenditures.[111]

This attempt to use offensive détente to escape from the constraints of political promises helped put Khrushchev on the slippery slope that led to his replacement in 1964 by the team of Brezhnev and Kosygin. Brezhnev learned from this that offensive détente could not be used to escape the strictures of coalition politics, but he did not learn that offensive détente was an inherently self-defeating policy. Indeed, the story of his own coalition building strategy suggests that he thought the distribution of political power in the 1960s still made offensive détente an indispensable tool in domestic politics.[112]

At first Brezhnev maneuvered to create a coalition on the moderate left. As part of this, he attracted ideologues and the moderate military with a foreign policy stressing support for "progressive" Third World states, notably the Arabs, and a military policy that emphasized a huge conventional buildup while opening the door to nuclear arms control. This isolated Kosygin and Nikolai Podgorny on the right, vulnerable because of their insistence on reduced defense spending, and Aleksandr Shelepin on the extreme left, apparently hoping to use a platform of even more reckless Third World adventures and domestic economic reform to attract a social-imperialist coalition.[113] But soon a flaw appeared in Brezhnev's policy of moderate appeasement of the cartels of the left. The strategy was extremely expensive, making him vulnerable to Kosygin's charge that it was wrecking the economy and scuttling indispensable reforms.

To parry this charge, Brezhnev developed a revised version of the "correlation of forces" theory and the strategy of offensive détente. The improved military balance and the liberation of progressive forces in the Third World would encourage realism in the West, leading to détente, arms control, and technology transfers that would solve the Soviet Union's economic problems without Kosygin's structural reforms, which threatened bureaucratic vested interests. The memoirs of defector Arkady Shevchenko show graphically how these pie-in-the-

111. Linden advanced the hypothesis that a victory in Berlin would give Khrushchev the prestige he needed to check his domestic opponents and push on with his economic program, but Richter is the first to show in convincing detail how it worked.

112. The following reconstruction draws on Gelman, Parrott, and Richter. The most detailed treatment of this period, Richard Anderson, "Competitive Politics and Soviet Global Policy: Authority Building and Bargaining in the Politburo, 1964–1972" (Ph.D. diss., University of California at Berkeley, 1989), argues that coalition making is the key source of Soviet foreign policy.

113. On Shelepin, see Gelman, *Brezhnev Politburo*; Parrott, *Politics and Technology*; Joan Barth Urban, "Contemporary Soviet Perspectives on Revolution in the West," *Orbis* 19 (1976): 1359–1402, esp. 1379; Christian Duevel, "The Political Credo of N. G. Yegorychev," Radio Liberty Research Paper no. 17, 1967; Anderson, "Competitive Politics," chap. 8.

sky arguments were crafted to appeal to a plenary meeting of the Central Committee before Nixon's 1972 visit to Moscow, which ratified Brezhnev's détente strategy and consolidated Brezhnev's commanding political advantage over his rivals.[114]

Despite this political victory, Brezhnev was nonetheless stuck with a strategy that was too costly and overcommitted. Through the mid-1970s he fought a running battle with Marshal Grechko and the military over the budgetary implications of détente in general and the Strategic Arms Limitation Talks in particular. Only after 1976, with Grechko's death and the installation of a civilian defense minister, did strategic force procurement flatten out and nuclear war doctrines wane.[115] The battle revived as a result of the Reagan defense buildup, with the chief of the General Staff, Nikolai Ogarkov, insisting that it would be a "serious error" not to increase military outlays. In the wake of the Polish crisis, however, the civilians were more worried about the danger of cutting social programs, and Ogarkov was fired.[116]

Signs of growing skepticism about backing radical Third World regimes also began to surface in the late 1970s,[117] though they could not proceed far until Suslov's death in 1982. A year later Andropov himself was stressing the need to limit the cost of Soviet counterinsurgency wars in support of pseudo-Marxist regimes, noting that "it is one thing to proclaim socialism, but another to build it."[118] Thus, through the failure of Brezhnev's strategy of offensive détente, some of the intellectual and political precursors to Gorbachev's new thinking were already in place.

In sum, Soviet expansionist behavior and strategic concepts have had their roots in the institutional and intellectual legacy of Stalin's revolution from above. Atavistic interests with a stake in military-industrial budget priorities and militant promotion of "progressive change" abroad have exploited the ideological baggage of Stalinism to legitimate their dominant social role. When Malenkov tried to change this, pushing forward new ideas and a new social constituency, Stalin was quoted to justify his removal from office: "In face of capitalist encirclement . . . 'to

114. Shevchenko, *Breaking with Moscow*, 211–12. This is corroborated by interviews with Oleg Bykov, a scholar at the Institute of World Economy and International Relations in Moscow, and Alexander Bovin, a Soviet journalist and former Brezhnev speech writer, reported by Onesti, "Portrait," chap. 5.

115. Bruce Parrott, *The Soviet Union and Ballistic Missile Defense* (Boulder, Colo., 1987), 27–39; MccGwire, *Military Objectives*, 61–62, 108–12; Richard F. Kaufman, "Causes of the Slowdown in Soviet Defense," *Soviet Economy* 1 (January–March 1985): 9–32.

116. Parrott, *Soviet Union and Ballistic Missile Defense*, 46–47; also Garthoff, *Detente*, 1018n.21.

117. Elizabeth Valkenier, "Revolutionary Change in the Third World: Recent Soviet Assessments," *World Politics* 38 (April 1986): 415–34, esp. 426.

118. *Pravda*, 16 June 1983; *CDSP* 35:8.

slacken the pace means to lag behind. And those who lag behind are beaten.'"[119] To gain power, an innovator like Khrushchev had to distort his policies to try to attract or outflank the atavistic interests and ideas, leading to contradictions and overcommitment at home and abroad.

The Gorbachev Revolution

Under Khrushchev and Brezhnev, Soviet politics became less unitary and increasingly cartelized, but the Gorbachev reforms have attempted to break this mold. Logrolled coalitions, cemented by an ideology of offensive détente, are no longer the prevailing pattern in Soviet politics and foreign policy. At least until the conservative turn in late 1990, Gorbachev's domestic strategy sought to curtail the power of the bureaucratic cartels of the Party, heavy industry, and the military by strengthening the unitary elements of the political system, in particular his own powers as president, as well as the democratic elements, enlisting grass roots political participation and market forces in his struggle against entrenched interests.[120]

Several factors made such a development feasible: the requirements of the intensive stage of economic development, the discrediting of the old institutions by the stagnation and foreign policy failures of the late Brezhnev period, and the increasing size and importance of the urban middle class and intelligentsia as a result of the natural processes of modernization.[121] Ironically, a final factor favoring the Gorbachev reforms was the Stalinist legacy of centralized institutions suited to the task of social transformation from above. Gorbachev realized, however, that the needed reforms could not simply be forced through in the tsarist and Stalinist "top down" manner, using administrative coercion and exaggeration of foreign threats to whip the population to greater efficiency. Intensive economic development would require economic decentralization, initiative from below, increased production for the consumer sector to provide incentives for initiative, and a fuller integration into the world market.

In its foreign policy component, such a reform strategy required not just a short respite from heavy military expenditures, but a durable, long-term détente. Unlike his predecessors, Gorbachev understood that "changes in the correlation of forces in the favor of socialism"

119. *Pravda*, 24 January 1955; *CDSP* 6:6.
120. For elaboration on the arguments presented in this section, see Snyder, "Gorbachev Revolution."
121. Moshe Lewin, *The Gorbachev Phenomenon* (Berkeley, Calif., 1988). Gorbachev's personal qualities and personal choices were obviously important too, but it was this broader social setting that made his choices necessary and possible.

hindered détente rather than promoted it, because they provoked balancing reactions from the West. Soviet military buildups only provoked a high-technology arms race that starved Soviet civilian sectors of scarce inputs and heightened Western vigilance against technology transfers to the East. Gorbachev needed a durable détente, moreover, to encourage increased economic integration with the West, which is essential for investment capital, technology, managerial know-how, and market discipline to make the reform work.

It remains to be seen whether Gorbachev will succeed in establishing a stable new pattern of politics in the Soviet Union. The democratic aspects of his strategy have unleashed forces he cannot adequately control: ethnic nationalism among Russians and non-Russians, as well as antimarket populism among average citizens who are disgruntled by poor economic performance during the mismanaged transition from plan to market. At the same time, threatened bureaucratic interests—the local remnants of the Party bureaucracy, industrial ministries, the KGB, and the military—retain the organizational ability to retard reforms, and they may adopt new coalition strategies suitable for the era of mass demagogic politics. The drift toward authoritarian economic, ethnic, and press policies in the winter of 1991 demonstrated that Gorbachev himself might choose to rely on old strategies, old institutions, and old justifications to keep the Soviet Union together and its command economy minimally functioning. This domestic shift coincided with developments that placed a cloud over the new foreign policy: the resignation of liberal Foreign Minister Eduard Shevardnadze, the use of military force to repress Baltic independence efforts, Western threats to curtail economic aid in response, disgruntlement from conservatives over the U.S. war against the Soviets' former ally Iraq, and Prime Minister Valentin Pavlov's allegation of financial machinations by Western banks as justification for draconian economic measures. Consequently the successful institutionalizing of a liberal, market-oriented democracy is only one of several political futures that are possible for the Soviet Union. Different domestic political coalitions might have quite different implications for the emergence of strategic ideas and for the survival of Gorbachev's strategy of cooperative integration with the West.[122]

CONCLUSIONS

The Soviet Union has three times flirted with overexpansion: in the early Cold War, during Khrushchev's missile diplomacy, and during

122. Jack Snyder, "Averting Anarchy in the New Europe," *International Security* 14 (Spring 1990): 5–42; Francis X. Clines, "Kremlin Accuses Banks in West of Plot," *New York Times*, 13 February 1991.

Brezhnev's overextension in the Third World. But each time the Soviet leadership has retrenched before major damage was done. Apart from these three interludes, Soviet grand strategy has been realistic and moderate.

The moderate periods, the effective learning, and even the over-aggressive behavior during the fluid period immediately after 1945 can all be plausibly explained as reasonable responses to prevailing international circumstances. But Khrushchev's and Brezhnev's misguided attempts to reconcile détente and expansionism cannot be explained in this way.

Cognitive explanations, such as the Bolshevik operational code and cognitive learning models, fare even worse, despite their current popularity. These explanations either are nonfalsifiable or, in their falsifiable versions, posit a largely mythical Bolshevik intellectual legacy. The offensive behavior depicted in the operational code became a hallmark of Soviet diplomacy in 1947–48, not in 1917. Moreover, even after Khrushchev ostensibly revised the philosophical basis of the operational code in 1956, Soviet behavior remained offensive. Finally, Gorbachev's successful learning about the realities of grand strategy may be the result of a cognitive process, but he has had more success in implementing a new strategy than previous good learners, like Malenkov and Kosygin, for domestic political reasons.

The Soviet Union's domestic political character as a late, late industrializer provides the most complete explanation both for periods of overextension and for periods of moderation. Stalin's realpolitik and, more generally, the Soviet Politburo's ability to learn from its mistakes reflect the encompassing interests of the elite dominating the top of the unitary polity, which was created by the late, late pattern of development. Two of the periods of moderate postwar overextension, under Khrushchev and Brezhnev, were caused by the increased cartelization of the political system, owing to the ossification of the institutions and ideas of Stalin's revolution from above. Finally, Gorbachev's more moderate foreign policy is made possible by his mobilization of centralized and grass roots power to hamstring atavistic cartels.

Though domestic structure offers the single best explanation for variations over time in Soviet expansionism, this does not mean that the international system was irrelevant to Soviet behavior. On the contrary, the international system shaped Soviet behavior in several ways. First, the international environment helped create the structure of the late, late polity by smashing the old domestic order in World War I and by providing the competitive environment that spurred Stalin's revolution from above. Second, during periods of relatively unitary politics, Soviet policy was closely shaped by the incentives of the balance of power system.

Finally, even during relatively cartelized periods, international conditions helped make or break strategic ideologies. Most episodes of Soviet belligerence or expansionism had international triggers—like the Marshall Plan, the rearming of West Germany, the U-2 affair, or the Jackson-Vanik Amendment and the post–Vietnam syndrome—that made the strategic arguments of some Soviet factions more plausible and those of others less plausible.[123] According to Herbert Dinerstein, Malenkov was done in by Dulles's massive retaliation speech.[124] Kosygin's attempt to promote a low-profile foreign policy was made more difficult by the escalation of the Vietnam War.

Conversely, Western balancing reactions have at other times served to discredit expansionist strategies. The huge American military build-up in response to the Korean attack gave Malenkov an opportunity to press his conciliatory line in foreign affairs. America's stiff response to Khrushchev's Cuban gambit, followed by President Kennedy's conciliatory American University speech, convinced Khrushchev to shift to a less offensive brand of détente. NATO's successful deployment of Pershing missiles undercut Brezhnev's notion that a one-sided military buildup was compatible with détente in Europe.

International events clearly influence the viability of strategic arguments in Soviet domestic politics, but which Western policies help the Malenkovs and the Gorbachevs and which help their foes? Two lessons stand out in this regard.

First, hard-line or highly competitive Western policies help Soviet soft-liners only when Soviet hard-liners are in power. American firmness after the Korean attack, the Cuban missile adventure, and the late Brezhnev imperialist binge helped Soviet doves, because the American action was clearly provoked by the Soviets' own assertiveness. America's deployment of B-29 bombers to Great Britain in response to the Berlin blockade, for example, allowed Malenkov's faction to argue persuasively that the Soviets' militant foreign policy had placed atomic-capable aircraft within range of the Soviet homeland for the first time.[125] Conversely, hard-line American positions simply discredit Soviet doves

---

123. The clearest cases are perhaps the U-2 (Tatu, *Power in the Kremlin*, part 1) and Jackson-Vanik (Gelman, *Brezhnev Politburo*, 161; Urban, "Contemporary Soviet Perspectives," 1379); see also Jack Snyder, "International Leverage on Soviet Domestic Change," *World Politics* 42 (October 1989):1–30.

124. Dinerstein, *War and the Soviet Union*, chap. 4. Khrushchev said that Dulles's "massive retaliation" speech revealed him to be "drunk with rage" (as quoted in Richter, "Action and Reaction," chap. 2).

125. Letteney, "Foreign Policy Factionalism," 77, citing V. Matveyev in *Izvestiia*, 22 July 1949. For more detail, see Snyder, "International Leverage," 15–21.

when they are already in power. This is the lesson of America's grudging response to Malenkov's thaw in 1953.

A second lesson is that Western firmness has a harmful effect on the credibility of Soviet doves when the Soviets cannot distinguish defensively motivated moves from offensive ones. The Marshall Plan undercut Varga's position in the Soviet policy debate because the economic instruments that were needed to shore up France and West Germany were indistinguishable from the means to lure Eastern Europe and create an American *place d'armes* on the continent.

In sum, Soviet expansion and its waning under Gorbachev are best explained as the result of Soviet domestic political structure. This does not mean that Western actions are irrelevant to Soviet behavior. Rather, it means that their effects are filtered through the medium of Soviet coalition politics. In the concluding chapter, I will offer some broader speculation on how Western policies might affect the course of Soviet political change in the future.

[7]

America's Cold War Consensus

In the late 1940s, two schools of thought vied for control of America's national security policy and foreign economic policy. Senator Arthur Vandenberg, a key architect of the bipartisan Cold War policy, called these two "the 'Eastern internationalist' school" and "the 'Middle Western nationalist' school."[1] The internationalists, epitomized by Truman's secretary of state Dean Acheson, favored a deep American involvement in multilateral economic and military institutions designed to stabilize Western Europe in the face of the Soviet threat, but they cautioned against entrapment in Asian quagmires.[2] The nationalists, epitomized by Republican senator Robert Taft, resisted costly commitments of American troops and money to Europe, favoring instead a free hand to use atomic air power to contain the global expansion of communism.[3]

Both these schools had a healthy sense of the limits of American power, the need to husband resources for priority tasks, and the importance of avoiding open-ended commitments to high-cost, low-benefit endeavors. They disagreed about what those priorities should be, but they agreed that priorities had to be set so as to have a solvent grand strategy.

Despite this, Cold War America fought two costly land wars in Asia, precisely the kind of morass both Acheson and Taft had warned must be avoided. The war in Vietnam was a classic example of strategic overextension, an unwinnable struggle fought for the mythical strategic purpose of maintaining the credibility of America's global commit-

---

1. Ronald Pruessen, *John Foster Dulles: The Road to Power* (New York, 1982), 223.
2. Dean Acheson, *Present at the Creation* (1969; New York, 1987).
3. Robert Taft, *A Foreign Policy for Americans* (Garden City, N.Y., 1951).

ments, a goal that fighting the war undermined.[4] The war in Korea is a more debatable case. In retrospect, significant strategic arguments can be seen to have weighed both in favor of and against having fought it. Nonetheless, it is an interesting case, because *all* the major strategic schools, factions, and bureaucracies warned against being dragged into this kind of a war in the years—even months—before its outbreak.[5] It is interesting also because it helped to solidify the "Cold War consensus" behind a globalist strategy of containment and thus contributed to the climate of opinion that led to American overextension in the Vietnam War.[6]

Compared with German and Japanese overexpansion, however, America's "imperial overstretch" has of course been relatively minor and was corrected before great damage was done to America's strategic position. The United States extricated itself from both the Korea and Vietnam quagmires through negotiation, and since Vietnam, the United States has avoided high-cost interventions. Thus, what needs to be explained is both America's Cold War penchant for limited overexpansion and also its ability to learn from its mistakes.

In this chapter I argue that one factor contributing to the Cold War consensus in favor of a globalist strategy of containment was the political competition and coalition building between "Europe-first internationalists" and "Asia-first nationalists." In the early postwar period, because of the separation of powers between the executive branch and Congress, and because the internationalist/nationalist cleavage cut across party lines, power over foreign policy was cartelized among several congressional voting blocs.[7] Globalist containment strategy resulted in part from a tacit logroll—organized especially by Republican internationalists like John Foster Dulles—between Europe-

4. John Lewis Gaddis, *Strategies of Containment* (New York, 1982), evaluates Vietnam and other periods of globalist containment strategy in terms of a disproportion between means and ends.

5. In discussing the Korean case, I draw on several recent books based on archival research, especially Rosemary Foot, *The Wrong War: American Policy and the Dimensions of the Korean Conflict, 1950–1953* (Ithaca, N.Y., 1985); John Lewis Gaddis, *The Long Peace* (New York, 1987); Michael Schaller, *The American Occupation of Japan* (New York, 1985); William Stueck, *The Road to Confrontation: American Policy toward China and Korea, 1947–1950* (Chapel Hill, N.C., 1981); and also Robert Blum, *Drawing the Line: The Origin of American Containment Policy in East Asia* (New York, 1982); and Nancy Bernkopf Tucker, *Patterns in the Dust: Chinese-American Relations and the Recognition Controversy, 1949–1950* (New York, 1983).

6. Robert Jervis, "The Impact of the Korean War," *Journal of Conflict Resolution* 24 (December 1980): 563–92.

7. On the separation of powers, see Theodore J. Lowi, "Making Democracy Safe for the World," in James N. Rosenau, ed., *Domestic Sources of Foreign Policy* (New York, 1967), 295–331, esp. 303–7 on the Marshall Plan and 315 for a more general argument. On foreign policy voting blocs in Congress, see H. Bradford Westerfield, *Foreign Policy and Party Politics* (New Haven, Conn., 1955).

first internationalists and Asia-first nationalists of both parties. Foreign policy consensus and harmony within the Republican party were achieved by giving both internationalists and nationalists what they wanted on the issues they cared about most. Blowback from domino arguments, which both the contending factions used to justify their preferred commitments abroad, contributed further to the ideology of global expansion.[8]

American overexpansion was ultimately limited, however, by democratic checks on the outcomes of these logrolls and by public scrutiny of strategic justifications for global intervention. Both Korea and Vietnam spurred effective public opposition to the high cost of strategically dubious interventions. Vietnam in particular split the elite foreign policy consensus down the middle, into hawkish and dovish branches of internationalism.[9] Since Vietnam, this has produced a more open debate on foreign policy issues, with the mass electorate leaning against presidents who stray too far from the middle-of-the-road position of "peace and strength."[10] Even hawkish internationalists shun high-cost military interventions, because they know the median voters will punish them.

Several qualifications to these arguments should be immediately be stressed. The cartelization and logrolling in American foreign policy in the early Cold War years differ qualitatively from the cartelization and logrolling in Germany, for example. In the case of Wilhelmine Germany, cartelization reflected fundamental characteristics of the domestic political economy and governing institutions of the country, having deep and long-lasting effects on coalition politics across all domestic and foreign issues. The political system as a whole was cartelized. In America cartelization was merely a transitory aspect of the handling of some foreign policy issues, caused by a temporary pattern of factionalism and partisanship. The political system as a whole was democratic.

Transitory cartelization and logrolling in a democratic system should not be expected to produce strong, permanent, or extreme effects on foreign policy. Such an outcome would require a significant revision of my coalition politics theory, which predicts weak effects—or none—in a democracy. Indeed, I do not claim that internationalist/nationalist logrolling and mythmaking were the sole force behind United States

---

8. This point is made by many historians, both revisionists and postrevisionists. Robert A. Pollard, *Economic Security and the Origins of the Cold War, 1945–1950* (New York, 1985), 194–95; Tucker, *Patterns*, 10–11; Richard Freeland, *The Truman Doctrine and the Origins of McCarthyism* (New York, 1974).

9. William Schneider, "Public Opinion," in Joseph Nye, *The Making of America's Soviet Policy* (New Haven, Conn., 1984), 11–13.

10. Schneider, "Public Opinion," 13–36; Miroslav Nincic, "The United States, the Soviet Union, and the Politics of Opposites," *World Politics* 40 (July 1988): 452–75.

interventionism during the Cold War. Nor do I claim there is direct evidence that specific instances of American overexpansion were solely and definitively caused by domestic coalition politics. I claim only that coalition dynamics contributed to the intellectual and domestic political underpinnings of a Cold War consensus favoring global containment of communism. This claim, despite its modesty, is still worth making. Though the effects of logrolling and mythmaking were more subtle and indirect in Cold War America than in Wilhelmine Germany, it is nonetheless important to understand them so that they can be recognized and controlled if they recur.

REALIST EXPLANATIONS FOR GLOBAL INTERVENTIONISM

The broad outlines of American containment policy during the Cold War fit a loose version of the Realist theory reasonably well. Given a bipolar distribution of power, the tasks of competing for influence with the Soviet Union, shoring up vulnerable economies and societies, organizing defensive military alliances, and balancing Soviet military power necessarily fell to the United States. But can Realism explain the global interventionism, leading to occasional overextension, through which the United States attempted to fulfill these tasks of containment? In particular, can Realism explain America's containment strategy in East Asia, including the decisions to fight in Korea in June 1950; to unify the Korean peninsula through military force rather than stop at the thirty-eighth parallel or Korea's "narrow waist"; to guarantee the Chinese Nationalist regime not only on Taiwan but on the small offshore islands of Quemoy and Matsu; and to fight in Vietnam?

Realism is itself divided about the strategic wisdom of direct commitments to defend such peripheral positions. Some Realists, such as George Kennan, have argued that the key to maintaining the balance of power is defending the major centers of industrial war making capacity.[11] Paul Kennedy, similarly, has warned that military overextension in a far-flung empire squanders resources that should be reinvested in the state's economic base.[12] For those who share this perspective, which I called "defensive Realism" in chapter 1, much of America's Cold War containment policy in East Asia was inexplicable in Realist terms: it wasted resources in strategically unimportant areas and made an enemy of China, a great power whose cooperation in balancing Soviet military power should have been enlisted earlier.

11. Gaddis, *Strategies*, chap. 2.
12. Paul Kennedy, *The Rise and Fall of the Great Powers* (New York, 1987).

A different brand of Realist strategists have argued the merits of a globalist approach to containment, however. They contend that commitments to defend threatened positions in the periphery are stabilizing. A staunch defense of peripheral positions makes clear to aggressors one's willingness to resist, they argue, and thus deters costlier subsequent challenges to more vital interests. Making and keeping commitments to peripheral allies encourages vital allies to balance against threatening powers, rather than joining the bandwagon with those powers, by demonstrating that strong, willing support is available.[13]

Finally, some Realists try to maintain both sides of this argument. For example, Kenneth Waltz argues on one hand that bipolarity is stabilizing, in part because it leaves no doubt about which great power has the task of resisting the other's expansionism around the globe. Constant tension and mutual opposition in a plethora of small conflicts at the periphery prevent larger conflicts by making the intention to resist aggression clear. On the other hand, he argues that the Vietnam War was a waste of resources in a region where no meaningful power assets were at stake.[14]

How well can any of these Realist perspectives explain American Cold War containment strategy, especially in East Asia and Southeast Asia? The Vietnam War is difficult to reconcile with any Realist criterion for intervention. Fighting and losing the war achieved precisely what it was designed to avoid: it undercut the credibility of American global commitments and created an anti-interventionist "Vietnam syndrome" just as Brezhnev was about to embark on his Third World adventures in the late 1970s. The war harmed the American economy by fueling inflation and forced the United States to reduce its troop strength in Europe to below 300,000.[15]

That the Vietnam War was a strategic misstep is clear not only in hindsight; even at the time, domino rationales for intervention were exploded inside the government by critics like George Ball and in the media by Walter Lippmann and others.[16] American allies denied that American credibility was at stake in Vietnam, but American decision

13. Gaddis, *Strategies*, discusses such arguments by U.S. officials. See chap. 4 on Paul Nitze and NSC 68, and chap. 7 on Walt Rostow and flexible response. For a scholarly statement of such arguments, see Thomas Schelling, *Arms and Influence* (New Haven, Conn., 1966), chap. 2.

14. Kenneth Waltz, *Theory of International Politics* (Reading, Mass., 1979), 171–72, 199, 205–8.

15. Gaddis, *Strategies*, chap. 8; Kennedy, *Rise and Fall*, 403–8; Phil Williams, *US Troops in Europe*, Chatham House paper 25 (London, 1984), 19.

16. John P. Burke and Fred I. Greenstein with Larry Berman and Richard Immerman, *How Presidents Test Reality: Decisions on Vietnam, 1954 and 1965* (New York, 1989), 170–72, 175, 235–38, 261, 266–67; Ronald Steel, *Walter Lippmann and the American Century* (Boston, 1980).

makers insisted that it was.[17] As Ball put it, the notion of an indivisibility of commitment linking Vietnam to Berlin was "a conceit invented at the top reaches of our government to justify what they wanted to do anyway."[18]

In the cases of Korea and Taiwan the balance sheet is more ambiguous, judging by various Realist criteria. American decision makers cited the risk that European allies would be discouraged and join the bandwagon as a key reason to fight in Korea. In June 1950 Europeans were in fact worried about American credibility and were briefly relieved when America chose to fight.[19] But they quickly swung in the opposite direction, fearing that the diversion of American resources to Asian theaters of war would weaken the defense of Europe. As early as 14 July 1950, Acheson wrote: "It is becoming apparent to the world that we do not have the capabilities to face the threat, and the feeling in Europe is changing from one of elation that the United States has come into the Korean crisis to petrified fright. People are questioning whether [the North Atlantic Treaty] really means anything, since it means only what we are able to do. Our intentions are not doubted, but our capabilities are doubted."[20] In November 1950 the British warned that proceeding past the narrow waist of Korea would provoke Chinese intervention, and in December Prime Minister Clement Attlee traveled to Washington to urge American concessions in pursuit of a negotiated settlement with China.[21] Accommodation of European fears thus can possibly explain the initial decision to fight in June 1950, but it cannot account for subsequent decisions to escalate and sustain the war.

Though the Korean War was costly in lives and resources, its net effect was to increase the military and economic resources available for the containment of Communist expansion. The Korean War, because it mobilized American domestic support for military spending against the heightened Communist threat, was a boon to American troop deployments in Europe, which peaked at 427,000 in 1953.[22] This was not an unintended benefit. In fact, George Marshall worried that if the war

17. George W. Ball, *The Past Has Another Pattern* (New York, 1982), 382–86.
18. Ibid., 386.
19. Deborah Welch Larson, "Bandwagon Images in American Foreign Policy: Myth or Reality," in Robert Jervis and Jack Snyder, eds., *Dominoes and Bandwagons: Strategic Beliefs and Great Power Competition in the Eurasian Rimland* (New York, 1991), 85–111; Thomas Christensen, "Strategies of Contentment: Truman, Domestic Politics and the Origins of the Korean War" (unpublished MS, Columbia University, 1987), 14–16.
20. Memorandum of conversation by Dean Acheson, *Foreign Relations of the United States* [hereafter *FRUS*], 1950, 1:344–45, cited in Christensen, "Strategies," 15.
21. D. C. Watt, "Britain and the Cold War in the Far East, 1945–58," in Yonosuke Nagai and Akira Iriye, eds., *The Origins of the Cold War in Asia* (New York, 1977), 95.
22. Williams, *US Troops*, 19.

ended too quickly, political support for the military buildup in Europe would evaporate.[23] Moreover, Japan was greatly strengthened by the economic stimulus of American military-related orders, though this was an unintended benefit that could presumably have been achieved through other means at less cost.[24]

Fighting a land war in Korea was a costly, inefficient way to achieve this military-economic mobilization. American decision makers were acutely aware of the strategic disadvantages of fighting in Korea. Russia was bleeding America white while committing minimal resources of its own, they recognized.[25] Because of the fighting in Korea, "There is no margin left. No additional commitments of United States support should be undertaken," said the military chiefs, "until [there is] a reappraisal of capabilities and priorities."[26]

The Soviets did not exploit this temporary advantage, possibly because America's decision to fight did what American leaders said it would—convince Stalin that American resolve to resist aggression was firm. Fighting in Korea and the attendant American arms buildup almost certainly helped strengthen Soviet leaders like Malenkov and Lavrentii Beria, who argued that Stalin's belligerent foreign policy was undermining Soviet security. By Stalin's death, the Politburo was eager to promote a Korean armistice, since the danger of provoking American war preparations was felt to outweigh the benefits of continuing to tie up American resources in a strategic backwater.[27]

Long-run effects on China were less positive. The Korean War turned a tense Sino-American relationship into one of long-run, active hostility.[28] It cemented the relationship between America and Chiang Kai-shek, leading to repeated crises over the offshore islands. Inflated notions of the Chinese threat also served as part of the backdrop necessary to spur American intervention in the Vietnam War. Arguably, this legacy of the Korean War undermined American Cold War strategy for two decades by postponing the geopolitically natural alliance between the United States and China against their common Soviet enemy. As Molotov told Dulles in 1954, America's "bankrupt" China policy "merely forced China closer to [the] Soviet Union."[29]

23. Stueck, *Road to Confrontation*, 256.

24. Schaller, *American Occupation*, 288–96. William Borden, *The Pacific Alliance: United States Foreign Economic Policy and Japanese Trade Recovery, 1947–1955* (Madison, Wis., 1984), 143–44, and Bruce Cumings, *Origins of the Korean War*, vol. 2 (Princeton, N.J., 1990), chap. 13, suggest that this might have been intentional.

25. *FRUS*, 1950, 4:1276; dispatch from Ambassador to the Soviet Union Kirk, 19 December 1950.

26. *FRUS*, 1950, 1:353. Also Foot, *Wrong War*, 103–5.

27. See chapter 6 above.

28. Jervis, "Impact of the Korean War," 563–92.

29. Gaddis, *Long Peace*, 185; Dulles to Eisenhower, 30 January 1954, *FRUS*, 1952–54, 14:354.

Conversely, it might be argued that America's policy of squeezing the Chinese hastened the Sino-Soviet split. Dulles explained his own strategy as "keeping [Communist China] under pressures which would, in turn, keep the Communists pressuring Russia for more than Russia would give."[30] This is precisely what came to pass during the 1958 Taiwan Straits crisis, when Chinese irritation at Khrushchev's unsupportive stance greatly deepened the rift.[31]

These mixed results of the Korean War must be judged against the likely results of some plausible alternative. Many analysts have pointed out that all the benefits and few of the disadvantages might have been achieved had the United States stopped its military advance at the thirty-eighth parallel or even farther north, at the narrow waist of the peninsula, since China's defensive intervention would not have been provoked. More speculatively, one can also argue that the United States could have achieved the main benefits of the war without having fought it at all. That is, the United States could have accepted the loss of South Korea but then shored up its positions in Europe and Japan by directly increasing its economic subsidies and military deployments in those core areas. This should have achieved the desired effect on the psychology of the Soviets, Europeans, and Japanese without turning China into a mortal enemy. Judged against this alternative, the decision to fight in Korea looks debatable, and the decision to march to the Yalu River on the Chinese border seems even more so.

In short, American intervention in the Vietnam War was a clear case of strategic overextension; it is difficult to explain in terms of any Realist criteria, judging either from hindsight or from information available at the time. The Korean intervention is a less clear case. Realist criteria were arguably consistent with the decision to intervene, and probably also with a decision not to intervene.[32] Though Realist explanations based on the strategic incentives of the international situation cannot be rejected out of hand, their looseness raises the possibility that domestic considerations affected the outcome of decisions within Realism's broad range of indeterminacy.[33]

30. David Allan Mayers, *Cracking the Monolith* (Baton Rouge, La., 1986), 119–20, citing a discussion with Taiwan's foreign minister, November 1952.

31. Donald Zagoria, *The Sino-Soviet Conflict, 1956–61* (New York, 1969), chap. 7.

32. Given the plausible range of uncertainty, Realist calculation might also be minimally consistent with the decisions to cross the Thirty-eighth parallel and to approach the Yalu. For a discussion of these uncertainties, see Foot, *Wrong War*, 69–87 on the crossing of the parallel, and 96–101 on the approach to the Yalu. For more general arguments about the rationality of hedging against the chance that domino processes might operate, see Douglas Macdonald, "The Truman Administration and Global Responsibilities: The Birth of the Falling Domino Principle," 134, and Jack Snyder, "Introduction," 9, in Jervis and Snyder, *Dominoes and Bandwagons*.

33. For a similar argument about containment in Europe, see Deborah Welch Larson, *Origins of Containment* (Princeton, N.J., 1985), 18–23.

Explanations of American policy in the Korean War and Vietnam War invariably stress decision makers' strategic beliefs, especially their fears of falling dominoes and bandwagon effects caused by a tarnished American reputation for resolve.[34] Secretary of Defense Robert McNamara's key aide on Vietnam even quantified reputational concerns as 70 percent of the reason for Americans to fight in Vietnam.[35]

Other elements of the typical syndrome of imperial ideology—such as the Thermopylae corollary to the domino theory—were present as well. Arguing in 1947 for an increased American commitment in China, for example, the Joint Chiefs of Staff argued that economic resources and morale were in danger of cumulating in a string of Communist victories, but that timely preventive action and verbal commitments could cheaply stem this tide.[36] Dwight Eisenhower, as army chief of staff in January 1947, argued that "in the long run the costs of our retreat from Korea would be far, far greater than any present or contemplated appropriations to maintain ourselves there."[37]

Many decision makers articulated a paper tiger image of the Soviet Union. Dulles, for example, argued that "the only way to stop a head-on collision with the Soviet Union is to break it up from within."[38] He also held to a big stick theory of alliance formation, contending that "if your major objective is to get a break [between a given Marxist state and] Moscow, the way to get that is to make the going tough, not easy."[39] Offensive advantages were commonly asserted. Acheson insisted that Western Europe could not be secure unless Soviet power was rolled back from Eastern Europe.[40] Some officials hoped the Marshall Plan would promote that end.[41] In a conflation of offensive advantage and reputational credibility, it was widely argued that failing to take offensive action to unify Korea would be showing weakness in the face of Chinese threats.[42]

34. Stueck, *Road to Confrontation*, 174, 253–55; Larry Berman, *Planning a Tragedy: The Americanization of the War in Vietnam* (New York, 1984); George McT. Kahin, *Intervention: How America Became Involved in Vietnam* (Garden City, N.Y., 1987).

35. John McNaughton's July 1965 memo underlying McNamara's escalation proposal, discussed in Kahin, *Intervention*, 357.

36. Stueck, *Road to Confrontation*, 44–45.

37. Ibid., 75.

38. Robert Divine, *Foreign Policy and U.S. Presidential Elections, 1952–1960* (New York, 1974), 51, quoting from remarks during the 1952 campaign.

39. Mayers, *Cracking the Monolith*, 119, citing February 1952 remarks on "Meet the Press"; also 92–93.

40. Pollard, *Economic Security*, 237, citing a memorandum of conversation, 24 March, *FRUS*, 1950, 1:207. On the fear that the Soviets would exploit offensive advantages, see Samuel Wells, "Sounding the Tocsin," *International Security* 4 (Fall 1979): 126.

41. Pollard, *Economic Security*, 137.

42. Stueck, *Road to Confrontation*, 255.

Windows of vulnerability were invoked as reasons for aggressive action while time remained. For example, a central implication of NSC 68, the grand strategy document written in spring 1950, was that the United States should take decisive action to reverse the tide of the Cold War before "the year of maximum danger," supposedly 1954. Some voices called for preventive war on those grounds, either outright or in code words.[43]

Every conceivable strategic rationale for security through expansion could be found in the intellectual arsenal of America's cold warriors. Equally striking, however, is the attempt of American statesmen in the early postwar years to identify strategic criteria that would impose limits on American commitments abroad. Both Achesonian internationalists and Taftite nationalists tried to establish such criteria, even as each undercut such distinctions by lapsing into Manichaean rhetoric about the monolithic Communist threat.

Acheson and the Europe-First Internationalists

Europe-first internationalists like Dean Acheson, Secretary of State (and later of Defense) George Marshall, State Department planner George Kennan, and newspaper columnist Walter Lippmann used realpolitik principles to distinguish the essential from the nonessential and effective from self-defeating uses of American power. They thought primarily in terms of the need to prevent Russia from controlling the major industrial centers of Eurasia, especially the Ruhr and Japan, and sought to focus resources on that task.[44] Consequently, they argued, the United States should avoid involvement in the "morass" of China, whose fate America could not affect and whose GNP in any event made it a geopolitical pygmy.[45]

They found the distinction between core and periphery difficult to maintain, however. Acheson believed, for example, that Japan needed Southeast Asia as an economic hinterland in order to stay out of the Communist orbit and so placed a high priority on American commitments to that peripheral region.[46] Similar calculations made Acheson want to maintain South Korea as part of Japan's hinterland.[47] Likewise

43. Marc Trachtenberg, "A 'Wasting Asset': American Strategy and the Shifting Nuclear Balance, 1949–1954," *International Security* 13 (Winter 1988–89): 5–59; NSC 68 appears in John Lewis Gaddis and Thomas Etzold, eds., *Containment* (New York, 1978), 385–442. Written early in 1950, it was approved only in September.

44. Gaddis, *Strategies*, chap. 2; Steel, *Lippmann*, esp. chap. 32.

45. On the China morass, see Acheson quoted in Blum, *Drawing the Line*, 40; also Steel, *Lippmann*, 444–45, 465–69.

46. Andrew Rotter, *The Path to Vietnam* (Ithaca, N.Y., 1987); Schaller, *American Occupation*, chaps. 8 and 12; Borden, *Pacific Alliance*.

47. Cumings, *Origins*, vol. 2, chap. 13.

Kennan believed, or at least argued, that what he called a Communist "bandwagon" in France would be set in motion by Communist successes in Greece or Turkey.[48] Still, in the years before the Korean War, the Europe-first internationalists tried to maintain the distinction between peripheral and core interests. They reduced commitments in the Far East in 1947, for example, when increased tension in Europe required a greater focus on the core.[49]

Domino effects between periphery and core were alleged more starkly when the internationalists made public pleas for financial support for their European aid schemes. Truman had to argue that the fate of the American way of life hinged on providing aid to Greece and Turkey in order to get the appropriations through Congress.[50] Similarly, NSC 68 was developed by Acheson and Paul Nitze in spring 1950 as a globalist manifesto to rally support for expenditures for the adminstration's containment policy, including assistance to Europe. Acheson claimed that "the purpose of NSC 68 was to so bludgeon the mass mind of 'top government' that not only could the President make a decision but that the decision could be carried out," but its arguments were also used as the basis for public propaganda. "If we made our points clearer than the truth, we did not differ from most other educators and could hardly do otherwise," Acheson later confessed.[51] Even when Acheson did not want to extend commitments to the periphery, he sometimes had to use the rhetoric of global containment. For instance, in 1949 Acheson accepted NSC 48's analysis of a monolithic Sino-Soviet bloc as a sop to Pentagon and Republican opponents whom he temporarily stalled in their bid to commit America to defending Taiwan.[52]

In addition to the Europe-first internationalists' distinction between core and periphery, these Realists also believed that the way to split the Soviet bloc was not by "making things tough," as Dulles put it, but by wooing China through appeasement. Specifically, Acheson argued that

48. From 27 March 1947, War College lecture, quoted in Larson, "Bandwagon Images," 85.

49. John Lewis Gaddis, "Korea in American Politics, Strategy, and Diplomacy, 1945–1950," in Nagai and Iriye, *Origins of the Cold War in Asia*, 277–98, esp. 281.

50. Joseph Marion Jones, *The Fifteen Weeks* (New York, 1955), 138–42.

51. Acheson, *Present*, 374–75. On the public use of NSC 68's arguments, see Christensen, "Strategies," 9. See also Borden, *Pacific Alliance*, 46–47; Cumings, *Origins*, vol. 2, chap. 13.

52. Schaller, *American Occupation*, 202–3, 206. Cumings, *Origins*, vol. 2, 420, suggests that Truman's 5 January 1950 statement that the United States had no intention of defending Taiwan "at this time" signaled a desire on the part of Truman and Acheson to do so if Chiang bowed out. This is part of Cumings's broader argument that in January 1950 Acheson wanted a much more assertive Asian posture than is generally believed. But Stueck, *Road to Confrontation*, 142, shows that this language was inserted not at Acheson's behest but at that of General Bradley, the chairman of the Joint Chiefs of Staff. See also, Foot, *Wrong War*, 51.

the United States should not defend Chiang Kai-shek's Nationalist regime on Taiwan. "We must not undertake from the Russians to ourselves the righteous anger, the wrath and the hatred of the Chinese people," he said in the January 1950 speech to the National Press Club that defined America's defense perimeter in a way that apparently excluded Korea and Taiwan. "It would be folly to deflect [this anger] to ourselves" by backing Chiang against Mao Tse-tung, he contended.[53] The force of these arguments was vitiated, however, by Acheson's frequent resort, for the aforementioned tactical purposes, to the rhetoric of monolithic, ideologically driven communism, which seemed to leave no room for exploiting nationalist differences among communists.

In sum, the Achesonian internationalists attempted to limit American global commitments by applying sound Realist principles, but their own arguments highlighting the grave consequences of American inaction in the zero-sum struggle with the monolithic opponent undercut their ability to maintain those limits.

Taft and the Asia-First Nationalists

Senator Taft spoke for a wing of the Republican party called the "Old Guard," intensely hostile to the New Deal and traditionally isolationist. On the floor of the Senate before American entry into World War II, Taft had said that "war is worse even than a German victory," because it would turn America into an imperial state with a bloated bureaucracy.[54] After the war he was critical of the Bretton Woods economic agreements as a subsidy for investment bankers, favoring instead an emphasis on protectionism and the development of domestic trade. He also resisted expensive schemes for global military commitments as a crippling tax burden and a foot in the door for big government.[55] His book *A Foreign Policy for Americans* prefigured Eisenhower's "New Look," with its emphasis on cheap atomic air power as a substitute for expensive ground forces stationed abroad.[56]

Most Old Guard Republicans, despite their reputation as "Asia-

53. Mayers, *Cracking the Monolith*, 53. Even in Europe, to which Acheson *did* want America to be committed, his Realism gave him a healthy skepticism about Adenauer's empty threats to join the Russian bandwagon if America failed to provide more backing. *FRUS*, 1950, 4:600. This raises questions about the argument that Acheson's real motive for fighting in Korea was to avert a bandwagon in Western Europe.

54. James T. Patterson, *Mr. Republican* (Boston, 1972), 243; Alonzo Hamby, *Liberalism and Its Challengers* (New York, 1985), 107. Also, Manfred Jonas, *Isolationism in America: 1935–1941* (Ithaca, N.Y., 1966), 85–86.

55. Justus Doenecke, *Not to the Swift: The Old Isolationists in the Cold War Era* (Lewisburg, Pa., 1979), 56–57, 61, 80–81.

56. Ronald J. Caridi, *The Korean War and American Politics: The Republican Party as a Case Study* (Philadelphia, 1968), 199.

firsters," were highly ambivalent about American commitments in both Europe and the Far East. Even relative moderates among them, like Senator Vandenberg, criticized President Roosevelt's Europe-first strategy in World War II, and others claimed that the policy of unconditional German surrender had opened the door to Soviet expansion.[57] This attitude did not mean, however, that old isolationists like Taft were eager for American entanglements in Asia. Most cared little about involvement in the Chinese civil war in 1945–46, and few had traditional ties to Asia.[58] Taft's book called for an offshore defense perimeter in Asia, which would use island bases for projecting air power and for logistic assistance to local forces resisting communism on the mainland.[59] Indeed, Taft's enthusiasm for the cause of Nationalist China increased only when Chiang's retreat to Taiwan made it easy to defend him.

Speaking shortly after Truman's decision to commit American troops to the fighting in Korea, Taft told the Senate that the peninsula was not vital to United States security. Taft called the president's action in committing forces without congressional approval a dangerous precedent and probably illegal. Nonetheless, America had no choice but to fight, he said, because a line against Communist aggression had to be drawn somewhere.[60] The Chicago *Tribune*, flagship newspaper of Old Guard isolationism, went further, flatly opposing the war at the outset.[61] After the Chinese intervention, the opinions of Taft and other Republicans swung wildly between calls for a retreat to Fortress America and calls for ending the war through atomic escalation.[62]

None of this suggests a deeply rooted Old Guard Republican orientation toward a high-profile American role in Asia. Such attitudes were held only by a hard core of China lobby supporters among Republican senators, such as William Knowland and Walter Judd. These were at first a small group with a strategic ideology that was almost a caricature in its pristine globalist logic. Judd's domino theory drew a direct line from Communist expansion in China and Taiwan to takeovers in Japan and Europe.[63] Accepting Britain's July 1950 proposal to seat Communist China in the United Nations would show weakness and consequently encourage Chinese intervention in the Korean War, Judd argued. Instead, Chiang should be promoted as a "thorn in their side"

57. Doenecke, *Not to the Swift*, 37–38.
58. Ibid., 173, 181–82; but for qualifications see Wayne S. Cole, *Roosevelt and the Isolationists, 1932–45* (Lincoln, Nebr., 1983), 239–40.
59. Taft, *Foreign Policy*, esp. 74–81.
60. Doenecke, *Not to the Swift*, 191.
61. Ibid., 190, 192–93.
62. Patterson, *Mr. Republican*, 485; Burton I. Kaufman, *The Korean War: Challenges in Crisis, Credibility, and Command* (New York, 1986), 122–23.
63. Thomas Paterson, "If Europe, Why Not China? The Containment Doctrine, 1947–49," *Prologue* 13 (Spring 1981): 19–38, at 21.

that would tie up Chinese strength and prevent such an intervention. "There are two philosophies," Judd explained. "One says, 'we will be nice to them and show we have no designs on them.' They know that already. They know we are not imperialists. They make that charge but they know it isn't true."[64]

Old isolationists like Taft took on this style of rhetoric relatively late in the game, after the loss of China made it almost irresistible to link foreign setbacks to innuendos of Communist infiltration of Acheson's State Department. Though Republicans had voted against aid to Korea in early 1950, and though Taft himself would soon urge an offshore defense perimeter in Asia, Taft nonetheless could not resist claiming that Acheson's defense perimeter speech had enticed the North Koreans to attack. Moreover, he claimed, the original decision to divide Korea at the thirty-eighth parallel had been part of the treachery of Yalta and Potsdam.[65] Isolationists like Taft were basically apathetic about the fate of China, but partisan considerations led them to join in the China lobby's charges that Acheson was hypocritical in blocking communism in Europe but letting it run wild in Asia.[66]

In short, Republican Old Guard nationalists like Taft had a fairly coherent conception of America's limited role in world affairs, rooted in an airpower-oriented Fortress America strategy and a laissez faire, domestically oriented economy. This conception lost its intellectual integrity when the Old Guard joined opportunistically in McCarthyite and China lobby attacks on the Truman-Acheson strategy of limited liability in Asia.[67] These attacks, which relied on the imagery of domino dangers and a monolithic Communist threat, fit awkwardly with Taft's underlying foreign policy beliefs. But they fit only too well with the tactical desire to link New Deal foreign policy to snowballing Communist victories. Thus rhetorical and tactical expediency undercut the sense of limits inherent in the nationalists' grand strategy, just as it had undercut that of the internationalists.

Pentagon Unilateralism

A third strategic school, which often cooperated with Republican "Asia-firsters," was Pentagon unilateralism. Defense Secretary Louis Johnson and the Joint Chiefs of Staff were particularly concerned to

64. U.S. Congress, Senate Foreign Relations Committee, Executive Sessions, *Reviews of the World Situation: 1949–1950* (Washington, D.C., 1974), session of 24 July 1950, 363.

65. Doenecke, *Not to the Swift*, 191; Patterson, *Mr. Republican*, 453.

66. Taft took up Taiwan's cause only when the rhetorical advantages were great and the geopolitical risks seemed low. See Doenecke, *Not to the Swift*, 179–80. See also Westerfield, *Foreign Policy*, chap. 12.

67. Michael Rogin, *The Intellectuals and McCarthy* (Cambridge, Mass., 1967).

acquire a reliable set of bases in the Far East that could be used for air attacks on the Soviet Union in a major war. Japan was one preferred location for such a complex of bases, but Johnson feared that the rush to sign a treaty returning Japanese sovereignty would prevent this solution. Suspicion of Japan's loyalty and the desire to maintain a convenient military infrastructure led Johnson and the Chiefs to favor a long occupation.[68]

The Chiefs favored the development of other strategic strongpoints and missions in East Asia, but only if sufficient resources would be poured in to make these positions more of an asset than a liability. When the military saw an opportunity to create an Asian strongpoint—whether on Taiwan, in Korea, or elsewhere—their memoranda insisted on its strategic value and foresaw falling dominoes if it was abandoned. Johnson and the Chiefs provided arguments to journalist Stewart Alsop, for example, for articles laying out his "bowling pin" theory and urging redoubled efforts to contain the Chinese "headpin."[69]

But when it seemed that insufficient resources would not be forthcoming, the Chiefs argued for scuttling exposed strategic positions. For example, though they initially saw Korea as a Thermopylae that would be much cheaper to save than to lose,[70] they soon feared they would get stuck defending an untenable position with insufficient resources. Then the military switched to the view that Korea was *not* a crucial domino, but rather a strategic irrelevancy, unimportant to Japanese defense.[71] Even after the North Korean attack, the military was reluctant to commit American forces or to cross the thirty-eighth parallel until they were assured that sufficient resources would be put at their disposal. But once assured of this resource commitment, the military quickly interpreted the buildup in Korea in offensive terms, as a chance to undermine the Communist position in Manchuria and drive a wedge between Russia and China through military intimidation.[72]

Pentagon unilateralism had simple decision rules. Forward bases in

68. Schaller, *American Occupation*, 248–49.

69. Ibid., 231–33. Johnson's motives in all of this were probably different from those of the Joint Chiefs. He favored an odd combination of low defense budgets, support for Chiang, and aggressive rollback rhetoric, probably because he thought these positions would gain support for his bid for the presidency.

70. Stueck, *Road to Confrontation*, 188.

71. Gaddis, "The Strategic Perspective: The Rise and Fall of the 'Defensive Perimeter' Concept, 1947–1951," in Dorothy Borg and Waldo Heinrichs, *Uncertain Years: Chinese-American Relations, 1947–1950* (New York, 1980), 102; Gaddis, *Long Peace*, 94.

72. Stueck, *Road to Confrontation*, 205–6. For similar inconsistencies in assessments of the strategic value of Taiwan, see ibid., 118, 140–41; Mayers, *Cracking the Monolith*, 42, 58–59; Warren I. Cohen, *Dean Rusk* (Totowa, N.J., 1980), 42; *FRUS, 1949*, 9:284–86, 466. Placing this in the context of bureaucratic politics are Pollard, *Economic Security*, 193; and Franz Schurmann, *The Logic of World Power* (New York, 1974), 156–59.

Asia were always good if sufficient resources were provided for their development, especially if they contributed to the development of an offensive posture threatening the Soviet Union and China. Domino and big stick theories were deployed as necessary to try to sell the expansion of the network of military bases. Such arguments were abandoned, however, when the military thought it was getting stuck with vulnerable positions and no resources to develop them. Then the domino theory was exchanged for a theory of economy of force, strongly distinguishing between the irrelevant periphery and the crucial strategic core.[73]

Like Acheson and Taft, the Joint Chiefs had no interest in starting down the road of global containment if that meant spreading American resources too thinly over too many commitments and entangling the United States on the Asian mainland. But also as with Acheson and Taft, the Pentagon's tactical use of domino arguments helped feed a public debate that was pushing American policy toward such overcommitment.

Cold War Globalism

A final school of thought, which emerged with full force in the months before the outbreak of the Korean War, was Cold War globalism, as exemplified by the views of Dean Rusk, Paul Nitze, and John Foster Dulles. At this time Europe-first internationalists like Acheson also increasingly espoused globalist ideas, especially in their public rhetoric. Though some of these men were sincerely dedicated to the strategy of global American military involvement, even these true believers resorted to disingenuous strategic exaggerations to sell their program. As a result, America's public debate was encrusted with a still deeper layer of mythology, perpetrated by men who in fact knew better.

Dulles became the major public figure most clearly associated with the policy and ideology of global containment. He extended the domino theory to include not only Formosa, but even the tiny offshore islands of Quemoy and Matsu, though the Europeans Dulles alleged would become despondent over the islands' loss were arguing that they should be abandoned.[74] At the same time Dulles was selling the domino theory, he also advanced the notion that communism was

73. Richard Betts, *Soldiers, Statesmen, and Cold War Crises* (Cambridge, Mass., 1977), makes a not dissimilar argument about the military's disinclination to engage in conflict with insufficient resources and its strong inclination to escalate the level of effort once involved.

74. Norman Graebner, "Conclusion: The Limits of Nuclear Strategy," in Norman Graebner, ed., *The National Security: Its Theory and Practice, 1945–1960* (New York, 1986), 284–85.

overextended and thus vulnerable to a counterattack. Writing in *Life* magazine in 19 May 1952, Dulles campaigned for secretary of state by calling for "A Policy of Boldness," shunning the reactive Truman policy of containment. Instead, Dulles called for regaining the initiative through nuclear striking power and a vague "liberation" doctrine.[75]

But beneath this public facade, Dulles in fact had more sophisticated views. While publicly depicting communism as ideological and mono-lithic, he privately recognized that there were profound differences between the Russians and the Chinese. In 1949 Dulles even entertained the possibility that Communist China should be recognized in order to encourage its independence, exactly Acheson's line at the time.[76] He was much more flexible than Republican senators on the subject of talks with Chou En-lai.[77] And in the 1948 Berlin crisis he had even warned that Politburo members' prestige was too deeply engaged to let them back out without a fig leaf.[78] While the public Dulles was doing his best to contribute to a stereotyped Cold War mythology, the private Dulles was often striving to implement the policy of global contain-ment in ways that managed its costs and risks.[79]

Globalists also engaged in exaggeration and rhetorical opportunism in the advocacy surrounding Paul Nitze's memorandum on American grand strategy, NSC 68. "A defeat of free institutions anywhere is a defeat everywhere," the document asserted. "The shock we sustained in the destruction of Czechoslovakia was not in the measure of Czecho-slovakia's material importance to us," but in its effect on morale and confidence.[80] Conflating balance of power thinking with such psycho-logical arguments, NSC 68 also asserted that any further Communist expansion would push past the critical point where a coalition strong enough to create a stable balance could no longer be mustered.[81]

Nitze, personally a believer in balanced budgets, wanted to raise taxes to pay for the military programs needed to implement NSC 68. Indeed, he lectured Truman's Keynesian chief economic adviser, Leon

75. Townsend Hoopes, *The Devil and John Foster Dulles* (Boston, 1973), 125–26. Once in office, Dulles told the Joint Chiefs that his political campaign rhetoric about liberation had turned out to be impractical. *FRUS*, National Security Affairs, 1952–54, part 1, 833.

76. H. W. Brands, *Cold Warriors* (New York, 1988), 14, Dulles to Luce, 24 February 1950.

77. David Mayers, "Eisenhower and Communism," in Richard A. Melanson and David Mayers, *Reevaluating Eisenhower: American Foreign Policy in the 1950s* (Urbana, Ill., 1987), 96–98.

78. Avi Shlaim, *The United States and the Berlin Crisis, 1948–1949* (Berkeley, Calif., 1983), 248.

79. Gaddis, *Long Peace*, chap. 6; Mayers, *Cracking the Monolith*; Brands, *Cold Warriors*, chap. 1; Richard Immerman, ed., *John Foster Dulles and the Diplomacy of the Cold War* (Princeton, N.J., 1990).

80. *FRUS*, 1950, 1:240.

81. George Herring, *America's Longest War* (New York, 1979), 10.

Keyserling, on the evils of deficit spending. Nitze soon saw, however, that a tactical alliance with Keyserling would help sell the economic feasibility of global containment. Keyserling had initially hoped to stimulate economic growth through deficit spending on domestic programs, not on military programs. He was nonetheless willing to defend Nitze's NSC 68, since he thought budget deficits would be beneficial to the economy regardless of the object of the expenditures.[82]

NSC 68 was used not only to "bludgeon the mass mind of 'top government,'" but also as a basis for preparing public speeches by administration officials on the need for full congressional funding of Truman's European aid program.[83] Indeed, globalist arguments caught on with mainstream journalists about this time. Edward R. Murrow argued that it was time to "draw a line across the globe," costs and risks be damned.[84]

There is also some evidence that Rusk's strategic arguments were calculated for their rhetorical effect, though he is perhaps the most sincere of the true believers in global containment. Rusk's biographer calls him "the consummate Wilsonian," committed to an idealistic struggle against communism in the developing world, less of a realist than his mentor, Acheson, and more interventionist than Acheson in East Asia.[85] Rusk gravitated easily to the domino theory as a strategic rationale behind his Wilsonian globalist convictions. Just before the Korea attack, Rusk collaborated with Dulles in reversing Acheson's policy of excluding Taiwan from the American defense perimeter. Their memorandum to Acheson justifying this change relied on a globalist, reputational version of the domino theory:

> Throughout the world, in Europe, the Mediterranean, the Middle East, Asia and the Pacific, governments and peoples are intently watching for the next move which will provide a measure of the extent of the power shift [in communism's favor], so that they can orient their policies accordingly. . . . If our conduct indicates a continuing disposition to fall back and allow doubtful areas to fall under Soviet Communist control, then many nations will feel confirmed in the impression, already drawn

82. Paul Nitze, interviewed in October 1988. On Keyserling's initial preference for nondefense spending, see Paul Nitze, "The Development of NSC-68," *International Security* 4 (Spring 1980): 173; and Paul Nitze, *From Hiroshima to Glasnost* (New York, 1989), 96–97. For general background, see Pollard, *Economic Security*, 239–41.

83. Christensen, "Strategies," 9.

84. July 1950, quoted in Lisle Rose, *Roots of Tragedy: The United States and the Struggle for Asia, 1945–1953* (Westport, Conn., 1976), 240. See also James Reston, New York *Times*, 8 January 1950, cited in Paterson, "If Europe," 35.

85. Cohen, *Rusk*, 109 and chap. 2; David Halberstam, *The Best and the Brightest* (New York, 1969), 308–23; Thomas J. Schoenbaum, *Waging Peace and War: Dean Rusk in the Truman, Kennedy, and Johnson Years* (New York, 1988), 193.

from the North Atlantic Treaty, that we do not expect to stand firm short of
the North Atlantic area.

To forestall "disasters," they told Acheson, the United States should
take "a dramatic stand that shows our confidence and resolution," and
Taiwan was the best place to achieve this.[86] Taiwan's defense was
feasible, even easy, with American help; without it, not only Taiwan,
but vast portions of the globe would be jeopardized. Even the European allies' confidence would be shaken.[87]

   In May 1951 Rusk gave a widely publicized speech calling the
People's Republic of China a "colonial Russian government, a Slavic
Manchukuo . . . driven by foreign masters."[88] Acheson and Truman,
who were still not ready to give up the idea of splitting the Soviet
Union and China through selective bargaining, were upset by the text,
which they had not cleared. Rusk himself was uneasy about the speech
in later years, admitting it had abetted McCarthyite attacks on Acheson.
Rusk acknowledged that his statements were "more polemical than
factual," exaggerations aimed at shaming the Chinese.[89] Rusk's most
recent and generally even-handed biographer, Thomas Schoenbaum,
puts the speech in the context of Republican pressure on the Truman
administration's China policy:

> Rusk also let himself be manipulated by John Foster Dulles to the point of
> adopting Dulles's memoranda on China as his own and forwarding them
> to Acheson. Domestic politics and McCarthyism also took their toll,
> putting the whole adminstration on the defensive, and the hardened
> attitudes toward the Chinese were embodied in a National Security Coun-
> cil Statement—NSC-48/4—which was signed by the President. The Repub-
> lican policy toward China was adopted by the Truman administration
> virtually intact.[90]

American thinking on grand strategy comprised the full panoply of
domino, bandwagoning, offense-dominance, window of vulnerability,
and Thermopylae arguments. These were tempered, especially in the
early years, by a sense of the limits of American resources and by the
need to distinguish between core and periphery in setting priorities.
Both internationalists and nationalists recognized these limits, though
they set priorities in a different way. Considerations of salesmanship

   86. *FRUS*, 1950, 6:349; Rusk's 30 May 1950 memo to Acheson, identical to Dulles's 18
May memo to Rusk.
   87. Foot, *Wrong War*, 52; Schaller, *American Occupation*, 259–60.
   88. Schoenbaum, *Waging Peace*, 223.
   89. Dean Rusk, as told to Richard Rusk, *As I Saw It* (New York, 1990), 173.
   90. Schoenbaum, *Waging Peace*, 224. For another example of Rusk's opportunistic use
of geopolitical arguments, see Cohen, *Rusk*, 24.

and political opportunism made the public arguments of the two schools more globalistic than their private views. By 1950 globalistic arguments increasingly came to dominate American public rhetoric. Even true believers in globalism exaggerated their beliefs in public, thus further feeding the strategic mythologies that prevailed in American political discourse.

Evaluating the Strategic Concepts

No one is expected always to be right in an uncertain world. Rational decision makers, however, are expected to conform to minimal standards of logical consistency, to be reasonably open to information that refutes their views, and to be joined in any errors by third-party observers. A variety of scholars have argued that American Cold War decision makers often failed these tests.

For example, it is widely acknowledged that American decision makers ignored ample warning signals that an advance to the Yalu River on the Chinese-Korean border would trigger a massive Chinese military intervention. Third parties, moreover, warned that the Chinese would intervene. Instead of heeding these warnings, Washington deferred to General MacArthur's reassuring bravado that the Chinese would not dare attack.[91]

Rather than recapitulating more of the alleged misperceptions behind American containment strategy, I will confine my own critique to the specific issue of logical inconsistencies and double standards used to justify global containment strategy. People can always disagree about what a decision maker "should have known" given the information available; logical errors, however, stand out more starkly. Examples from the Korean War period strongly suggest that rationalization, not rationality, underlay many of the arguments for the escalation of American commitments in East Asia. Three logical oddities pervade the Korean case: first, a contradictory paper tiger image of the enemy; second, an image of an enemy that is both oblivious to and cowed by threats, and finally, opposite perceptions leading to the same policy.

American decision makers saw the Communist opponent as an overwhelming threat, almost impossible to deter, yet somehow also inert in the face of American opposition. For example, MacArthur thought the Chinese would be extremely easy to deter if the United

---

91. Foot, *Wrong War*, 91–101; Allen Whiting, *China Crosses the Yalu* (Stanford, Calif., 1960); Alexander George and Richard Smoke, *Deterrence in American Foreign Policy* (New York, 1974), 184–234; Richard Ned Lebow, *Between Peace and War* (Baltimore, 1981), 149–64, 172–84. For transcripts showing MacArthur's confidence about Chinese nonintervention at his Wake Island meeting with Truman, see Schoenbaum, *Waging Peace*, 218.

States was completely uncompromising: they would not dare attack because they must know that America would then bomb Peking with devastating force. But he also believed they would be difficult to deter if the United States gave the slightest quarter: "To give up any portion of North Korea to the aggression of the Chinese Communists would be the greatest defeat of the free world in modern times," because anything less would be insufficient punishment of aggression. Stopping at the thirty-eighth parallel or the narrow waist of Korea would be Munich all over again.[92]

American characterizations of Soviet strength incorporated a similar duality, if not outright contradiction. One of the spurs toward global containment was the perception of a huge increase in Soviet power, owing to the atomic test and the Communist victory on the Chinese mainland, both in 1949. And yet American proponents of unifying Korea by force justified this on the grounds that the Soviets would surely not intervene, having revealed their abject weakness by not even protesting the crossing of the thirty-eighth parallel.[93]

I do not claim these views are mutually contradictory, but they come close. American proponents of global expansion alternated between extreme overestimates of Soviet and Chinese power and extreme contempt for it. Both exaggerations were used to underpin arguments for global expansion. As William Stueck has put it, American leaders showed a "mixture of arrogance and insecurity," "overestimating their nation's ability to shape events" but also "exaggerating America's need to hold firm" in Korea and China.[94]

In a related paradox, Americans simultaneously argued that China knew it was not threatened by the American advance, and also that China would be intimidated by American power. On one hand, the Chinese must know the United States did not intend to go beyond the Yalu, and consequently they had no reason to be provoked by the proximity of U.S. military power. On the other hand, MacArthur argued, the advance would cow them because "it is the pattern of Oriental psychology to respect and follow aggressive, resolute and dynamic leadership—to quickly turn on a leadership characterized by timidity or vacillation."[95]

Third, American leaders frequently derived identical policy conclusions from opposite analytical premises. For example, global anticommunists argued that the Chinese would not intervene in the Korean

92. Stueck, *Road to Confrontation*, 245, 255; Foot, *Wrong War*, 85, 100.

93. Foot, *Wrong War*, 75.

94. Stueck, *Road to Confrontation*, 257. For a similar observation about the United States in Vietnam, see Herring, *America's Longest War*, 170–71.

95. Robert Jervis, *Perception and Misperception in International Politics* (Princeton, N.J., 1976), 70–71; Stueck, *Road to Confrontation*, 207.

War, because they would recognize that monolithic communism had already missed its opportunity for expansion. According to this argument, the "logical" point for the Chinese to intervene would have been early in the war, when the anticommunist forces were on the ropes. But Acheson, arguing from the opposite premises, came up with the same conclusion. His view hinged on the notion that communism was not monolithic and that Chinese motives were primarily defensive. He deduced from this that China, instead of intervening in Korea, would husband its strength to deal with its real enemy, Soviet Russia.[96] When opposite premises lead to the same conclusions, one might surmise that policy choice comes first and arguments are aligned as required.

Other double standards and inconsistencies litter the history of American Cold War argumentation. Taft argued in January 1951, for example, that deploying three additional American divisions in Europe might goad the Russians to attack, whereas three months later he denied that bombing along the Soviet border in Asia would be the slightest bit provocative.[97] In Vietnam, a double standard of proof dismissed Ball's well-reasoned refutations of the domino theory, while McNamara's apocalyptic obiter dicta were allowed to go unchallenged. Lyndon Johnson probed the validity of neither the domino theory nor his obsession with the risk of Chinese intervention.[98] Knowing that gradual escalation was the safest political course in the short run, he avoided examining the beliefs that justified that course.[99]

All these logical twists have one thing in common: they helped to portray a policy of forward containment as necessary, feasible, and safe. Almost nobody who argued for aggressive containment admitted that it would be risky. An exception was John Allison of the State Department's Office of Northeast Asian Affairs. He conceded that his proposal to advance as far north as the Manchurian and Siberian borders "may mean war on a global scale." Nevertheless, he said, "the American people should be told [about this risk] and told why and what it will mean to them. When all legal and moral right is on our side why should we hesitate?"[100] No one else took this attitude. Those who had doubts about the prudence of the advance were not impressed by Allison's "grit our teeth" attitude. Only when they convinced themselves—or when MacArthur convinced them—that the risks were nil did American decision makers jump on the bandwagon for the

96. Foot, *Wrong War*, 80–81.
97. Doenecke, *Not to the Swift*, 205.
98. Larry Berman, "Waiting for Smoking Guns: Presidential Decision-Making and the Vietnam War, 1965–67," in Peter Braestrup, ed., *Vietnam as History* (Washington, D.C., 1984), 17.
99. Daniel Ellsberg, *Papers on the War* (New York, 1972), 42–135.
100. Foot, *Wrong War*, 73.

northern advance.[101] Sugarcoating the risks and costs of forward containment was necessary because without it the policy would not have been accepted.

COGNITIVE EXPLANATIONS

The most influential cognitive explanations for American Cold War interventionism stress the intellectual impact of formative lessons. For example, Ernest May's account of the decision to intervene in the Korean War emphasizes the American leaders' fixation on an oversimplified lesson of the Hitler era: that aggressors must be firmly resisted from the start, not appeased. He supports this with numerous quotations showing that Truman and other American officials invoked analogies to the 1930s in explaining their decision to intervene.[102] Subsequently Robert Jervis has developed a more general argument, drawing on cognitive theory, that suggests that the dogmatized lessons of decision makers' formative experiences often bias their subsequent perceptions and choices.[103] Thus cognitive theory can apparently explain both the decision to intervene in Korea and most of the strategic conceptions behind the decision: the domino theory, bandwagon fears, and the image of the adversary. In this view American Cold War leaders, in fighting their wars in Korea and Vietnam, were simply reliving their intellectually formative epoch of the 1930s.

There is one fundamental problem, however, with May's otherwise well-constructed argument. By May's own account, the American leaders' obsession with the Munich analogy came out of the blue in June 1950. Before that, May stresses, Acheson and other responsible officials had taken the opposite view—that failure to fight for Korea would *not* have devastating consequences for America's credibility or geopolitical position. May thinks this helps his argument: "Because of the earlier studies and decisions, evaluating Korea as of negligible importance and concluding that warfare there should be avoided, the 1950 decision [to intervene] provides a particularly vivid illustration of the potency of beliefs about history. When events in the peninsula were perceived as analogous to certain events in the recent past, an axiom derived from the analogies came into play, and all previous calculations lost their force."[104]

In fact, these "earlier studies and decisions" seriously undermine

101. Stueck, *Road to Confrontation*, 204–5; Foot, *Wrong War*, 73–74.
102. Ernest R. May, *"Lessons" of the Past* (London, 1973); Ernest R. May, "The Nature of Foreign Policy: The Calculated versus the Axiomatic," *Daedalus* 91 (Fall 1962): 653–68.
103. Jervis, *Perception*, chap. 6.
104. May, *Lessons*, 83.

May's case. These studies explicitly considered the risks of failing to resist an aggressor,[105] but American officials, by May's own account, found those risks a secondary consideration. If the lessons of the 1930s had indeed created obsessions for American decision makers, then they should have been obsessed with the Munich analogy in 1949, when American troops were withdrawn from Korea, and in January 1950, when Acheson made his defense perimeter speech, not just during the intervention decision in June.

Deborah Larson's study of the origins of American Cold War beliefs finds that the Munich analogy did not play a major role in the thinking of the late 1940s.[106] Instead, she finds that perceptions were guided by a variety of cognitive biases and, above all, by post hoc rationalization of behavior. Larson uses the cognitive psychological terminology of "self-perception theory," which holds that people act first and afterward construct beliefs that help them explain to themselves and to others why they acted as they did. Translated into the language of my own study, they engaged in strategic rationalization of actions they took for other reasons. Those other reasons are not well specified by self-perception theory. Larson suggests that "the pressure of external events" directly determined the behavior around which beliefs developed.[107] My own conjecture is that those other reasons included domestic consensus building. In any event, the dominance of the Munich analogy was an effect of policy and its rationalization, not its cause.[108]

A study similar to May's by Yuen Foong Khong argues that U.S. decisions to escalate the Vietnam War were influenced by analogies to the Korean War, which he contends had been a formative experience for some of the key decision makers.[109] Khong demonstrates clear and convincing connections between the Korea analogy and some aspects of strategic thinking during the Vietnam War, especially the exaggerat-

---

105. Gaddis, "Defensive Perimeter," in Borg and Heinrichs, *Uncertain Years*, 103–4; Gaddis, *Long Peace*, 95.
106. Larson, *Origins of Containment*, xi, 350–51.
107. Ibid., 49.
108. If analogies had a powerful causal effect, one would expect there to be strong opinion differences across generations with different formative experiences—for example, the Munich generation versus the Vietnam generation. According to Ole Holsti, "Public Opinion and Containment," in Terry Deibel and John Gaddis, *Containing the Soviet Union* (Washington, D.C., 1987), 20–58, that relationship does not hold.
109. Yuen Foong Khong, "The Lessons of Korea and the Vietnam Decisions of 1965," in George Breslauer and Philip Tetlock, *Learning in U.S. and Soviet Foreign Policy* (Boulder, Colo., 1991); also, Khong, "From Rotten Apples to Dominoes to Munich: The Problem of Reasoning by Analogy about Vietnam" (Ph.D. diss., Harvard University, 1987). Jervis, however, raises the possibility that Korea was not formative for people like Rusk but rather reflected attitudes that led them to seek out responsibility in this area. See *Perception*, 219, 221, 227.

ed fear of Chinese military intervention. But there is a larger problem with Khong's argument. United States decision makers in the mid-1960s drew selectively on the potential lessons of the Korean War, ignoring the one that had been most salient in the immediate aftermath of the Korean War: "No more land wars in Asia." That lesson was the one that heavily influenced the Eisenhower administration's decision not to intervene with United States troops in the 1954 Indochina crisis.[110] Thus an analogy that can justify any policy and its opposite has limited explanatory value.

Arguments based on the formative lessons of history, like May's and Khong's, are the only fully developed cognitive explanations for American Cold War policy in East Asia.[111] Robert Jervis's *Perception and Misperception in International Politics*, however, offers a number of other hypotheses that might be developed into such an explanation. Still, it is far from clear which of these hypotheses would survive systematic historical scrutiny. One of his most promising propositions, for example, is that biases in the availability of information will lead statesmen to exaggerate the unity of opposing states and alliances and thus to perceive their adversaries as more monolithic, calculating, and malevolent than they really are.[112] One might try to explain Dulles's public assertions about the monolithic Sino-Soviet bloc as a result of this cognitive bias. Recent archival research has demonstrated, however, that privately Dulles was well aware of Sino-Soviet divisions.[113] Public relations strategy, not cognitive bias, explains the monolithic imagery in this case.

DOMESTIC POLITICS

I have argued that democratic political systems are likely to engage in only limited overexpansion and that they are apt to learn to reverse their overextension before doing irreparable damage to the state's strategic position. Indeed, the United States settled its two costly, peripheral wars at the bargaining table, and since Vietnam it has been careful to avoid such quagmires. Compared with the overexpansion of the cartelized great powers, Germany and Japan, America's "imperial overstretch" has been moderate and self-correcting.

But I have also argued that even democracies may suffer from limited

110. Burke and Greenstein, *How Presidents Test Reality*, 17, 30, 64.
111. I exclude Larson's study, because it focuses on Europe and because in her account behavior causes beliefs, not vice versa.
112. Jervis, *Perception*, chaps. 8 and 9.
113. Mayers, *Cracking the Monolith*; Gaddis, *Long Peace*, chap. 6; Gaddis, "The Unexpected John Foster Dulles: Nuclear Weapons, Communism, and the Russians," in Immerman, *Dulles*, 47–78; Brands, *Cold Warriors*, chap. 1.

cartelization, which can produce imperial logrolling and mythmaking to a lesser degree. Such a process contributed to the formation of the Cold War consensus, the emergence of the domino theory, and the adoption of a globalist strategy of containment. In the early Cold War period, grand strategy became a subject for logrolling and mythmaking among factions because of the temporary stalemate between internationalist and nationalist economic interests in American society, and because the internationalist/nationalist cleavage cut across party lines. As a result of these conditions, competing approaches to containment strategy never confronted each other directly in presidential elections but rather became the subject of complicated coalition making between Congress and the executive branch. Therefore the politics of American grand strategy reflected logrolling among cartels and opinion groupings more than it did a direct two-party competition for the favor of median voters.[114]

Though presidents were always internationalist after 1945, they still needed Congress to approve their programs. Even when Democrats controlled Congress after 1948, Truman could not count on forcing through a Europe-first internationalist program by a party-line vote. On most issues the votes of moderate Republicans were needed to offset defections by significant numbers of southern Democratic nationalists. Former vice president Henry Wallace's advocacy for continuing the wartime U.S.-Soviet alliance caused a further splintering of the Democratic majority. This left internationalist Republicans like Vandenberg as the swing votes for the adminstration's European programs such as Greek and Turkish aid and the Marshall Plan. To maintain harmony within the Republican party, and also to win credit as people who could deliver on issues the nationalists cared about, Republican internationalists used the leverage of their swing position to move the administration's Asia policy closer to the nationalist position.

This cartelization within Congress also affected the development of strategic ideology. As the price of Republican support for Europe-oriented internationalist programs, Vandenberg urged that they be justified in terms of a fundamental ideological struggle against communism. This played into the hands of the Old Guard Republicans, who were scrapping isolationism in favor of a more attractive platform of ideological anticommunism, especially in Asia. Because Democratic internationalists needed moderate Republican votes, a direct ideological showdown attacking the premises of the Asia-first Republicans was difficult.

114. For a broader analysis of the political stalemate at this time, which emphasizes the breakup of the Democrats' New Deal coalition, see Samuel Lubell, *The Future of American Politics* (New York, 1951), esp. 5.

To achieve internationalism's main objectives in Europe despite this stalemate, statesmen like Eisenhower, Dulles, and Rusk created a new strategic vision to underpin a stable Cold War consensus. That vision, rooted in strategic myths like the domino theory, tacked together the strategic programs of the Europe-first and Asia-first schools into a globalist, anticommunist consensus. The political result was more prone to geopolitical overextension than either of its constituent parts taken separately.

Some historians argue that this domestic political context affected to some extent the decision to intervene in the Korean War; many more accept that it affected the decisions to cross the thirty-eighth parallel, to march to the Chinese border at the Yalu River, and to align with Nationalist Chinese on Taiwan.[115] Many of them place greater stress, however, on the American foreign policy elite's belief in the danger of appeasing aggressors, the importance of America's reputation for standing firm, the likelihood of a European bandwagon, and in general the domino theory.[116] But I argue that such strategic ideas were in part a product of the domestic political environment; consequently the domestic component in these explanations must be given greater weight.

Roots and Character of Internationalism

Europe-first internationalism springs from two main sources: internationally oriented business and the executive branch of government. Its proponents for the most part favored a limited, realpolitik approach to American international commitments, focusing on essential security and on economic interests abroad, rather than on undifferentiated expansionism. In this brief review of the foundations of internationalism, I will stress economic interests, not because cultural and other factors were irrelevant, but because they were often intertwined with economic interests, which provide the simplest focus for telling the story.

In the decades before World War I, America pursued a free-rider

---

115. For mainstream historians accepting some role for domestic factors, see Waldo Heinrichs, "Summary of Discussion," in Borg and Heinrichs, *Uncertain Years*, 119–29; Stueck, *Road to Confrontation*, esp. 143–46; Blum, *Drawing the Line*, esp. 187–91; Foot, *Wrong War*, 42–45. For the interaction of international and domestic politics on the conduct and termination of the war, see Rosemary Foot, *A Substitute for Victory: The Politics of Peacemaking at the Korean Armistice Talks* (Ithaca, N.Y., 1990), 1–19. Gaddis, *Long Peace*, 82 and throughout chap. 4, stresses the impact of domestic politics on the Taiwan issue more than on Korea. Revisionist works that place greater stress on the domestic environment include Joyce Kolko and Gabriel Kolko, *The Limits of Power: The World and United States Foreign Policy, 1945–1954* (New York, 1972); and Lewis Purifoy, *Harry Truman's China Policy* (New York, 1976), chaps. 7 and 8.

116. Stueck, *Road to Confrontation*, esp. 6–8; Gaddis, *Long Peace*, chap. 4.

strategy in world affairs, maintaining a protectionist coalition of workers and capitalists in import-competing industrial sectors while exploiting Britain's unconditional openness to American exports. As the American economy grew, other states began to retaliate more systematically against American goods. As a strategic response to this retaliation, officials in the executive branch promoted the emergence of a domestic coalition, which included internationally oriented business, in favor of a conditional reduction of American tariffs, contingent on other states' reciprocity. This culminated in the Underwood tariff of 1913.[117]

The growth of the Europe-oriented sectors of the American economy was given a huge boost by trade with Europe during World War I and by American loans to Britain and other European states.[118] The United States emerged from the war as the world's major creditor and with an increasingly internationalized business and financial sector.[119] International lawyers like Sullivan and Cromwell's John Foster Dulles and their financier sponsors were actively involved in negotiating the Versailles Treaty and prepared to play a central role in the postwar economic order in Europe.[120] Though these internationalist interests were themselves divided over the appropriate conditions for American entry into the League of Nations, they were united in opposing a retreat to isolationism. To plan strategy and proselytize the internationalist faith, they formed the Council on Foreign Relations, with its *Foreign Affairs* magazine, as well as more mass-oriented international organizations.[121] In this effort they also enlisted northeastern, Anglophile, old-stock Protestants, forming a cadre of internationalist bankers, lawyers, editors, professors, and ministers.[122] Within the executive branch of the government, they used sympathetic State Department channels, technical expertise, and J. P. Morgan's economic clout to try to promote internationalist financial and trade policies against the Commerce Department's more nationalist stance.[123] Because experience in international

117. David Lake, "The State and American Trade Strategy in the Pre-hegemonic Era," *International Organization* 42 (Winter 1988): 33–58; and David Lake, *Power, Protection, and Free Trade: International Sources of U.S. Commercial Strategy, 1887–1939* (Ithaca, N.Y., 1988).

118. Jeff Frieden, "Sectoral Conflict and U.S. Foreign Economic Policy, 1914–1940," *International Organization* 42 (Winter 1988): 59–90; Melvin Small, "Woodrow Wilson and U.S. Intervention in World War I," in John Carroll and George Herring, *Modern American Diplomacy* (Wilmington, Del., 1986), 21–34.

119. Sources cited in Frieden, "Sectoral Conflict," 62n.3.

120. Pruessen, *Dulles*, chaps. 3–5.

121. Robert D. Schulzinger, *The Wise Men of Foreign Affairs: The History of the Council on Foreign Relations* (New York, 1984); Robert Divine, *Second Chance: The Triumph of Internationalism in America during World War II* (New York, 1967), chap. 1; Frank Costigliola, *Awkward Dominion: American Political, Economic, and Cultural Relations with Europe, 1919–1933* (Ithaca, N.Y., 1984), 69–75.

122. Divine, *Second Chance*, 22.

123. Frieden, "Sectoral Conflict," 74; Costigliola, *Awkward Dominion*; Melvin Leffler,

finance conveyed the skills needed for reconstructing the international order after 1945, the bulk of the postwar foreign policy elite—including such figures as Acheson, Dulles, Robert Lovett, Harriman, and John McCloy—were recruited from business-internationalist circles.[124]

Sources and Character of Unilateralist Nationalism

Opposition to free trade, foreign aid, collective security, and other international commitments has come at various times from a variety of sources within American society. In the interwar period, economic nationalism was supported by import-competing industrial sectors with no foreign operations, which still dominated the American economy despite the rise of Wall Street international financial ties.[125] Farmers were also economic nationalists, since they saw international markets as largely closed to additional exports anyway, and they calculated that foreign loans would lead to increased interest rates on their heavy debts.[126] Inflationary monetary policy, necessitating a protectionist international stance, was always a favorite of rural isolationist populists.[127] This helps explain the concentration of isolationist sentiment in the rural Midwest and West.[128] These groups and regions were selectively internationalist, however, on issues where it helped their pocketbook. They supported, for example, the federally financed Saint Lawrence Seaway project.[129]

The South was an exception to rural isolationism in the interwar period, because cotton was a successful export crop and because of an opportunistic alliance between Democratic internationalists and southern white segregationists.[130] After 1945, however, southern Democrats

---

The Elusive Quest (Chapel Hill, N.C., 1979); Thomas Ferguson, "From Normalcy to New Deal," *International Organization* 38 (Winter 1984): 41–94.

124. Walter Isaacson and Evan Thomas, *The Wise Men* (New York, 1986).

125. Frieden, "Sectoral Conflict"; Helen Milner, "Trading Places: Industries for Free Trade," *World Politics* 40 (April 1988): 350–76.

126. James R. Connor, "National Farm Organizations and United States Tariff Politics in the 1920s," *Agricultural History* 32 (January 1958): 32–43. Costigliola, *Awkward Dominion*, 67–68, shows farmers' high export dependence, but Judith Goldstein, "The Impact of Ideas on Trade Policy: The Origins of U.S. Agricultural and Manufacturing Policies," *International Organization* 43 (Winter 1989): 31–72, explains why high-cost American farmers determined that an export strategy had little prospect of success.

127. Cole, *Roosevelt*, 49, 191.

128. Leroy Rieselbach, *The Roots of Isolationism* (Indianapolis, Ind., 1966), 106–14, shows that the regional hypothesis holds in congressional voting when party is controlled. See also George Grassmuck, *Sectional Biases in Congress on Foreign Policy*, Johns Hopkins Studies in Historical and Political Science, vol. 68, no. 3 (Baltimore, 1951).

129. Connor, "National Farm Organizations," 41–43; Cole, *Roosevelt*, 133–34.

130. Charles O. Lerche, *The Uncertain South* (Chicago, 1964), 43–47; Connor, "National Farm Organizations," 35.

were unreliable partners in the Democrats' internationalist coalition. Many of them took a "unilateralist" stance, favoring firm opposition to Communist expansion, for example, but opposing economic aid to allies.[131] This pattern accelerated during the 1950s, as southern politics became less dominated by traditional landed gentry and more influenced by populist demagogy.[132]

Small businessmen have been the group most consistently nationalist in their foreign policy attitudes. Taft's attitudes capture their thinking well. Lacking international business interests themselves, they see overseas entanglements as raising taxes, subsidizing East Coast financiers, and promoting big government bureaucracies. Before World War II this expressed itself as isolationism; after the war, as Asia-first, anti–New Deal, anti–United Nations, pro–air power, anticommunist unilateralism. This outlook was interventionist, but "at places and times of our own choosing."[133]

These small businessmen wielded considerable power, because their seniority gave them disproportionate membership on key congressional committees and because of their dominant role in local politics in many areas of the country.[134] Stephen Ambrose details the role of a committee of local small businessmen—people hurt by New Deal taxes, regulations, and union policies—in promoting Richard Nixon's meteoric rise in California politics. Contrary to later Democratic charges, his brand of anti–New Deal, anticommunist demagogy arose from that small business climate of opinion, not from southern California's big oil interests.[135]

Isolationism was not entirely an economic affair. The isolationism before World War II may have been correlated to some degree with German or other anti-British ethnic groups.[136] Some authors argue that isolationism stemmed in part from small-town, xenophobic, or "pietistic" attitudes or from the combining of such factors with class or sectoral economic interest.[137] Isolationism may also be connected more broadly

131. Westerfield, *Foreign Policy*, 46, 203–6, 366.

132. Lerche, *Uncertain South*, chaps. 7–9.

133. Barton Bernstein, "The New Deal," in Barton Bernstein, ed., *Towards a New Past* (New York, 1968), 275; Doenecke, *Not to the Swift*, 26–67, 243–44; Lynn Eden, "The Diplomacy of Force: Interests, the State, and the Making of American Military Policy in 1948" (Ph.D. diss., University of Michigan, 1985), 184–87; Jonas, *Isolationism*, 86–88.

134. Kathleen Kemp, "Product Cycles, Industry-Party Coalitions, and the Growth of Federal Economic Regulation, 1860–1986," paper prepared for annual meeting of the American Political Science Association, Washington, D.C., September 1988, 14–15.

135. Stephen Ambrose, *Nixon: The Education of a Politician, 1913–1962* (New York, 1987), 127–31.

136. Lubell, *Future*, chap. 7, argues this, though Rieselbach's statistical tests of congressional voting, *Roots of Isolationism*, 120–26, suggest that this effect was quite weak.

137. Doenecke, *Not to the Swift*, 23–25; Paul Kleppner, "Coalitional and Party Transformations in the 1890s," in Seymour Martin Lipset, ed., *Party Coalitions in the 1980s* (San

to America's geographical isolation and ideological differences from Europe, which caused U.S. foreign policy to oscillate between withdrawal from Europe's realpolitik and intervention to remake Europe in America's image.[138] Such considerations notwithstanding, it is clear that unilateral, nationalist attitudes were rooted in a social base opposite from that of Europe-first internationalism.[139]

The Postwar Showdown

In the interwar period, neither the internationalists nor the nationalists were strong enough to achieve a decisive victory. But World War II provided what one historian has called the internationalists' "second chance" to seize the initiative in American foreign policy.[140] Several factors worked in their favor. The war itself convinced the American public that international involvements were unavoidable. In a 1944 poll, only 10 to 15 percent were isolationists, though this did not necessarily make them internationalists. A majority favored the United Nations, but a majority also doubted it would succeed in preventing war.[141]

Urgent tasks of reconstructing the international order, which necessarily fell to the economically most powerful member of the victorious alliance, strengthened the hand of internationalist military and diplomatic bureaucracies of the American state.[142] It also brought internationalists with foreign-economic and military expertise into dominant positions in government service.[143] Underlying economic trends probably aided the emergence of internationalism too. As one scholar has put it, "the Depression and eventually World War II weakened the economic nationalists and allowed the state to reshape both policies and policy networks" through its "internationalist bureaucracies."[144] "Long range socioeconomic developments in the United States, including urbanization and industrialization, laid fundamental groundwork for these changes," argues another.[145]

Yet the wartime disruption of the international economy left Ameri-

Francisco, 1981), 87–106. Rieselbach, *Roots of Isolationism*, 114–20, finds high correlations between rural districts and isolationist voting.

138. Louis Hartz, *The Liberal Tradition in America* (New York, 1955), chap. 11.
139. Eden, "Diplomacy," 181–96.
140. Divine, *Second Chance*, chap. 2.
141. Ibid., 182–83.
142. Schurmann, *Logic*, 3–202, 401–41; Daniel Yergin, *Shattered Peace: The Origins of the Cold War and the National Security State* (Boston, 1977).
143. For discussion of the relationship between group and national interests in this regard, see Eden, "Diplomacy," 91–92.
144. Frieden, "Sectoral Conflict," 88.
145. Cole, *Roosevelt*, 365.

cans with a temporarily diminished stake in foreign trade. The low point since 1920 for American foreign direct investment was 1946.[146] The U.S. export surplus with Europe in 1946 and 1947 amounted to only 2 percent of U.S. GNP.[147] Economic nationalists, consequently, could still advance powerful arguments and find a sufficient constituency to defeat internationalists' plans for the International Trade Organization.[148]

The Tactic of Threat Inflation

Competing for preeminence in shaping the postwar order, internationalists, nationalists, and bureaucrats all found that inflating the Soviet threat was a good way to argue for their particular programs. For example, according to Robert Pollard, State Department officials who had originally conceived of a loan to Britain as economically beneficial to the United States found that it could be sold only as a national security necessity: "The loan had failed, and once again, Europe was clamoring for more American aid [in 1947]. After the Republican resurgence in the autumn of 1946, the administration could scarcely count on enthusiastic Congressional backing for additional foreign aid programs. The administration had learned that economic self-interest did not impress Congress and the public as much as the specter of Communist aggression."[149] Only in this way could they overcome Taft's arguments that such loans amounted to taxpayer subsidies for European socialists and New York investment bankers.[150]

In some parts of the globe, the bureaucratic interests of State and Defense sometimes made them work at cross-purposes in their threat assessments. State Department officials stressed the threat of monolithic communism to Indochina, for example, in order to promote economic aid programs to develop an economic hinterland to fuel Japan's

146. Milner, "Trading Places," 360–61; Pollard, *Economic Security*, 205.

147. Yergin, *Shattered Peace*, 309.

148. For general discussions of conflicts over international economic issues in this period, see Fred Block, *The Origins of International Economic Disorder* (Berkeley, Calif., 1977); and Michael Hogan, *The Marshall Plan* (Cambridge, 1987).

149. Pollard, *Economic Security*, 71–72; Jeffry Frieden, *Banking on the World: The Politics of American International Finance* (New York, 1987), 67; David S. McLellan, *Dean Acheson: The State Department Years* (New York, 1976), 94.

150. Patterson, *Mr. Republican*, 292; Pollard, *Economic Security*, 15–17. A study by John Gimbel contends that State Department and army bureaucracies used the Soviet threat to sell European aid programs that would ease their own organizational tasks. The army's main interest in Marshall Plan aid was to avoid being chained to the dead body of occupied Germany, while State Department bureaucrats wanted to further their agenda of reorganizing the international economic order. The Soviet threat was the main motive for neither of these organizations, though it was featured in their public relations efforts. John Gimbel, *The Origins of the Marshall Plan* (Stanford, Calif., 1976), 25, 30, 267–68.

industrial revival. The Pentagon tried to divert these same aid funds to its own purposes by exaggerating the strategic value of a base on Taiwan.[151] To counter this, Acheson sent out an internal memorandum ordering Foreign Service officers to minimize the consequences of Taiwan's fall, but General MacArthur outmaneuvered him by leaking the memo.[152]

Acheson, in turn, had access to information that the China lobby was using narcotics money and laundered U.S. aid funds to publicize its cause in the U.S. press.[153] This included hiring an American public relations firm to, in its own words, "conduct a 'fear' campaign through all the press and radio media which will emphasize the dangers to this country of the spread of Communism over China and the necessity of maintaining a democratic foothold in China to stop the spread of Communism in the Far East."[154] Acheson did not make his information public because, as Walter Lippmann speculated, too many highly placed Democrats might be implicated.[155]

Other examples of the manipulation of strategic images for bureaucratic or partisan purposes abound. Clark Clifford wrote a memorandum to Truman pointing out the advantages of talking up the Cold War as a means to undercut Henry Wallace's bid for the presidency.[156] General Lucius Clay, U.S. commander in Berlin, used the occasion of the Communist coup in Czechoslovakia in 1948 to wire Washington his view that "war may come with dramatic suddenness," a bit of hyperbole that historians now agree consciously targeted upcoming decisions on defense appropriations.[157]

These internationalist and bureaucratic efforts to publicize the need for greater foreign involvement by overselling the foreign threat seem to have been highly effective. This is proved not just by the hardening attitude of U.S. public opinion during the year following the campaign to sell the Marshall Plan. This, after all, could have been caused by international events themselves rather than by elite interpretations of them.[158] Public opinion specialists have been more impressed by the

151. Schaller, *American Occupation*, 211, 216–20; Stueck, *Road to Confrontation*, 111; Schurmann, *Logic*, 156–58.
152. Foot, *Wrong War*, 51.
153. Steel, *Lippmann*, 469.
154. Memo to Joseph Ku from Norman Paige, Wellington Koo papers, Columbia University, box 180, 9 June 1949. There is no evidence that Acheson had this specific piece of information.
155. Steel, *Lippmann*, 469.
156. Robert Divine, *Foreign Policy and U.S. Presidential Elections, 1940–48* (New York, 1974), 171–83; Freeland, *Truman Doctrine*, 192.
157. Hannes Adomeit, *Soviet Risk-Taking and Crisis Behavior* (London, 1982), 70; Yergin, *Shattered Peace*, 351; Jean Edward Smith, *The Papers of General Lucius D. Clay: Germany 1945–49*, 2 vols. (Bloomington, Ind., 1974), introduction.
158. Freeland, *Truman Doctrine*, 7, misses this point.

high correlation between acceptance of Cold War internationalist attitudes and level of education. They interpret this in terms of a "followership" model, in which an attentive public imbibes the interpretations put forward by opinion leaders.[159] The elites oversold, and the public overbought.

One of the biggest oversellers was Dulles. In an extraordinary 1942 pamphlet, he even admitted that religious faith was a great way to sell imperial expansion. All empires, he noted, had been "imbued with and radiated great faiths" like "Manifest Destiny" and the "White Man's Burden." We Americans "need a faith," Dulles said, "that will make us strong, a faith so profound that we, too, will feel that we have a mission to spread it through the world."[160] Dulles's most assiduous biographer concludes that Dulles's religiosity lay dormant for decades until this more practical use for it occurred to him.[161]

Throughout the late 1940s, in this analysis, Dulles consciously overinflated his rhetoric on the Soviet "challenge to civilization."[162] This proclivity was reinforced when Thomas Dewey restrained Dulles from crude Red-baiting in his role as Dewey's chief foreign policy adviser in his unsuccessful 1948 presidential campaign. Attributing the defeat in part to this self-restraint, Dulles ran a campaign unsurpassed in anticommunist innuendo in his bid for the Senate in 1949, though he still lost.[163]

In general, Republicans were stunned by their surprise defeat in 1948. Consequently they pulled out all the stops in exploiting the loss of China, Communists in government, and Acheson's support of Alger Hiss in maneuvering toward revenge in the 1950 election.[164] Like the internationalists' sales campaign for the commitment to Europe, the Republicans' and Asia-firsters' anticommunist and pro-Chiang campaigns also convinced many. Henry Luce's publicity blitz in *Time* and

159. William R. Caspary, "United States Public Opinion during the Onset of the Cold War," *Peace Research Society (International) Papers* 9 (1968): 25–46, esp. 30, 34, 43; William R. Caspary, "The 'Mood Theory': A Study of Public Opinion and Foreign Policy," *American Political Science Review* 64 (June 1970): 536–47; Ralph Levering, *The Public and American Foreign Policy* (New York, 1978), 22, 97–99; John Mueller, *Wars, Presidents, and Public Opinion* (New York, 1973), 122–23; Divine, *Second Chance*, 253. Robert Shapiro and Benjamin Page, "Foreign Policy and the Rational Public," *Journal of Conflict Resolution* 32 (June 1988): 211–47, esp. 225, argue that public opinion normally responds rationally, given the information it has about international events, though sometimes, as in the late 1940s, elite threat inflation may have manipulated public responses. See also Benjamin Page and Robert Shapiro, *The Rational Public* (Chicago, 1991), chaps. 5 and 6.
160. Pruessen, *Dulles*, 200.
161. Ibid., 3–4, 178–210.
162. Ibid., 285–89, 296–97.
163. Ibid., 400.
164. Stueck, *Road to Confrontation*, 143–46; David Reinhard, *The Republican Right since 1945* (Lexington, Ky., 1983), 65–67; Foot, *Wrong War*, 96.

Life reversed American opinion on aid to Taiwan between February and April 1948.[165] And by May 1950 more people agreed than disagreed with the statement that McCarthy's charges about Communists in the State Department were true and "a good thing" to have exposed.[166]

By way of summary, let me quote some of the most recent archival studies of the years leading up to the Korean War. In this period, says David Mayers, "the administration had managed, clumsily, to hobble its own diplomacy. Some high officials, by making excessive public statements about the monolithic nature of communism, had inadvertently cultivated a public opinion unreceptive to the subtleties of Acheson's diplomacy."[167] Moreover, says Rosemary Foot, the terms in which the Truman Doctrine was sold allowed the China lobby "to capitalize on the global rhetoric to promote their demands for military assistance."[168] Acheson said that he would simply "explain why Greece is not China." "Having once utilized global rhetoric," however, says Nancy Tucker, "the White House and State Department found it almost impossible to channel the militancy the rhetoric engendered."[169]

Nationalist Republicans like Taft were no less caught up in this rhetorical competition, which was dragging them toward international commitments about which they were highly ambivalent. As Representative Carl Vinson told Secretary of Defense James Forrestal after the Truman Doctrine speech, the isolationist Republicans "don't like Russia, they don't like the Communists, but still they don't want to do anything to stop it. But they are on the spot now, and they all have to come clean."[170]

The upshot of this spiral of mythmaking, born of the internationalist-nationalist power competition and the self-seeking of government bureaucracies, was political and intellectual pressure toward global military entanglements, including some that none of these factions had initially advocated.

THE KOREAN WAR AND THE COMMITMENT TO TAIWAN

Between January and June 1950 the Truman administration shifted from a policy of excluding South Korea and Taiwan from the perimeter of U.S. defense commitments to a policy of including them. During this

---

165. Stueck, *Road to Confrontation*, 60.
166. Thomas C. Reeves, *The Life and Times of Joe McCarthy* (New York, 1982), 283.
167. Mayers, *Cracking the Monolith*, 62.
168. Foot, *Wrong War*, 44.
169. Tucker, *Patterns*, 11.
170. Pollard, *Economic Security*, 124.

period there occurred pivotal international events like the signing in February of a Sino-Soviet alliance and the North Korean invasion of the South in June, as well as dramatic domestic events like the launching of Senator Joseph McCarthy's charges of Communists in the State Department. Consequently it is difficult to separate the effects of international and domestic developments in causing the expansion of U.S. defense commitments in East Asia.

Most historians have attributed a major role to domestic factors in the decision to guarantee Chiang Kai-shek's regime by interposing the U.S. fleet between Taiwan and the Chinese mainland.[171] Truman's Republican critics were directly clamoring for support for Chiang, so these historians have found the link to domestic political pressure to be clear and persuasive, even though direct quotations from Acheson or Truman acknowledging the link are lacking. Fewer historians, mainly those of the revisionist school, have argued that the decision to intervene in the Korean War was a direct result of domestic politics.[172] This skepticism stems from the Republican critics' stress on Taiwan, not Korea, and from the scarcity of direct statements by Truman or Acheson acknowledging domestic political pressures during the decision making on the Korean intervention.[173]

These qualifications notwithstanding, the process of domestic coalition making contributed to changes of administration attitudes on Far Eastern questions during the spring of 1950, paving the way for a Cold War consensus behind expanded military commitments. The need to appease Republican critics in order to gain votes for European programs encouraged this outcome; so did the blowback effects of globalist propaganda, which all factions used to mobilize support for their preferred programs. These programs were, for Acheson, aid to Europe and the Japanese Treaty; for the China lobby, support for Taiwan; for the military, its base structure in the Far East; and for Taft, the opportunity to defeat the Democrats. Every one of the principal decision makers and factions except Rusk expressed strong reservations between January and June 1950 about the prudence of fighting a land war in defense of Korea, even in the scenario of an attack supported by China or Russia. But everyone's globalist rhetoric and coalition making

---

171. Gaddis, *Long Peace*, 82.
172. Kolko and Kolko, *Limits of Power*; Purifoy, *Truman's China Policy*, chaps. 7 and 8. For a sympathetic review of such literature, see Stephen E. Pelz, "When the Kitchen Gets Hot, Pass the Buck: Truman and Korea in 1950," *Reviews in American History* 6 (December 1978): 548–55.
173. A thorough airing of this debate, with discussion by Alexander George and others, is recorded in a transcript of a colloquium given by Stephen E. Pelz, "America Goes to War, Korea, June 24–30, 1950: The Politics and Process of Decision," Woodrow Wilson Center, Smithsonian Institution, 11 July 1979.

helped create a domestic climate that loaded the dice in favor of such military commitments.

Between January and June 1950, Acheson shifted from extreme wariness about a military commitment in South Korea to forceful advocacy for military intervention. Though Truman and Acheson appreciated Korea's economic and symbolic importance, they also recognized the limits of American power, which precluded open-ended military commitments in peripheral areas.[174] Acheson did not oppose the U.S. troop withdrawal from Korea in 1949.[175] He went along with the recommendation of a State Department task force, which feared that the situation in Korea might be "untenable even with expenditure of considerable US money and effort." Though recognizing that simply abandoning the U.S. commitment would create an unfortunate impression, the task force suggested that the United States should aim for some kind of "settlement of the Korean problem which would enable the US to withdraw from Korea as soon as possible with the minimum of bad effects."[176]

Pursuing a similar line of limited liability in a January 1950 speech to the National Press Club, Acheson defined both Korea and Taiwan as outside the defense perimeter of the United States. He added, however, that the United Nations might choose to act if South Korea was attacked, in which case the United States would support such a decision.[177] But in secret testimony to the Senate Foreign Relations Committee, Acheson pointed out that the United Nations probably would not take action under the charter because the Soviets would veto it:

SECRETARY ACHESON. South Korea could now take care of any trouble that was started solely by North Korea, but it could not take care of any invasion which was either started by the Chinese Communists or powerfully supported by them or by the Soviet Union. I think that is clear. It is also clear that in that case we would take every possible action in the U.N. I do not believe that we would undertake to resist it by military force.
SENATOR VANDERBERG. Independently.
SECRETARY ACHESON. Independently. Of course, if under the charter action were taken, we would take our part in that, but probably it would not be taken because they would veto it.[178]

174. Even Cumings, *Origins*, vol. 2, chap. 13, allows that "for Acheson, who favored containment, the limits to American power meant one could not guarantee defense of all these places" from Iran to Indochina to Taiwan to Korea.
175. Stueck, *Road to Confrontation*, 154.
176. Gaddis, "Defensive Perimeter," 104; minutes of a meeting of State Department Far East advisers, 29 September 1947. Also in Gaddis, *Long Peace*, 95.
177. Foot, *Wrong War*, 58.
178. Acheson to Senate Foreign Relations Committee executive session, 13 January 1950, in U.S. Senate, *Reviews of the World Situation*, 191. Cumings, *Origins*, chap. 13,

In short, except for the quirk of fate that the Soviets were boycotting the United Nations in June 1950 over the seating of Red China, Acheson foresaw precisely the kind of scenario that occurred, and he anticipated that the United States would probably not fight. And yet by the time of the Blair House meetings immediately following the North Korean attack, Acheson had become the most insistent advocate of American intervention.[179]

At various points between January and June 1950, other key figures expressed similar reluctance to support military commitments for South Korea. Amid intelligence reports of a North Korean tank buildup in May 1950, Tom Connally, the Democratic chairman of the Senate Foreign Relations Committee, said that the United States would not intervene even if Russia seized South Korea.[180] The Republican minority report opposing an aid package for Korea early in 1950 called it a "dike of sand" that was "foredoomed to failure."[181] John Vorys, a senior Republican member of the House Foreign Affairs Committee, called it "rathole money."[182] Earlier MacArthur, the Joint Chiefs, and Defense Secretary Johnson had all proposed withdrawal of American troops from Korea, citing pressing commitments elsewhere and the unfavorable nature of the terrain, which would make Korea a strategic liability in a serious showdown with the Soviets.[183]

After the attack, Johnson, Dulles, MacArthur, and the Joint Chiefs were all initially reluctant to commit ground troops.[184] At the Blair House meetings Johnson and General Omar Bradley seemed preoccupied by the effect of Korea on Taiwan.[185] On 13 July Dulles wrote Walter Lippmann that he "had doubts as to the wisdom of engaging our land forces on the continent of Asia as against an enemy that could be nourished from the vast resources of the USSR."[186] The Chicago

---

argues that Acheson *did* favor a military commitment to Korea, but he could not say so, because it would spur calls for a similar commitment to Chiang and because it might encourage South Korea to attack the North. Cumings certainly succeeds in showing through documentary evidence that Acheson hoped to preserve America's position in Korea. But the argument that in January 1950 Acheson would have been willing to commit significant American ground forces to combat in Korea, despite the contrary implications of the defense perimeter speech, goes beyond what can be proved by available documents.

179. Schaller, *American Occupation*, 278–86.
180. Stueck, *Road to Confrontation*, 153; Caridi, *Korean War*, 31. Cumings, *Origins*, vol. 2, 431, notes that Acheson refused to "correct" Connally's statement.
181. James Matray, *The Reluctant Crusade: American Foreign Policy in Korea, 1941–1950* (Honolulu, 1985), 204–5.
182. Doenecke, *Not to the Swift*, 189.
183. Gaddis, "Defensive Perimeter," 103, 105; Gaddis, *Long Peace*, 94–96; Stueck, *Road to Confrontation*, 154.
184. Gaddis, "Defensive Perimeter," 107; Gaddis, *Long Peace*, 96–97; Pruessen, *Dulles*, 455; Schaller, *American Occupation*, 283.
185. Schaller, *American Occupation*, 283; Cohen, *Rusk*, 52.
186. Steel, *Lippmann*, 472.

Tribune opposed the intervention immediately, whereas it took Taft
until January 1951 to say that the United States should scuttle and that
he would not have intervened in the first place.[187] Rusk, who had
helped draw the border at the thirty-eighth parallel, was the only
figure not on record as opposing U.S. intervention in the event of a
Communist attack.[188]

Acheson stands out as the most hawkish of the advisers in the Blair
House meetings. Had some new evidence cropped up that might have
rationally changed Acheson's mind? One common claim is that Acheson's
defense perimeter speech did not envision a conventional cross-border
attack. Thus the June invasion had to be resisted because the reputational
costs of accepting this kind of blatant armed aggression were higher
than those of losing a civil struggle. But Acheson's secret congressional
testimony in January 1950 casts doubt on this interpretation.

Another possibility is that the February Sino-Soviet friendship treaty
and the ill treatment of American diplomatic personnel during the
winter of 1950 changed Acheson's view of the appeasability of the
Chinese Communists. Acheson's proposal to interpose the fleet between the mainland and Taiwan after the Korean attack might be
interpreted as giving up on his pro-Mao, anti-Chiang line. But the bulk
of the evidence suggests that Acheson resisted these changes down to
the last minute. Secret congressional testimony from Acheson at the
end of March reveals no change in his views, though this was after
Mao's proclamation about "leaning toward one side," that is, toward
the Soviet side, in the Cold War.[189]

Another change between January and June was the intensification of
the political attacks mounted on Acheson's Far Eastern policy and on
Acheson personally by McCarthyites who resented his public defense
in January of Alger Hiss.[190] Immediately after the defense perimeter
speech, the press thought that Acheson had scored a great success
with his popular policy of peace and "no adventures" in Asia.[191]

187. Doenecke, *Not to the Swift*, 190; Patterson, *Mr. Republican*, 485.

188. Christensen, "Strategies," 7, citing *FRUS*, 1950, 7:65, notes that even Rusk stated
in a top secret May 1950 document that the United States "is not in a position to provide
the Korean government with such a [military] commitment," though Christensen uses
this as evidence of American policy rather than Rusk's personal preference.

189. Testimony of 29 March, in U.S. Senate, *Reviews of the World Situation*, 276. Foot,
Wrong War, 47, citing *Reviews*, 273, quotes Acheson as saying that, despite the treaty, the
"very basic objectives of Moscow are hostile to the very basic objectives of China," and
therefore that the January strategy for splitting them should still remain in force.
According to Foot, State Department analysts had information suggesting the continuation of deep Sino-Soviet differences despite the treaty. But Acheson said already in March
that Korea was covered by the "Truman Doctrine." It is unclear whether this was caused
by the Sino-Soviet Friendship Treaty or by Republican attacks on the defense perimeter
speech. Schaller, *American Occupation*, 280.

190. On the Hiss affair, see McLellan, *Acheson*, 219.

191. Westerfield, *Foreign Policy*, 365, 368.

Beginning with public attacks on the speech by Dulles, Vandenberg, and Knowland, the Republicans set out to reverse that impression.[192] At the same time, McCarthy revealed his "list" of Communists in the State Department. Acheson's China experts were subjected to congressional grillings that questioned their loyalty.[193] This Red-baiting understandably preoccupied the department. Acheson and his aides frequently met to discuss the handling of the charges.[194] Foreign Service officers felt inhibited from passing along information regarding the shortcomings of anticommunist Asian politicians, even inside State Department channels.[195]

In this climate, Rusk volunteered to help appease the Senate Republicans by replacing the anti-Chiang Walton Butterworth as the assistant secretary for East Asia. Dulles reciprocated by telling McCarthy to "lay off Rusk."[196] Dulles himself was named a special adviser to the State Department as a result of pressure from Vandenberg.[197] Dulles's coercion of Acheson in this context was breathtaking. Just before Dulles's appointment, Dulles wrote to Rusk reminding him that the Democrats "had tried to smear me" in the 1949 Senate campaign, and that now Dulles's stance "would depend on the attitude of the Administration. If they really wanted bipartisanship, they could have it so far as I was concerned. If they did not want it, that would be their choice, not mine." Threatening another run for the Senate as a forum to air his attacks on Truman's policy, Dulles "authorized" Rusk to report this to Acheson.[198] Dulles also promised that he would provide a defense against Taft and other Republican critics "if Truman allowed ... 'early affirmative action' against the Communist menace."[199] And indeed Dulles got the group of China lobby senators to agree that "we would start no 'fireworks' until Dulles has a chance to move in on this with Acheson."[200]

Truman himself was very cool to the idea of taking Dulles into the administration, but he decided he had no choice, since Vandenberg was still crucial to the passage of the administration's European program.[201] Despite an attempt to enforce unanimous support for Acheson's Taiwan policy at a Senate Democratic caucus, southern Democrats' support was passive at best. After Acheson's remark in

192. Gaddis, "Defensive Perimeter," 84–85; Gaddis, *Long Peace*, 84.
193. Reeves, *McCarthy*, 356, 461; Purifoy, *Truman's China Policy*, 206–7.
194. Schaller, *American Occupation*, 250, 332n.7.
195. Ibid., 240–41.
196. Schoenbaum, *Waging Peace*, 199–201; Rusk, *As I Saw It*, 161.
197. Schaller, *American Occupation*, 252.
198. Hoopes, *Devil and John Foster Dulles*, 87.
199. Foot, *Wrong War*, 43.
200. Gaddis, "Defensive Perimeter," 86–87; Gaddis, *Long Peace*, 85.
201. Hoopes, *Devil and John Foster Dulles*, 88.

support of Hiss, party solidarity was further undermined.[202] Consequently a coalition of southern Democrats and Republicans might at any time jeopardize key pieces of foreign policy legislation. In the House, for example, Republicans voted six to one to defeat Truman's economic aid package for Korea; Democrats voted only three to one in favor. Owing to southern Democratic defections, the bill was defeated.[203] A similar coalition managed to cut 10 percent from the European aid bill.[204] Obviously the full support of internationalist Republicans like Vandenberg and Dulles would be increasingly needed to keep the Truman program intact.

By the end of May, Dulles and Rusk felt strong enough to try to force a change in China policy on an unwilling Acheson. First, Dulles prepared a domino theory justification for defending Taiwan, to be forwarded to Acheson under Rusk's signature. Even before carrying this task through, Rusk signed an agreement with General John Burns, an aide to Johnson, to give maximum aid to the Nationalist Chinese within "existing United States policy," which of course was *not* to give such aid.[205] Just before the Korean attack, Dulles held a press conference with MacArthur where he said that the administration's foreign policies were "constantly under review, taking account of changing situations. This generality applies to Formosa also."[206] Meanwhile the China lobby senators continued to play their role. After the North Korean attack, but before the completion of the Blair House conferences, Republican senators were already attacking the Truman adminstration as appeasers.[207] In this political context, pressure from Rusk, Dulles, Johnson, and their Republican senatorial backers was making some change on Taiwan policy inevitable. Acheson merely decided to preempt the inevitable in order to implement it in the least damaging way—a two-way blockade that would leash Chiang as well as protect him.[208]

Historians are less willing to conclude that this domestic political background decided the outcome of the Blair House decisions on Korea. Walter Lippmann, however, wrote in his newspaper column that it had: Acheson's "real views could not command general support

202. Westerfield, *Foreign Policy*, 109–10.
203. Ibid., 366.
204. Ibid., 379.
205. Schaller, *American Occupation*, 261. Nancy Tucker argues that Dulles and Rusk were collaborating on a plan to remove Chiang and make Taiwan a United Nations trust territory, but that Acheson demurred. See Nancy Tucker, "John Foster Dulles and the Taiwan Roots of the 'Two Chinas' Policy," in Immerman, *Dulles*, 237, and Tucker, *Patterns in the Dust*, 187.
206. Hoopes, *Devil and John Foster Dulles*, 96.
207. Glenn D. Paige, *The Korean Decision* (New York, 1968), 151–54.
208. Foot, *Wrong War*, 66; Mayers, *Cracking the Monolith*, 82; *FRUS*, 1950, 6:391, 396.

in Congress," Lippmann claimed, implying that Acheson's changed policy and "his refusal to debate the great issues" were due to political expediency.[209] Still, there is no smoking gun in the archives to prove this. Such direct evidence appears only at later stages on the Korean intervention.

For example, Truman's December 1950 interview with British Prime Minister Clement Attlee is revealing in this regard. Attlee was trying to press Truman into negotiations with the Communist Chinese, leading to diplomatic recognition and a settlement of the Korean War, in order to head off the risk of escalation and of getting bogged down in a strategically disadvantageous conflict. Truman and Acheson tried out a series of strategic arguments, prominently featuring domino and bandwagon theories, to explain why this would be a bad idea. Finally, in evident frustration at Attlee's obtuseness, Truman blurted out that recognizing the People's Republic was out of the question because it would be "quite a political issue" in the United States. Acheson admitted that the American people would not accept a rapprochement with Communist China for at least another ten years.[210]

THE COLD WAR CONSENSUS

The Europe-first/Asia-first logroll that Dulles and Rusk cobbled together in the spring of 1950 lived on as the globalist Cold War consensus. Eisenhower made it one element in what some have called his consensual, "corporatist" governing style.[211] Though using the language of globalism and sometimes adopting its substance, he and Dulles succeeded in implementing the Cold War consensus in a fashion that avoided egregious strategic overextension. By the 1960s, however,

---

209. Steel, *Lippmann*, 474. Schaller, *American Occupation*, 281–82, speculates that Acheson was influenced by the attacks on him by Secretary of Defense Johnson and the McCarthyites. On Johnson's plotting, see Cohen, *Rusk*, 45; see also Koo conversation with Johnson aide Paul Griffith, 3 June 1950, Wellington Koo papers, Columbia University, box 180, document 95/50, p. 5. Johnson himself was later fired for such machinations. See McLellan, *Acheson*, 285.

210. This account draws on an interpretation by Christensen, "Strategies," 34–38, and also Mayers, *Cracking the Monolith*, 93. For Truman's remark as paraphrased in the official minutes of the meeting, see *FRUS*, Western Europe, 5 December 1950, 3:1733.

211. Robert Griffith, "Dwight D. Eisenhower and the Corporate Commonwealth," *American Historical Review* 87 (February 1982): 87–122; Richard Melanson, "The Foundations of Eisenhower's Foreign Policy: Continuity, Community, and Consensus," in Melanson and Mayers, *Reevaluating Eisenhower*, 31–66; Ambrose, *Nixon*, 512. Eisenhower's coalition strategy might also be likened to Palmerston's—governing with the help of liberal Democrats in foreign affairs and conservative Republicans and southerners in domestic matters. See James Sundquist, *Politics and Policy* (Washington, D.C., 1968), 422; Stephen Ambrose, *Eisenhower*, 2 vols. (New York, 1983–84), 1:489.

the new generation of true believing cold warriors who replaced them, inheritors of a decade of rhetorical blowback, proved unable to match their flexibility.

Eisenhower and Dulles stressed a Europe-first internationalism in the 1952 campaign, but they also pandered to the "primitives" by promising liberation of Eastern Europe and by failing to condemn McCarthy's slanders of Eisenhower's mentor, George Marshall.[212] Vice presidential candidate Richard Nixon proved crucial in bridging the gap with Taft's disappointed supporters, though Eisenhower's East Coast establishment advisers cringed at Nixon's foreign policy rhetoric.[213]

Once in office, Eisenhower continued the strategy of appeasing the Republican Old Guard on military, Asian, and domestic security issues in order to gain their support for Europe-first internationalism. In the area of grand strategy, the Solarium study sketched out three alternative approaches: Kennan-style containment, Taft-style massive nuclear retaliation, and Dulles-style liberation rhetoric and ideological warfare.[214] These three strategies were tacked together as the New Look, and Admiral Arthur Radford was named chairman of the Joint Chiefs to oversee it. According to one "confidential" source, Radford was picked to please Taft.[215] One problem with this strategic amalgamation was that Kennan's containment idea stressed the need for negotiation once the Soviets saw they could get nowhere by force. But Dulles's "massive retaliation" speech, the striving for ever greater nuclear superiority that went along with it, and the talk of liberation undercut the position of those Soviets who wanted détente.[216]

In Asia, Eisenhower "unleashed" Chiang by withdrawing the fleet from the Taiwan Straits, a move that allowed the Nationalist Chinese to build up their forces on the offshore islands, provoking a crisis in which Eisenhower resorted to nuclear threats.[217] In the midst of this

212. Robert F. Burk, *Dwight D. Eisenhower* (Boston, 1986), 121–25; Paige, *Korean Decision*, 197–201; Caridi, *Korean War*; Divine, *Foreign Policy*, chaps. 1 and 2.

213. Ambrose, *Nixon*, 265 and passim.

214. Reports to the National Security Council by Task Forces A, B, and C of Project Solarium, Washington, D.C., 16 July 1953.

215. Herbert Parmet, *Eisenhower and the American Crusades* (New York, 1972), 296. See also Douglas Kinnard, *President Eisenhower and Strategy Management* (Lexington, Ky., 1977), 3–4; Melvin Gurtov, *The First Vietnam Crisis: Chinese Communist Strategy and United States Involvement, 1953–1954* (New York, 1967), 53; Robert Divine, *Eisenhower and the Cold War* (New York, 1981), 34–37; Ambrose, *Eisenhower*, 2:33. Taft reportedly prevented Nitze from obtaining a Defense Department post under Eisenhower. See Strobe Talbott, *The Master of the Game: Paul Nitze and the Nuclear Peace*, Vintage ed. (New York, 1989), 62.

216. Solarium A, 131–32; Herbert Dinerstein, *War and the Soviet Union* (New York, 1959), chap. 4.

217. Ambrose, *Eisenhower*, 2:47; Gordon Chang, "To the Nuclear Brink: Eisenhower, Dulles, and the Quemoy-Matsu Crisis," 96–123, and H. W. Brands, "Testing Massive Retaliation: Credibility and Crisis Management in the Taiwan Strait," 124–51, both in *International Security* 12 (Spring 1988).

crisis, Eisenhower wrote to his NATO commander, Alfred Gruenther, that "at home, we have the truculent and the timid, the jingoists and the pacifists." In making decisions about the Taiwan problem, Eisenhower wrote that he was considering "what solutions we can get that will best conform to the long term interests of the country and at the same time *can command a sufficient approval in this country so as to secure the necessary Congressional action.*"[218]

Likewise, during the encirclement of Dienbienphu Eisenhower told his cabinet that he could not afford to let the Democrats ask who lost Vietnam.[219] But he saw a host of disadvantages to intervening, including the reputational costs of fighting and then losing, as well as the opprobrium that would come from using nuclear weapons.[220] In his handling of the crisis, Eisenhower used the domino theory to create support for aid to the remaining "healthy parts" of Indochina. But at the same time he consulted with Congress and the allies in a way that placed on them the onus of avoiding an unpopular land war in Asia.[221]

Finally, on domestic security issues Eisenhower refrained from confronting McCarthy head-on. Dulles also bowed to the security hysteria by firing loyal, experienced Foreign Service officers.[222]

This strategy for co-opting the Republican unilateralists was both necessary and effective. At the beginning of the Eighty-third Congress Republicans were typically hostile to military and other aid to Europe. To prevent a new "Yalta," most of them favored the Bricker amendment to the Constitution, which would have forced executive agreements to be ratified like treaties. A modified version of Bricker lost by only one vote.[223] Though Eisenhower continued to suffer cuts in his foreign aid requests, the strategy of co-opting the Republican right nonetheless paid off. A quantitative study of roll call votes shows that by the end of the Eighty-third Congress, Eisenhower had won a

218. Fred Greenstein, *The Hidden-Hand Presidency* (New York, 1982), 24, Eisenhower's original emphasis. For more on the domestic political considerations behind Dulles's Taiwan policy, see Ronald Pruessen, "John Foster Dulles and the Predicaments of Power," 21–46, esp. 28–31, and Richard Immerman, "Conclusion," 267, 269, both in Immerman, *Dulles*.

219. Ambrose, *Eisenhower*, 2:173.

220. Divine, *Eisenhower*, 49; for a related point about Eisenhower's strategy in Korea, see Ambrose, *Eisenhower*, 2:34–35.

221. Richard Immerman, "Eisenhower and Dienbienphu," in Melanson and Mayers, *Reevaluating Eisenhower*, 120–54; Burke and Greenstein, *How Presidents Test Reality*, chap. 4, p. 38, chap. 5, p. 23; Ambrose, *Eisenhower*, 2:177; Fred Greenstein, "Dwight D. Eisenhower," in Fred Greenstein, ed., *Leadership in the Modern Presidency* (Cambridge, Mass., 1988), 88, 107.

222. Greenstein, *Hidden-Hand Presidency*, chap. 5; Griffith, "Eisenhower," 114–15.

223. Burk, *Eisenhower*, 129; Phillip Henderson, *Managing the Presidency* (Boulder, Colo., 1988), 41–50.

number of converts to Europe-first internationalism among this group.[224]

This came at a cost, however. To appease McCarthyite, Asia-first Republicans, Eisenhower and Dulles had to continue with exaggerated Cold War rhetoric, which made it difficult to distance themselves from even worse outbursts by Nixon. Eisenhower's domino theory statements about Vietnam, for example, provoked Nixon to say that America had better "face up to it" that military intervention would probably be needed. Eisenhower tried to make the best of it, remarking privately that at least it would keep the Communists guessing.[225]

In the long run, however, the price for this was heavy. In the 1960 election debates on Quemoy and Matsu, the press and the public, conditioned by a decade of strategic mythmaking, were more persuaded by Nixon's domino/Munich/Yalta litany than by Kennedy's limited liability realpolitik.[226] By the end of his tenure in office, says biographer Stephen Ambrose, Eisenhower came to believe that aggressive Cold War fever had been artificially manufactured by politicians like Stuart Symington, arms manufacturers, Pentagon missile gap exaggerators, and the like.[227] He failed to recognize, however, the extent to which his own administration's rhetoric had legitimized this fever, creating a political consensus in which frank criticism of Cold War views was seen as illegitimate.

Eisenhower may even have been a victim of mythological blowback himself. In a taped conversation with Nixon, for example, he asserted that "the reason we lost China . . . was because [Marshall] had insisted upon Chiang Kai-shek taking Communists into his government."[228] And in his last days in office, he lectured the incoming Kennedy administration people about the dangers of falling dominoes in Southeast Asia.[229]

VIETNAM

America's military escalation in Vietnam was justified largely in terms of the underexamined domino theory. Government strategists exaggerated the probability of success only a little.[230] Rather, they

---

224. Gary Reichard, *The Reaffirmation of Republicanism: Eisenhower and the Eighty-third Congress* (Knoxville, Tenn., 1975), 96.

225. Ambrose, *Eisenhower*, 2:180–81.

226. Divine, *Elections*, 260–66.

227. Ambrose, *Eisenhower*, 2:513–18.

228. Ibid., 2:202.

229. Berman, *Planning a Tragedy*, 16–17.

230. Leslie Gelb and Richard Betts, *The Irony of Vietnam* (Washington, D.C., 1979), chap. 11; Ellsberg, *Papers on the War*, 49–71; Herring, *America's Longest War*, 178; Kahin, *Intervention*, 357.

justified intervention by overstating the costs of withdrawal.[231] Can the politics of the Cold War consensus account for this outcome?

Daniel Ellsberg has contended that this approach was indeed the decisive factor. He argues that domestic politics created a "stalemate machine" whereby no president could risk either the political repercussions of losing Vietnam to communism or the risk of provoking Chinese intervention by taking the war decisively to the North. In his view the domino theory was, in Vietnam and earlier, a mere rationalization for policies that had to be adopted for political reasons.

Though Ellsberg's argument is exaggerated, subsequent historians have in fact uncovered evidence that the prospect of domestic criticism for abandoning Vietnam was discussed among Kennedy and Johnson administration officials. As early as November 1961, a Rusk-McNamara memo warned that the fall of South Vietnam would "stimulate bitter domestic controversies in the United States and would be seized upon to divide the country and harass the Administration."[232] Lyndon Johnson told Doris Kearns of his fear of a "mean and destructive debate." "There would be Robert Kennedy out in front leading the fight against me, telling everyone that I had betrayed John Kennedy's commitment to South Vietnam."[233] Both John Kennedy and Johnson have been quoted as saying that they thought the loss of Vietnam would bring a revival of McCarthyism in America.[234] On the eve of the crucial 1965 escalation decisions, McGeorge Bundy told Johnson that "even if it fails, the policy will be worth it. At a minimum it will damp down the charge that we did not do all that we could have done, and this charge will be important in many countries, including our own."[235]

Yet Bundy also gave Johnson an excellent summary of the kinds of attacks he would suffer if he *did* escalate.[236] "I knew from the start I was bound to be crucified either way I moved," Johnson told Kearns.[237] Why then did Johnson run the political risks of escalation rather than the risks of withdrawal? Bundy's assessment was that the "Goldwater crowd," who would slam him if he pulled out, were "more numerous, more powerful and more dangerous than the fleabite professors" who would attack him if he stayed in.[238]

---

231. For domino quotes, Kahin, *Intervention*, 191–92, 352, 376–78, 383.

232. Ibid., 138.

233. Doris Kearns, *Lyndon Johnson and the American Dream* (New York, 1976), 252–53; see also Kathleen J. Turner, *Lyndon Johnson's Dual War* (Chicago, 1985), 83, 270n.53; Berman, *Planning a Tragedy*, 22–23, 94; Gelb and Betts, *Irony of Vietnam*, 221; Kahin, *Intervention*, 214.

234. Kearns, *Johnson*, 282; Kahin, *Intervention*, 147.

235. Ellsberg, *Papers on the War*, 91, citing *The Senator Gravel Edition: Pentagon Papers* (Boston, 1971), 3:690.

236. Kahin, *Intervention*, 386.

237. Kearns, *Johnson*, 251.

238. Herring, *America's Longest War*, 141–42, quoting McGeorge Bundy to Johnson, 14 July 1965.

John Burke and Fred Greenstein have contested this judgment. They make a powerful case that Johnson could have extricated himself from Vietnam after his landslide victory over Barry Goldwater without suffering great domestic damage. Public opinion polls were not unambiguously pro-war, southern conservatives in Congress were wary of escalation, and journalistic opinion was mixed.[239]

If Burke and Greenstein are right, the domestic political "stalemate machine" was only a very loose constraint on Johnson's policy in Vietnam. There is clear evidence, however, that a related domestic consideration did affect Johnson's decison for gradual escalation: Johnson believed that any disruptive debate on the war—over ending it or escalating it abruptly—would kill "the woman I really loved—the Great Society."[240] This point is definitively established as regards abrupt escalation. Cyrus Vance cabled to McNamara on 17 July 1965 that Johnson believed a large supplemental appropriation for Vietnam "will kill [his] domestic legislative program."[241] Bundy recalled that Johnson wanted to avoid a reserve call-up so that it would "not derail his legislative calendar."[242] A broad consensus of historians believes that Johnson's preoccupation with the Great Society led him to do the minimum not to lose the war, in order to postpone attacks from both hawks and doves until the domestic program had passed.[243]

Once this gradual trajectory of escalation was established, the habits and practices of the Cold War consensus helped keep public debate to a minimum. Senator William Fulbright agreed to push through the Tonkin Gulf resolution and deflect questions about the details of the incident, because he saw it as necessary to defuse the Goldwater threat.[244] Richard Russell, Johnson's mentor and a skeptic about escalation, agreed not to criticize the decision to introduce large numbers of ground forces once American prestige was already committed.[245] The media also held back at first. The government convinced the National Broadcasting Company, for example, not to air clips of rough treatment of Vietcong prisoners by the South Vietnamese army.[246] And the U.S. Army in Vietnam had every incentive to aid the whitewash. As one

239. Burke and Greenstein, *How Presidents Test Reality*, 146–49, 167, 192–94. For similar arguments, see Kahin, *Intervention*, 147, 240, 284; Ellsberg, *Papers on the War*, 97.

240. Kearns, *Johnson*, 251.

241. Burke and Greenstein, *How Presidents Test Reality*, 214.

242. Berman, "Waiting for Smoking Guns," 17.

243. Ball, *Past*, 375; Kearns, *Johnson*, 298; Berman, *Planning a Tragedy*, 150–51; Kahin, *Intervention*, 320, 387, 394–98; Burke and Greenstein, *How Presidents Test Reality*, 248–54; Richard Betts, "Discussion," in Braestrup, *Vietnam as History*, 47; Gelb and Betts, *Irony of Vietnam*, 17, 201–26.

244. Herring, *America's Longest War*, 2d ed. (New York, 1985), 123; Kahin, *Intervention*, 219–25.

245. Burke and Greenstein, *How Presidents Test Reality*, 249.

246. Kahin, *Intervention*, 142.

division commander told an inexplicably honest junior officer reporting on the failure of the pacification program: "Son, you're writing your own report card in this country."[247]

But beyond the workings of the Cold War consensus, one also gets the sense that the people who decided to escalate the war in Vietnam were true believers in a simplistic version of the domino theory in a way that most of the early Cold War leaders were not. Eisenhower and Dulles had invoked the domino theory in the 1954 Vietnam crisis, but they had not let it trap them into an inflexible policy. In contrast, Johnson's advisers presented him with oversimplified, inexorable scenarios for cascading dominoes in Asia and Europe once South Vietnam fell.[248] Rare were suggestions like William Bundy's that the reputational consequences of losing Vietnam could be handled by pointing to "special local factors that do not apply to other nations we are committed to defend."[249]

CONCLUSIONS

The domino theory and other arguments for security through expansion underpinned the globalist containment strategy accepted by the American Cold War consensus. These strategic concepts arose at least in part out of the political competition between internationalist and nationalist elements of American society. Neither side favored unrestrained expansionism, but each used the rhetoric of global struggle against the Communist threat to promote its favorite projects and to attack its political enemies. This ideological competition was exacerbated by divisions within the Democratic and Republican parties, which created a cartelized structure of power in the Congress. Internationalist Republicans, serving as a pivot between internationalist Democrats and nationalist Republicans, forced Democratic internationalists to use anticommunist rhetoric to sell their program and to logroll with nationalist Republicans. Under these conditions, political entrepreneurs like Dulles and Eisenhower found it advantageous to use the rhetoric—and if necessary the policies—of global interventionism in order to govern effectively and to maintain support for essential European commitments. Likewise, these circumstances made it politically possible for true believing globalists like Rusk to rise to positions of great authority.

Historians disagree about how central domestic political dynamics were in globalizing American containment policy, though most agree

247. Ellsberg, *Papers on the War*, 117.
248. See, for example, Kahin, *Intervention*, 383, also 360; Burke and Greenstein, *How Presidents Test Reality*, 211–12.
249. Burke and Greenstein, *How Presidents Test Reality*, 142.

that such domestic factors played some role. My main aim in this chapter has been to put forward a more theoretically informed interpretation of how this domestic dynamic worked and what domestic political forces kept it in check.

As my theory of coalition politics would predict, America's democratic political system was able to learn to reevaluate its strategic myths and to retrench from its strategic overextension. The defeat in Vietnam broke the Cold War consensus, splitting the internationalist establishment down the middle.[250] As a result, the elite's mutual nonaggression pact was no longer observed. Strategic debate was more open, and public information more available. Under these conditions of open, democratic competition in foreign affairs, median voters have tended to punish presidents who deviate too far in either direction from a moderate policy of military strength and nonintervention abroad.[251] Thus the American case is consistent with my hypothesis that cartelized politics produces overextension, as in the Cold War consensus, whereas two-party electoral competition over foreign affairs, as in the post-Vietnam period, does not.

This more democratic foreign policy arena has created a strong deterrent to imperial overextension. For example, the Reagan administration sought to compete aggressively with the Soviet Union in the Third World, but it was politically constrained to compete in ways that kept the cost in American lives very low. Secretary of Defense Caspar Weinberger issued a list of very restrictive prerequisites for the use of U.S. forces abroad, stressing in particular the need for broad public support.[252] Given the fresh lessons of Vietnam in the mind of the American public, in practice this meant limiting the direct use of U.S. forces to quick, virtually bloodless operations like the invasion of the

250. See Schulzinger, *Wise Men*, chap. 8; Joan Hoff Wilson, "Richard M. Nixon," in Greenstein, *Leadership*, 164–65. For qualifications, see Ole Holsti and James Rosenau, *American Leadership in Foreign Affairs: Vietnam and the Breakdown of Consensus* (Boston, 1984), chaps. 2–3. Using evidence from elite surveys, they argue that the split on Vietnam had only a limited effect on other issues.

251. The most systematic statement of the case that electoral constraints have exerted a moderating effect on recent American foreign policy is Nincic, "United States, the Soviet Union, and the Politics of Opposites," 452–75. Page and Shapiro, *Rational Public*, chap. 1, note that the Vietnam War led to a "more politically attuned American voter." James Sundquist, *The Decline and Resurgence of Congress* (Washington, D.C., 1981), discusses Congress's more critical role as a result of the Vietnam War. Benajmin I. Page, *Choices and Echoes in Presidential Elections* (Chicago, 1978), 220, 282, passim, updates Anthony Downs's arguments about the moderating effects of democratic competition. Other analysts, however, have argued that the breakdown of elite consensus causes foreign policy to oscillate between extremes of dovish optimism and hawkish hysteria, according to the moods of public opinion. See, for example, Joseph Nye, "The Domestic Roots of American Policy," in Nye, *Making of America's Soviet Policy*, 1–10.

252. Caspar Weinberger, *Department of Defense Annual Report, Fiscal Year 1987* (Washington, D.C., 1986), 78–79.

island of Grenada. Consequently the "Reagan Doctrine" sought indirect means of intervention, especially proxy wars against new Soviet client states in the Third World.[253] When Congress placed limits even on indirect intervention in Nicaragua, the Reagan administration resorted to private and clandestine funding for the insurgent forces.

The Bush administration's war to eject Iraq from Kuwait does not necessarily signal a waning of democratic constraints on imperial overextension. Indeed, there was no overexpansion, no disproportion between strategic costs and benefits. Preventing Saddam Hussein from dominating half of the world's oil reserves was a vital national interest, and the economic cost of fighting was shared among several wealthy countries. The strategy of a prolonged air campaign before the start of the ground offensive took into account the public's desire to minimize casualties.

True, the sales pitch for the war included most of the myths of empire. Kuwait was portrayed as a crucial domino: if Iraq were allowed to retain it, Saddam would soon hold sway over the entire Arab world, which would join the Iraqi bandwagon in a holy war against Israel. Saddam was a paper tiger: easy to defeat now, but certain to grow stronger in the future. Benefits would be of El Dorado proportions because defeating Saddam would safeguard the "new world order." The costs of not fighting would be enormous, it was claimed, since other aggressors would be emboldened.[254]

But experts and political figures critically evaluated these assertions in widely publicized debates. Congress and the public had a much fuller airing of diverse views and pertinent evidence before the Gulf War than they had before Congress voted on the Gulf of Tonkin resolution, for example. The use of the myths of empire to justify the Gulf War shows that democratic scrutiny of strategic assertions is still needed. The fact that after such scrutiny Congress voted for war does not necesarily mean that democratic oversight was a failure.

253. Stephen Van Evera, "The Case against Intervention," *Atlantic* 266 (July 1990): 72–80, shows that the costs of these proxy wars were very high for Third World societies, even though they were low for the United States.

254. For example, George Bush, "Text of the Radio Address by the President," *New York Times*, 6 January 1991; also, Congressional debates on 11 and 12 January 1991.

[8]

Overexpansion:
Origins and Antidotes

All the nations examined in this book exhibited a tendency toward overexpansion, in the sense of provoking self-encirclement by their belligerent behavior, blundering into quagmires on the periphery, or both. These cases include all the industrialized great powers except France, covering the periods of their greatest relative power and imperial activism.[1] The tendency toward overexpansion varies greatly, however, both across cases and over time.

The Pattern of Outcomes

Germany and Japan were most inclined toward disastrous overexpansion; Britain, the Soviet Union, and the United States were less so. When Germany and Japan encountered resistance, they usually took this as a signal to redouble their efforts to achieve security through expansion. When the other states met resistance they typically retrenched, attempting to defuse mounting opposition by offering concessions to their opponents.

Even the worst of the overexpansionist states went through periods where this impulse was kept under control however. Germany was least inclined toward overexpansion under Bismarck and during the Weimar period. Japan was least inclined toward overexpansion under the Meiji *genro* in the late nineteenth and early twentieth centuries and during the Taisho period of the 1920s. Conversely, even the states that were less self-destructive occasionally flirted with overextension. For Britain, in the periods I examined, this included certain interludes in

1. See chapter 2 for a discussion of case selection criteria.

the Palmerstonian period and the scramble for Africa in the 1890s. For the Soviet Union it included the militant period between 1947 and 1950, the period of Khrushchev's missile diplomacy from 1958 to 1962, and Brezhnev's overextension in the Third World. For the United States, incidents of overexpansion occurred during the period of the Cold War consensus, from the Korean War through the Vietnam War.

STRATEGIC CONCEPTS

All the states justified their policies through a recurring set of arguments for security through expansion. These included the domino theory, its Thermopylae corollary, paper tiger images of the adversary, bandwagon and big stick theories of alliance formation, belief in offensive advantages, perception of windows of opportunity for preventive action, and El Dorado arguments about the benefits of conquest. The prevalence of such ideas correlated closely with the inclination toward overexpansion. Such ideas were most common, most extreme, and least tempered by openness to contradictory evidence in Germany and Japan, and during the periods of greatest overextension in the other countries.

The very structure of these ideas suggests they were ex post facto justifications for policy and elements of a strategic ideology rather than mere beliefs or perceptions. In many cases the concepts underlying the policy of security through expansion came close to self-contradiction. Opponents were seen as unappeasably aggressive, yet somehow inert in resisting aggressive measures to contain their expansion. In other cases decision makers used analytical double standards to support their conclusions or argued from opposite premises to support the same conclusion. Frequently they failed to search systematically for relevant information, and they punished people who discovered disconfirming evidence. These pathologies of logic and information processing were worst in the cases and periods of greatest overexpansion.

POSITION IN THE INTERNATIONAL SYSTEM

The tendency toward overexpansion correlated at least roughly with each state's position in the international system. Of the five powers, Germany and Japan were the least buffered by size, geographical location, or resource endowments from the dangers of international anarchy. Consequently they had the most to gain by attempting to expand to a position of economic and military self-sufficiency.

[306]

Likewise, changes in a state's international position over time often correlated with its inclination to overexpand. Germany and Japan had relatively moderate foreign policies in the relatively benign international economic and security environment of the mid-1920s, though German weakness also helps explain this. Both turned to expansionism in the wake of the world depression and protectionism at the end of the 1920s, which increased their incentives to use military power and make a grab for autarky. Wilhelmine expansionism, however, had no similar international trigger. Germany in that period was increasingly prosperous and secure in the prevailing international order until belligerent German diplomacy gratuitously provoked an encircling alliance.

One of the worst periods of Soviet and American overexpansion coincided with the time of fluid global power relations in the late 1940s. In this period the postwar power vacuum in Europe, the rise of revolutionary movements in Asia, and significant fluctuations in the nuclear balance created an environment that spurred domino fears and worries about windows of vulnerability.

Thus, in several cases a state's position in the international system correlated roughly with its propensity to overexpand. The tighter the state's security dilemma, the more likely it was to adopt a strategy of expansion. The more vulnerable it was economically, the greater was its urge to run risks to achieve autarky. The more fluid the power situation it faced, the more it acted on the assumption of falling dominoes, bandwagons, and military first-strike advantages.

Consequently the international explanation might be seen as passing a relatively undemanding test: in most of the cases, the policy adopted had some minimally plausible relation to the prevailing international conditions. The international explanation would fail more demanding tests, however. Were international conditions in themselves *sufficient* to explain the outcome? Was the expansionist policy the best available option under those conditions? Even more stringently, was that policy compelled by the international circumstances facing the state?

Judged against this standard, in no case can the adoption of a strategy of security through expansion be explained by the international conditions facing the state. As I argued above, Germany and Japan were not doing badly in security or economic terms by the mid-1930s. Moreover, Germany was doing very well in the years before World War I. Similarly, militancy and belligerency have always been inappropriate and counterproductive ways for the Soviets to mitigate their security problems. Fighting in Korea had questionable value for promoting American security, and Vietnam was counterproductive. Britain's aggressive role in the scramble for Africa left it less secure, and Palmerston's inclination to expand the Crimean War would have done so had he had free rein to act on it. In all these cases the economic and security interests of the state would have been better secured by retrenchment, selective appeasement, shoring up vital rather than peripheral areas, or simply benign neglect. Manageable economic or security problems were invariably made worse by militant, expansionist policies that provoked sharp international resistance.

COGNITIVE EXPLANATIONS

Cognitive theory might offer a variety of explanations for the belief in security through expansion. In the case studies I have carried out a fairly systematic test of one cognitive explanation—that strategic ideas are rooted in intellectually formative lessons. I found remarkably little support for this explanation. Typically, lessons of the past were invoked as rationalizations to advocate policies preferred on other grounds. People drew different lessons from similar experiences if their interests were different. They switched their preferred historical analogies when their policy preferences changed.

I do not claim that in all cases these findings decisively refute cognitive theory as an explanation for strategic beliefs. Sometimes ingrained lessons from formative experiences are unquestionably important. For example, the lessons of the trench stalemate in the First World War had a powerful impact on European military doctrine in the interwar period, counteracting emerging offensive technological possibilities and the usual offensive proclivities of military organizations. Moreover, I have not attempted systematic tests of a host of other cognitive hypotheses about strategic perceptions. Nor have I eliminated the possibility that certain cognitive biases—attribution errors, for example—create a weak but widespread predisposition to overexpand, which interacts with geopolitical or domestic political variables in triggering specific instances of overexpansion. Nonetheless, my cases suggest that cognitive explanations for the belief in security through expansion should be approached critically.

DOMESTIC COALITION POLITICS

For the most part, the coalition politics theory passed both cross sectional and time series tests. Cartelized political systems like Germany and Japan were the most recklessly overexpansionist; democratic systems and systems ruled by unitary oligarchies were less so. Each of the countries was most expansionist when it was most cartelized; it was less so when it was more unitary or democratic. One period deviates from this pattern; two others are questionable.

The obvious deviant is Hitler's Germany, a comparatively unitary political system that was extreme in its expansionism. Nonetheless, this case does not falsify the coalition politics theory for two reasons. First, as I argued in chapter 2, unitary systems ruled by a single individual lack the political checks that are characteristic of systems ruled by unitary oligarchies. The coalition politics theory does not necessarily predict that individual dictators will always overexpand, but it is not falsified if they do.

Second, in accord with most recent historians, I argue that Hitler internalized the geopolitical concepts that had become common currency in German strategic discourse as a result of the mythmaking of the cartelized Wilhelmine period. In this way the coalition theory, in amended form, can explain the Hitler period. It would obviously be even better for the coalition theory if one could argue that strategic myths helped Hitler come to power or stay in power. Some historians have tried this argument, but most do not find it fully convincing.

Another possibly deviant case is Stalin's aggressively militant policy between 1947 and 1950, a period of rule by an individual dictator. Thus, a unitary period produced the same overexpansionist outcome as did the later cartelized periods under Khrushchev and Brezhnev. Conversely, this unitary period produced a different outcome from the unitary but generally nonexpansionist interwar period. Though this pattern of outcomes is awkward for the coalition politics theory, it does not clearly refute that theory, for two reasons.

First, as in Hitler's case, the theory makes no hard predictions about individual dictatorships, so such cases are not decisive for the theory. Second, a number of scholars have argued that internal political needs strongly shaped Stalin's foreign and domestic policy in this period. He needed a tense, two-camp international environment to help consolidate Soviet power in Eastern Europe and reconsolidate the Soviet Union itself after the political relaxation of the war years. Part of Stalin's aim, in this view, was to divide and stymie institutionally based social groups, which became logrolling cartels after his death. Thus a variant of the cartelization argument might help explain Soviet overexpansion in the late 1940s.

Finally, the American case embodies a weaker variant of the domestic coalitions theory. Unlike the other cartelized cases, I do not claim that American politics as a whole became more cartelized during periods of global overexpansion, but only that policy-making on some foreign policy issues was affected by logrolling among cartels. This qualification notwithstanding, the case fits the coalition politics theory well:

America was inclined toward overexpansion while the logrolled Cold War elite consensus lasted; it was anti-interventionist in the more democratic period that followed the breakup of that consensus.

In the case studies and in these conclusions, I have often labeled each country or period as simply cartelized, unitary, or democratic. It should be obvious, however, that most political systems are hybrids, embodying different mixes of these three types. For example, Gladstonian Britain combined strong unitary elements (an oligarchy with diffuse interests) and strong democratic elements. In contrast, Brezhnevite Russia combined strong unitary elements (the Politburo oligarchy) and strong cartels. Gorbachev from 1987 to 1990 tried to create a more Gladstonian constellation of power, using pressure by unitary forces from above and democratic forces from below to reform the recalcitrant cartels. In Taisho Japan, unitary (*genro*), cartel, and democratic elements were all present to a significant degree.

For these various hybrids, different patterns of overexpansion are predicted. When cartels are weak but unitary and democratic forces are both strong, overexpansion should be minimal. When strong cartels are combined with strong unitary forces, overexpansion may occur, but it should be tempered by the restraining effect of the unitary elements, which can broker and control the ill effects of cartel logrolling. When strong cartels combine with strong democratic pressures but there is no significant unitary element, the result is less clear. On one hand, democratic forces might be expected to restrain the worst excesses of cartel logrolling. On the other hand, cartel mythmakers might find fertile ground among the masses, making things even worse. As the Wilhelmine case shows, elite interest groups may even compete among themselves in using strategic ideologies to recruit mass allies.

My hypothesis is that the outcome depends on the balance of power between the cartelized and democratic forces. If the forces of cartelization face a well-institutionalized electoral democracy with open public debate and multiple sources of strategic information, then democracy will act as a check on the cartels' inclination toward overexpansion. This is the American pattern. If strong cartels face a situation of weakly institutionalized democracy and truncated debate, however, then increasing mass participation will exacerbate the cartels' tendency toward overexpansion, because selling strategic ideology to the masses will probably produce blowback effects that constrain the elite mythmakers themselves. This is the Wilhelmine pattern. It is also a current danger in the Soviet Union and Eastern Europe, where mass participation in politics is increasing rapidly and democratic institutions are not fully formed.[2]

2. See Jack Snyder, "Averting Anarchy in the New Europe," *International Security* 14 (Spring 1990): 5–41.

In contrast, if democratization occurs under a relatively unitary system in which the leadership favors imperial restraint, then increasing political participation should do no harm. Strategic myths will be neither excessively manufactured nor excessively consumed. This is the Gladstonian case. It is also the likely outcome if Gorbachev succeeds in institutionalizing his democratic reform program.

Table 3 summarizes the tests of the domestic structure hypothesis and their results. The "overall" characterization is based on a comparison with other states. The characterization of different periods is a based on a comparison with other periods in the development of the same country. For example, when I say that Taisho Japan is "more democratic," I mean compared with Meiji Japan or the Japan of the 1930s, *not* compared with other countries in the 1920s.

Table 3. Tests of the coalition politics theory

Country and period	Domestic structure	Outcome
Germany		
Overall	Cartelized	Overexpansion
Bismarck	More unitary	More moderate
Wilhelmine	Cartelized	Overexpansion
Weimar	More democratic	Moderate
Hitler	Unitary dictator	Overexpansion
Japan		
Overall	Cartelized	Overexpansion
Meiji	More unitary	More moderate
Taisho	More democratic	More moderate
1930s	Cartelized	Overexpansion
Britain		
Overall	Unitary oligarchy/ democratic	Moderate
Palmerston	More cartelized	More overexpansion
Gladstone	More democratic	Moderate
Unionist coalition	More cartelized	More overexpansion
Soviet Union		
Overall	Unitary	Moderate
1930s	Unitary dictator	Moderate
1947–50	Unitary dictator	More overexpansion
1953–85	More cartelized	More overexpansion
Gorbachev	More unitary/democratic	Moderate
United States		
Overall	Democratic	Moderate
Cold War	More cartelized	More overexpansion
Post-Vietnam	More democratic	Moderate

Variants of the Domestic Explanation

In chapter 2 several variants of the domestic argument were advanced, stemming from the logical deduction that narrow interest groups normally lack the power to hijack state policy to their parochial, overexpansionist ends. Conversely, encompassing groups like the state and the ruling class would have the power but normally lack the motive. Thus the variants differ in the mechanism whereby parochial interests hijack state policy. One variant stresses the role of strategic ideologies propagated by individual groups. Another stresses logrolling. The most inclusive variant posits a role for the ideologies of separate groups, for logrolling processes, and for the ideologies propagated by political entrepreneurs managing logrolled coalitions.

Though the simpler, less inclusive variants can explain some aspects of some of the cases, the most inclusive variant is needed to explain most of the outcomes. In several cases the overexpansion extended far beyond what any single group would have individually preferred. Ideology and logrolling explain these unintended consequences. The cases strongly support the logical deduction that individual groups, without exploiting ideology, will lack either the power or the motive to hijack state policy for self-interested overexpansion. The only partial exception was the Kwantung army's fait accompli in Manchuria. In this instance a narrow, parochial group simply acted on its own authority and dared its superiors to renounce the action. But to sustain the policy of imperial expansion, the Japanese army propagated an ideology of security and prosperity through expansion and entered into a logrolling arrangement with the navy.

All the cases included instances when individual groups used strategic ideology to sell parochial programs. Often this hinged on monopolies of information or expertise, but advantages in organizing and paying for publicity were also factors. Examples include the overselling of the Russian threat by British Near East specialists and Tirpitz's selling of the battle fleet through the Navy League.

In none of the cases was this the whole story, however. When a single interest group's overcommitted policies started to get the country into trouble, its strategic ideology inevitably came under intense scrutiny from other groups in society. The outcome of that scrutiny seems to have hinged more on broad political constellations than on the individual group's power or persuasiveness. Democracies and unitary systems tended to pull misbehaving cartels into line, whereas logrolled systems tended to make excuses (coalition ideologies) to cover up the real causes of disastrous policies.

In the British case, for example, the interventionists' strategic ideology helped get Britain into an Afghan war at the end of the 1830s, but the obvious failure of their strategic program led to its termination after an open parliamentary debate. Conversely, in the German case Bulow was fired for recognizing that the Tirpitz battle fleet was provoking Britain and that the Junkers had to be taxed to pay for the arms race on land and sea. In his stead, Bethmann propounded the comforting idea of "risk diplomacy," through which Germany could expand and neutralize its enemies without actually fighting.

In short, cartelized political systems build a Rube Goldberg contraption of strategic justifications to keep the logroll alive. Noncartelized systems seek out and destroy the strategic myths propagated by individual interest groups once they have independent means for evaluating those myths.[3]

Further evidence supporting the key role of coalition dynamics is that coalition managers were often among the most expansionist figures in their countries. This applies most clearly to Palmerston, Khrushchev, and "the best and the brightest" who managed America's Cold War consensus. Separate groups wanted expansion only on a particular front, but the coalition managers were placed in a position where they had to accept it on every front. Indeed, they gained their positions by devising schemes that purported to reconcile all the conflicting imperial programs.

Coalition managers have crafted their political alliances in one of two ways. The first is the straight logroll. In this process, each major group in the ruling coalition gets what it wants on the issue it cares about most. The clearest examples are the Wilhelmine iron-rye-army-navy coalition, Brezhnev's ideologue-army-détente coalition, and the Japanese army-navy logroll.

A second approach is the creative straddle. In this process, the political entrepreneur comes upon a stalemated political system in which no stable coalition seems possible owing to the sharp differences among all the groups. Even a straight logroll seems impossible because things that one group wants strongly are strongly opposed by other groups. To square this circle, political entrepreneurs engage in one form or another of prestidigitation. They may, for example, use ideological appeals to change the preferences of individual groups, making them available for more feasible logrolls. Thus Palmerston convinced middle-class Britons that imperialism was a "liberal" activity and so was able to logroll their support for imperialism with Tory support for the domestic status quo. Alternatively, political entrepreneurs may

---

3. On strategic evaluation in this context, the seminal work is Stephen Van Evera, "Causes of War" (Ph.D. diss., University of California at Berkeley, 1984), chap. 10.

come up with a creative synthesis that purports to solve everyone's problems simultaneously, in a way no single group had conceived. The best example would be Khrushchev's attempt to use the ICBM and other policy innovations to satisfy or rebut everyone's concerns. Some historians also describe Hitler's role in this fashion. In such cases coalition leaders may wind up pursuing foreign adventures that literally no member of their coalition would have initially preferred, in order to validate their strategic vision. Some scholars argue that Khrushchev's Berlin crisis of 1958 emerged in this way.

The American Cold War consensus falls somewhere between the straight logroll and the creative straddle. On one hand, Europe-first and Asia-first figures reconciled their differences through a backscratching alliance, as in logrolling. On the other hand, the element of prestidigitation was much stronger in this case than the element of straightforward group interest. Many Republican Asia-firsters merely pretended to care about Chiang for tactical political purposes. Internationalist coalition managers appeased this pretended interest in order to neutralize this tactical advantage. Eisenhower's strategy of governing through a pseudoliberal globalist alliance on foreign policy and a Republican–southern Democrat alliance on domestic policy is strongly reminiscent of Palmerston's method.

This raises a final point: simple logrolling does not explain most of these cases without resort to ideology. In some cases ideology was so integral to the political process that it played a central role in determining what the individual "interest groups" wanted. This happened, for example, with mid-Victorian middle-class imperialists and with post-1945 Republican Asia-firsters. Economic or other tangible interests were less relevant to these groups' preferences than were ideological interests in liberal imperialism in the former case and anticommunism in the latter.

Sometimes ideological dynamics merely exaggerated the outcome of interest group logrolling and made it harder to reverse. But in other instances ideological blowback outlived the political circumstances that gave rise to the strategic ideologies. In this case, without reference to ideology there is no explanation at all. Hitler's Germany is the clearest instance of this; America in Vietnam is a partial example.

DETERMINANTS OF THE DEGREE OF CARTELIZATION

The industrialization process was the major factor affecting the degree of cartelization of politics in four of my five cases. Comparing across the countries, late industrializing Germany and Japan were more cartelized than early industrializing Britain or late, late industrializing Russia. Comparing within each country over time, cartelization was greatest in Britain and Germany during the most rapid stage of industrialization. Arguably this was because rapid industrialization brought about the historical concurrence of too many different social classes with deeply opposed interests. But this did not happen in the Soviet case, since social revolution had swept away the old classes before the stage of rapid industrialization. Nor did such a pileup occur during rapid industrialization in Japan, where the Meiji restoration had swept away some of the old classes.

The character of the industrialization process was thus the single most important factor determining the degree of cartelization in four of the five cases. In part my case selection affected this finding. For example, I chose not to examine America's period of rapid industrialization in the late nineteenth century but to focus on the Cold War period. Bias in case selection cannot be much of a problem, however, since I looked at a long historical sweep for most of the great powers of the industrial era. Though the industrialization process was important, it was not the only factor causing or exacerbating cartelization. I offer no theory to organize these other causes; I will simply report what some of them were.

International depression and protectionism helped promote cartelization in Germany and Japan. It did so directly, by spurring industrial sectors to organize behind protectionist barriers and more generally to pursue a strategy of organized markets. It also did so indirectly, by undercutting labor-export democratic coalitions and by playing into the hands of military bureaucracies' programs for expansion to achieve autarky. Theoretical literature has already examined the links among depression, protectionism, and cartelization.[4]

In the Soviet case, cartelization was due to the completion of the transformational phase and the self-interested ossification of the institutions originally designed to carry out the transformation. This generally fits Mancur Olson's argument that the mere passage of time is associated with increasing cartelization, though in Soviet Russia the highly centralized character of its institutions also aided their organization as self-interested cartels. Similarly in Britain, ossified atavistic institutions promoted cartelization and expansionism. In particular, declining Midlands industries seeking protection within an expanded empire provided a key base of support for Joseph Chamberlain's Africa policies.

4. David Lake and Jeffry Frieden, "Crisis Politics: The Effects of Uncertainty and Shocks on Material Interests and Political Institutions," paper presented at the annual meeting of the International Studies Association, London, March 1989.

The breakup of cartelization was most often associated with dramatic failures of the cartels' policies: for example, Vietnam led to the demise of the elite Cold War consensus; the consequences of Brezhnevite stagnation spurred Gorbachev's reforms. When cartels were exceptionally strong, as in Wilhelmine Germany and imperial Japan, defeat in a major war was required to break their hold.

In short, not only the industrialization process, but also international influences and lesser kinds of domestic social change can affect the degree of cartelization. So can policy failure. To predict patterns of cartelization in the future, a theory might focus on social changes associated with advanced industrial or postindustrial society, as well as on other international or domestic influences.

IMPLICATIONS FOR THEORY

What kind of theory of international politics would be consistent with these findings? It would have to accept most of the basic insights of Realist balance of power theory, since balancing against aggressors is a dominant feature of all my cases. But it would also have to reject contemporary Realism's assertion that, in anarchy, international competitive pressures necessarily override pressures from domestic interests and coalitions in the formulation of national strategy. It would also have to allow a major role for ideology. I will not attempt here to offer a fully developed theory of international politics based on the findings of this book. Rather, I will give a rough sketch of the kind of theory my findings imply should be developed.

Such a theory would start with the assumption that any individual belongs to a number of conflict groups, that is, groups of people who combine to use their resources in pursuit of common interests in competition against other groups.[5] These conflict groups include classes, ethnic groups, industrial sectors, firms, bureaucracies, political parties, and national states.[6] Some groups are stronger than others owing to the intensity of their members' interests, their size, their wealth, monopolies of information and expertise that they enjoy, or other characteristics.

Groups seek to advance the interests of their members through a variety of methods that involve conflict and cooperation with other groups. These methods include competing with other groups (e.g., making war on them, bankrupting them, beating them at the polls) as

5. Georg Simmel, *Conflict and the Web of Group Affiliations* (Glencoe, Ill., 1955), 11–124, esp. 17.
6. Jeff Frieden, *Debt, Development, and Democracy: Modern Political Economy and Latin America, 1965–1985* (Princeton, N.J., 1991), chap. 1.

well as entering coalitions with them (e.g., interest group logrolls or international treaties). Under conditions of uncertainty, another important method is using misinformation to steal members from other coalitions and reduce other groups' opposition to one's own policy preferences. As a by-product of this kind of ideological activity, members of one's own group might also be inadvertently misled—the blowback phenomenon.

In the modern era, the national state plays a particularly central role as the focal point for much of this activity. It regulates the behavior of groups within its jurisdiction, while at the same time those groups form coalitions to try to capture state power. The state also organizes competition against states that control other territorial units. Thus the state is a pivot between the domestic and international realms as well as a pivot of competition within the domestic realm.[7]

What is the character of this state, and how does it play its pivotal role? Is it to be considered, in Realist fashion, a hierarchical organization whose strategies are governed by the exigencies of the international competition? Or is it the captive of domestic interests, carrying out their will in disregard of the requirements of rational international strategy?

The answer suggested by the cases examined in this book is, "It depends." At the most general level, it depends on whether international pressures are more threatening, insistent, and immediate than domestic pressures. It is by no means obvious that vulnerability to international pressure is more worrisome than vulnerability to domestic pressure. Faced with extreme threat, statesmen must worry about both international subjugation through war and domestic overthrow through revolution. Under less extreme threat, they must worry about the collapse of their government, which in principle could be triggered by some weakening of the state's international position, by the alienation of a crucial domestic coalition partner, or by some interaction of the two. Whether international or domestic woes are more pressing, and how they interact, is an empirical question. It cannot be dismissed out of hand by Realist axioms about the *Primat der Aussenpolitik*.

Some hypotheses about the relative salience of domestic and international-pressures might focus on international-level variables. Great powers with big internal markets and large reserve capabilities for fighting long, difficult wars enjoy a substantial buffer from the pressures of international competition. In contrast, small states are more exposed to the vagaries of international security and economic

7. For the pivot idea, see Robert Putnam, "Diplomacy and Domestic Politics: The Logic of Two-Level Games," *International Organization* 42 (Summer 1988): 427–60; G. John Ikenberry, David Lake, and Michael Mastanduno, eds., "The State and American Foreign Policy," special issue of *International Organization* 42 (Winter 1988).

competition. Whereas great powers adapt their foreign strategies to their domestic circumstances, small powers adapt their domestic circumstances to the strategy that their foreign environment dictates.[8]

A focus on the structure of domestic politics within the state generates other hypotheses about how the state plays its role as pivot. States in cartelized systems may be highly responsive to interest group pressures, even if this requires international behavior that makes little sense in terms of the objective constraints and incentives posed by the international environment. Conversely, states dominated by unitary oligarchies with encompassing interests will be more responsive to international pressures, since no powerful domestic groups with parochial interests are pressing the state. States in democratic systems may be highly responsive to their electorate, though median voter preferences should typically drive the state to do what is internationally rational in any event.

Still other hypotheses might focus on the effects of interaction between international and domestic variables. A given international stimulus might have opposite effects, for example, depending on domestic conditions. One might argue that an increase in foreign threat will cause any state to pay more attention to its international environment and less to domestic concerns. Barry Posen hypothesizes, for instance, that in periods of low external threat, military doctrines will be shaped by military organizational biases, whereas in periods of high external threat civilians will intervene in military decision making and force doctrine to conform to the exigencies of the state's international circumstances.[9] Case studies of grand strategy before World War II support this conclusion, but pre-1914 case studies do not. In those instances, increasing threat played into the hands of military officers, who used the situation of impending war as an excuse to elude civilian control and indulge their organizational biases for offensive doctrines.[10] The difference between the World War I and World War II cases may have been that by the 1930s civilians had developed much better systems for institutionalizing civilian control of modern, professionalized military specialists. In the changed domestic institutional environment, a similar international impetus had an opposite effect.[11]

In short, the findings of this book suggest the need for a theory of international politics based on competition and alliances among various

---

8. Peter Katzenstein, *Small States in World Markets* (Ithaca, N.Y., 1985).

9. Barry Posen, *The Sources of Military Doctrine* (Ithaca, N.Y., 1984).

10. Jack Snyder, *The Ideology of the Offensive* (Ithaca, N.Y., 1984).

11. Barry Posen suggested this argument to me. For elaboration, see Jack Snyder, "International Leverage on Soviet Domestic Change," *World Politics* 42 (October 1989): 7–9, 25–28.

kinds of conflict groups, in which national states play a pivotal but not an exclusive role. Under uncertainty and asymmetry of information, ideological manipulation should play a major part in such a theory. In general, a research program based on this theory should pay more attention to interactions between international and domestic politics and less to making assertions about the "primacy" of one or the other political arena.

IMPLICATIONS FOR POLICY IN THE PRESENT ERA

The arguments advanced here have implications for how we understand the contemporary period of international relations and how we should act in it. The dramatic developments in Europe in 1989 have spurred statesmen and scholars to ask fundamental questions about the nature of international politics with a fresh eye. Some of the most fundamental concern the consequences of the end of the bipolar division of Europe and the boom in mass political participation in its eastern half.

Some optimists argue that these developments will lead to a peaceful democratic utopia in which life under international anarchy will no longer be "nasty, brutish, and short." They contend that the new thinking in Soviet foreign policy reflects an irresistible trend toward liberal democracy and toward the peaceful foreign policies that democracy brings in its wake.[12] In contrast, some Hobbesian pessimists argue that it was the bipolar division of Europe that kept the peace among the great powers since 1945 and that a return to multipolarity will mean a less stable international scene.[13]

My findings about the past sources of aggressive great power overexpansion can help in assessing the probable consequences of these two developments for the stability of the international order and in predicting which of the two will have the greater impact. First, regarding the arguments of the Hobbesian pessimists, my findings suggest that their extreme emphasis on the causal priority of the international structure of power is unwarranted. The Realists may be right that bipolar distributions of power are more stable than multipolar ones.[14] The historical record is at best ambiguous on this point, but the logic of the argument for bipolar stability has considerable power.

12. Snyder, "Averting Anarchy."
13. John Mearsheimer, "Back to the Future: Instability in Europe after the Cold War," *International Security* 15 (Summer 1990): 5–56.
14. John Lewis Gaddis, *The Long Peace* (New York, 1987), chap. 8; Kenneth Waltz, *Theory of International Politics* (Reading, Mass., 1979).

Such structural effects may be weak and easily overwhelmed by domestic sources of stability or instability, however. In the twentieth century, multipolar periods were unstable, and the bipolar period was highly stable, but my findings suggest that this correlation may be spurious. That is, the multipolar periods were unstable because extraordinarily aggressive states, Germany and Japan, were poles in the system. Conversely, the bipolar period was stable because Germany and Japan were eliminated as poles; the only remaining poles had domestic systems that produced much more moderate foreign policies.

My findings lend only qualified support to those who foresee the dawn of a peaceful democratic utopia. I argue that well-institutionalized democracies are more likely to have moderate foreign policies than are most undemocratic states. Even such democracies will still compete in an anarchic setting, however, so limited conflicts over power and security are likely to continue. Moreover, my British and American cases show that even democracies can become partially cartelized, partially internalize ideas of security through expansion, and behave immoderately for a time. A world of democracies may be more stable than most international systems of the past, but it will not be a utopia.

A second qualification to the arguments of the democratic utopians is even more grave. In this book I argue that booming mass political participation may stimulate strategic mythmaking if it takes place in a partially cartelized society whose democratic practices are weakly institutionalized. Wilhelmine Germany and Palmerstonian Britain provide cautionary tales about the foreign policy consequences of booming mass political participation when new entrants are socialized into politics by elites with a parochial interest in fostering nationalism and imperialism. It remains to be seen whether the new half-democracies in the Soviet Union and Eastern Europe will recapitulate this pernicious historical pattern.

If the program of the liberal democratic Soviet reformers succeeds, the Soviet domestic environment will become less cartelized, Soviet strategic concepts will be less myth-ridden, and consequently Soviet foreign policy will be even less inclined toward overexpansion. But this program may fail, because voters may reject the market reforms needed to make it work and because old elite cartels—the military, local party bosses, and monopolistic industrial ministries—may retain their ability to block key changes. If so, the Gorbachev coalition or its successors may have to govern in chaotic conditions by resort to populist or nationalist appeals. This could prove a fertile field for mythmaking of all kinds, including strategic mythmaking.

If Gladstonian and Wilhelmine outcomes are both possible for the Soviet Union, then it seems a high priority for Western policy to exert pressure in ways that favor the former. The case studies in this book shed a little light on how this can be done. Once imperialist coalitions are firmly established, the paper tiger images of opponents that they espouse make it difficult for other states to break the pattern either through threats or through concessions: threats will confirm their view that preventive aggression is necessary, whereas concessions will confirm their view that one can get away with it cheaply. But fortunately the current task is not to discredit Soviet paper tiger images, which Gorbachev has for the most part overthrown. Rather, the task is to reinforce Gorbachev's relatively benign strategic ideology and to prevent its replacement with more dangerous views.

Inhospitable international conditions played a major role in undercutting the political base and strategic concepts of the relatively benign Weimar and Taisho regimes. Russia played into the hands of Palmerston's social imperialism through its gratuitously belligerent diplomacy at the Turkish Straits. Stalin's invasion of South Korea helped solidify the American Cold War consensus. The West's unyielding policies repeatedly undercut Soviet doves, liberals, and reformers: Chicherin, Varga, Malenkov, Khrushchev in his later years, and Kosygin. As a rule, conciliatory policies, open international trading environments, and nonoffensive security postures help maintain the credibility of the opponent's doves and benign reformers when they are in power. Deterrent firmness may help the doves when hawks are in power, but this is not yet the case in Gorbachev's Russia.[15]

Some opportunities to promote favorable institutional changes in the Soviet Union have already been missed. During the summer of 1990, when Gorbachev publicly agonized over the adoption of a "500 days" plan for radical market reform, the United States insisted that a West European proposal for a multibillion dollar financial-aid package for Moscow be referred to a committee for "study." If instead the West had offered a concrete proposal for substantial aid, tied to the acceptance of the 500 days plan, the political balance in Moscow might have been tipped in favor of the reformist camp. Similar infusions of capital from the liberal democracies briefly helped to create favorable conditions for Weimar and Taisho democracy, whereas adverse international economic conditions helped usher in their collapse. At this turning point in the Soviet reform process, the Western allies spent their billions on a military buildup in the Persian Gulf, and Gorbachev retreated towards a command economy.[16]

In short, the Soviet Union is the only great power that still has not

---

15. In addition to the cases above, see Snyder, "International Leverage."

16. Jack Snyder, "East-West Bargaining over Germany: The Search for Synergy in a Two-Level Game," in Peter Evans, Harold Jacobson, and Robert Putnam, eds., *International Bargaining and Domestic Politics: An Interactive Approach* (forthcoming); also, remarks by Jeffrey Sachs, New York, 7 February 1991.

fully resolved the social crisis inherent in the transition to industrial society and increasing mass political participation. It may deal with the remnants of this crisis in either of two ways: through a Gladstonian model of benign mass mobilization, or through a more pernicious Wilhelmine model. The West has a powerful interest in ensuring that international conditions are made as propitious as possible for the success of the liberal model. Zigzags in the Soviet reform process, including the partial reversion to strong-arm methods in economic and nationalities policy, will complicate Western efforts. But as long as Soviet reformers retain any political base, the West should devote substantial resources to strengthening their hand. If the arguments advanced in this book are correct, there is no investment more crucial to the long-run prospects for international peace.

Finally, this book has implications not only for affecting the strategic debates inside other great powers, but also for understanding America's own debates on grand strategy. It suggests that readers should turn a skeptical eye toward much of America's strategic discourse, reevaluating many U.S. strategic concepts in light of the social and institutional context that produces them. If the United States and the other democratic great powers can do that, and if reform takes hold in the Soviet Union, the long peace among the great powers should become even more permanent.

Index

Library of Congress Cataloging-in-Publication Data

Snyder, Jack L.
    Myths of empire : domestic politics and international ambition / Jack Snyder.
        p. cm.—(Cornell studies in security affairs)
    Includes index.
    ISBN 0-8014-2532-8 (alk. paper)
    1. Imperialism. 2. World politics—19th century. 3. World politics—20th cen-
    tury. I. Title. II. Series.
    JC359.S577   1991
    325'.32—dc20   91-55052